T0301557

Philosophy, Politics, and Economics

Philosophy, Politics, and Economics

AN INTRODUCTION

GERALD GAUS

JOHN THRASHER

PRINCETON UNIVERSITY PRESS

PRINCETON & OXFORD

Published by Princeton University Press
41 William Street, Princeton, New Jersey 08540
6 Oxford Street, Woodstock, Oxfordshire OX20 1TR

press.princeton.edu

ISBN 9780691211251
ISBN (pbk.) 9780691219790
ISBN (e-book) 9780691219806

Library of Congress Control Number: 2021944858

British Library Cataloging-in-Publication Data is available

Editorial: Matt Rohal
Production Editorial: Karen Carter
Jacket/Cover Design: Layla Mac Rory
Production: Danielle Amatucci
Publicity: Alyssa Sanford
Copyeditor: Karen Verde

This book has been composed in Arno

10 9 8 7 6 5 4 3 2 1

CONTENTS

PREFACE

This book grew out of decades of teaching in a variety of different types of classrooms. While there are many excellent introductory texts in decision theory, economics, game theory, social choice theory, and public choice, we were at a loss to find a single book that worked as an introduction to Philosophy, Politics, and Economics (PPE) for advanced undergraduates or graduate students. In response, Jerry Gaus published what he called his "little book" on PPE in 2007, versions of which he used at the University of Queensland, the University of Minnesota–Duluth, Tulane University, the joint UNC–Chapel Hill/ Duke Philosophy, Politics and Economics program, the Di Tella University Law School in Buenos Aires, and the University of Arizona. I also taught a modified version of that material at Monash University and at Chapman University.

Over the course of the last several years, though, we both saw the need for a more comprehensive and focused approach that would cover some additional ground and make certain points more clearly. During that time, there was also an explosion of interest in PPE and a corresponding growth in the number of PPE programs that were seeking to teach classes in this area. We saw the need for a book that could cover the basic methods that inform the PPE approach in a way that was both philosophically rigorous and technically accessible. This book is a culmination of that pursuit.

I had been encouraging Jerry to write just such a book ever since I started teaching from his previous book on the topic. We both recognized that the older book, as good as it was, didn't do everything we wanted it to do. The opportunity to write a new and better book arose when Princeton University Press became interested in the idea. Given my interest in a new and improved introductory PPE text, Jerry asked if I would be interested in coming on board as a co-author. At the time, I had just moved from Monash University in Melbourne, Australia to Chapman University in southern California and was excited to help craft the kind of book that I wanted to teach. I also relished the opportunity to collaborate with Jerry on the book, who was not only a teacher and mentor, but also a friend. I looked forward to discussing the material and to the inevitable debates on topics where we disagreed. We talked about plans for the book over the spring and early summer of 2020 and signed the contract for the book with Princeton on August 15, 2020. I looked forward to spending the next several months immersed in this material and in discussion with Jerry. Only a couple of days later I heard from a close mutual friend that Jerry had died in his sleep the night before. The news was devastating and totally unexpected.

Following Jerry's untimely death, there was the obvious question of whether to continue the project. After talking to Jerry's surviving family, several colleagues (many of whom were students or friends of Jerry's), and our Princeton editor Matt Rohal, I decided to complete the book. Doing so presented several serious challenges, however. Jerry and I had already developed a fairly detailed plan of how we wanted the book to go and had even decided who would write the first drafts of each chapter. He also left extensive notes that formed the basis of his PPE lectures at the University of Arizona that I could draw on, as well as the previous PPE book. Using this material as a starting point, I wrote the book with the spirit of Jerry in mind, aiming to keep his distinctive voice at the forefront. Where I know that we disagreed on some issue or question, I either present both views or err on the side of Jerry's preferred view. Even so, this is a different book than we would have written together. We will never get to see that book. Nevertheless, I have tried to write a book that comes closest to the one that I believe would have emerged from our collaboration. His spirit was with me every day while I wrote, and I took the responsibility of completing this project in his name very seriously. Jerry is irreplaceable as a teacher and a writer, but my hope is that, with this book, a part of him will live on to inform the teaching of others and to continue to illuminate the minds of students even though his direct presence is gone.

Many thanks are due to those who worked hard to bring this book to fruition during the difficult plague year of 2020 and after the loss of Jerry. Matt Rohal, our editor at Princeton, has been especially understanding, compassionate, and helpful during this process. Without his encouragement and interest, this book would not exist. Jerry's surviving family, his daughter Kelly and his beloved wife Andrea, gave me their blessings to proceed with the project, as well as encouragement and support, which was essential. Several of Jerry's students and friends, most notably Keith Hankins, Chad Van Schoelandt, Kevin Vallier, and Ryan Muldoon, were generous in their friendship and time in discussing crucial issues in this book. Some of my other colleagues at the Smith Institute for Political Economy and Philosophy have also discussed many of the book's ideas with me (sometimes without knowing it)—to my enormous benefit. These include Erik Kimbrough, David Rojo-Arjona, Bart Wilson, and Vernon Smith. I thank them, as well as the other members of the Smith Institute and their families, for making it such a hospitable, vibrant, and fun place to be.

The person I owe the most gratitude to is my wife Molly. The unusual circumstances of completing this book without Jerry, combined with the stress and strain of life during a pandemic, put more demands on me and, in turn, on my family than it would have otherwise. This has not always been easy, but it would have been impossible without her fortitude and compassion. I also thank her and my three-year-old son Jack for reminding me every day what is really important. Although completed under strange and difficult circumstances, writing this book was a labor of love in more ways than one.

John Thrasher
Orange, California
The waning days of 2020

Philosophy, Politics, and Economics

Introduction

Social scientists and political philosophers are concerned with both how people act, and how they interact. One way to go about studying how people act and interact is to appeal to psychological or social laws that allow us to predict what they will do in certain situations. But we almost always want more than to merely predict the behavior of others—we want to make sense of what they do, to see it as an intelligible way of acting. We seek a genuine *explanation* as well as a *justification* of their behavior.

Making others intelligible to us is closely bound to seeing them as rational. True, sometimes it is intelligible to us why people are not rational, as we can understand all too well, for example, why someone who is drunk accepts a dangerous and silly dare. But usually, when we are confronted by simply irrational behavior, we don't understand what it is really all about. To explain behavior, we need to understand the choices that caused the behavior. And to understand rational choice, we need to understand the reasons that militated in favor of this rather than that choice. Sometimes it is easy to understand the choices of others and to see their reasons for making the choices they did, but sometimes it is not so easy.

Consider the case of Socrates, the most revered of all philosophers. What should we conclude from Socrates' choice to drink hemlock rather than to seek exile or escape? To understand why Socrates did what he did, we can't only look at his choice (drinking hemlock), we also need to look at the underlying reasons he chose that path rather than others that were open to him. From reading Plato's *Apology* of Socrates and the *Crito*, we come to understand how Socrates saw his death as an affirmation of his integrity and his values, and it is his dedication to those values and his courage to philosophize that we still honor today.

At the core intersection of the three disciplines of Philosophy, Politics, and Economics is a concern with understanding rationality and how rational choice and rational belief explain and justify human behavior. Of these, economics has developed the most sophisticated and elegant model of rational choice. Starting with a set of simple building blocks, we are able to build a model of individual and then strategic choice. By making a few other assumptions, we can then extend that model to collective and political choice. Along the way, we encounter a number of philosophical questions about the status of rationality and the underlying economic model of human nature. It is commonplace to think of economic models of rationality as based on a narrow conception of humans as selfish, or even worse, "greedy," and such assumptions, even if appropriate to economics, are inappropriate to politics and social philosophy. Economists, in turn, wonder why a model of human rationality that has been so enlightening in one domain should suddenly be inappropriate when applied to others.

This model of human rationality, *Homo economicus*, is at the heart of this book. We seek to understand it and to judge its strengths and weaknesses. In the end, whether one accepts or rejects the general applicability of *Homo economicus* within PPE, we believe that one must understand *Homo economicus*—either to apply it or to reply to and challenge it. In this book, we believe that once we do try to understand *Homo economicus*, what we find is a far more sophisticated model of rational choice than many critics—and indeed supporters—of economic rationality believe. The theory of rational agents at the heart of economics does not inherently imply a "selfish" or "greedy" acquisitive consumer; the model is quite general and encompasses a wide diversity of concerns and goals. And that is why, we think, all students of social interaction must know the basics of the economic approach to society.

PPE is a unified way to make sense of our common social life by using methods and approaches at the intersection of the three PPE disciplines. We see it as an interdisciplinary pursuit meaning that students of PPE will need to understand, from the inside, the economic model of rationality that underlies both economics and political science. But PPE is the study of philosophy, politics, and economics: how does philosophy enter this picture? In two ways. First, reflecting on the nature of rational agency and its explanatory power is essentially a distinctly philosophical enterprise—the philosophy of economics. But second, and far more important, we believe, moral and political philosophy are themselves concerned with questions about how rational people will interact, whether such people will act cooperatively or competitively, and whether they need a sort of "social contract" if they are to live together in peace. Thomas Hobbes (1588–1679) constructed his political philosophy on an analysis of humans as rational agents engaged in strategic interactions, which, as we will see in chapter 5, many believe can be understood in terms of the famous Prisoner's Dilemma analyzed by economists. But though Hobbes is the most obvious example, all moral and political philosophers must be concerned with understanding what is involved in being a rational agent and what is required for such agents to live together cooperatively and according to common rules. We do not believe that one can be a good moral or political philosopher without understanding the economic model of rationality and related approaches to social interaction. One of the things that made John Rawls (1921–2002) among the greatest political philosophers of our time was his deep knowledge of economic approaches to studying society. Often Rawls drew on this knowledge in his own work, but even when he declined to do so, his decision was informed by a thorough appreciation of economic analysis and its shortcomings.

Our aims in this book, then, are first to provide an introduction to those areas of the economic approach to society that are of most interest to students of political science, political philosophy, and PPE more generally. Second, we aim to analyze the economic model of rationality, so that we can better understand its presuppositions and commitments. This second task, we believe, should be of special interest to students of economics. In our many years of teaching these topics, we have found that economics students are familiar with basic concepts and theorems, especially in their formal presentations, but often have not reflected on just what they mean. When we have asked students who have completed intermediate microeconomics to explain what they mean by "efficiency," "utility," or "cost," they frequently respond by saying they have not really thought about it. It is our hope that this book will spur them to do so.

In writing this introductory text to philosophy, politics, and economics, we have tried to avoid two extremes. Rather than simply reporting the standard results, we have endeavored to explore the reasoning behind various claims, to show where we think mistakes have been made, and to take positions on some controversial issues where such positions are warranted. When doing so, we have tried to be clear where there is a difference of opinion and why we take the positions we do. Because of this, much of what we say should be of interest to students in economics, as well as to graduate students in philosophy and political science. On the other hand, we have also sought to make this book accessible to undergraduates outside economics. This means, first, that we have tried to survey the main issues and report what we see as the standard results. Second, it means that no mathematics (beyond some basic algebra) is employed. Where there are formal points to be made, we have made them graphically or via simple notation that is explained in the text. This book assumes no prior knowledge of economics, though students who have had several courses in economics will, no doubt, take away more from reading the book.

So, what, specifically, do we discuss in this book? We begin in the first chapter by exploring the concept of rationality that lies at the core of economic analysis. This chapter is the most "philosophical," since the aim here is to explore the idea of "rationality" itself and the notion of "instrumental" or goal-based rationality and to see how it relates to "economic rationality." The second and third chapters continue the analysis of rationality by considering the relation of instrumental rationality to a more precise understanding of utility theory. Utility theory is the foundation for the rest of the book, so it is important to understand just what it means to say that "rational individuals are utility maximizers." We argue that there is a great deal of confusion about the meaning of this claim. Many people who reject the "economic approach"—and, alas, even many who accept it—do so on the basis of misconceptions about what it means to say that rational agents are utility maximizers. After clarifying the formal characteristics of utility maximization, we close chapter 3 by briefly looking at the work of psychologists and behavioral economists who have investigated whether actual people act in the ways predicted by utility theory.

Chapter 4 introduces the idea of efficiency, another idea about which non-economists tend to have misconceptions. A basic claim of chapter 4 is that efficiency is very closely tied to rationality: rational individuals will seek efficient exchanges. This leads to the important notion of Pareto efficiency. The chapter concludes with a brief discussion of basic failures of efficiency in relation to externalities and public goods.

Chapter 4 also introduces the idea of social interaction between rational individuals in the form of market exchanges and contracts; Chapter 5 and 6 continue this focus on rational interactions as analyzed in the theory of games. Just about every student in the social sciences or political philosophy will at some point encounter game theory, if only in the form of the ubiquitous Prisoner's Dilemma. Chapter 5 introduces the main ideas in game theory, while arguing that a deeper knowledge of game theory can help us avoid many of the pitfalls and mistakes that characterize the analysis of social life. Chapter 6 complicates the models we introduced in the previous chapter by introducing repeated encounters, evolution, imperfect information and signaling, as well as cooperative bargaining.

Chapter 7 responds to a number of anomalies that we see in rational choice by arguing for the importance of conventions, social norms, and institutions in understanding rationality in the context of social life. We begin by looking at the classic analysis of conventions of coordination developed by the great philosopher David Lewis (1941–2001). Conventions rely on chance and other non-rational factors to generate a coordination equilibrium. As such, they introduce considerable path dependence and contingency into our understanding of rationality in a social context. They also help to explain many of the ubiquitous and enduring phenomena that seem to defy obvious rational explanation. Norms do something similar in the context of cases of conflictual coordination, where there is often an incentive to want to deviate from the cooperative equilibrium. We take our bearings there from the impressive work of Cristina

Bicchieri, while also discussing other accounts of social norms along the way. We conclude chapter 7 by discussing, in a briefer fashion than it deserves, the important role that institutions understood to be sets of norms and guidelines that laid out the "rules of the game" of social interaction play. We argue that conventions, norms, and institutions serve as the "friction" that acts upon the abstract theory of economic rationality and efficiency that we have examined so far.

Chapter 8 turns to the application of economic analysis to large-scale social interaction in the form of collective choice. The chapter commences by examining the contrast between two views of politics, one of the political arena as a sort of market and the other as "forum" in which economic analysis is somehow inappropriate. Although the contrast captures an insight, we suggest that rather too much has been made of it, and even the "forum" view in the end has to see collective choice as having a crucial "economic" component. The chapter then reviews collective choice and democracy in light of the pure logic of collective choice, "axiomatic social choice theory," which investigates how the preferences of many people might be aggregated into a social decision. The core topic of this chapter is Arrow's impossibility theorem.

The last chapter brings us back to where we began, namely the question of whether *Homo economicus* is an appropriate unified model of the domains at the core of PPE. James Buchanan (1919–2013) and others have developed what is sometimes called "public choice theory," which seeks to explain politics by depicting political actors as economic actors in a political context. Politics, on this approach, can be modeled as a form of exchange that differs from economic exchange because of the different rules of the game. As William Riker (1920–1993) emphasized, though, the background rules of political "exchange" often make inefficiency the norm rather than the exception. This led Riker to characterize politics as the "truly dismal science" since mutually advantageous interactions are often not even possibilities. The lesson that Buchanan and his colleagues have drawn from public choice analysis is that if we are going to achieve a politics that avoids these regrettable outcomes, we must fix the rules of the game so that interest of political actors, driven by an economic conception of rationality in the political arena, will align with the public good.

By the close of this work, we hope the reader will have a better grasp of why we think economics, politics, and philosophy are closely related disciplines and why PPE as a unified, disciplinary approach is crucial to a basic understanding of individual rationality and social life. But even those who disagree—who believe that *Homo economicus* and formal models of rationality more generally are not relevant to politics or philosophy—should have a much better idea of just what it is they find inappropriate about the economic approach.

1

Rationality

This chapter considers basic questions concerning the nature of rationality. We begin by looking at rationality and choice generally before connecting these ideas to economic rationality in the form of the *Homo economicus* model of rationality. Rationality, we argue, is goal oriented: rational choice is about choosing actions to achieve one's chosen goals. This simple idea, though, has a number of potential complexities hidden within it and getting clear on these is a big part of this chapter. After developing the idea of rational choice and rational beliefs, we add more content to that notion to generate the *Homo economicus* model of rationality that we will use and interrogate throughout the rest of this book.

Rationality and Choice

In the course of a day and over the entire course of a life, we are constantly confronted with choices. Some are comparatively minor, like the choice of what to have for breakfast. Others are decidedly less so, like the choice of what career to pursue, where to live, and whether to have children. Retrospectively, we look at the choices we have made and ask whether we made the "right" choice in the circumstances. We can and do also ask this about the choices we see others make and even of imaginary or long dead characters. Should Hamlet have looked for his father's killer? Did it make sense for Lear to turn Cordelia away? Was it a good idea for Abraham Lincoln to go to Ford's Theater on the night of April 15, 1865? We all know how these decisions turned out (not well), but the question of whether those characters made a good decision can't be wholly answered by what we know of the actual results of those decisions.

The world presents us with challenges, inconveniences, and opportunities. We make choices and act to make the world a more comfortable place to live. We find things we care about, things we value. We attempt to act to achieve our goals and values. When we deliberate about what we should do, we look for something to justify one choice over another. We want some reason to act in a particular way. The goal of all action or choice is to improve our lot by our own lights, and when we look at the world and see a state of affairs that we believe could be made better, this judgment gives us a reason to take action. There are intricacies to what it means to have a reason, but at its simplest level, a reason is just a justification for an action. If I am thirsty, I have a reason to drink some water.

In ordinary life as well as in the social sciences and philosophy, we evaluate choices and decisions on the basis of whether they are rational. In that sense, rationality is the basic norm of decision-making. In a sense, all of economics is about rationality. Economic analysis is based on a certain conception—or, as we shall see, conceptions—of rational choice.

The (very) short answer to the question "what is economics?" is "the theory of rational choice, and its consequences, under constraints." It is because this basic idea is so powerful, and economists have developed it in such sophisticated ways, that economic approaches have come to dominate other social sciences such as political science, as well much of political philosophy. The core of the economic model—and indeed, all our thinking about rational action—is a theory of rationality. We call this "rational choice theory" or "decision theory," but in all its forms it amounts to developing basic norms for evaluating choices and decisions.

This theory was developed, in one strand, by Thomas Hobbes and later British empiricists and through them became basic to the emerging science of political economy in the nineteenth century. The model has given rise to a variety of specifications. Some follow David Hume (1711–1776) and argue that all rational action is intended to satisfy desires. Another strand comes out of the development of probability theory and statistics. These strands fused into a general theory of rationality in the twentieth century by Oskar Morgenstern (1902–1977), John Von Neumann (1903–1957), Frank Ramsey (1903–1930), Leonard Savage (1917–1971), and others. The theory they developed became the rational choice theory that is the basis of contemporary economics, game theory, political science, and is used in political philosophy.

What Is Rationality?

The basic material of any theory of rational choice consists of three elements. These are states of the world (states), actions that one might take (actions), and ways the world can be after one acts (outcomes). The world is one way, we want it to be other than it is, and we act to bring that better world about. This is the basic model of rational choice.

It is important to note that while this is a model of choice, one is always choosing actions, which are causal interventions on the world. In this sense, we can agree with John Milton (1608–1674) that "reason is but choosing." States of the world and outcomes are both just ways the world happens to be or how it might be. The difference between them is temporal or, rather, causal. Actions transform states into outcomes and not vice versa, and this is what distinguishes one from the other.

We choose actions, not outcome. If I am thirsty (state), I can't decide to have my thirst sated (outcome). I can, however, choose to take a drink of water (action) in an attempt to bring about the outcome that I want. In this case, choosing this action will very likely lead to a positive outcome. This is the trivial case where it is pretty clear what the right or rational choice is, but knowing what is rational is not always so easy. Indeed, it is not always possible to clearly evaluate the paths from actions to outcomes. Some of these subtleties will be discussed in the next chapter, for now it is only necessary to say that rationality is an evaluative standard that we apply to choices of actions that aim at outcomes.

We can begin to think about what a standard of rationality might look like by considering some obvious failures of rationality. We are unlikely to believe that choices that seem random are rational. This is not because randomness is contrary to rationality; indeed, as we will see in later chapters, adopting a policy to choose randomly may be a perfectly rational strategy in some situations. What makes randomness seem non-rational, when it is not done as the result of a larger strategy, is that it makes the choice in question seem to lack a point or an aim. Rational choice aims at having a positive impact by one's own lights at least.

All rational choice aims at an end, which is to say that all rational choices aim to bring about some kind of outcome. In this sense, rational choice is *teleological* since the choice of an action is parasitic on the end that the action is meant to achieve. This is also described as *instrumental* rationality, since the idea is that rationality is an instrument for connecting means (actions) to ends (outcomes). Rationality, in this sense, is a norm or evaluative standard for assessing choices on the basis of how the choice of actions is related to various outcomes. As a norm, rationality is distinct from thinking, reasoning, or deliberating. One may deliberate at length and still not make a rational choice, or one may make a rational choice without deliberating at all.

This last point is very important. Since rationality is an evaluative standard—a norm—and not, in the first instance, a process, we can often attribute rationality to choices that we may not have understood at the time or that seemed otherwise strange. Much of the social sciences, especially psychology, is the search for an explanation, in rational terms, for otherwise puzzling behavior. We see this in literature and history as well. Think of Abraham and Isaac. Although he spared him in the end, Abraham's willingness to sacrifice his only son Isaac appears inexplicable until you know the aim of his intended action. The same can also often be said of seemingly perverse or insane behavior like the mass sacrifices that were so common in pre-Columbian Mesoamerica. These sacrifices had complex political and social functions, aside from the obvious religious explanations, and cannot be explained as merely irrational bloodlust.

What these examples should highlight is that rationality is a pretty capacious standard. Even if we know a choice is rational, there are a number of other questions we can ask about it, like whether it was a sensible or morally right. One might also think that rationality is so expansive a notion that it doesn't rule out any choices except the truly random, but this would not be correct. To get a fuller sense of what a norm of rationality amounts to, we need to look more closely at different possibilities for how to specify such a standard.

Rationality as Effectiveness

One question we might ask at the outset is why we can't just judge choices and decisions by their fruits. In other words, if your choice has a good outcome, it was a good choice and vice versa. This is probably the simplest way to think about rationality; so much so that we might even think of it as a "folk theory" of rationality. We can call this view *Rationality as Effectiveness*.

Rationality as Effectiveness

An agent A's choice to φ is rational if and only if φ-ing is an effective way to achieve A's desire, goals, end, or taste G.

Certainly, this makes sense; if choice is an instrument for achieving one's goals, then it would seem a choice is rational if it is effective in that end. Simple, right?

Ah, philosophy is seldom simple. Rationality as effectiveness is both too narrow and too broad. To see how it is too narrow, suppose that our agent is a hiker who tries to be careful about the weather by always checking multiple weather forecasts before any hike in the mountains. As it happens on this occasion, all the forecasters concur that it is going to be a gorgeous day. On the basis of all this information, our prudent hiker goes out dressed for a pleasant day but gets caught in a freak snowstorm and ends up with frostbite. According to rationality as effectiveness, the hiker's decision not to dress for snow is a failure of rationality since it was anything but effective. More generally, rationality as effectiveness deems "not rational" any action that harms one's goals, no matter how diligent the agent was in gathering information and hedging against risks. So, any risky action—such as an investment—that turns out badly is irrational.

This seems wrong to most philosophers—and perhaps to you too. Remember that we wanted our account of rationality to provide a defensible evaluative standard for choices and to accord, more or less, with how we use the idea of rationality in ordinary life. On both of these counts rationality as effectiveness fails. Rationality as effectiveness says that the hiker was irrational and yet, when we think about it, we would definitely call her rational. This is good reason to be skeptical of this account of rationality. When we reflect on what it means to be a rational agent, it doesn't seem that, no matter how diligent one is, if an act with risks turns out badly, one has been shown to be irrational. We don't want the idea of whether a choice is rational to depend on whether one happens to be lucky or unlucky. Rationality cannot simply be reduced to effectiveness.

This concept becomes even clearer when we consider the way in which rationality as effectiveness is too broad. Suppose that another hiker never bothers with weather forecasts of any sort but flips a coin to decide whether the weather will be good or bad, heads, good weather and tails, bad weather. The coin came up tails the day of the storm, so this hiker was prepared for the snow. In this case, rationality as effectiveness deems this hiker's choice to flip a coin to determine what to wear as rational. After all, being prepared for the snow was an effective way to avoid frostbite! But, on reflection, this seems like a case of dumb luck, not rationality. Instead, rationality should help us distinguish between better and worse choices given our goals and options.

Subjective Rationality

Rationality, properly understood, should concern the *quality* of a given choice, not simply the effectiveness of the outcome that arises from it. Of course, to choose an option is still to *do* something: it is to buy the Honda rather than the Ford, or to go out to dinner rather than stay in. When we evaluate a choice to do this or that, our focus should not be only on the actual consequences of what is done (whether, in the end, the choice to do this or that achieved one's goals), but whether, at the time of the choice, one chose what they believed to be the best option available to achieve their goal. This standard suggests anther account of rationality, *Subjective Rationality*.

Our first hiker believed that it would not snow, so subjective rationality deems this hiker's actions rational even though, despite all the precautions, they resulted in frostbite.

Subjective Rationality

An agent *A*'s choice to φ is rational if and only if when *A* chooses to φ:

(i) *A*'s choice was based on her beliefs (*B*),

(ii) if *B* were true, φ-ing would have best satisfied *A*'s desire, goal, end, purpose, or tastes *G*.

This account of rationality relies on a counterfactual, conditional claim. *If* the hiker was right that it was not going to snow, *then* the hiker's actions would have achieved the hiker's goals. So, subjective rationality absolves the hiker from irrationality, which seems correct.

Subjective rationality also implies that our second, coin-flipping hiker was rational, however. Given the flip of the coin, this hiker believed it would snow. Indeed, even if the coin had come up heads (indicating it was going to be a gorgeous day), this hiker would still be rational even though frostbite would have been the result. *If* the beliefs based on the toss of the coin *were* true, things would have worked out well, which is all that subjective rationality requires.

Despite this rather odd implication, subjectivist theories of rationality have appealed to many, and we can see why. If we take one's beliefs as given, and we know one's goals, we can understand how an action was *intended* to promote one's goals. Insofar as our only concern is to make choices intelligible, we can understand choices as displaying a sort of rationality as long as they sensibly relate goals, beliefs, and choices. Although thoroughly subjective theories of instrumental reasoning have their attractions in social scientific explanation, almost all attempts to develop the idea of rational action have sought to justify some constraints on what constitutes reasonable beliefs that underlie an instrumental choice.[1] It seems to most philosophers that an account of instrumental rationality must build in some criterion of how sensible the beliefs are.

Consider a case described by Sigmund Freud, that of "Little Hans."[2] Little Hans refused to go out into the street because he was afraid of horses. He believed that if he went out into the street, a horse would bite him. If Little Hans's beliefs *were* correct, then his choice not to go out into the street would be completely rational—nobody wants to get bitten by a horse. But Little Hans strikes us, as he did Freud, as not being rational, since Little Hans had no more reason than anyone else to believe that a horse would bite him if he went out into the street. Thus, Freud set out to uncover why Little Hans believed such an odd

---

1. This is true even regarding those decision theorists who describe themselves as "subjectivists." As one of the most eminent subjectivists insists, "your 'subjective' probability is not something fetched out of the sky on a whim." Richard Jeffrey, *Subjective Probability*, 76.

2. Sigmund Freud, "Inhibitions, Symptoms and Anxieties," 229–315.

thing. Freud's explanation was that Little Hans, because he desired his mother and feared retribution from his father, transferred his fear that his father would castrate him onto horses. Little Hans's fear of horses was really a fear of his father. Leaving aside how plausible Freud's explanation of Little Hans's fear was, the point is that if you question the rationality for his original fear, as Freud did, you are thereby rejecting the pure theory of Subjective Rationality.

Rationality and Sound Belief

In our rather more mundane cases, our conscientious hiker seems to be rational while not wearing snowshoes, even though doing so undermines the hiker's goals, given that this hiker's beliefs about the weather were well-grounded, though false. Even though our coin-flipping hiker was successful, flipping coins to determine what the weather will be is hardly rational. Little Hans is also irrational since not only were horses unlikely to bite him; if he was afraid that his father would castrate him, avoiding horses wouldn't help very much.

Given all of this, then, an adequate characterization of Rationality must go something like this:

Rationality

An agent's *A*'s choice to φ is rational if and only if *A soundly believes* φ-ing is the best prospect for achieving *A*'s goals, values, ends, etc. *G*.

Rational choice, in light of one's goals, must be based on at least minimally sound beliefs to exclude cases of luck and delusions from the realm of rationality.

Rational Belief and Choice

Here we might seem to be in dangerous territory, since we are beginning to blur the epistemic conception of rationality, which aims at truth, with the practical conception of rationality that aims at good choices. We might embrace this possibility and lean on epistemic concepts like justification, reliability, knowledge, or truth to fill out our notion of "sound beliefs." Doing so, however, would mean that our search for a norm of rationality would be parasitic on some further set of epistemic norms and standards, which are likely to be as or more fraught than the original notion of rationality that we started with. This would also detach our philosophical conception of rationality from the mainstream of economics and political science.

Fortunately, there is another way, which relies on fusing rational beliefs and choice together. This approach was developed by a number of theorists in the twentieth century, most notably by the philosopher Frank Ramsey. The idea is that we can measure the degree to which one believes something based on the price at which one would be willing to take a fair bet on whether that belief turns out to be true. So, if you believe that there is a 50–50 chance that a coin will either turn up heads or tails if flipped, you should be willing to bet on any offer where the probability of heads turning up, multiplied by price, is greater than zero. We can think of this as the expected value of the bet. Given your belief, anything less than a 50–50 odds would not be worth taking, and anything higher would be, because the expected value would be greater than zero. In this way, we can model rational belief on the choice that one would make if one had to bet on this or that option. The better the odds one is willing to take, the higher the credence one puts in the claim being true.

This approach to thinking about beliefs has a number of advantages. Perhaps most importantly, it allows us to ultimately generate a complete theory of rational choice in the form of utility theory, which we will explore in the next chapter. It does this by linking belief to choice through probability theory. Ramsey argued that we can "measure beliefs" by imposing a scale on beliefs from 1 to 0 where believing with a credence of 1 means that one is absolutely certain, while a credence of 0 is the opposite. While credences or degrees of belief are technically continuous from 0 to 1, in practice it is very unusual for the probability of anything to be either 0 or 1 and the same is true of credences.

On this view, beliefs as credences are still subjective, so one might wonder whether we have really moved beyond subjective rationality and its problems. To do so, we need a criterion of soundness. The criterion used in science is a rule for evaluating the probability of a hypothesis about the world being true given some evidence related to that hypothesis. This rule for evaluating hypotheses conditional on evidence was developed by the Reverend Thomas Bayes (1701–1761) and is now used across numerous disciplines.

Bayes' Theorem

The probability (P) of a hypothesis (H), given some evidence (E), is determined by

$$P(H \mid E) = \frac{P(E \mid H) \times P(H)}{P(E)}.$$

The result of this equation, $P(H|E)$, is called the "posterior probability" and is the probability of a given hypothesis H being true given that we have observed evidence E. The first term in the numerator, $P(E|H)$, is called the "likelihood odds" and is the probability that we would observe evidence E if hypothesis H were true. We multiply this by our "prior," which is our antecedent belief in the hypothesis H, represented as a probability, $P(H)$. That product is divided by the "normalizing constant" of the independent probability of observing some evidence E.

So, imagine Alf is concerned that he may have cancer. He gets a test that comes back positive. How likely is it that Alf has cancer? There are basically four possible ways the world can be given the test results, represented in table 1.1.

TABLE 1.1. Type I and Type II Errors

	Has Cancer	Doesn't Have Cancer
Test Positive	True Positive	False Positive (Type I Error)
Test Negative	False Negative (Type II Error)	True Negative

Since Alf has tested positive, we know that a Type II error (false negative) and a true negative aren't plausible states of the world. Instead, we need to decide how likely it is that Alf has cancer (H), given that he has received a positive test result (E). We can determine this using Bayes' theorem. If we know that this cancer test is 95% accurate with a 2% false positive rate, and that 1% of the population is likely to have this cancer, we can determine the likelihood ratio of a positive test result given cancer is actually present $P(E|H)$ at .95.[3] Since we know the underlying probability of any given person having this type of cancer is 1%, we can set our prior $P(H)$ at .01.

Now we just need to figure out what the normalizing constant is. This can be a little tricky. In this case we need to know what the probability of testing positive is. Remember, testing positive is a combination of both the true positive and the false positive. So, to find it, we need to multiply the probability of the true positive with the probability of the false positive given the likelihood in the population, so

$$P(E) = P(E|H) \times P(H) + P(E|\neg H) \times P(\neg H).$$

3. Since probabilities are represented on a continuous interval between 0 and 1, all probabilities can be represented as a real number between 0 and 1.

TABLE 1.2. Test Accuracy

	Positive Result (E)	Negative Result (¬E)
Has Cancer (H)	95%	5%
Doesn't Have Cancer (¬H)	2%	98%

$P(E|H) \times P(H)$ is just the test accuracy (95%) multiplied by the percentage of the population likely to have cancer (1%), which in this case is .95 × .01 = .0095 or .95%. $P(E|¬H) \times P(¬H)$ is the false positive rate (2%) multiplied by the percentage of the population that is likely to be cancer free (99%), which amounts to .02 × .99 = .0198 or 1.98%. Add these together and we have the complete normalization constant .0095 + .0198 = .0293 or 2.93%.

Now we can use the theorem to determine the likelihood that Alf has cancer given his positive test with the formula in figure 1.1.

$$\frac{P(E \mid H)[.95] \times P(H)[.01]}{P(E)[.0293]}$$

FIGURE 1.1. Bayesian Likelihood

The answer, in this case, is .324 or about 32.4%. So, despite his positive test, there is only about a 1 in 3 chance that he has cancer! With these rates and this test, we would need to get the false positive rate down to .1% before we could be 90% certain that a positive test result indicates cancer.

The representation of Bayes' theorem is presented here as a way to test hypotheses, which is a clear way of thinking about it, but it is also a general rule for updating conditional probabilities or, as we have seen, credences. We can think of our beliefs as "priors" that are rationally updated according to Bayes' rule when we encounter new evidence. All our beliefs or credences are the result of previous "experiments." For instance, if I am thirsty, I might have the belief that water will quench my thirst. If I drink water and it does indeed quench my thirst, this evidence is consistent with my prior. Given my past experience, my credence that water will quench my thirst is high, the probability of finding countervailing evidence is low. If I do find such evidence, the fact that it is so unlikely means I have to reevaluate my priors.

Bayes' theorem is a simple, though far from obvious, application of the logic of conditionals, but it can function as an all-purpose testing and learning rule. As such, it can buttress the general conception of subjective rationality by anchoring those subjective probabilities in a constant interaction with the world. In this way we have a standard for rationality in belief based on rules for what consistent belief or credence updating would look like. Given some arbitrary set of credences and beliefs, one could use Bayes' theorem to update those credences over time. Someone who did this consistently would be rational regardless of whether their beliefs happened to be correct. In this way, we avoid both rationality as effectiveness and the dangers of the extreme form of subjective rationality.

Rationality and Goals

Rational choice is about choosing actions in order to achieve outcomes. We just saw how Bayes' rule can help set our credences about states of affairs and about prospects from actions to outcomes. To choose an action rationally, though, we need to be able to rank outcomes. That is, we need to be able to evaluate which outcomes are more attractive and consistent with our larger goals. Rationality is about connecting our choices consistently given our beliefs about states of affairs, prospects from actions to outcomes, and our ranking of outcomes. We have already seen that it is crucial that one's beliefs also be soundly based on evidence and learning. Do values and goals have a similar requirement?

David Hume answered this question with a firm "No," arguing that rationality is merely a tool to achieve whatever aims we happen to have. As he argued:

> 'Tis not contrary to reason to prefer the destruction of the whole world to the scratching of my finger. 'Tis not contrary to reason for me to chuse my total ruin, to prevent the least uneasiness of an Indian or person wholly unknown to me. 'Tis as little contrary to reason to prefer even my own acknowledg'd lesser good to my greater, and have a more ardent affection for the former than the latter.[4]

For Hume, rationality is a "slave of the passions," which is to say that our goals, aims, values, and desires are in the driver's seat; rationality works for the passions to get what they want. Rationality, on this view, cannot tell us what to want, so *no desire or goal* can ever be against reason.

Contemporary philosophers, however, often resist embracing the radicalism of Hume's thesis. Although, as Robert Nozick (1938–2002) acknowledges,

4. Hume, A Treatise of Human Nature, sec. III.3.

"we have no adequate theory of the substantive rationality of goals and desires, to put to rest Hume's statement," there are still ways we can make sense of more or less rational goals by applying some basic consistency requirements.[5] We can think of two basic types: diachronic and synchronic, which is to say those that are and are not related to time.

Of these, synchronic consistency is the least demanding and least controversial since it only involves consistency between one's beliefs and goals. So, if one wants a martini and is offered two different clear liquids, gin or kerosene, with which to make, gin is the proper choice.[6] If we notice that Betty reaches for the kerosene rather than the gin, we can assume either that she doesn't know it is kerosene or that she doesn't want a martini. Either she (wrongly) believes that choosing this clear liquid is the best prospect for generating a martini or her goal is not, in fact, to make a martini.

Nozick advocates a further consistency requirement between beliefs and goals. According to Nozick, someone who wants one thing, while at the same time not wanting it, lacks "proper integration." One wants a thing, while wishing that one didn't. Alf may want an additional slice of pizza, but, since Alf is fighting a losing campaign in the battle of the bulge, he may wish he didn't want that extra slice. We can call the desire to desire our evaluation of our own values, desires, and goals "second-order" aims or desires. They are what we want to want. When such a second-order desire (a desire directed at another desire) conflicts with a "first-order" desire (the desire for x), Nozick argues, "it is an open question" which should be given up, but it is clear that "they do not hang together well, and a rational person would prefer that this not (continue to) be the case."[7]

Perhaps. Take a standard case where this story appears to make sense: a desire to get drunk. We can imagine a person with a desire to get drunk, and also with a desire to get rid of his desire to get drunk. Let's say he loves the taste of IPAs but doesn't love the weight gain and hangovers that come with overindulgence. When asked if he'll have another, he often says "yes," while also thinking that he shouldn't. There appears to be the sort of conflict of desires that Nozick has in mind, a conflict between a desire and a desire directed at that desire. And this, he believes, is an irrational inconsistency. Yet this inconsistency isn't obvious. Why can't our man love two things: hops and feeling well rested? These two aims often conflict, but why isn't that inconsistency just

5. Nozick, The Nature of Rationality, 63, 148.

6. A proper martini is made with a 3:1 ratio of Plymouth gin to dry vermouth, stirred until properly chilled and diluted, then served with a twist of lemon.

7. Nozick, The Nature of Rationality, 141.

the kind of tragic necessity that is the stuff of human life, rather than an error in rationality?

Take a parallel case: suppose Alf desires fame, but he also thinks it would be wiser if he didn't care about popular opinion of his work and uses this to temper or counter his first-order desire for fame. Alf both wants fame and wishes he didn't. Does this make him irrational? To be sure, Alf can't satisfy both desires, but so what? All sorts of desires are incapable of being fulfilled together. LeBron James was, by all accounts the best basketball and football player at his school and he desired to play both sports, but he knew that he could only achieve all-time greatness in one of the sports, not both. As long as one can consistently order one's desires and goals for purposes of choice, one is a rational chooser, even though one may want incompatible goals.

Now consider a conflict between a "first-" and "second-order" desire. This is certainly more complicated. A second-order desire is a desire about a desire, and this immediately raises questions. Whenever we have an idea that applies to itself (a desire about a desire), things get messy and we confront what philosophers call "reflexivity." And of course, if I can have a second-order desire not to have a desire, I can have a third-order desire not to have *that* desire not have a desire. This is not far-fetched. Imagine the plight of a gay man who was brought up to be a devout Catholic and so he has a desire not to have a sexual desire for other men. But he may rebel against this upbringing, and so have a desire not to have that second-order desire. People often feel guilty about things that they personally don't see as having any reason to be guilty about.

Nevertheless, leaving all these puzzles and questions aside, it does not seem more irrational to have a conflict between first- and second-order desires than it is to have a conflict between two "first-order" desires. Suppose Alf has a "first-order desire" (to be famous) and a "second-order" desire (to want to not desire fame). Alf is *ambivalent* about his desire for fame, but is he irrational? If Alf can rank his two desires for choice purposes, he can consistently choose, though there will always be a desire that he won't be able to satisfy. But that can happen with a conflict of first-order desires too. Some say this is irrational: it is like believing that the world is a sphere and that it is flat. But this seems wrong. With beliefs we eliminate conflict by *abandoning* one of the beliefs (I can't believe that it is both raining and not raining outside my window), whereas we eliminate conflicts of desires by *ordering* them. We are often ambivalent creatures who, perhaps typically, are not fully satisfied with our choices because we have a hankering after the opposite.

Ordering goals imposes synchronic consistency, but we might think that there must be an ultimate hierarchy of such goals in order to completely order all of them. At the top of such a hierarchy we might find a "master goal" that can organize all of one's other goals. According to Nassau William Senior (1790–1864), an important nineteenth-century political economist, economics can reasonably assume that everyone seeks wealth because "wealth and happiness are very seldom opposed."[8] The ultimate goal is happiness: no matter what one desires, it is a manifestation of the pursuit of happiness or pleasure. Our goals, then, have a rational structure to them: they all serve the end of achieving the master goal of happiness.

This "hedonistic" view of our ends—which was common among political economists in the nineteenth century but rejected in the twentieth century—has been making something of a comeback: a number of works have been published recently about how we measure happiness, and whether market economies really make people happy. Still, the old criticisms remain. If hedonism is intended as an account of rationality, it follows that those who aim at goals that do not serve their own happiness are ipso facto irrational. That seems a very restrictive notion of rational action: the action "Alf sacrificed his own happiness to help others" would be, by definition, irrational. In response to the oddness of defining such actions as intrinsically irrational, many hedonists switch ground, arguing, as did the early utilitarian Jeremy Bentham (1747–1832), that:

> Nature has placed mankind under the governance of two sovereign masters, pain and pleasure. It is for them alone to point out what we *ought to do*, as well as *to determine what we shall do*. . . . They govern us in all we do, in all we say, in all we think: every effort we can make to throw off our subjection, will serve but to demonstrate and confirm it.[9]

We ought to pursue pleasure *and* we must do so. If it is impossible not to pursue one's own pleasure, then we clearly can't have cases of rational action that don't aim at pleasure, since it is impossible not to aim at pleasure.

This psychological claim seems dubious: people aim at a variety of goals, and it is hard to see how they all are ways to gain pleasure. Consider helping the poor: is that a way to give you pleasure?

It is said that Thomas Hobbes argued it was. Hobbes, who was famous for arguing that people only cared about themselves, was once seen giving money to a beggar. When pressed about why he did so, Hobbes replied that it gave him pleasure to see the poor man happy. But was that what Hobbes really cared about? Is helping the poor, just like drinking beer, a way to gain pleasure? After all, unless one gets a lot of pleasure from it, there seem to be cheaper

8. Nassau William Senior, An Outline, 187–88.

9. Jeremy Bentham, Introduction to the Principles of Morals, 65. Emphasis added.

ways to get pleasure than giving money away! Suppose that we can and do act for other goals besides our own pleasure, then surely it is not irrational to do so. If Hobbes thought that his reply was necessary to show that he wasn't being irrational, I think it is safe to say that he was mistaken.

One reason that we might look for some master value to order all of our goals is to induce diachronic consistency, which is to say consistency in a series of choices. If Alf drinks coffee with breakfast and wine with dinner, we might think that his behavior signals some kind of inconsistency. After all, if wine is good enough for dinner, why not for breakfast as well? But we could look to Alf's higher goals to see that it wouldn't serve those goals for him to be groggy at breakfast and amped up at dinner. We can use some master value as a way of organizing and ordering the goals and values that led to specific choices. As we will see, economists do something like this by assuming some minimal structuring requirements for the goals of their agents, typically that they prefer more to less money or the equivalent value. We will return to this assumption several times in this book, so we leave it aside for now.

Another common way of taking a small step beyond Hume's thesis is to provide a test that distinguishes rational from irrational desires. Two sorts of tests are widely used; one ties the rationality of one's goals or desires to their origin, while the other links their rationality to their stability.

The *Autonomous Formation Test* claims that only desires that were formed free of undue pressure or force, free of manipulation by others, or were formed under conditions of adequate formation, are rational desires. For example, it might be argued that if a desire to smoke cigarettes has been induced by advertising and peer pressure, and so was formed in a procedurally objectionable way, it is not rational. The idea here is that we can distinguish between rational and irrational goals by looking at where the goals come from. If they came from our authentic self, we could assume they are rational, but if we have reason to think that they didn't, this makes them suspect.

The *Critical Reflection Test* claims that only desires that *could* survive a process of critical reflection are truly rational. An adherent of the Critical Reflection Test might hold that the desire to smoke is not rational because it cannot withstand critical reflection: if people reflected on smoking and the risks, it is said, they would not continue to desire to smoke. On this view, people who smoke only maintain their desire by refusing to look at the evidence, or engaging in wishful thinking, and so on. The idea here is that rational goals should be counterfactually stable in the face of new evidence or changing circumstances.

Although there is merit to both of these amendments to Hume's thesis, their comparative strength in filtering out "bad" desires or goals is also a weakness in that it also filters out "good" ones. Consider the Autonomous Formation Test. The procedure by which people come to develop a desire to be moral, for example, seems to have a lot to do with a desire to please one's parents and conform to their commands—not a desire formation process that would seem to pass muster. Even the Critical Reflection Test can have counterintuitive consequences. As many physicians know, giving people too much information, or asking them to vividly picture the recommended procedure, may lead people not to desire things that are clearly good for them, and which they realize are good for them. Suppose a patient has a desire to have a colonoscopy, but if the agent really reflected on what this involved, he would no longer desire the procedure. Would this render the desire irrational? Or is that just a good reason not to think too much about some things?

Actions and Goals

On this account of rationality, all rational action is a means to achieve a goal. Actions are merely prospects for realizing some outcome given some state of affairs. An implication of this theory is that all actions are chosen instrumentally to bring about a desired outcome, we never act just to act. That is, actions cannot be their own outcomes.

Sometimes, though, this assumption seems at odds with how we normally think about our choices. Some actions do directly satisfy one's goals; the action itself is what we want, not the outcome that it produces. Say, for example, that Betty is eating ice cream and she explains her behavior by proclaiming "I like ice cream." If all rational action is a means to achieve a goal, what is the goal and what is the action?

A hedonist might explain Betty's action by saying that it was an instrumentally effective way of achieving pleasure. If pleasure is the sole end, and if we are constructed in ways such that we always pursue pleasure and avoid pain, then indeed all action is instrumental to experiencing this mental state.

But, as we saw, aiming at happiness has conceptual problems and is not as general as one might like. Perhaps we can replace hedonism—a master goal of all action—with another master goal, "desire satisfaction." Suppose Betty had a desire for an ice cream cone and so she ate one. Some will say that her decision to eat the ice cream cone aimed at "satisfying her desire for an ice cream cone." There is a distinct thing called a "desire to eat the ice cream cone" that her eating somehow assuaged.

We can interpret this in two ways. First, "satisfaction" might simply mean "a pleasant experience," but then we are back to hedonism. Alternatively, satisfaction might mean something like *extinguishing the desire*—as if it were an itch that she sought to get rid of. On this "itch" theory of desires, we perform acts that satisfy desires because we actually have the aim of getting rid of the desire. But the itch theory seems wrong. Betty does not eat the ice cream cone to get rid of her "itch" to eat the ice cream cone. Instead, she eats the ice cream cone because she likes ice cream cones. The "aim" of her eating the ice cream cone is, well, to eat an ice cream cone. If she could either take a pill to get rid of the itch, or eat the ice cream cone, the itch theory says she should do whatever is least expensive. But surely, she desires to eat the ice cream, not get rid of the itch.

We seem to have a problem. Unless we accept some master goal at which all action aims, the goal of some action seems to be to engage in that action itself. Instrumental rationality can explain when I do one thing (walk to the pizzeria) in order to secure a goal (eat a pizza). The first is a means to the second. But what happens when I get to the pizzeria: why do I eat the pizza? Is that instrumental to some further goals? It seems that at some point my action and goal are the same: my goal is to eat the pizza.

This, however, raises the specter of entirely vacuous explanations of people's actions. We see Betty φ-ing (eating the vanilla ice cream cone) and we "explain" it by saying that "Betty's goal is to φ (eat the vanilla ice cream cone), so φ-ing (eating the vanilla ice cream cone) satisfies her goal." But now that which is doing the explaining (Betty has a goal to φ) and that which is to be explained (Betty φ-ed) look as if they are the same thing. The worry is that the only way we can really know that Betty has a goal of φ-ing is by observing her φ-ing. Our explanation would then be of the form shown in table 1.3.

TABLE 1.3. Goal-Based Explanation of Betty's Actions

Explanandum (what is to be explained):	Betty φs.
Explanans (what is to be explained):	Betty's reason for φ-ing is that he has a goal to φ.
which looks too much like . . .	Betty φs because she is observed to φ.

This does not seem very promising as a way to explain her action; the *explanans* is essentially a restatement of the *explanandum*.

Although it is tempting to revert to the "itch theory," we can solve the problem without resorting to the itch theory. Betty's specific act, φ, can be genuinely *explained* (as opposed to merely restated) if it is an instance of a general disposition to φ, or engage in φ-type acts—i.e., a disposition to engage in actions of a certain *type*. Thus, for instance, when Betty explains eating ice cream cones by saying "Vanilla is my favorite!" this counts as an explanation if Betty is generally disposed to eat vanilla ice cream cones. The explanation here is one of token and type, or specific instance and general kind. Now, this sort of explanation is not altogether empty. Consider table 1.4.

TABLE 1.4. Consumption-Based Explanation of Betty's Action

Explanandum (what is to be explained):	Betty φs.
Explanans (what is to be explained):	Betty's reason for φ-ing (in this instance) is that she has a goal of φ-type consumption.

In this case what is doing the explaining is not a restatement of the thing to be explained; the specific act is explained by showing it to be an instance of a general type. Again, one may be tempted to reduce this to an explanation of the form: Betty φs as a way to bring about her goal of φ-typing. But this really is to get the relation of the specific act and the general type wrong: φ-ing is not a means to φ-typing, it is an instance of it.

It follows from this that, if Betty has a general goal of eating ice cream, and if she is rational, then she should display *consistent choice behavior* when confronted with identical choice between ice cream and alternatives. If, say, she has a general goal of eating ice cream but not cake, then a rational person will consistently choose ice cream over cake.

Note that the core of this idea is *consistency of choice*, not traditional means-end reasoning. We can explain Alf choosing act α over β either because:

(1) α is a better means to Alf's goals than β.
(2) Alf displays a consistent tendency to choose α or β when confronted by the choice (thus showing that he has a general goal of consuming α rather than β).

We can, then, complement the idea of rationality with a consistency criterion after all.

Consumption Consistency

When deciding among actions that are performed purely for their own sakes, a rational person chooses consistently.

This is a very minimal notion of consistency. It says that a rational person may have a goal of eating dirt, but she must be disposed to always eat dirt when given the opportunity; she can't sometimes choose to eat dirt and other times have no disposition to do so. Of course, it all depends on what the options are—our options change, and so our choices do too. But, at a minimum, we can say that consumption consistency requires that, if presented with an identical set of options (and all other circumstances are equal) on Monday and Tuesday, if the person chooses dirt on Monday, a person chooses it on Tuesday too.

Let us, then, combine Rationality and Consumption Consistency for a preliminary fuller account of Rationality:

Rationality

An agent's *A*'s choice to φ is rational if and only if *A*

(a) *soundly believes* φ-ing is the best prospect for achieving *A*'s goals, values, ends, etc *G*; and
(b) demonstrates consumption consistency.

This conception of rationality, as we will see, can form the basis of the general theory of individual rational choice, strategic choice, and social choice.

Although the full explication of this conception of rationality allows for both instrumental and consumption rationality, its power and persuasiveness stem from instrumental explanations. The theory of rational choice derived from this conception of rationality rests much of its claim to our allegiance on the "almost unbelievable delicacy and subtlety"[10] of its analysis of the market. And this analysis shows that individuals with diverse goals engage in certain sorts of economic activity because they believe that such activity is instrumentally effective in achieving their different goals. Thus, for instance, the economic model can explain the choice of medicine as a career by citing relative costs of training, opportunity costs, etc., and showing how occupational choices are instrumentally rational in achieving an agent's ends. For some economists, the crux of the economic model is to explain how different actions in different situations are instrumentally rational to satisfying a stable set of goals.[11] Choices, such as the choice of an occupation, are ways of achieving the satisfaction of stable goals in different circumstances. Such economists, then, would not explain occupational choice by appeal to the goal to be a doctor but, rather, as a way to satisfy one's stable goal for income and prestige.

However, it is important to note that citing the brute desires or goals of people to be doctors does not entail abandoning the notion of consumption consistency: after all, people must have ultimate desires or goals if the economic model is to work. But direct appeal to a desire to φ-type as a way to explain φ-ing is not the preferred mode of economic explanation. We might say that it is an explanation of the last resort, for while it is not empty, neither does it explain much. The preferred explanation is to show that action φ is instrumentally rational for agents with a wide variety of goals, which are not directly about the merits of φ-ing.

---

10. Stigler, Economist as Preacher, 21.
11. Becker, Economic Approach to Human Behavior.

From Rational Choice to *Homo Economicus*

Thus far, we have been developing a general conception of rationality. Economists typically do not concern themselves with these matters but, as will become clear in the following topics, it is important to have in hand a general and nonformal understanding of economic rationality before we begin to look at ways to formalize the theory of rationality.

But much more needs to be added to our informal model of economic rationality before we describe *Homo economicus*. "Economic man" builds on but goes far beyond a basic Humean theory of rationality. *Homo economicus* pursues multiple goals and operates on general principles that determine when one goal rather than another will be sought. Whereas the rational agent—as we have defined it so far—captures part of rational action, *Homo economicus* looks more like a full-fledged model of an instrumentally rational agent. Let us consider five formal traits that characterize *Homo economicus*.

Optimizing—More Is Better than Less

Hume, it will be recalled, argued that "'Tis as little contrary to reason to prefer even my own acknowledg'd lesser good to my greater, and have a more ardent affection for the former than the latter." *Homo economicus* definitely rejects this. Consider a case where Hume's theory looks irrational. Suppose Betty adores Australian wine of a certain winemaker and vintage and is confronted with a choice: she can have either one bottle or two bottles of that wine and vintage. And suppose she chooses one bottle over two.

Why might she do this? We can think of a variety of reasons. She might be drinking too much wine these days and knows that she'll drink both bottles right off. Or perhaps she is riding her bike home and really can't carry a second bottle. Note, though, that explanations like these appeal to some other goal (health) or consideration (the second bottle can't be transported). These other considerations make sense of what seems to be an irrational choice: a choice for less rather than more of something I desire. Imagine, though, that confronted with the choice between one or two bottles of her favorite wine she simply chooses the one, saying she desires less of what she likes to have more of it. A sign that we are confronting an irrational desire here is that it seems unintelligible why someone would want it: we need to tell more of a story to make the action sensible to us.

As Russell Hardin puts it, "[t]he simplest definition of rationality . . . is that one should choose more rather than less value."[12] When faced with a choice

---

12. Hardin, Indeterminacy and Society, 16.

between the satisfaction of a goal at a higher or lower level of satisfaction, it seems paradigmatically irrational to choose the lesser level of satisfaction. Rationality involves optimization, which is to say choosing the best option, given what one values. Hardin puts this claim in terms of "value," which is fine as far as it goes, but we can generalize by thinking in terms of goals.

For example, we do not think eating a ten-pound steak is better than eating a two-pound steak, even if we love steak. More steak is not necessarily better than less steak. If we redefine our goal in terms of, say, pleasure of having a satisfying meal, then the anomaly is removed, for the bigger steak does not, presumably, make for a more satisfying meal: it does not yield a greater degree of goal fulfillment. Although we need not adopt hedonism, it probably is the case that rationality more obviously endorses "more is better than less" when goals are not understood as aiming at specific goods, but as more abstract aims, ends, and states of being. "Lumpiness" can also be a problem if we focus on specific goods; it may well be that we only have use for a good in "lumpy" increments, so that an extra amount that does not get us to the next increment is of no use. If I am building a new bicycle, two new (identical) seats are probably not better than one, since I can't use the second. But here the problem seems to be that my goal is not really better satisfied by a second seat, so the second seat does not achieve a higher level of goal satisfaction. One way to avoid these problems is to simply assume that goods are continuous (not lumpy), and that an extra increment always better satisfies our goal than a smaller increment does. The good of money probably satisfies this assumption fairly well.

Decreasing Marginal Value

Homo economicus, other things equal, will always prefer a greater over a lesser degree of goal satisfaction. However, although we always prefer the greater amount over the lesser, the increase in value diminishes as we accumulate units of a goal. This idea of diminishing marginal utility was one of the revolutionary developments in modern economics. In the words of Carl Menger (1840–1921), one of the economists usually credited with its discovery:

> The satisfaction of every man's need for food up to the point where his life is thereby assured has the full importance of the maintenance of his life. Consumption exceeding this amount, again up to a certain point, has the importance of preserving his health (that is, his continuing well-being). Consumption extending beyond even this point has merely the importance—as observation shows—of a progressively weaker pleasure, until it finally reaches a certain limit at which the satisfaction of the need for food is so complete that every further intake of food contributes neither to the

maintenance of life nor the preservation of health—nor does it give pleasure to the consumer, becoming first a matter of indifference to him, eventually a cause of pain, a danger to his health, and finally a danger to life itself.[13]

Menger's basic insight was that the amount of extra value we place on additional increments of a good decreases as we gain more of the good. As we see from the last lines of this quote, Menger himself thought that at some point we reach satiation and beyond that we *dis*value increments; so not only does the extra value of an increment become smaller, but at some point there is no increment at all (this then conflicts with "more is better than less," at least when applied to the good of food). If, though, we accept that "more is better than less," then we suppose that we never quite reach the point in which a person is entirely indifferent, though the extra value he achieves from the increment might be miniscule.

Somewhat surprisingly, although decreasing marginal utility is fundamental to economic analysis, its grounding is not obvious. Some treat it simply as an empirical generalization about how people do in fact typically make choices rather than a basic feature of rationality itself or a deep psychological law.[14] Hedonists can provide a more secure foundation for it, claiming that since everything we do aims at pleasure, it is a deep psychological law that the more we have of something, the less extra pleasure we get from each additional unit: the first slice of pizza gives a lot of pleasure, the second less, the third even less. While this makes sense of decreasing marginal utility, it does so only if we accept hedonism, something we have already questioned.

Another possibility is to see decreasing marginal utility as fundamental to the concept of a rational agent with multiple goals. Thus far we have been treating instrumentally rational agents as if they had only one goal, desire, etc. Rational agents, though, must act on a variety of goals. Now suppose one has a variety of goals, but the satisfaction of each goal has no diminishing marginal effect. Suppose further that this goal is the most important goal for you, and you could always do something to achieve it. Suppose that this goal is watching Australian Rules Football. If so, you would do nothing but watch Australian Rules Football, all day every day. Agents whose goals are not characterized by decreasing marginal utility would tend to be monomaniacs: they would be apt to seek the same the thing over and over and over again.

We can, then, see decreasing marginal utility as crucial to the idea of a *rational multiple-goal pursuer* who seeks to satisfy different goals at different times. As one goal is achieved, its importance tends to decline so that other

---

13. Menger, *Principles of Economics*, 124.
14. Hausman, The Inexact and Separate Science of Economics, 32.

goals rise to attention. To say that a goal's "utility" decreases, then, is simply to say that its relative importance decreases as it is increasingly satisfied; at some point then the agent will choose an action that secures a basic satisfaction of a less important goal over an act that yields ever more satisfaction of a more important goal. Insofar as we think a rational agent is not a monomaniac who pursues just one thing all the time, we will have to include in our model some version of decreasing marginal utility.

Consider another example: suppose a person is deeply conservative, and she performs the same religious ritual over and over again. One might think this means that the value of performing the ritual does not decrease at the margins for her. Are we saying that she is *economically irrational*, because her choices do not reflect decreasing marginal utility of rituals? No, we would tend to think that her choices *do* reflect decreasing marginal utility: after all, she does not perform the ritual all day every day. Having performed her religious ritual, she then chooses to eat, work, or read.

That we do something repeatedly is not a counter-example to decreasing marginal utility. One of the authors, Jerry, used to watch old movies every day, sometimes two in a day. He put great value on them, but despite the great value he put on them, he would do other things—like write PPE books—that he apparently "valued less." Why would he ever do anything but watch old movies if he loved them so much? Why does our traditionalist ever do anything other than perform her valued ritual? Decreasing marginal utility explains why.

Much the same idea can be put in terms of *decreasing rates of substitution*. Suppose we have two goods, pizza and ice cream. And suppose Betty has a total amount of money to spend on some combination of pizza and ice cream. We then get figure 1.2.

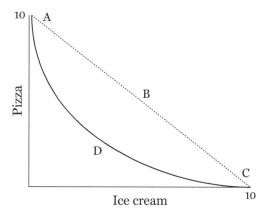

FIGURE 1.2. An Indifference Curve

At point A, Betty spends all her money on ten pizzas. At point C, she spends all her money on ten quarts of ice cream. At B, she divides her expenditure. Given decreasing marginal utility, Betty prefers B to either A or C. This can be put in terms of decreasing rates of substitution between pizza and ice cream: when you have all pizza, you will give up quite a bit to get some ice cream; but as you get more and more ice cream, you will give up less pizza to get the same increment of additional ice cream.[15]

This leads to the important idea of an *indifference curve*: Betty is *indifferent* between all bundles of ice cream and pizza on the convex line (A-D-C). Betty is, of course, not indifferent between B and A since she prefers B to A; she is, though, indifferent between A, D, and C and this even though D is a smaller bundle of goods than A or C—because of decreasing marginal utility, D, as it were, manages to squeeze more utility out of the goods. Vilfredo Pareto (1848–1923), who is often credited with the modern development of indifference curve analysis, described them as contours on the "hill of pleasure." Like the contours on a map, each line connects points of equal elevation, or in our case equal value; as we go up the hill, we go up in value.

The Law of Demand—Downward Sloping Demand Curves

We have suggested that an important ground for accepting the assumption of decreasing marginal utility is that we are pursuers of multiple goals. In many ways the heart of economic thinking is that we always have to choose between our goals and values. The crucial contribution of economic analysis is the idea of *opportunity costs*: the cost of getting one good thing is that we forego the opportunity to have something else that is good. This is not a lesson easily learned. When Jerry's daughter was around five years old, she would sometimes get money from a relative on a special occasion, and she would promptly go to the toy store. But it was always a tragedy for her: although she desperately wanted the toy, she desperately wanted to keep the money too. She could not bear to pay the cost of the toy but could not bear to forego the toy either. Typically, the trip ended with her bursting into tears (and Jerry buying the toy!). The tragedy resulted because she sought an action without opportunity costs.

Given that choice always involves opportunity costs, as the cost of a choice increases it becomes less attractive to a rational chooser. We can say that *Homo economicus*'s willingness to act to satisfy goal G_1 decreases as the costs of

---

15. Decreasing marginal utility and decreasing rates of substitution are closely related but not the same idea: whereas the idea of decreasing marginal utility requires a cardinal measure of utility, decreasing rates of substitution can be expressed in purely ordinal terms.

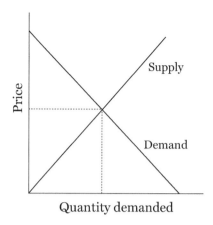

FIGURE 1.3. Supply and Demand

achieving G_1 (in terms of lost opportunity to achieve G_2) increase. This is a gloss on the "law of demand," the notion that the demand curve for any good is "downward sloping": the more a good cost, the less of it is demanded.

The law of demand can be combined with its inverse, the "Law of Supply," which states that as the price of a good increases, more of it will be supplied. Both of these laws together form the basic model of supply and demand. This model shows that the equilibrium price and quantity demanded of a good should exist where the supply and demand curves intersect.

Unlike our simple model of an instrumentally rational agent with which we began, we now see that *Homo economicus* is a much more complicated fellow: he must be able to choose between competing actions promoting different ends through a system of trade-off rates according to which the "demand" for a goal/end decreases as its cost relative to other goals/ends increases. This is the crux of what we mean by an efficient pursuit of goals.

Self-Interest

Homo economicus is generally understood as an egoist or, even more narrowly, a wealth maximizer. Many of the best economists believe that the core of the "economic approach" to society has been the explanatory power of self-interest. Assuming that people are self-interested, only looking out for their material well-being, is in most people's minds what economics is all about. And it is precisely this aspect of *Homo economicus* that has attracted so much criticism from social scientists resisting the economic approach.

It remains, though, a matter of dispute whether narrow motivations such as egoism or wealth maximization are really basic to the economic conception of rationality or whether they are best understood as simplifying assumptions that allow for more determinate applications of the model. The latter, we think, is more plausible. This is especially clear regarding wealth maximization: it surely is not part and parcel of being a rational agent that one maximizes wealth. However, to *assume* that people are, generally, devoted to maximizing wealth allows for determinate applications of some economic models by allowing us to specify what the agents' goals are, and so see what actions are indeed instrumentally rational given those goals. In many contexts, it does well enough to suppose that what people are really interested in is wealth and income. However, the usefulness of this assumption is surely context dependent. It makes sense in a few areas of economics, but most of economics does not suppose that people are wealth maximizers.

One of the core insights of economics is related to the ability to explain mutually beneficial behavior solely by reference to the self-interest of the parties involved. In *The Wealth of Nations*, Adam Smith (1723–1790) argues that:

> It is not from the benevolence of the butcher, the brewer, or the baker, that we expect our dinner, but from their regard to their own interest. We address ourselves, not to their humanity but to their self-love, and never talk to them of our own necessities but of their advantages. Nobody but a beggar chuses [*sic*] to depend chiefly upon the benevolence of his fellow-citizens. Even a beggar does not depend upon it entirely.[16]

Smith is making an important point here that economic exchange does not presuppose benevolence (or altruism). If I act benevolently, I act for the sake of giving benefits of the person I am exchanging with. In the passage about the butcher and baker, Smith is certainly denying that benevolent motivation is behind market exchanges. Now most readers suppose that if one is not altruistic, one must be selfish or egoistic. But this really isn't so. If one acts egoistically, one acts with no other concern than benefits to one's self, so one is certainly not acting for others (altruistically). But it doesn't follow that everyone who is not an altruist is an egoist. Between altruism and selfishness is reciprocity (or conditional cooperation), according to which "if you benefit me then I will return the benefit; I will not benefit you if you do not benefit me." This seems to be what Smith is talking about. Recall that he says, "Give me that which I want, and you shall have this which you want, is the meaning of every such offer."

The difference between selfishness and reciprocity will only emerge after we consider game theory: selfish agents, we will see, have great difficulty

---

16. Smith, An Inquiry, bk. II.2.ii.

cooperating, while reciprocal agents are able to easily cooperate for mutual benefit. Selfish agents would prefer not to respond to benefit with returned benefit: they would just like to keep the benefits that others confer on them without reciprocating. In our view, markets couldn't work if people were truly selfish: there are just too many opportunities to cheat, steal, and commit fraud. To the extent that many people are selfish, markets do not work well. On the other hand, if the large majority are reciprocators, mutual benefit is easy to achieve, and cheating is not as serious of a problem.

Indeed, much of economics does not even suppose the modest sort of self-interest characteristic of Smith's reciprocators. Certainly, such a supposition is questionable when applied generally to political science or analysis of the law. We have tried to show that the real crux of rational choice can be explicated without any reference to self-interest: more is better than less, decreasing marginal value, and downward sloping demand curves all can be explained without any reference to self-interest. They simply assume that people have goals they wish to pursue and are devoted to pursuing their own goals in the most efficient manner. Just what those goals are is another question.

According to Philip Wicksteed (1844–1927), "the specific character of an economic relation is not its 'egoism,' but its non-tuism."[17] By this Wicksteed meant that each party to an economic relation is seeking to advance her own goals, desires, and ends and not those of the other party. As Smith recognized, economics is not a study of transactions among altruists, but of *non-tuists*. The important feature in an economic transaction between Alf and Betty is that Alf is not seeking to achieve Betty's goals, and she is not seeking to achieve his: each is seeking to advance their own goals. Their goals, though, may not be at all self-interested. Parents engage in economic transactions with universities: they pay large tuitions to educate their children and the universities use this money to support their own academic and social goals. Neither party need be concerned with its own self-interest.

To be sure, we can save the characterization of rationality as inherently self-interested by describing all goal pursuit as "self-interested": if it is your goal, then it is in your interest to pursue it. This, though, is to expand the meaning of "self-interest" so that it includes anything the self is interested in. If my values lead me to give to charity, educate my children, and help my neighbors, then on this view I am being just as "self-interested" as one who keeps all her money, ignores her children, and dumps her garbage in her neighbor's yard. The idea of being "self-interested" loses its typical meaning and simply becomes just another name for non-tuism.

17. Wicksteed, Common Sense, 180.

Even Wicksteed's non-tuism is merely a simplifying assumption: it allows us, in an economic transaction, to calculate your "utility" as, in principle, independent of my "utility" (see the next chapter for more on utility). If my aim is to promote your aim, and your aim is to promote my aim, calculating what actions further our aims is exceedingly complicated. In such cases our utility functions are not independent, and the mathematics of modeling such interdependent functions is quite complicated. If we accept Wicksteed's non-tuism, things are much simpler—but that is the point, it is a simplifying supposition, not something inherent to the economic understanding of rational agents.

Constrained Maximization

The picture of *Homo economicus* that emerges is of a basically instrumentally rational agent, who seeks more rather than less, who is responsive to the costs of her choices, and who does not pursue one goal again and again but acts on a variety of goals. In this way, she maximizes the achievement of her goals or ends. Economists, though, understand this maximization to occur against a background of constraints. Individuals maximize given budget constraints: in figure 1.2, the line A-B-C is the budget constraint, showing possible combinations of goods for a fixed budget. More broadly, economic agents operate within a set of rules and institutions that constrain what they can do. That a person may maximize by attacking others is not included in most economic models, as noncoercion is usually understood as a constraint.

Need *Homo economicus* maximize? Given her goals, must she always seek the greatest possible amount of goal satisfaction? Herbert Simon (1916–2001), a Nobel prize–winning economist, has famously argued for an alternative to "*Homo economicus* the maximizer"—a "satisficing" agent.[18] Instead of seeking the best outcome—maximizing the achievement of her goals—an agent who "satisfices" seeks an outcome that is satisfactory or "good enough." Many insist that rational agents often satisfice rather than maximize.[19]

However, it is not always clear whether satisficing is really an alternative to maximizing. On one view, satisficing is simply a strategy that a maximizer might follow. People who *try* to maximize—who always seek the best—are apt to waste a lot of time; they incur search and information costs while trying to determine whether they can do a little bit better than the "good enough" choice, and in so doing may not achieve as many of their goals as a satisficing agent, who finds a good enough option and then moves on to something else.

18. See Simon, "Theories of Decision-Making," 253–83.
19. Here we use "maximize" as a synonym for "optimize."

Conceived thus, satisficing is not an alternative to maximizing, but a *way to maximize* (you can do best by settling for good enough and then moving on to a different goal). More radically, though, some see satisficing as an inherently rational way of acting that does not turn on a claim to ultimately maximize. It is rational to settle for good enough even if one could, all things considered, do better. Understood in this way, satisficing requires a fundamental revision of *Homo economicus*: "more is better than less" must be abandoned, since sometimes, on this satisficing view, "good enough is as good as more."

Conclusion

This chapter explored the foundation of all rational choice and economic analysis: the notion of a rational agent. Underlying this idea is the even more fundamental notion of rationality. We saw that rationality is best characterized as consistency between one's beliefs and goals. Rational choice means acting on the basis of one's sound beliefs in order to secure some goal. We also argued that economic or consumption rationality in the form of *Homo economicus* goes beyond the basic idea of a rational agent and includes additional assumptions. We also challenged the idea that *Homo economicus* is essentially selfish rather than non-tuistic. In the following several chapters, we will add more precision to this basic model of rational choice.

Discussion Questions

(1) Can it pay in business to be irrational? How? If it would pay, would it be rational after all?

(2) Can a person who always fails to achieve her goals really be rational?

(3) Hume writes, "'Tis not contrary to reason to prefer the destruction of the whole world to the scratching of my finger." Do you agree? Would such a person be rational?

(4) Can it be rational to desire pain over pleasure?

(5) Rationality is often thought of as a special kind of consistency. Can one be entirely consistent in one's choices, and yet irrational? Are there any cases in economics, politics, or ethics that you can think of?

(6) Why do you think economists assume that more is always better than less when we know that sometimes more is worse—at some point one becomes ill from eating or drinking too much, or perhaps from having too much leisure time?

(7) According to James M. Buchanan and Geoffrey Brennan, "Homo economicus offers a better basic model for explaining human

behavior than any comparable alternative," but it is a "useful fiction," indeed a "caricature of human behavior." People are not always consumptively rational, but a useful social theory employs *Homo economicus* as a generalization. Can a productive science rely on useful fictions?

(8) What proportion of people do you think are basically selfish? What proportion of market participants?

(9) Think about the market exchanges you have had in the last week. Which best explains the behavior of others—selfishness, reciprocity, benevolence, or some combination? Which best explains your behavior?

2

Ordinal Utility Theory

In the last chapter, we examined the idea of rationality and what it means to make a rational choice. As we saw, there are a number of thorny philosophical issues that the seemingly straightforward idea of rationality raises. In the end, we learned that rational choice is best understood as choosing the best prospect that one soundly believes will get the best result, given one's goals and values. In this chapter, we will make that idea more precise and develop the formal apparatus for rational choice theory as it is used in decision theory, economics, and political science, by introducing the ideas of preferences and utility. Rationality is about choosing the best way to get what one wants, and utility theory is a way of representing that idea precisely through the notion of preferences. By using preferences to signify rankings of possible outcomes, we will be able to construct ordinal as well as cardinal utility functions to represent what rationality in terms of optimizing looks like given a specific set of preferences.

Building Blocks

Rationality is about choosing consistently given one's beliefs and values, desires, and goals. Beliefs are one's representations of states of the world—how things are and how certain actions are likely to change things. These can be represented, as we saw in the last chapter, as credences (e.g., "there is a one in five hundred chance of the Cincinnati Reds winning the World Series"), but they can also be represented as propositions (e.g., "it is raining today"), or as comparative claims (e.g., "it is more likely than not to rain today" or "it is more likely that we will find definitive evidence of Bigfoot this year, than that the St. Kilda Saints will win the AFL Premiership this year"). Outcomes are future states of the world—how things might be. Actions are probabilistic prospects or paths from current states of the world to outcomes.

- States (ways the world is)
- Outcomes (ways the world could be)
- Actions (ways to transform the world from how it is into what it could be)

Using these basic notions, choice is a function of the form Action: State $\rightarrow$ Outcome.

When we are thinking about rational choice in these terms, we will often think in terms of sets of actions, outcomes, or, later, of preferences. Sets are simply collections of things that have certain well-known logical properties. Sets are collections of basically anything. One can have a set of ducks, animals, people, real numbers, fictional characters, or even other sets. Sets are represented as brackets, e.g. $\{\ldots\}$, where the members of the set are within the brackets. For instance, if we have a set A with three members $x, y,$ and z, we can represent this as $A = \{x, y, z\}$. We can also say that x, y, z are members of A with $x, y, z \in A$. There is a special set called the null set which has no members and is represented with $\varnothing$. We can make sets out of sets by placing brackets around them so, for instance, $\{A\}$ is distinct from A and $\varnothing$ is distinct from $\{\varnothing\}$.

The elements of a set are unordered, so $A = \{$apples, oranges, strawberries, grapes, tomato$\} = \{$apples, oranges, strawberries, tomato, grapes$\}$. This is important since one of the critical concepts we will introduce is an ordering on a set, which will impose a structure on the elements in a set. A union of two sets A and B, $A \cup B$, includes all the elements of A and of B. The intersection of two sets A and B, $A \cap B$, includes all the elements of A that are also in B. Two sets, A and B, are considered disjoint if $A \cap B = \varnothing$, which is to say their intersection has no members in it. A is a subset of B, $A \subseteq B$, if all the elements in A are also in B. A is a superset of B, $A \supseteq B$, if all the elements in B are also in A. For two sets, A and B, the complement of A and B, $A \setminus B$ or $(A\text{-}B)$, consists of all the elements of A that are not in B.

Preferences

Preferences are the primitive unit of rationality in utility theory—it is fundamental to utility theory. As we have seen, rational choice is about optimizing, i.e., choosing the best option as one sees it. Sometimes we think of this as "satisfying a preference," but, unfortunately, "preference" is an especially ambiguous term. We can identify at least three interpretations of preference:

(1) a noncomparative "taste" for something
(2) choice behavior itself
(3) the agent's deliberative rankings of her outcomes and options

Let's consider each.

Preferences as Tastes or Desires

Philosophers, lawyers, and even some economists tend to equate the idea of a preference with a *liking*. To have a "preference for pizza" is to *like* pizza, or to have a *taste* for pizza. "I prefer it" means "I like it" or "I have a taste for it." Thus, for Louis Kaplow and Steven Shavell to say a person has a preference for a fair outcome is simply to say that she has a "taste" for fairness:

> [I]f individuals in fact have tastes for notions of fairness—that is, if they feel better off when laws or events that they observe are in accord with what they consider to be fair-—then analysis under welfare economics will take such tastes into account.[1]

Notice the echo of hedonism and egoism; a person's sole aim seems to be to "*feel* better off." Although we sometimes talk this way, there are two reasons why this notion of preference cannot enter into utility theory. To see why, let's look at a couple of illustrative cases.

First, consider the famous "ticking time bomb" case from Michael Walzer:

> a politician who has seized upon a national crisis—a prolonged colonial war—to reach for power. He and his friends win office pledged to decolonization and peace; they are honestly committed to both, though not without some sense of the advantages of the commitment. In any case, they have no responsibility for the war; they have steadfastly opposed it. Immediately, the politician goes off to the colonial capital to open negotiations with the rebels. But the capital is in the grip of a terrorist campaign and the first decision the new leader faces is this: he is asked to authorize the torture of a captured rebel who knows or probably knows the location of a number of bombs hidden in apartment buildings around the city, set to go off in the next twenty-four hours. He orders the man tortured, convinced that he must do so for the sake of the people who might otherwise die in the explosions—even though he believes that torture is wrong, indeed abominable, not just sometimes, but always.[2]

If we think of a "preference" as something akin to "liking" or "having a taste for," we can interpret this case in two ways. We can say:

(a) that the politician has a preference (taste) for torture, or
(b) that he does not have a preference to torture the terrorist rather than to let the buildings blow up, though he still chooses to torture the terrorist.

---

1. Kaplow and Shavell, Fairness versus Welfare, 431.
2. Walzer, "The Problem of Dirty Hands," 161–62.

The first interpretation is obviously wrong. As Walzer tells the story, the politician despises torture; he certainly does not have a taste for it. That would make him a sadist! So perhaps we should adopt interpretation (b) and say that the politician chooses to torture but does not have a preference for it (since he certainly does not like it or enjoy it). But this would mean that the politician both chose the best option as he saw it and, thereby, acted rationally, while also acting against his preference. In this case, rationality and preferential choice would come apart. Utility theory is a way of representing rational choice, so it is no good if choosing according to one's preferences and choosing rationally are distinct.

In utility theory, preferences are rankings of outcomes, and choosing according to one's preferences is the same as choosing the optimal option available. So, if our politician ranks option x as more choice-worthy than y, then he prefers y even if he detests both—though he detests x a little less than y. If he is rational and chooses x then he *must* (analytically) prefer x to y, even though he doesn't *like* either. So, we need to make sure that we do not confuse the technical notion of a preference with the ordinary language conception of a "liking."

Second and more important, understanding preferences as tastes or desires makes them *noncomparative*: one likes x, has a taste for x, or desires x. If preferences are rankings of outcomes—as they are in utility theory—preferences are always understood as *comparative*: one always prefers one thing (or option) to another. A preference always and necessarily relates two options and compares them in terms of choice-worthiness. One does not simply have a preference for one thing. In this way, "preference" is more like "bigger" than "big." One thing can be "big," but "bigger" relates two things: it is inherently comparative.

We now see why it is confusing to interpret "preference" as synonymous with "goals," "desires," or "values." The latter are all non-comparative: my goal can be just x (to get a pizza), I can desire just x, or I can simply value x. But in utility theory I cannot simply have a preference for x (pizza)—it must be a preference for x over y, some second option—for pizza *over* (rather than) tacos.

Preference

Preference is a binary relation "R" or "$\geq$" such that $x \geq y$ or $x\, R\, y$ **means** x is preferred to y.

A binary relation like R is a way of ordering two elements of a set.[3] Think of a set of numbers $N = \{2,1,4,5,3\}$. We can impose a binary relation "greater than" or $>$ on these numbers to order them so that $5 > 4 > 3 > 2 > 1$. Some

---

3. Technically a powerset of two other sets.

binary relations like "greater than" are asymmetric so that $2 > 1 \neq 1 > 2$. Being a father is also an asymmetric relation. If Abraham is the father of Isaac, it doesn't follow that Isaac is the father of Abraham. The binary relation of being "equal to" is symmetric, however. If $x = y$, then $y = x$. As we will see, the preference relation is asymmetric. It is also reflexive, which is to say that xRx is always true or that x is always as choice-worthy as itself. This may seem like a weird property but think about Socrates' admonition to "know thyself"; the assumption must be that even though we may know others, it is possible that we don't sufficiently know ourselves. We will have more to say about the properties of preferences in utility theory below.

Revealed Preferences: The Behavioral Interpretation

Economists often insist—at least in their more official pronouncements—on a purely behavioral conception of preference. On this view, Alf is said to have a preference for x over y if and only if *Alf actually* chooses x over y, when both are choices are available and feasible. On this interpretation, to prefer x to y is simply to choose it over y; if one has never made the choice then one does not have the preference. Preference so understood is, then, equivalent to actual choice. When pressed, economists are apt to say that a preference is simply choice behavior, and if one has consistent preferences this means simply that one chooses consistently. Thus, it is said, one's actual choices "reveal" one's preferences.

The very term "revealed" preference is somewhat misleading. If preferences just *are* choices, what sense can be made of saying that a choice *reveals* a preference? To use this sort of language is to suggest that the choice is "revealing" something else, something hidden and mental, as when a person makes a "revealing statement," showing something previously hidden about her character. However, avoiding all appeal to such mental entities was the explicit aim of the economists who stressed "revealed preference "theory."[4] But if the choice behavior does not reveal anything mental, what does it reveal?

Leaving aside the confusion about what is supposed to be "revealed," we have powerful reasons to question the plausibility of the most radical version of behaviorism; the attempt to rid the mental from social science appears doomed to failure. Choice is an intentional concept and any effort to describe Alf's choice of x over y will necessarily involve a reference to his understanding

---

4. The classic formulations of revealed preference theory are by Paul Samuelson. See Samuelson, "Consumption Theory in Terms of Revealed Preference."

of what he is doing—his *intentions*—and what he sees as the nature of the choice confronting him.

Voting for candidate *x* over *y*, for example, is not a piece of behavior qua movement of a body, it is not simply puling a lever or filling out a ballot. A description of an act as "a vote for *x*" necessarily turns on the intentions—mental states—of actors involved. The behavior of "raising an arm" may be the act of asking a question or casting a vote (or innumerable other acts); only reference to the intentions of the agent can distinguish the two. And very different pieces of behavior (raising a hand, marking a piece of paper, or shouting "yea!") all may constitute the *same act* of "voting for *x*." This is not to say that an intention is sufficient (Neither of the authors can vote for the president of Russia even if we intend to), but it seems quite impossible to rid the intentional from our conception of choice. If so, we can hardly purge the mental from our explanation of choices.

Nevertheless, the idea of revealed preferences can make sense if we think of preferences in terms of what economists call "choice functions." The idea is that, given some set of options and a "menu" or a "budget set," which is a subset of those options that are feasible, the choice of options within a menu when other choices are possible "reveals" a preference. In other words, if one is presented with two choices of equally priced wine to have with dinner, e.g., Shiraz and Cabernet, and one chooses Shiraz (as the authors would), then we can infer that one prefers Shiraz to Cabernet. We can do this not because preferences are identical with choice as the behaviorist interpretation would have it, but precisely because they are not. The assumption in the background is that the binary preference relation "rationalizes" choice within a certain menu by making them consistent. However, this only makes sense if we view the idea of preference as basic rather than choice. We assume that choice is rational and then use preference to rationalize choice. As we will see, this approach creates some problems, but it is consistent with the appropriate way of thinking about preferences.

We cannot do without appeal to the mental in accounting for what is involved in choosing on the basis of one's preferences. Although in their official pronouncements many economists are apt to adopt a behavioristic notion of revealed preference, most economic writing, and almost all accounts of rational action, suppose that actual choice is taken to *reveal* (or advance) preference qua a deliberative ranking of the options by the agent. The agent is assumed to order the options in the feasible set of options. Her actual choice from the feasible set would then *reveal* her deliberative preference over the feasible set of options.

Deliberation, Actions, and Outcomes

Actions and Outcomes

This leads us to a fundamental issue in utility theory: what ultimately do our preferences range over? There are two clear possibilities:

(a) outcomes, and
(b) possible actions that we might undertake.

Say you prefer to live in California rather than New York (outcomes), but now you have to consider how this preference over outcomes relates to what action you choose. Perhaps the actions open to you are to accept an offer of going to surf school in California or law school in New York. If your preference over outcomes is to live in California, perhaps the action you should choose is to accept the surf school offer because that action option will better satisfy your deliberative preference over outcomes. It looks like we must, then, consider both a person's ranking of *outcomes* and a person's ranking of *action-options* in terms of which action is most choice-worthy: that is, which actions best satisfy one's preferences over outcomes.

Consequence Domain

The *consequence domain* of a choice involves everything relevant to a person's ranking of states of the world that might obtain.

   The important point here is that one's ranking of outcomes must include all the considerations that lead one to the judgment that it is more or less desirable than an alternative. Thus, the consequence domain of living in California would include the wonders of its climate and landscape, its diversity, one's job, what one's partner thinks of moving, tax rates, and so on.

   Once one factors in all of these considerations, one is then ready to map actions on to consequences. Suppose you can rank all these states of the world in terms of which best satisfies your goals and desires, etc. Here $C_1 \succcurlyeq C_2 \succcurlyeq C_3$. However, the important point for utility theory is not *why* you rank states of the world the way you do, but that you are *able* to rank them. Now suppose that you confront a variety of action-options, and their consequences. In this case, actions w and x are both correlated with C_1, y is correlated with C_2, and z is correlated with C_3. Thus, your preferences over outcomes determine your preferences over options. We can think, then, of a *mapping* of an ordering of outcome-consequences on to the action-options, producing an ordering of action-options as in figure 2.1.

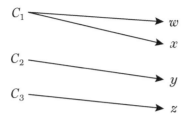

FIGURE 2.1. Mapping Actions to Outcomes

Although the ordering of action-options (w, x, y, z) will be correlated with the ordering of outcome-consequences (C_1, C_2, C_3), a unique one-to-one relation is not necessary. As we see in the figure, two actions (w, x) may be correlated with the same consequence C_1. In such cases, a rational agent will be *indifferent* between w and x since they are associated with the same consequence. If, on the other hand, w is correlated with C_1 and y is correlated with C_2, where C_1 is a higher ranked consequence than C_2, then a rational agent will prefer x over y.

Preferences Over Actions

We tend to model preferences over outcomes as simply given; one's preferences over action-options are determined by their relation to outcomes. On this standard view, actions are simply routes or prospects to outcomes. However, preferences over action change as one gets new information about the relation of the acts to one's rankings of outcomes. The distinction between preferences over outcomes and over actions is especially important when we study utility theory under risk and strategic situations (chapters 3–6), where one cannot be certain what action-options produce certain outcomes.

Nevertheless, as we shall see a little later, we can complicate things by building in preferences that directly concern actions as well as outcomes. That is, rather than the preferences over the outcomes determining the preferences over actions (one prefers action w to x if and only if w leads to more preferred outcomes than x), we can suppose that people also have preferences over what actions they perform. Perhaps Alf just prefers action w to x—perhaps because he thinks x is immoral. This complicates things but helps us to capture important cases that are especially relevant to political philosophy and moral aspects of social life.

Although most standard views of rational choice don't allow for the possibility of preferences directly over actions, we think that this assumption is a serious mistake. There is no reason we cannot have preferences over actions as well as outcomes. Rather than actions being simply instruments to securing states of the world, they may themselves be things we care about; an action may be its own outcome in some cases. One of Alf's preferences over outcomes may be that he performs act x, say, "telling the truth when under oath today." If in his current set of options one action-option is to tell the truth under oath, he will rank that act highly. Given this, the action of telling the truth under oath may be an action that one has a direct preference to perform.

Another way we can describe this point is in terms of Amartya Sen's distinction between comprehensive and culmination outcomes. Sen writes:

> A person's preferences over *comprehensive* outcomes (including the choice process) have to be distinguished from the conditional preferences over *culmination* outcomes *given* the act of choice. The responsibility associated with choice can sway our ranking of our narrowly-defined outcomes (such as commodity vectors), and choice functions and preference relations may be parametrically influenced by specific features of the *act* of choice (including the *identity* of the chooser, the *menu* over which the choice is made, and the relation of the particular *act* to behavioral social norms that constrain particular actions).[5]

Sen distinguishes the *comprehensive* outcome, which can include the utility of the choice process like choosing to do the fair act, from the distinct state of affairs that is produced by a choice, which he calls the *culmination* outcome or the outcome that one thinks is best overall. Insofar as part of the outcome's utility derives from what it shows about one of the options confronting our choice, this is part of the comprehensive, but not the cumulative, outcome.

Sen has in mind cases in which the utility of the states of affairs depends on the fact that one passed up what looked to be a more attractive option. Again, according to Sen:

> You arrive at a garden party and can readily identify the most comfortable chair. You would be delighted if an imperious host were to assign you to that chair. However, if the matter is left to your own choice, you may refuse to risk it. You select a "less preferred" chair. Are you still a maximizer? Quite possibly you are, since your preference ranking for choice behavior may well be defined over "comprehensive outcomes," including choice processes (in particular, who does the choosing) as well as outcomes at culmination (the distribution of chairs).[6]

Or, consider the case where Alf is presented with a choice of taking a mango from a basket that also has two apples. Alf generally prefers mangos to apples,

---

5. Sen, "Maximization and the Act of Choice," 159.
6. Sen, "Maximization and the Act of Choice," 161.

but he also knows that this is the last mango and that his host also loves mangos. Knowing all of this, Alf chooses the apple over the mango.

Sen asks whether the choice of the lesser preferred option shows either that Alf really did prefer apples to mangos, as revealed preference theory would have it, or that the simple choice function is obscuring important information about the choice in question. In these cases, the person prefers an outcome—getting the comfortable chair, getting the last mango—but also has independent preferences about the route that would produce these actions. Alf, for instance, prefers being polite to not being polite. So now the overall evaluation depends not just on the outcome, but the route taken to the outcome as well as the outcome itself. Another way of putting this point is that the evaluation of outcomes can be conditional on what routes there are to reach it.

Utility theory thus will look very different depending on how we restrict the scope of "preferences." If rational people can have preferences over actions themselves, then a person who acts on a moral principle is nevertheless acting to promote one's "preferences." Thus, we can understand a sort of Kantian agent, who seeks to follow correct moral principles regardless of their consequences, as nevertheless acting on her "preferences." And that means that we will be able to model her actions as rational in utility theory.

We can see why it was so important not to confuse the idea of a "preference" with something one "likes." A person may not "like" being polite—what she really likes are mangoes!—but nevertheless, she can "prefer" being polite to having something that she likes.[7]

Ordinal Utility Theory

For now, we will focus on the core idea of preferences over outcomes, since they are clearly at the heart of the story. Before we can continue, we need to introduce a complication to the idea of preference. So, if for Betty $x \succcurlyeq y$, we can read this as "x is at least as good as y." This leaves open the possibility,

---

7. While we have followed Sen in accepting that the route to an outcome can independently matter to an agent, he nevertheless seems attracted to the idea that a preference must be something that a person likes. For instance, he advises us to distinguish actions that follow from "adhering to a deontological principle" from those that are "actually 'preferred.'" The idea is that a moral obligation (say, to tell the truth) may require one to act in a way that sets back one's goals or welfare. Perhaps one's best friend will be convicted if one tells the truth under oath: his conviction is not an outcome "one prefers." Here, Sen is pushing the idea of "preference" closer to its ordinary meaning of "liking," where one can rationally do what one does not prefer ("I had reason to do it, but I sure did not prefer it."). But, as we have argued, there is no good reason to think that the technical conception of preference has anything to do with "liking."

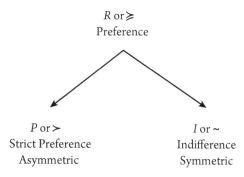

FIGURE 2.2. The Preference Relation

however, that Betty ranks x and y as good as one another. We call this indifference and represent it as "I" or "$\sim$" where xIy or $x \sim y$ means that Betty is indifferent between x and y. This is a symmetric binary relation, so $x \sim y$ is equivalent to $y \sim x$. If Alf is indifferent between a pizza and a taco, he is also indifferent between a taco and a pizza.

There is also the strictly asymmetric binary relation, represented as P or $\succ$, so if xPy or $x \succ y$, we read this as "x is strictly preferred to y." The strict preference relation is, then, *asymmetric*: $\forall$ (for all) $(x,y) \neg$ [i.e., not] $[(x \succ y)$ & $(y \succ x)]$. If Alf strictly prefers a pizza to a taco, it must be the case that he does *not* strictly prefer a taco to a pizza.

With the material we have introduced so far, we can generate an *ordinal utility function* for any person in terms of their preference rankings for the different outcomes if that ranking satisfies the following standard conditions for a *weak* ordering.

The first is completeness. The orderings are *complete* if Alf can always rank all the relevant options in his feasible set. That is, he can always decide whether one possible outcome is better than another, worse than the other, or equally choice-worthy. Note that in this sense Alf "orders" a pizza and a taco if either (a) he strictly prefers one to the other or (b) he is indifferent between them: a pizza and a taco are equally worthy of being chosen.

More formally, we can say that for every pair of outcomes (x,y) it must be the case that in Alf's ordering: (a) x is strictly preferred to y; (b) y is strictly preferred to x; or (c) y and x are indifferent.

Completeness

$\forall(x,y)$: $(x \succcurlyeq y) \vee$ [or] $(y \succcurlyeq x)$. That is, either x is at least as good as y or y is at least as good as x (or both).

We also need a rather obvious but uninteresting axiom: Alf must hold that a pizza is at least as good as a . . . pizza! The general preference relation is *re-flexive*: $\forall(x): x \succcurlyeq x$. From that we can derive $x \sim x$, which makes a lot of sense!

Reflexivity

$\forall(x): (x \succcurlyeq x)$ That is, x is at least as good as itself.

More interesting, Alf's preferences must be transitive. If Alf prefers a pizza (x) to a taco (y), and a taco (y) to a cup of yogurt (z), then Alf must prefer a pizza (x) to a cup of yogurt (z). Also, if Alf is indifferent between a pizza (x) and a taco (y), and indifferent between a taco (y) and a cup of yogurt (z), then Alf must be indifferent between a pizza (x) and a cup of yogurt (z).

Transitivity

$\forall(x,y) \ (x \succcurlyeq y) \ \& \ (y \succcurlyeq z) \rightarrow (x \succcurlyeq z)$.

From this it follows: $(x \succ y) \ \& \ (y \succ z) \rightarrow (x \succ z)$ and $(x \sim y) \ \& \ (y \sim z) \rightarrow (x \sim z)$.

We can now define *utility* in terms of preference. Letting U stand for utility, we can say that $x \succ y \equiv U(x) > U(y)$, i.e., "$x$ is strictly preferred to y" is equivalent to "the utility of x is greater than the utility of y."

Utility

If a set of options is weakly ordered (i.e., is complete, reflexive, and transitive),

$x \succ y \equiv U(x) > U(y)$.

It is, then, an error to say (as is all too often said) that a person prefers x to y *because* x gives him more utility. The utility does not explain the preference: the utility is simply a mathematical representation of the preference. Utility is not something apart from, or additional to, preference satisfaction, it is a numerical function that represents the degree to which a person's preferences are satisfied.

Ordinal utility functions map preferences over outcomes to numbers. We can assume that the most preferred outcome is mapped onto the highest number, then the next preferred is mapped onto a smaller number, the next onto an even smaller number, and so on. The only information we have, however, is the ranking, not the intensity; the sizes of the differences, or ratios between the numbers, provide no additional information. A person's preference ranking can generate an infinite number of different ordinal utility measures; there is no unique way to represent an ordinal utility function. For instance, the strict preferences $x \succ y \succ z$ might be represented by any of the three utility functions, as shown in table 2.1.

TABLE 2.1. Three Equivalent Ordinal Utility Functions

Preference	Utility Function A	Utility Function B	Utility Function C
x	3	10	1000
y	2	5	999
z	1	0	1

It should be clear that it makes no sense to add together different people's ordinal utilities, or even to add a single person's ordinal utilities for different outcomes. All the ordinal utility function tells us is that, for a specific person, a higher-numbered outcome is preferred to a lower-numbered one.

Why Accept the Axioms?

Can we show people that they *should* order outcomes according to the ordinal axioms? Suppose someone challenges the transitivity axiom:

> Yes, I can understand what transitivity is. According to transitivity, if I prefer a pizza (x) to a taco (y), and a taco (y) to a cup of yogurt (z), then I must prefer a pizza (x) to a cup of yogurt (z). But I simply *do* prefer a cup of yogurt (z) to a pizza (x)! Given any pair of options I can always make a choice. So, what's wrong with that?

Before we proceed, we should point out that this is an extreme case: we assume that the person *simultaneously* asserts all three strict preferences ($x \succ y$, $y \succ z, z \succ y$). With actual agents, we would expect them to choose x over y at one point in time, y over z at another, and finally z over x at yet another. In these sorts of sequential choices, we can only infer that the person violates transitivity if we assume that her preferences are *stable*, which clearly is not always the case. One possible explanation of her third choice (of z over x) is that she has now tired of pizza; in that case she has undergone preference change and we cannot say that she violates transitivity. If her preferences shift back and forth from moment to moment, we could never infer that her ordering violates transitivity. Thus, we need to suppose either stable preferences over outcomes or a nice case in which at one moment the person entertains all three preferences.

Many respond to the above challenge by invoking the idea of rationality as consistency, providing an *instrumental* justification for the transitivity axiom. This is the "money pump" argument. Suppose Betty has the preferences just described. If she prefers a taco to a cup of yogurt, there must be a trade of the following type that she will agree to. Alf tells her that he will give her a taco in return for her cup of yogurt and one cent. Since she strictly prefers the taco to the yogurt, she will hand over a penny to Alf (along with her yogurt) in exchange for a taco. So, she makes the trade. Alf then proposes another trade: in return for another one cent and the taco, he will give her a pizza. Since she strictly prefers the pizza to the taco, she will hand over the penny and the taco to Alf in exchange for a pizza. So, she makes the trade. At this point she has traded her cup of yogurt, her taco, and two cents for a pizza. This makes sense, since she prefers pizza.

But now Alf makes another offer: in exchange for her pizza and one more cent, *he will give her yogurt back*. Since her preferences are not transitive, and so $z \succ x$ (she strictly prefers yogurt to pizza), she will make the trade. Now she is back where she began, with the yogurt, but she has spent three cents—all to get back to her original yogurt. And of course, if Alf offers again to trade her a taco for her yogurt plus one more cent, again she will take the trade, and around and around she will go, serving as a money pump, making Alf richer and richer while she ends up where she started. So, it is said, we can see an instrumental or pragmatic justification for the transitivity axiom: agents who reject it could not possibly achieve their goals.

The money pump argument depends on the "more is better than less" axiom of *Homo economicus*: more money is better than less. That Betty ends up with less money is, other things equal, a bad outcome. Putting aside any worries that "more is better than less" may not hold to goods without qualification, the main worry is that the "more is better than less" axiom is itself an application of transitivity to amounts of goods. If quantity $2q$ of a good is better than quantity q, and if quantity $3q$ is better than $2q$, "more is better than less" requires that $3q$ is better than q. This, though, is just transitivity applied to quantities of goods. If one *really* questioned transitivity, one would also question whether more is better than less; and if so, then one would not be convinced by the money pump argument. If Betty holds that $q\$ > 3q\$$ the money pump argument won't move her.

This is not to deny that there is something deeply irrational about Betty; agents like her probably would have died out a long time ago. The money pump argument is persuasive in demonstrating to *us* how important transitivity is, but we should not expect it to move Betty. What it really shows is that *we* are deeply committed to transitivity. It does not, though, provide an instrumental justification for transitivity if by that we mean a route to *accepting* transitivity, because only someone already committed to transitivity has the instrumental justification.

Rather than trying to provide instrumental or pragmatic justifications for the axioms of ordinal utility, it is better to see them as constitutive of our conception of a fully rational agent. Failure to recognize relations of transitivity is characteristic of schizophrenics.[8] Those disposed to blatantly ignore transitivity are unintelligible to us: we can't understand their pattern of actions as sensible. This is even more obviously so with, say, the *asymmetry* of strict preference. If someone prefers a pizza to a taco *and* a taco to a pizza, we just do not know what to make of his choices. To say that he would fail to satisfy his preferences, or be unsuccessful in practice, misses the point: we can't even understand *what his preferences are.* We cannot even make sense of ascribing a preference to an agent who does not conform to the *asymmetry* of strict preference.

Some claim that the axioms of ordinal utility are more demanding than our understanding of a practically rational agent. Completeness seems especially strong and controversial. Completeness requires that for every possible pair of outcomes (x,y), $(x \succcurlyeq y) \vee (y \succcurlyeq x)$. But suppose the agent never has to choose between x and y; perhaps x and y only occur in the presence of z, and the agent always prefers z to both x and y. Say that x is a pizza with pepperoni, y a pizza with salami, and z a plain cheese pizza; perhaps our plain-cheese-loving pizza eater just has no preference relation between pepperoni and salami pizzas, but this doesn't matter, since she never has to make a choice between them. If we are impressed by such cases, we may insist that the agent simply be able to have a *choice function* over *options* such that for any set of options (x,y,z), the agent can select the *best* option—that which is preferred to all others.

It looks as if our plain-cheese-loving pizza eater has such a choice function even though for her $\neg [(x \succcurlyeq y) \vee (y \succcurlyeq x)]$. But unless the agent is able to order all options, even her ability to choose may break down. If she goes to the Philosophy Department's Christmas party and finds only pepperoni and salami pizzas, she will not be able to choose. Because she does not have a complete ordering, she cannot say that pepperoni is worse or better than salami, or even that she is indifferent to both of them. She just cannot relate to them at all. For her the choice between pepperoni and salami pizza is *incommensurable*: should she be confronted with the choice, she simply has no way to choose between them. It is this that makes her look potentially irrational as a chooser. If we require that a person *always* has a choice function open to her (over all possible sets of options there is always a best choice), then she must conform to completeness.

Conclusion

In this chapter, we made the *Homo economicus* model more precise by representing our rankings of outcomes as preferences and thinking of utility as a representation of that ranking. Preferences, we saw, are inherently relational

8. Argyle, Psychology of Interpersonal Behaviour, 211.

and comparative. For instance, Alf prefers coffee to tea. Because of this, preferences cannot be the same as desires or likings, which are not inherently relational and comparative. Betty may desire a Ferrari or like ice cream, but her liking these things doesn't tell us anything about her preferences. In ordinary English, the idea of preference covers both notions, but we must keep them distinct here. To construct an ordinal utility function, preferences need to be structured according to the axioms of ordinal utility theory, which is to say they have to be complete, reflexive, and transitive. Although in simple cases, these seem like undemanding assumptions, we saw that there are challenges to each of them.

In the next chapter, we will go beyond the idea of a utility function as an ordinal ranking and see how we can, by building in a few more assumptions, generate a cardinal conception of utility that represents not only the brute comparative ranking of outcomes, but also the intensity; not only that Alf prefers coffee to tea, but also that he thinks that coffee is much better than tea. This will, in turn, provide us with the basic foundations that we need to generate a formal theory of rational choice.

Discussion Questions

(1) In the "ticking time bomb" case that we discussed, would you say that the politician

    (a) has a preference to torture the terrorist over not torturing him,
    (b) has a desire to torture the terrorist,
    (c) likes to torture the terrorist, or
    (d) has a commitment to torturing?

(2) Does a rational person have to have good reasons for her preferences? Or are preferences simply passions, and it is reason's job to figure out how to satisfy them?

(3) What do you think the relation is between the informal idea of rationality that we looked at in the last chapter and the interpretation of utility theory according to which all actions are "routes" to outcomes?

(4) Martin Luther is traditionally thought to have said at the Diet of Worms, "Here I stand, I can do no other." Suppose he did. Does this make any sense given what you have thus far learned of utility theory? Can you model this claim given what you have learned in this chapter?

(5) Suppose that a scientist is experimenting on a person to test his sensitivity to pain. She begins at levels 1 and 2, where the numbers

indicate increasing pressure of a needle on his skin. She asks, "which is worse?" He says, "They are the same." She then uses levels 2 and 3, and again asks, which is worse, and again he says they are the same; the same happens when she tries levels 3 and 4. She then uses level 1 and level 4, and he says "Oh, 4 is worse!" Does this cause any trouble for the axioms we considered?

(6) What is the difference between Alf being indifferent between x and y, and Alf's ordering being incomplete regarding x and y?

(7) Is transitivity really a requirement of rationality? Is the person who is susceptible to a "money pump" irrational?

(8) Can you think of cases where it looks like choice is intransitive? Are these examples of irrationality?

(9) Can you think of cases where reflexivity might not hold?

3

Cardinal Utility

We have seen that an ordinal utility function for a person can be generated if her rankings satisfy completeness, reflexivity, and transitivity. But recall table 2.1, the utility table from chapter 2: ordinal utility function A, which numerically represents the options (x, y, z) as $(3, 2, 1)$, is equivalent to ordinal utility function C, which represents them as $(1000, 999, 1)$. We cannot say whether option y is "closer" to x or to z: the numbers only represent the ordering of the options. We can get some idea of the relative preference distances between the options (roughly, *how much* one thing is preferred to another) by developing *cardinal utilities,* using some version (there are several) of additional axioms. We then look at a number of challenges that have been raised against these axioms. We conclude by reviewing challenges to cardinal utility theory raised by psychologists, who show that real people seem to violate the basic principles of utility maximization in their decisions.

Cardinal Utility

On one accessible view, four further axioms are required. The key to this approach—pioneered by John von Neumann and Oskar Morgenstern—is to assume certain preferences over lotteries (risky outcomes), and then confront an agent with lotteries involving her ordinal outcomes.[1] Her ordinal preferences *over the lotteries* allow us to infer a cardinal scale (or, rather, as we shall see, a set of such scales). This is an incredibly powerful idea: it generates a cardinal utility measure from a series of ordinal preferences. Lotteries are denoted $L\{p, x, y\}$ where x is a state of affairs that occurs with probability p and y is a state of affairs that arises with probability $(1-p)$.

One version of developing the idea goes like this. Continuing with our axioms, in addition to the ordinal axioms we need to include some other assumptions. The first is *continuity.* Alf's preferences must be *continuous.* Suppose Alf has ranked three possibilities: having a pizza, having a taco, and having a cup of

---

1. Von Neumann and Morgenstern, Theory of Games and Economic Behavior.

yogurt. Now suppose we give Alf a taco (his middle choice). He has the taco, but now we offer him a gamble: he can give up his taco and take a lottery ticket, in which the good prize is his first choice, and the booby prize is his third choice (a cup of yogurt). Now we can easily imagine him rejecting many possible lotteries and keeping his taco. For example, suppose we offer him a lottery that gives him a .01 chance of getting a pizza and a .99 chance of getting a cup of yogurt. He probably will say, "thanks, but no thanks; I'll keep my taco." But suppose we offer Alf the opposite: a lottery that gives him a .99 chance of getting the pizza and only a .01 chance of getting the yogurt. Now we wouldn't be surprised if he gave up his taco for the lottery ticket. For Alf's preferences to be continuous, it has to be the case that there is always some lottery in which the chances of getting his first choice and ending up with his third choice are such that he is indifferent between keeping his taco and accepting the lottery ticket.

Continuity

$\forall (x, y, z) \in$ S: if $x \succ y \succ z$, then $\exists p \in [0,1]$ such that $L\{p, x, z\} \sim y$.

There must exist some lottery L that gives Alf a probability p of getting x (and so a $1 - p$ of getting z) such that he is indifferent between having y and playing L.

For every state of affairs there's always some probability that will make us willing to trade a worse chance at a more preferred outcome for a better chance at a less preferred outcome.

The next additional axiom is *better prizes*. Imagine that Alf is now confronted with two lotteries. In each lottery he is certain to end up with one of two prizes. The first lottery, say, is between a pizza and a cup of yogurt. The second lottery is between a taco and a cup of yogurt. Suppose the lotteries have the same probabilities of prizes: in Lottery 1 there is a .6 chance of a pizza and a .4 chance of a cup of yogurt; in Lottery 2 there is a .6 chance of a taco a .4 chance of the yogurt.

To conform to better prizes, Alf must prefer Lottery 1 since the chances of the best prizes in the lotteries are the same, and the second prize (and chances of getting it) are the same in both lotteries, but in Lottery 1 the first prize is better, since Alf prefers a pizza to a taco. So, if Alf is confronted with lotteries L_1 over (w,x) and L_2 over (y,z), and L_1 and L_2 have the same probability of prizes while having an equal prize in one position and having unequal prizes in the other position, if L_1 is the lottery with the better prize, then $L_1 \succ L_2$; if neither lottery has a better prize, then $L_1 \sim L_2$.

Better Prizes

If $L_1 = \{p, x, y\}$ and $L_3 = \{p, x^*, y\}$, then: $U(L_3) > U(L_1)$ if and only if $x^* \succ x$.

The next axiom is similar and is called *better chances*. Imagine that Alf is again confronted with two lotteries. In each lottery he is certain to end up with one of two prizes. Both lotteries are between a pizza and a cup of yogurt. In Lottery 1 there is a .7 chance of a pizza and a .3 chance of a cup of the yogurt; in Lottery 2 there is a .6 chance of a pizza and a .4 chance of the yogurt. To conform to better chances, Alf must prefer Lottery 1 since the prizes are the same, but Lottery 1 gives him a better chance of his more preferred prize.

Better Chances

If $L_1 = \{p, x, y\}$ and $L_2 = \{p^*, x, y\}$, then: $U(L_2) > U(L_1)$ if and only if $p^* > p$.

So, if Alf is confronted with a choice between L_1 and L_2, and they have the same prizes but L_1 has a better chance of the better prize, then $L_1 \succ L_2$. If neither lottery has a better prize, then $L_1 \sim L_2$.

Given the complexity of lotteries being nested within one another, we need an additional axiom called *reduction of compound lotteries*. If the prize of a lottery is another lottery, this can always be reduced to a simple lottery between prizes. This eliminates utility from the thrill of gambling: the only ultimate concern is the prizes. As we shall see, this does not mean that people's attitudes toward risk are not factored into the utilities, only that the fact that something is a gamble between x and y cannot itself be a source of utility.

Reduction of Compound Lotteries

If $L_1 = \{p, x, y\}$ and $L_2 = \{p^*, x, y\}$, then we can also have

$L_3 = \{q, L_1, L_2\}$ where L_3 is a lottery in which q is the probability that L_1 obtains and $(1-q)$ is the probability that L_2 obtains.

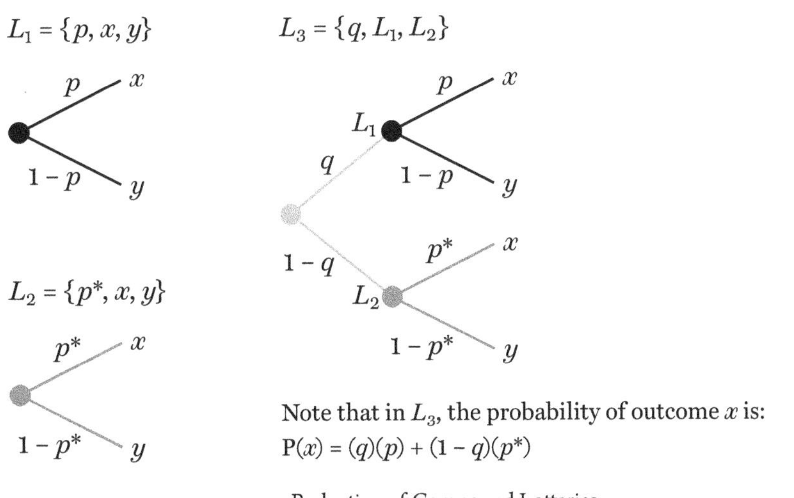

Note that in L_3, the probability of outcome x is:
$$P(x) = (q)(p) + (1-q)(p^*)$$

FIGURE 3.1. Reduction of Compound Lotteries

The final axiom and perhaps the most controversial is the *independence of irrelevant alternatives*, which is often referred to simply as *independence*. So, if there are two lotteries, each with the same chances, and one of the prizes is preferred to the other, the lottery with the more preferred option is also preferred, regardless of whether any other, less preferred, option is added to the lottery.

Independence

$\forall(x, y, z)$ if $x \succ y$ and $\neg[z \succ (x \vee y)]$, then $L_1\{p, x, z\} \succ L_2\{p, y, z\}$

If Alf prefers x to y and doesn't prefer z to either x or y, then Alf should prefer a lottery with x to one with y, given the same chances, regardless of whether z is included in the lottery.

Imagine that Betty is presented with two identically priced three-course meals. The first has soup for the starter and steak for the main with a raspberry tart for dessert, while the second has salad for the starter, lobster for the main course with a cheese plate for dessert. Betty is indifferent between soup and salad as well as between raspberry tarts and a cheese plate, but she prefers lobster to steak. In this case, only the preference between lobster and steak is relevant to the decision. If she would order lobster over steak when given the choice, she should also order it in the presence of other options that she is indifferent between. Although this condition is plausible, it has come under frequent attack, as we will see below. It also reappears in a slightly different form in social choice theory and in voting theory, where it is even more controversial.

If Alf meets all of these conditions, we can convert his ordinal utilities into cardinal utilities, which not only gives the ordering of the payoffs but the size of the differences in the payoffs for each (or, more strictly, the ratios of the differences) where the higher the number, the better the outcome.

Generating Cardinal Utilities

To grasp the crux of this method for generating cardinal utilities, assume that we have our three options: a pizza (x), a taco (y), and a cup of yogurt (z), where $x \succcurlyeq y \succcurlyeq z$ and we define the best option (x) as having a utility of 1, and the worst, (z), as 0. The question, then, is where on the scale of 1–0 we should place y, the taco.

If we were dealing simply with ordinal utilities, any number less than 1 and greater than 0 would suffice, but this kind of representation can't make sense of the distinction of the intensity of preference or the "distance" between, on the one hand, the taco, and on the other, the pizza and the cup of yogurt. Suppose that Alf is confronted with a lottery which gives him a p chance of getting the pizza and a 1-p chance of getting the yogurt. If he wins, he gets his pizza and if he loses, he gets the cup of yogurt. Now we give him a binary choice: he can either have y, the taco (for certain), or he can play the lottery.

It seems that Alf is very likely to prefer playing the lottery, in cases where it gives a near 1 (perfect) chance of getting the pizza and a tiny chance of getting the yogurt, to the certainty of the taco. In that case, he is essentially trading his second choice for the near certainty of his first choice. As p (the probability of winning the better prize in the lottery) decreases toward zero, we would expect Alf to prefer to keep his taco (certainty of getting his second choice) to a lottery that gives a tiny chance of a pizza and a very large chance of the booby prize—the cup of yogurt. At some point in between, the continuity axiom says there is a value of p for which Alf is indifferent between the lottery $[L(x,z)]$ and y.

Suppose it turns out that the lottery gives him a p of .9 of getting x and .1 chance of getting z. What we infer from this is that it takes a very large chance of getting his first option (.9) to lead Alf to give up his second. He must, then, see y (the taco) as pretty good, if he will only play the lottery when he has a very great probability of winning. So, we can say that on our scale of 1 (x, the pizza) to 0 (z, the yogurt), y, the taco, is at .9. In contrast, suppose that Alf was indifferent between having the taco for certain and playing a lottery that gave him a small chance (say .1) of getting the pizza and a .9 chance of ending up with the yogurt. From this we can infer that the taco must not be much better than the cup of yogurt, but the pizza must be a lot better, so we now give the taco a score of .1. We thus can generate a measurement in which the ratios between the numbers are significant from purely binary (ordinal) preferences involving lotteries.

It should be noted that we have also factored in Alf's attitude toward risk. He might refuse lottery L_1 between x and z, and prefer the certainty of y, because he is risk-averse and prefers a "y-in-the-hand" to the possibility of z. If Alf is risk-averse, he will require a better of chance of getting x before he plays the lottery. But the continuity axioms require that at some point he will be indifferent between y and some lottery between x and z.

We have argued that the new cardinal measures tell us something about the "preference distance" between the options, but not everyone accepts this interpretation. If we wish to be *extremely* careful, we will restrict ourselves to saying that these "von Neumann–Morgenstern" utilities tell us are a person's preferences between lotteries or gambles, and so what he will do in certain situations that involve *risk*—where the agent does not know for certain what outcomes are associated with a given set of action-options but can assign a specific probability p that a certain action-option x will produce a certain consequence C_1.

We also must not lose sight of the fact that the axioms are ways to generate cardinal measures out of ordinal preferences. This means that ordered ordinal preferences over outcomes and lotteries are all that are required. This is an especially elegant idea, but the very idea of cardinal utility does not depend on it. We should expect that doing something as neat as deriving the cardinal from the ordinal may invoke some contestable axioms. Although it is sometimes claimed that all uses of cardinal utility measures implicitly rely on the existence of the von Neumann–Morgenstern axioms, in practice economists and game theorists are quite happy to appeal directly to the idea of a cardinal scale on which outcomes can be placed.

Indeed, John Pollock has developed a computationally realistic model of rational decision-making according to which cardinal, not ordinal, utility is fundamental.[2] Pollock argues that a cognitive system that stored its basic values in an ordinal ranking would have to relate to so many possible pairs of options that it would be unable to function—essentially such an agent would require an infinite data structure. Pollock shows that a person who used pairwise comparisons to relate every possible state of the world over which she might choose would have more comparisons than the number of elementary particles in the universe! Thus, rather than taking ordinal data as basic and trying to show how we might derive cardinal data from it, Pollock argues that real agents store their utility information in cardinal form. Some cognitive scientists and philosophers of mind also argue that preferences, as they are represented in the mind, are cardinal, not ordinal.

Representation of Utility

One of the problems we noted with simple ordinal utility was that we could not sensibly add the utility of different people into an overall, aggregate measure of utility. Think back again to the discussion of ordinal utility. Given the very different sets of numbers that represent the same preference structure, it was clear that ordinal utility functions do not lend themselves to addition. To add we need a cardinal measure. Now suppose that in Alf's utility function option y gives him, say, .7 utility and y gives Betty .5. Can we proceed to add these nice cardinal numbers together and say that the total utility of y is 1.2? Can we say that Alf gets more utility than Betty from y? Not without a lot more argument. We have assumed arbitrary highs (1) and lows (0) for each person, but there is nothing to say that Alf's score of 1 for his best option identifies the "same utility" as Betty gets from her best option, to which she gives a score of 1.

2. Pollock, Thinking about Acting, chap. 2.

Given that the end points cannot be equated as the same, none of the ratios of distances that we identify in between can be automatically identified.

While ordinal rankings can be preserved by *any* monotonic transformation of a utility function, cardinal rankings can only be preserved by linear (or positive affine) transformations. If our function is U then any function U^*, where $U^* = aU + b$ (where a is a positive real number and b is any real number), gives exactly the same information about ratios of differences between the options, and so serves equally well to describe a person's preferences. Because of this, summing the utilities identified by one of the functions is not meaningful without an independent account providing a rationale of how they should be combined and at what ratios. There is no reason to suppose that Alf's .5 is the same as Betty's .5.

Linear Transformation

For a given set of cardinal preferences, $u(x)$ and $u^*(x)$ are equally valid representations if: $u^*(x) = m[u(x)] + c$ where m is a positive real number and c is any real number.

The easiest analogy is to temperature. The Celsius scale sets the temperature that water freezes at 0° and the temperature that water boils at 100°. On the Fahrenheit scale, water freezes at 32° and boils at 212°. The Celsius scale can be converted into Fahrenheit by the linear transformation Fahrenheit $= (9/5 * \text{Celsius}) + 32$. Applying this, we can see that 0° C $=$ 32° F, but it would also be obviously wrong to think that two temperatures on either scale feel the same even though they are represented by the same number. For instance, 35° Fahrenheit is very cold (just above freezing), while 35° Celsius is very hot (95° F). With temperature we have set ways of comparing a temperature on one scale with that on another; can we do the same with utility scales between people?

Interpersonal Comparisons

Whether or not (and how) we might be able to compare utility representations between people is a hotly contested question in economics and philosophy. On one view, associated especially with Lionel Robbins (1898–1984), as a science, economics cannot compare one person's utility to another's.

> [I]t is one thing to assume that scales can be drawn up showing the order in which an individual will prefer a series of alternatives, and to compare the arrangement of one such individual scale with another. It is quite a different thing to assume that behind such arrangements lie magnitudes which themselves can be compared. This is not an assumption which need anywhere be made in modern economic analysis, and it is an assumption which is of an

entirely different kind from the assumption of individual scales of relative valuation. . . . It is a comparison which necessarily falls outside the scope of any positive science. To state that A's preference stands above B's in order of importance is entirely different from stating that A prefers *n* to *m* and B prefers *n* and *m* in a different order. It involves an element of conventional valuation. Hence it is essentially normative. It has no place in pure science.[3]

Robbins is arguing that by comparing the utility scales of two different people, we are forced to make a normative or evaluative claim about their relative importance. He takes the position that to do so is to move away from science toward ethics. Kenneth Arrow (1921–2017), along the same lines as Robbins, leaves no question where he stands on this issue. He argues that interpersonal comparisons of utility have "no meaning."[4]

Ken Binmore clarifies the central issue, arguing that "the problem isn't at all that making interpersonal comparisons is impossible. On the contrary, there are an infinite number of ways this can be done."[5] This is too strong, for there may be an infinite number of mathematical formulas for doing it, but many of those might not be plausible or justified in actual cases. Still, the larger point is correct. The problem here is indeterminacy rather than impossibility. It is a bit like asking what the "right" temperature or measurement scale is. In principle, any are acceptable just as a base 8 or a base 10 system are all acceptable for counting.

Robbins's point was that *any* way of comparing them must be a normative issue drawing on social values, not a scientific question. To Robbins, political economy—our subject in PPE—was distinct from economic science just because it could draw on normative considerations to make such judgments. On Robbins's view, most political economy has held, as a moral proposition, that all persons are essentially equal, and so in some ways one person's utility should be counted as of equal importance to another's. But, he says, this is a moral view that need not be a part of economics as such: one can have a science of the effective relation between means and ends that did not make this assumption. Insofar as our conception of science is broader than Robbins's, in tandem with an interest in taking an explicitly philosophical approach to many of these questions, we can still meaningfully ask whether such normative evaluation makes sense.

In open societies, we assume, for certain purposes, that persons in similar circumstances are capable of equal satisfactions. Just as for purposes of justice

3. Robbins, An Essay on the Nature & Significance of Economic Science, 138–39.
4. Arrow, Social Choice and Individual Values, 9.
5. Binmore, Natural Justice, 121.

we assume equality of responsibility, in similar situations as between legal subjects, so for purposes of public finance we agree to assume equality of capacity for experiencing satisfaction from equal incomes in similar circumstances as between economic subjects. But, although it may be convenient to assume this, there is no way of proving that the assumption rests on ascertainable fact.[6]

As a result, it is by no means impossible to add cardinal utilities—but we should not be misled by their arithmetical form which suggests addition is unproblematic. To justify interpersonal comparisons is a philosophical-normative project. As we will see in later chapters, this question becomes more fraught when we get to the question of social welfare.

Expected Utility

An attractive feature of cardinal utility that does not raise these deep normative questions is that it can be employed to perform expected utility calculations. This is done by applying cardinal measures of credence or probability to cardinal measures of utility to determine what action is most likely to produce the best result.

Assume that Betty has a cardinal utility scale according to which the following outcomes are scaled: $w = 9$, $x = 8$, $y = 5$, $z = 3$. Suppose further that she is confronted with two action-options (a, β). Option a has two possible consequences (x, y); β has two possible consequences (w, z). Say that the probability of a producing x is .7; so, the probability of a producing y must be $(1 - .7)$, or .3 since there is a probability of 1 that if she performs the act either x or y will occur, the probabilities must always sum to 1; similarly, if we assume that the probability of β producing outcome w is .5, the probability of producing z must also be .5.

We can now calculate the expected utility of a and β using the formula that the expected utility (EU) of an action-option is the expected utility of its outcome multiplied by the probability that the outcome will be produced. Hence $EU(a) = .7(8) + .3(5) = 7.1$; $EU(\beta) = .5(9) + .5(3) = 6$. Thus, because $EU(a) > EU(\beta)$, then $a \succ \beta$. Based on her cardinal preferences over outcomes, Betty has been able to generate a preference over action-options even in cases where she is not certain what outcomes will be produced by her action-options. Notice that we can only make sense of expected utility theory by distinguishing a person's preferences over outcomes from her preferences over action-options.

We can give the general formula for expected utility of an action as the sum of expected values of all of the outcomes associated with that act where the expected value is calculated by discounting the value of the outcome by the

---

6. Robbins, An Essay on the Nature & Significance of Economic Science, 140.

probability that it will occur. So, if one stands to gain $100 on a bet that a coin lands heads and $0 if it lands tails, the expected value of the bet as a whole is $50 (.50 * $100 + .5 * $0).

Expected Utility

For an action a, the expected utility of that action is the sum of all the outcomes that action can bring about u, discounted by the probability p that the given action will cause that outcome.

$$EU(a) = \sum_{i=1}^{n} p_i u_i$$

Despite the example from above, it is important that the expected utility is different than "expected value." Say there is a lottery with a probability of .8 of giving you $10 and another lottery with .2 of giving you $40. The expected value of both lotteries is $8, but this does not imply they have the same expected utility for Betty. She may be risk-averse and find the first lottery more attractive—it gives an 80% chance of winning. The way we constructed von Neumann–Morgenstern utilities, a person's cardinal scale was generated by lotteries incorporating her attitude toward risk, so whether Betty is risk-averse is already factored into her utilities. Given that, we are warranted in simply multiplying the utility by the probability, and the option with the highest expected utility will be preferred.[7]

It is because expected utility is not the same thing as expected value that it is often hard to deduce from economic experiments what a person's utilities, and so preferences, must be. We know her choices over expected values—typically, a certain probability of a certain monetary amount—but it does not follow that rationally she must choose the option with the highest expected value. We will see this in more detail when we look at several economic experiments in later chapters.

Questioning the Axioms

Despite the elegance and simplicity of the method of generating utility functions out of pairwise preferences, many have questioned the basic axioms. The von Neumann–Morgenstern axioms are especially controversial: there are well-known paradoxes associated with them and they are the object of continued debate.

---

7. For a theory of rational choice that puts risk aversion at its center, see Buchak, Risk and Rationality.

Continuity

Consider first a simple objection. According to the continuity axiom there always must be some lottery L in which a rational agent is indifferent between certainty of y and lottery L between x and z. As R. Duncan Luce and Howard Raiffa argued in their classic work, some choices may not be continuous.[8] To use their example: even if we all agree that \$1 $\gtrsim$ 1¢ $\gtrsim$ death, not too many people are indifferent between 1¢ and a lottery with chance p of \$1 and a $1 - p$ chance of death! Yet, many people will travel an extra mile to save a few cents on a gallon of gasoline. But in the extra traveled mile, they were at greater risk of death due to a possible fatal traffic accident. They apparently decided that the cheaper gas was worth the risk—just as the continuity axiom requires!

Better Prizes

A more complex objection to the better prizes axiom is discussed by James Dreier.

> Suppose you have a kitten, which you plan to give away to either Talia or Horace. Talia and Horace both want the kitten very much. Both are deserving, and both would care for the kitten. You are sure that giving the kitten to Talia [x] is at least as good as giving it to Horace [y, so $x \geqslant y$]. But you think that would be unfair to Horace. You decide to flip a fair coin: if the coin lands heads, you will give the kitten to Horace, and if it lands tails, you will give the kitten to Talia.[9]

The problem is that you seem to have violated the better prizes axiom, according to which, if you are confronted with lotteries L_1 and L_2 and both have the same probability of prizes with the equal prizes in one position and the unequal prizes in the other, if L_1 is the lottery with the better prize, then $L_1 \geqslant L_2$ (in the story, $x \geqslant y$.)

To see the problem, suppose that L_1 has the prizes (x,z) and L_2 has the prizes (y,z), where z is simply a variable for the same outcome. Suppose further that L_1 and L_2 both give a .5 probability of winning z, so there must be a .5 probability of winning the other prize (either x or y). L_1 and L_2 have equal prizes in the second position, so one's concern is only the first position. Since $x \geqslant y$—it is at least as good to give the kitten to Talia as to Horace—then according to the better prizes axiom, $L_1 \geqslant L_2$.

8. Duncan Luce and Raiffa, Games and Decisions, 27.
9. Dreier, "Decision Theory and Morality," 156–81.

Now let us substitute for the variable z a particular prize: x (Talia gets the kitten). So now L_1 is a .5 chance of (x,x), that is, x—that Talia gets the kitten—for certain, since it is the prize in both positions, and L_2 a .5 chance of (y,x), that is, a .5 chance that Horace will get the kitten and a .5 chance that Talia will. In the first lottery (heads it's Talia's kitten, tails it's Talia's kitten); in the second lottery (heads it's Horace's kitten, tails it's Talia's). By better prizes, one prefers the first lottery. But this violates one's commitment to justice through a fair lottery; the person concerned with fairness holds that $L_2 \succcurlyeq L_1$, so better prizes is violated.

We confront the deep issue of how to identify the correct description of the outcomes and options. Still, however we characterize the outcomes, it looks like a rational person should conform to better prizes in this case. Suppose first that the only relevant differences between the outcomes concern who gets the kitten: all preferences are "who-gets-the-kitten" preferences. Now it looks as if the chooser ought not to violate better prizes by employing the fair lottery. To use the fair lottery to give away the kitten seems irrational if we suppose that all you care about is who gets the kitten. Why would you select a mechanism that sometimes gives the kitten to your preferred person and sometimes to the other if the only thing you had preferences over was who ended up with the kitten? So here, violating better prizes seems objectionable. Assume, though, that you do not simply have preferences over "who-gets-the-kitten" but over "the process by which kittens are distributed." Here you opt for the fair lottery, which can distribute to either Talia or Horace.

Now the options may be better described as (a) "giving the kitten to the person who would be a better owner" and (b) "giving the kitten in a fair way," and you might hold that $b \succcurlyeq a$. If we understand the options in that way—that one of the things you have preferences over is the fairness of the process of distribution—the outcomes, and so the value of the action-options (your preferences over them), change and there is no violation of better prizes. So here, though it is rational to employ the fair lottery, employing it is consistent with better prizes.

The Allais Paradox

The most famous challenge to the axioms of cardinal utility theory was presented by Maurice Allais (1911–2010). Suppose that an eccentric billionaire offers you two lotteries, each with two options. In both lotteries, you reach into an urn that contains one hundred balls, of which there is one red ball, ten blue balls, and eighty-nine white balls. Each lottery associated the prizes from the lottery with the ball you end up pulling out of the urn.

TABLE 3.1. Allais Paradox

	Options	Red Ball (1)	White Ball (89)	Blue Ball (10)
Lottery 1	A	$1 million	$1 million	$1 million
	B	$0	$1 million	$5 million
Lottery 2	C	$1 million	$0	$1 million
	D	$0	$0	$5 million

Intuitively, we can see that according to better prizes and better chances, one's preferences over lotteries are to be determined only by differences in the size of the prize and the chance of getting it; if two lotteries have the same prize configurations and the same chances of winning the prize, then one will have the same preferences in the lotteries.

Now in Lottery 1, your preference for option A can't be determined by the white ball, since both options give you the same chance of getting the same prize (an 89% chance of getting $1 million). Better prizes and better chances tell us that when choosing between lotteries we should ignore in each the equal prizes with equal chances and make our choice on the basis of better prizes and better chances. So, *if* you do choose option A, then it must be the case that, in your estimate, the 10% chance of gaining an extra $4 million in option B should the blue ball come up does not make up for the 1% chance of getting $1 million less in option B if the red ball comes up. So (roughly) if you choose A, you essentially prefer a gamble that, out of every eleven times, you get $1 million each time to a gamble that, out of every eleven times, you get $5 million ten times and nothing once.

If this is your reasoning, then you must also prefer option C in Lottery 2. Again, your choice cannot be made on the basis of what happens if the white ball comes up, since there are equal prizes with equal chances in both lotteries. Everything turns on the prizes and chances if the red or blue balls come up, but these are exactly the same prizes and chances as in Lottery 1. So, the axioms commit you to option C.

But many people who take option A in Lottery 1 take option D in Lottery 2. In Lottery 2, the idea of getting $5 million ten out of eleven times and nothing one in eleven times seems like a reasonable bet, but it doesn't seem like a reasonable bet in Lottery A. This seems to be because in Lottery 1, if one chooses A, one is certain of getting a million dollars no matter what happens, and people have a hard time turning down the certainty of $1 million. In contrast, in Lottery 2, there is no certain outcome, and one is forced to gamble, and people do seem to prefer a good chance of getting $5 million, at the cost of a small chance of getting nothing. This means that what makes people choose differently in Lotteries 1 and 2 are the prizes concerning the white balls, but we have seen that since in both lotteries the white ball has equal chances of equal prizes, it should not affect one's choice between A and B, or between C and D.

The question, then, is whether people's tendencies to select A and D show that the axioms of cardinal utility are flawed insofar as rational people make choices that violate them, or whether we are often irrational in the way we judge probabilities. A crucial question here is whether rational people only seek to determine how well they might do, or whether rational people also seek to avoid regret. In Lottery 1, if we select B and lose, we might have deep regrets—"I had a million for sure and now I have nothing!"; but in Lottery 2 everything is a matter of chance, so we have little cause to regret our choice ("I made a good bet and just had bad luck").

As we see it, the Allais paradox doesn't show either (a) that the axioms of cardinal utility fail to adequately capture our understanding of rational choice or (b) that those who choose A in Lottery 1 and D in Lottery 2 are irrational. Rather, it looks like people's utility functions—their rankings over outcomes— are often far more complicated than the monetary bets would indicate, e.g., one lottery leaves a person with the possibility of regrets and the other does not. As we saw when we looked at comprehensive outcomes, one's utility function can depend on the menu of options one faced, not just on the option one chose.

The Ellsberg Paradox

Consider another case that is similar to the Allais paradox, but that highlights different issues. This example is called the Ellsberg paradox and is named after the Pentagon Papers leaker, Daniel Ellsberg, who developed the problem in his economics doctoral dissertation.[10] As in the Allais paradox, an eccentric billionaire presents you with two urns, each urn contains one hundred balls, with a mix of red and black balls. You don't know the exact mix of red and black balls in the first urn, but you are told the second urn has a mix of fifty red and fifty black balls. You will be able to select a ball from each urn and you may bet on whether you will get either red or black in each case. Which bets do you prefer?

---

10. The version here follows Ellsberg, "Risk, Ambiguity, and the Savage Axioms."

TABLE 3.2. Ellsberg Paradox

	Red I	Red II	Black I	Black II
Red	$100	$100	$0	$0
Black	$0	$0	$100	$100

Most people say they are indifferent between red or black in the first urn, and between red and black in the second urn. This makes sense, as the chances in the first urn are unknown so there is no reason to think that red or black is more likely, and we know that the chances of selecting red or black in the second urn are equal. But, what about between betting on Red I and Red II or Black I and Black II? Most people prefer either bet in the second urn to either bet in the first. Some may also prefer either bet in the first urn over either bet in the second. Put slightly differently, assume you can bet on either red or black and then choose which urn you pick from. If you bet on red and pick from the first urn, we can assume you think you are more likely to find a red ball there and vice versa if you pick from the second urn.

Unless you are indifferent between both urns, there is a problem. If you prefer Black II to Black I, we can infer that you think you are more likely to select a black ball from the second urn than from the first. Since the prizes are the same, you must think your chances are higher with the second urn to prefer that bet. This would mean, though, that you think you are more likely to select a red ball from the first urn than the second since the second urn has a 50:50 ratio of black to red. So, if Black II ≻ Black I, then Red I ≻ Black I and Red I ≻ Red II. This means that you will violate either the completeness axiom or independence.

Ellsberg believed that this was the result of what he called "ambiguity" in the first urn. Although there is no reason to antecedently prefer either red or black in either urn, the first urn, since it lacks precise probabilities, is ambiguous and people tend to be averse to ambiguity in choice. This type of ambiguity is also called *uncertainty* in contrast to *risk*. When we choose under risk, we can assign precise probabilities to the possibilities, which we cannot do in cases of uncertainty. The psychological explanation is that people prefer risky to uncertain choices. This may be so, but does it make them irrational to do so since it violates the principles of utility theory, which are just formulations of rationality? Maybe. Another possibility that has become popular is that the aversion to ambiguity is actually just a symptom of risk aversion more generally. We will look at risk aversion in greater detail in the next chapter.

Prospect Theory

"Prospect Theory" seeks to explain the sort of choice we find in the Allais paradox and in at least some interpretations of the Ellsberg paradox.[11] Economists, as we have seen, usually understand utility theory as only concerning the evaluation of end states. Prospect theory contends that individuals have a reference point that affects their ranking of options, in particular what they *now have*. Actions are judged not simply in terms of outcomes, but rather they increase or decrease a person's utility as measured from that reference point. When considering whether to risk their present endowment for a gain, people are risk-averse. If a person now has $100, they are not likely to take a bet that would give them a 49% chance of losing $100 and a 51% chance of gaining $100: even though the expected value of the bet is positive, most people will not take the bet (perhaps they will only take the bet when they have a 50% chance of winning $120). On the other hand, if confronted with a bet between a 51% chance of losing their $100 and a 49% chance of winning $100, they are likely to take the bet: they are *risk-prone when faced with the possibility of avoiding losses*. Note that the Allais paradox seems to exemplify this: consider a person's attitude toward the bet in Lottery 1, where faced with losing the $1 million from the sure-thing Option A—here the reference point is adjusted to "I already have $1 million," so one is wary of losing it. In the second lottery the reference point is set at what you now have, so the lottery holds out the possibility of a *gain*.

Clearly, good questions can be raised about the cardinal utility axioms. We can safely conclude that its axioms are far more controversial than the ordinal axioms: it is by no means hard to imagine rational agents who have noncontinuous preferences or who simply prefer to gamble (and therefore violate the reduction of compound lotteries). In general, however, we think philosophers have been rather too skeptical of the axioms: while some are rationally rejectable, they are not implausibly strong. The much-maligned better prizes and better chances axioms are not as vulnerable as is often thought.

Psychology and Expected Utility Theory

Expected utility theory provides a highly formal and developed theory specifying how rational agents choose under conditions of *risk*—that is, where they are not certain about what consequences are produced by their action-options but can assign probabilities relating each action-option and possible consequences. If they cannot assign probabilities, they are said to operate not under

11. Kahneman and Tversky, "Prospect Theory: An Analysis of Decision under Risk."

risk, but under *uncertainty*, which leads to still more complications about rational expectations. We have seen, though, that many people have reservations about the axioms, especially the better prizes and better chances axioms. People often seem to choose in ways inconsistent with their requirements. In the last twenty-five years, cognitive psychologists, led by Daniel Kahneman and the late Amos Tversky, apparently have uncovered ways in which normal reasoners systematically violate the requirements of expected utility theory. We briefly review some of their findings and then consider what implications they have for expected utility theory.

Errors in Probability Judgments

The most basic and obvious problem is that most people are simply bad at making probability judgments. Even people of above-average intelligence don't assign probabilities in the way that is consistent with the probability calculus, leading to rankings that are contrary to what expected utility theory would indicate.

Consider this example. You are a fighter pilot who runs the risk of being killed by enemy fire. You can be killed in one of two ways: either by flak or by burns. You may also wear a jacket that will protect you entirely against one hazard, but is useless against the other, that is, you may wear a flak jacket or a burn jacket but not both. Two-thirds of the casualties result from flak; one-third from burns. You can wear either jacket all or part of the time. Which jacket do you choose to wear and why?[12]

Even rather sophisticated reasoners who have taken courses in statistics tend to say, "the flak jacket two-thirds of the time, and the burn jacket one-third of the time." But that is wrong. Suppose there are 99 flights, each of which gets hit by enemy fire (we can ignore the flights that do not get hit). Assume each pilot wears the flak jacket two-thirds of the time: that is, for 66 missions. On those 66 missions, two-thirds of the deaths will be prevented (those from flak) while a third of the pilots will die. So, on those 66 missions, there will be 22 deaths. What about the remaining 33 missions (those for which only burn jackets are worn)? Here, one-third will be saved (11) and two-thirds will die (22). So altogether, the two-thirds/one-third strategy will yield 22 + 22 deaths, or 44, which clearly is worse than wearing the flak jacket all the time, which will result in one-third of 99, or 33, deaths. But people have a strong tendency to respond to mixed threats with mixed responses, even though in cases like this a single response is best.

12. This example is recounted by Epstein, Skepticism and Freedom, 229.

Highly trained people make these sorts of errors, especially when they must calculate probabilities given base rates in the population. Consider a simple problem posed by Richard Nisbett and Lee Ross:

> The present authors have a friend who is a professor. He likes to write poetry, is rather shy, and small in stature. Which of the following is his field (a) Chinese studies or (b) psychology?[13] What would you say?

Tversky and Kahneman's research indicates that people will overwhelmingly select (a). The diagnostic information is *representative* of a professor of Chinese studies and, because of this, people tend to be quite certain that the friend is a Chinese scholar. Yet, if we consider the relative size of the two populations, professors of psychology and Chinese studies, the probability is very much that the person is a psychology professor. To be sure, the diagnostic information would justify some small departure from the probabilities given by the base rates, but the evidence indicates that in such situations, people tend to wholly ignore base rate information, even when it is supplied to them.[14] Tversky and Kahneman conclude that "people's intuitions about random sampling appear to satisfy the law of small numbers, which asserts that the law of large numbers applies to small numbers as well."[15]

This bias can lead to serious errors when people rely solely on probability estimates of the accuracy of medical tests and ignore the base rates of the disease (or characteristic) in the population. We saw a version of this in a previous chapter when we looked at Bayes' theorem. Suppose we have a relatively rare disease, say one that occurs at a rate of 1 in 1,000 (or 10 in 10,000). Suppose further that we have a test for the disease which is 99% accurate. We administer it to everyone in a population of 10,000. You test positive. Is it likely you have the disease? No, as table 3.3 shows.

TABLE 3.3. Likelihood of Having a Disease After Testing Positive

	Have disease (10)	Don't (9,990)
Test +	9.9	99.9
Test −	.1	9,890.1

13. Nisbett and Ross, Human Inference, 25.
14. Kahneman and Tversky, "On the Psychology of Prediction."
15. Tversky and Kahneman, "Belief in the Law of Small Numbers," 25.

Of the entire randomly selected population who test positive, there is still only around a one-tenth chance that any one of them has the disease. Many people find this extremely surprising; if you do, then you will have trouble applying expected utility theory.

Another source of error in probability judgments is that "information is weighted in proportion to its vividness." Thus, for instance, concrete or emotionally salient information is more vivid, and hence is apt to play a dominant role in deliberating. Consider Richard Nisbett's tale:

> Let us suppose that you wish to buy a new car and have decided that on the grounds of economy and longevity you want to purchase one of those solid, stalwart, middle-class Swedish cars—either a Volvo or a Saab. As a prudent and sensible buyer, you go to *Consumer Reports*, which informs you that the consensus of their experts is that the Volvo is mechanically superior, and the consensus of the readership is that the Volvo has a better repair record. Armed with this information, you decide to go and strike a bargain with the Volvo dealer before the week is out. In the interim, however, you go to a cocktail party where you announce this intention to an acquaintance. He reacts with disbelief and alarm. "A Volvo! You've got to be kidding. My brother-in-law had a Volvo. First, that fancy fuel injection computer thing went out. 250 bucks. Next he started having trouble with the rear end. Had to replace it. Then the transmission and the clutch. Finally sold it in three years for junk.[16]

Nisbett acknowledges that this gives you a reason to make a very small adjustment in the repair rates given by *Consumer Reports*; assuming that it wasn't in the original survey, you now have one additional observation. But is it likely to be weighed that lightly? More to the point, would one have the nerve to go out and buy a Volvo? This bit of information is so vivid that it is apt to drive out the bland statistics found in *Consumer Reports*.

Now, as we argued earlier, credences or probabilities of this sort are subjective appraisals of likelihood, so there is likely to be some variation between persons based on what evidence they find compelling. Still, using Bayesian updating, agents concerned with making the best assessment of the relative probabilities will use the best evidence available, and this will usually mean taking more seriously the type of information that one gets from something like *Consumer Reports* than vague claims from someone at a cocktail party. Not in every case, though. There are likely to be cases where testimony and first-hand knowledge, even in small samples, will be important. This case, however, is not one of them.

---

16. Quoted in Nisbett and Ross, Human Inference, 15.

Framing Effects

Different ways of putting the "same choice" can yield different preferences over options. Consider another example (the percentages in parentheses are those who select this option).[17]

(1) Imagine that the United States is preparing for the outbreak of an unusual infectious disease that is expected to kill 600 people. Two alternative programs to combat the disease have been proposed. Assume that the exact scientific estimates of the consequences of the programs are as follows:
   A. If program A is adopted, 200 people will be saved. (72%)
   B. If program B is adopted, there is a one-third probability that 600 people will be saved and two-thirds probability that no people will be saved. (28%)
(2) The same basic story is told with the following options:
   C. If program C is adopted, 400 people will die. (22%)
   D. If program D is adopted, there is a one-third probability that nobody will die and a two-thirds probability that 600 people will die. (78%)

The pair A,C will result in the same number of lives saved and lost; the pair B,D will also result in the same number of lives saved and lost. A and C are just different descriptions of the same program, as are B and D. Yet people are apt to make very different choices depending on the way the choice is "framed" or described—saving lives or letting people die.

If one's choices are "framed" in this way—if the *same option* is described in different ways—it can affect how people judge the expected utility of the choices.[18] The cognitive psychologists refer to the "framing" of questions, the effect of the way they are formulated on the answers. A fundamental element of rationality, so elementary that we hardly notice it, is, in logicians' language, its *extensionality*. The chosen element depends on the opportunity set from which the choice is to be made, independently of how it is described.[19] That is, the options must be stable in the sense that they describe *outcomes*, and people will have their preferences over action-options determined only by the outcomes associated with each option, not the way in which those outcomes are described.

17. Kahneman and Tversky, "Choices, Values and Frames," 5.
18. Tversky and Kahneman, "Rational Choice and the Framing of Decisions," 211.
19. Arrow, "Risk Perception in Psychology and Economics."

Endowment Effects

We have already mentioned prospect theory in the last section. Prospect theory insists that people make choices from a reference point—the status quo—not simply in terms of best outcomes. A part of this "anchoring" of one's reasoning concerns the "Endowment Effect." In one experiment students were given a free coffee mug and asked whether they wanted to exchange it for a Swiss candy bar of roughly equal market value. About 10% of the students elected to give up the mug for the candy. In another group, the students were given the candy and were offered the mug in exchange; again, about 10% of the students made the trade. Finally, in a third group no initial distribution was made, and students could choose either a mug or a candy bar; they split roughly equally in their choices.[20]

This suggests that the students valued the exact same goods differently depending on whether they had one in hand or did not. The prospect of losing a good for another of, presumably, equal value to them is treated differently to the prospect of gaining either.

Do These Findings Undermine Expected Utility Theory?

The findings of cognitive psychologists such as Kahneman and Tversky must give pause to any advocate of expected utility theory since they point to well-documented shortcomings in people's ability to calculate probabilities and make choices based on them. However, to evaluate just how much of a challenge they pose, we need to distinguish several different ways in which they might lead us to doubt our account of rationality.

Certainly, the often-replicated findings about the systematic errors people make in probability judgments show that expected utility is an idealization that most individuals never fully approach. That, though, should not be a great surprise: to assume rational choice is to assume a certain sort of ideal chooser, which perhaps few agents ever entirely approximate. The question is whether the idealization—rationality as a normative standard—is so far removed from reality as to be useless. If people are really *awful* at probability judgments, then it will not help much to try to understand their actions in terms of maximizing expected utility, although we may still see their actions as manifesting a funny sort of subjective rationality. It is not clear, though, that the findings are as troublesome as they first appear.

20. Knetsch, "Endowment Effect," 172–73.

There is also evidence that, while people tend to be bad at calculating probabilities, they are much better at estimating frequencies and drawing the right conclusions about them.[21] Think again of our case of testing for the rare disease. People seem to have a hard time thinking of the case in terms of probability calculations involving not only the probability that the test is right but also the probability that a random person in the population has the disease. But once explained in terms as we do, it is clear. So too with the flak jacket example: a case that is puzzling to many when put in terms of probability becomes much easier when redescribed in terms of frequencies. This suggests that people may be considerably better at making the probabilistically correct choices when they are able to conceive of the choice in terms of frequencies.

Endowment effects (and prospect theory) pose more of a challenge for *Homo economicus* than for expected utility theory. Economists typically (though not always) suppose that consumers simply have preferences over goods but not preferences whether they move from a certain starting point. *If* our preferences were only over goods, then endowment effects imply a sort of inconsistency: sometimes we prefer mugs to candy and other times, candy to mugs. This implies a violation of independence. But, of course, the crux of the issue is that the individuals do not have preferences simply over goods, but over outcomes, so there is no real problem with preferring to keep what they have to getting something else if each outcome is identified precisely.

Such preferences may be basic to what it means to "own" something; once you see something as your property, you may be reluctant to give it up, just because it is yours. "It ain't much, but it's mine" suggests that its being yours makes it more valuable. Having such preferences may be important to living a happy life; having them is apt to make each more pleased with the goods she ends up with, which she wouldn't trade "even for a lot of money." Again, to the extent that endowment effects are strong, economists may have to weaken their assumption that preferences are only over goods, but that is not a challenge to expected utility theory per se.

We are back to Talia, Horace, and the kitten from above. If all preferences are over outcomes characterized independently of process, then there is something odd going on. But if agents have preferences not only over outcomes but also over the processes that produce the outcomes (was the kitten given away by a fair lottery? was the mug something of mine that I have to give up to get the candy?), then the oddness disappears. This, finally, leads us to the most fundamental issue: *framing*. Arrow, remember, argues for *extensionality*: preferences over outcomes must be independent of our description of them, and

21. See Steven Pinker, *How the Mind Works* (New York: Norton, 1997), 347–48.

under framing we see that our evaluation of the "same" outcome changes as the description changes.

Is this so? Think of Sen's polite guest who refuses to take the last mango. Can we say that she *really* has a choice between eating a mango and an apple, but she responds to different descriptions and so changes her preferences, and that is why her choices violate the contraction and weak expansion properties? But this assumes either that action-option descriptions are given to us in some sense—that is, that the description of these options is somehow part of the furniture of the world—or that there is a uniquely correct way of representing those states, actions, and outcome. We think both of these options are implausible; there is no such thing as a set of brute action-options that are independent of the descriptions (intentional states) of the choosers. Are Betty's true options: a mango or an apple to eat, a soft object or a hard one, a dull-surfaced object or a shiny-surfaced one, the superior piece of fruit to throw at a disliked political speaker, the superior fruit to put on the teacher's desk, or between being rude and being civil? Meaning is bound up with all of these options, and different meanings will change the attractiveness of the options.

One of the hopes of revealed preference theory, with its behavioral underpinnings, was that we could describe an unambiguous "choice behavior" that had no reference to the chooser's intentional states and so to her descriptions of what she is up to. But as we have argued, action is inherently intentional. We can't read the intentions directly from choice. This doesn't mean, however, that a choice theory drawing from revealed preference is useless. We can't infer meaning and intentions directly from choice, but we can't easily infer it any other way either. Choice behavior gives us evidence that we need to interpret the values, reasons, and intentions of agents, but we can only do so indirectly.

So "framing" cannot simply be understood in terms of different descriptions of the "same" option, for what is the "same" option depends on the relevant description. On Sen's view framing explains *inconsistent choices*, but our person who refuses to take the last mango does not really seem inconsistent.[22] When an agent changes her action when the action is redescribed, this does not imply an objectionable "framing." As Betty is about to perform what looks like the same action she performed yesterday ("picked up the mango from the tray"), she suddenly redescribes it to herself ("It's the last mango today!") and draws back. The new description alerted her to something of relevance to her evaluation of her action and the result that brings it about ("it isn't just about

---

22. Sen, "Maximization and the Act of Choice," 168n.

choosing fruit; it is also about civility"). To show Betty is in some way irrational we might show that she has manifestly relied on an *irrelevant*
consideration.

A full account of framing, and its relation to a plausible version of Arrow's
condition of "extensionality," must then involve a notion of *irrelevant* differences in description or a criterion of choice inconsistency.[23] In our obvious
framing case it seems that there is something amiss because there is apparently
no good reason for drawing a distinction between A and C, or B and D, yet the
respondents do. But if there is a good reason for drawing the distinction, no
framing occurs. What this suggests, then, is that we need some account of
which distinctions are relevant and which are not or, as John Broome says,
what justifies a preference.[24] Underlying or justifying a preference ordering
must be a system of principles, goals, ends, or values, and that is what can
justify distinguishing outcomes in terms of their descriptions. If this is so, then
preferences over states of affairs cannot be basic. There are an infinite number
of descriptions of any one state of affairs. Our resistance to obvious cases of
framing shows that we do not think every change in description makes for a
different outcome. But, then, which do and which don't? It looks as if the only
way to justify making a distinction is to draw on some other evaluative criteria
to justify our representations of states of affairs.

One method principle for doing so comes from Leonard Savage who, in
The Foundations of Statistics, introduces what he calls the "sure-thing principle"
(STP) with this story:

> A businessman contemplates buying a certain piece of property. He consid-
> ers the outcome of the next presidential election relevant. So, to clarify the
> matter to himself, he asks whether he would buy if he knew that the Demo-
> cratic candidate were going to win, and decides that he would. Similarly, he
> considers whether he would buy if he knew that the Republican candidate
> were going to win, and again finds that he would. Seeing that he would buy
> in either event, he decides that he should buy, even though he does not
> know which event obtains, or will obtain, as we would ordinarily say.[25]

From this story, Savage extracts the general principle that if Alf prefers to
choose x over y, whether or not an event E occurs, then Alf should prefer x to
y regardless of what he knows about E. Savage reports that he knows of "no

23. Arrow himself refers to people being moved by "irrelevant" events in his "Risk Perception
in Psychology and Economics," 7.

24. See Broome, "Rationality and the Sure-Thing Principle," 74–102.

25. Savage, The Foundations of Statistics, 21.

other extra-logical principle governing decisions that finds such ready acceptance."

The STP is a version of the independence axiom from above and Savage is probably right that it does tend to find ready acceptance. But he is also right that it is an extra-logical principle in the sense that it cannot be derived directly from his definitions of actions, states, and affairs. Savage goes beyond the von Neumann utility representations, which take probability assessments over lotteries as basic. Savage wants a more general theory, but to do so, the STP requires the introduction of causal considerations since we need to know how states, actions, and outcomes are causally linked. What is needed is causal exclusion between states and acts. Which is not to say that states and acts need to be wholly independent, only that there cannot be a direct causal link between states and acts for the STP to hold.[26]

An alternative version of expected utility theory was developed by Richard Jeffrey to avoid any reference to causal claims by identifying acts and outcome jointly as events.[27] This approach has some controversial implications and other drawbacks, though it does have the advantage that, since it makes events into propositions, it is partition-invariant. For this and several other reasons it has been popular among philosophers, but largely ignored by economists.[28]

The Relation Between Utility Theory and Rationality

Many—perhaps most—see utility theory as an account of instrumental or goal-oriented reasoning. Those who believe that all reasons are instrumental typically embrace formal utility theory because they think it is essentially a formalization of their view. Just as an instrumentally rational agent aims to maximize the satisfaction of her goals, it seems that an agent who corresponds to the axioms of ordinal and cardinal utility theory seeks to maximize the satisfaction of her preferences—her utility. Further, if "goals," "ends," and "preferences" are the same thing, decision theory is simply a formal version of instrumental rationality. To be sure, the axioms add constraints on the structure of the preferences, but the core of the model is still seen as instrumental rationality.

---

26. There has been a revolution in our understanding of causality over the last decade or so that should be able to put a causal theory on a firmer foundation; for overviews of the recent developments, see: Glymour, Thinking Things Through; Pearl and Mackenzie, The Book of Why.

27. Jeffrey, The Logic of Decision.

28. Two prominent examples of philosophers who use the Jeffrey-Bolker approach are Joyce, The Foundations of Causal Decision Theory; Bradley, Decision Theory with a Human Face.

We think that this belief, when properly understood, is a serious mistake, albeit a common one. Utility theory allows us to model choice based on one's notion of the overall ordering of outcomes by whatever criteria one thinks appropriate. What is required to generate a utility function is that one has some way to determine what is the best outcome, what is the next best outcome, and so on—but "best" need not be that which leads to the highest satisfaction of one's goals. There is no reason whatsoever to suppose that Alf's set of evaluative criteria are all about Alf's *goals*, *welfare* or *goods*. Although standard utility theory distinguishes acts from outcomes (or consequences) and holds that the ranking of acts is determined by the ranking of outcomes, we should not confuse this sort of decision-theoretic consequentialism with the theory of rational action.[29] Anything of normative relevance for choice is part of the consequence domain.[30] One of Alf's preferences over outcomes may be that he performs act *a*, say, "telling the truth when under oath today." If, in his current set of options, one action-option is to tell the truth under oath, he will rank that act highly. Given this, the action of telling the truth under oath has "high utility"—that is, the action Alf has most reason to perform.[31] If then one's normative criteria include moral principles, and these lead to ranking outcomes in ways that meet the basic axioms, then a person acting on her moral principles can be modeled as maximizing a mathematical cardinal function.

That is why we stressed that one can have preferences over actions—what Sen calls "comprehensive" outcomes. One can be concerned not only with what happens, but what you had to do to bring it about. One may care not only about the ultimate result but how that result came about. Given that, there is no reason why utility theory cannot model a principled moral person who is more concerned with the nature of her acts than their outcomes.

It is true that some sorts of principled action cannot be modeled in terms of a cardinal utility function. One who is an "absolutist" about some principle, and so will never contemplate a lottery between acting on it and her second-best option, violates *continuity*, and so we cannot develop a cardinal utility function for her. Think of a sort of Kantian who will absolutely never lie, regardless of the circumstances. Such an absolutist still can have complete,

---

29. The Jeffrey-Bolker version of utility theory does not directly distinguish between acts and outcomes, but even here one needs to conceptually distinguish in some way between the attractiveness of the way the world is, the way it could be, and how to make it so.

30. As Paul Anand recognizes in Foundations of Rational Choice Under Risk, 84.

31. Stanley Benn has modeled deontological requirements in this way. See A Theory of Freedom, chap. 3.

reflexive, and transitive ordinal preferences (at least, so long as she has only one absolute principle).[32]

The important point, though, is that these sorts of worries cannot show that decision theory is confined to instrumental reasoning in any interesting sense: they are objections to the lottery axioms and the development of *cardinal* utility. The difference between ordinal and cardinal utility pertains to the information implied about the relation between the ranked outcomes. More precisely, it may not be possible to construct a real valued representation of one's utility function.

Consider what has been called a "plural intuitionist"—someone who holds that there is a set of moral principles $\{P_1, P_2, P_3, \ldots P_n\}$ that one should *always* follow, but in any given case one must "weigh" one principle against the others. So, if one principle is "Don't lie" and another is "Don't endanger innocent lives" in cases where the only way to avoid endangering innocent lives is to tell a lie, one must "weigh" the two principles to decide which is the most important. This sort of moral theory is usually described as "deontological," as opposed to "consequentialist," since it is not only concerned with good consequences. But there is no reason why such a "deontological" theory cannot be modeled in terms of utility theory.[33]

Rationality and Maximizing Utility

The power of decision theory is that modest principles of consistency and transitivity of preference allow us to construct a mathematical representation of a person who consistently chooses higher- over lower-ranked options and has a complete ordering of outcomes; for cardinal representations, as we have seen, additional and somewhat more contentious principles are required, but they too are relatively intuitive. This mathematical representation allows us to depict consistent choices for higher- over lower-ranked options as maximizing a utility function.

32. If one has two absolutist principles, it would seem likely that one would violate either completeness or asymmetry of strict preference. As John Rawls notes, a strict lexicographic preference ordering prevents formulating a cardinal utility function. He writes, "A utility function is simply a mathematical representation of households' or economic agents' preferences, assuming these preferences to satisfy certain conditions. From a purely formal point of view, there is nothing to prevent an agent who is a pluralistic intuitionist from having a utility function." Political Liberalism, 332n.

33. Jamie Dreier has argued that all moral theories can be "consequentialized," making them susceptible to decision theoretic analysis. See Dreier, "Structures of Normative Theories." Also important is Dietrich and List, "What Matters and How It Matters."

Utility theory formalizes a person's *all-things-considered considerations* in favor of action-options. It is crucial to stress that utility theory simply does not maintain that anyone *seeks* to maximize utility—that idea is a remnant of utility qua hedonism. A utility function is a formal representation of an ordering of outcomes meeting certain conditions, acting in a way that maximizes utility model choices that are consistent with this ordering. Maximization of utility is not itself a goal. That is just as well, since utility is a mathematical representation, and few of us want to maximize mathematical representations!

Because utility theory can represent consistent choice for the best option as *maximization* of a mathematical function, it is very easy to think that utility theory, like instrumental rationality, is about the most efficient way to *maximize* the satisfaction of a set of goals. However, utility theory is not about the most efficient means to one's ends, but about consistently choosing what one deems the best option. This confusion can occur so readily that even experts are prone to it. But it still is a confusion. Utility theory can indeed model the rationality of an instrumentally rational agent, but it can also model the rationality of an agent who thinks it is better to act on moral principles or what Sen calls "commitments," as we saw above.

Conclusion

The ability to represent utility as a continuous, cardinal function is a tremendous advance that allows us to formulate a general, formal account of rationality. We looked at the axioms of cardinal utility theory derived from the approach made famous by John von Neumann and Oskar Morgenstern. This approach takes preferences over outcomes and embeds them in probabilistic lotteries. Doing so allows us to construct relative intensities of preference given the same chance of getting an outcome. The axioms that we use to generate this utility representation are subject to a number of challenging counterexamples or complications, including the Allais and Ellsberg paradoxes. Psychologists have also questioned whether utility theory of this sort is a descriptively accurate representation of the way agents chose and whether it should be used as a normative standard for choice. In the next chapter, we use the utility theory we have generated here to model rational individual choice and see how it can be used to make sense of joint choice in the market.

Discussion Questions

(1) Using Venn diagrams, graph the relation between rationality, selfishness, *Homo economicus,* and utility maximization.

(2) Lionel Robbins argued that deciding on the proper way to compare people's cardinal utilities is a normative task of political economy. Here are some proposals:
   a. Each person's utility should count equal to everyone else's.
   b. People who work hard should count for more than others.
   c. The poor should count for more than the rich.
   d. Fellow nationals should count for more than outsiders.
   e. There is no useful way to compare one person's utility to another's.

   As a budding political economist, which do you think is the best answer?

(3) Of the psychological doubts explored in this chapter, which do you think is the biggest challenge to the idea that economic agents are utility maximizers?

(4) Recall our case of Talia, Horace, and the kitten. How does its significance change if (a) we hold that preferences are only over outcomes, (b) that they can be over acts and outcomes, or (c) that our kitten-giver believes he has an absolute duty to protect the kitten's welfare?

(5) Suppose a person says, "under cardinal utility theory everything has a price." Is this true? Remember, prices need not be understood in terms of money, but relative prices. What does your answer say about the application of cardinal utility theory when it comes to human life?

(6) In his famous theory of social justice, John Rawls argues for "Two Principles of Justice." The first requires equal liberty for all, the second concerns egalitarian distributions of opportunities and resources. Rawls imposes a "lexical ordering" on the two principles so that satisfaction of the first principle can never be compromised in any way to satisfy the second. We can never trade the satisfaction for some of the first for any degree of satisfaction of the second. Why does this show that, while we can represent Rawls's theory in terms of ordinal utility, we cannot do so in terms of cardinal utility? Do you think this shows an irrationality in Rawls's theory, or a flaw in cardinal utility theory?

4

Efficiency and Contract

We have thus far focused on individual rationality: what is it to be a rational actor, and how can we formally model such an actor? This chapter begins with that concern, but then turns to an analysis of how rational actors interact, which will form the subject of the remainder of the book. The main concern of this chapter is to explore the relation between rational action and the idea of efficiency: it begins with efficiency of the consumption decisions of one person, and then moves to the idea of an efficient exchange: an interaction between two economically rational agents. We can think of the model of exchange as a model of rational contracting. The important ideas of Pareto superiority and Pareto optimality are introduced. The second part of the chapter briefly sketches well-known failures of efficiency, involving various notions of "externalities," before turning to a discussion of welfare and rights, the Coase theorem, and public goods.

Rationality and Efficiency

Everyone knows that economics is about efficiency, and most of us have some pro or con attitude about that. Some of us are all for efficiency while others insist that efficiency is a cold economic value that must not come before equity, concern for the needy, or protection of the environment. Thus, it is said we need to "trade off" efficiency against other values.[1] But while most of us know whether we are "for it or agin' it," we are often not sure what "it" is. Just what is efficiency? Is it simply one value among others—one that economists but not the rest of us find very attractive—or is it somehow a fundamental idea that we cannot do without, which we ought not to sacrifice for other good things?

An efficient state of affairs is best thought of as a state of affairs without waste—where everything is put to productive use. We can make that idea

---

1. See Okun and Summers, Equality and Efficiency.

more precise with utility theory. The particular understanding of efficiency used in political philosophy and economics means that some state of affairs (e.g., possible policy outcome, trade, or political regime) is efficient insofar as it is not possible for any reallocation of goods, rights, or whatever to make anyone better off by their own lights (according to the theory of rationality and utility detailed in the last two chapters) without making someone else worse off.

It is helpful to understand this idea in the single individual case, before looking at the general case. Let's reflect on what we know about our rational "economic man." As a fully rational chooser, *Homo economicus* has a well-formed utility function satisfying the requirements of utility theory we examined in chapter 2. His preferences are characterized by the concepts of more is better than less, decreasing marginal utility, and downward sloping demand curves. Suppose, then, that *Homo economicus* has a preference for pizza. How much pizza is it rational for *Homo economicus* to consume?

Suppose that the utility cost of pizza is constant at $U(c)$. By "cost" we mean the total opportunity costs of consuming the pizza—the foregone opportunities to satisfy other preferences. Thus, cost is understood in terms of foregone utility, not money prices. It is important to stress that "cost" does not necessarily mean a monetary payment, or something that you don't like, for example, "a cost of taking this course is that I have to take tests."

In the economist's sense, the "cost" of getting your first choice of a pizza is that you had to forego your second choice of a box of chicken wings: when you have to choose between good things, the cost of your decision is that good thing you didn't choose. This can be specified in terms of *Homo economicus*'s foregone utility—call this $U(c)$. It is the utility you would have received from your second choice. Now consider Alf's decision to consume the first slice of pizza. It satisfies his preference for pizza over something else; given his utility function we can represent this by some utility benefit—call it $U(b)$. If $U(b) \geq U(c)$ (that is, if the utility benefits are greater than, or equal to, the utility costs), then it will be rational for him to purchase the slice of pizza. But should he buy only one slice?

Well, we know that since the cost of pizza is constant per unit, in this case 2X the cost of the foregone utility, so the cost will be $2[U(c)]$. But because of decreasing marginal utility, the benefits of the second slice will be less than twice $U(b)$: call this $[x(U(b))]$—where x is a positive number less than 1. The crucial idea here is that whatever the utility benefits of the first piece $[U(b)]$, the utility of the second piece will be positive (because more is better than less) but smaller than the utility of the first piece (hence it will be $U(b) + [x(U(b))]$; that is what is meant by decreasing marginal utility. It will be rational for Alf to consume two slices if the utility benefits of two slices are greater than, or equal to, the utility costs of two slices—$U(b) + [x(U(b))] \geq 2[U(c)]$.

Because the costs are constant but the marginal benefits are decreasing, at some point it will be the case that the additional, or as economists say, "marginal" (utility) benefits that Alf gets from some slice of pizza will be less than the marginal (utility) costs he had to incur in order to get that slice; in that case it would be irrational for *Homo economicus* to consume that additional slice of pizza because the preferences he then would be satisfying are ranked below the preferences he is foregoing.

Figure 4.1 is a graphic representation of a specific example of this simple choice problem. On the left vertical axis, we measure *Homo economicus*'s total utility costs, while on the right vertical axis we measure his total utility benefits. In the figure, it is rational for *Homo economicus* to purchase three slices of pizza.[2]

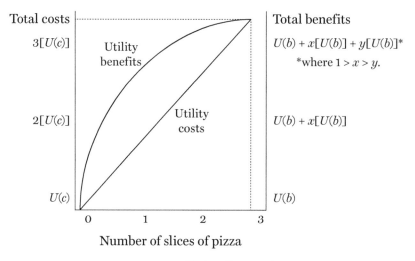

FIGURE 4.1. Efficient Consumption

Homo economicus will consume up to the point where marginal benefits equal marginal costs or MB = MC. This is one definition of efficiency. *Homo economicus* chooses in this way not because he "values efficiency" any more

2. This graph may look unfamiliar: it graphs total utility gains, not just utility gains at the margin. It is a good thing to present the same idea in different ways—we have to pause and examine the unfamiliar, rather than just nodding because we have seen "that graph" so many times.

than a rational actor seeks to "maximize utility"—this decision is simply required by rationality as utility theory understands it. To choose any other way would be to choose a lower- over a higher-ranked preference, and that, of course, is the essence of irrationality. In this sense, then, efficiency is simply rationality.

There is, then, a close relation between efficiency and the rational choice since to be rational is to choose in a way that best satisfies one's preferences—and that means that the marginal gains are at least as great as the marginal costs. At a later point we shall examine paradoxical situations where rationality and efficiency break apart; in such cases many are uncertain just what is the truly rational thing to do.

Note, though, that efficient consumption is not simply an implication of instrumental rationality, or of utility maximization per se. Suppose a person's consumption was not characterized by decreasing marginal utility. Then, unless the price for the good rises, the "marginal" benefit of the nth unit would be the same as the marginal benefit of the nth unit. Or, more radically, suppose a person followed Hume, and preferred *less over more*. Then what would their rational consumption look like?

Exchange and the Edgeworth Box

Let's move to a two-person case. We will represent the choice problem in terms of indifference curves, which, as recalled from chapter 1, plot one's preferences over bundles of goods given decreasing marginal rates of substitution between them. Suppose that Alf has four slices of pizza and Betty has eight Buffalo chicken wings. And suppose that they have pretty much the same preferences over pizza and chicken wings, so that their indifference curves are essentially the same.

Figure 4.2 shows their indifference maps; Betty's (solid) indifference curves start in the lower left, Alf's (dotted) indifference curves come down from the upper right. Suppose that in this *Edgeworth Box*, Alf and Betty are at point P_1: Alf has four slices of pizza and no wings, while Betty has eight chicken wings and no pizza.[3] The key point to note is that every single allocation pair on each indifference curve is efficient. From the point of view of efficiency, there is no difference between any allocation along a particular indifference curve.

---

3. Named after Francis Edgeworth (1845–1926) who depicted alternative allocation of resources, and possibilities for contracts, in this way.

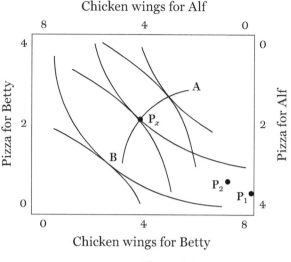

FIGURE 4.2. Edgeworth Box

It is important to remember that Alf is indifferent between all combinations of pizza and chicken wings on any of his indifference curves; however, he prefers all bundles on curves to the left to all bundles on curves to the right. As Alf moves southwest, he receives increasingly preferred combinations of pizza and chicken wings. If he moves all the way to the southwest corner, he receives all the pizza and all the chicken wings. Betty prefers to move starting at the lower left corner, she prefers combinations of chicken wings and pizza that are to the northeast.

Now any point in the "lens" formed by the Alf_1-$Betty_1$ indifference curves improves the utility of both Alf and Betty: any point in the "lens" moves each to a higher indifference curve. Pick any point in the "lens": you will see that Betty and Alf have both moved from moved from P_1 in their preferred directions. What this shows is that both can be made better off by exchange, even though no additional goods have been created. An exchange that moved both Alf and Betty to point P_2 would make both of them better off. We can say then that point P_2 is *Pareto-superior* to point P_1—at least one person is better off, and no one is worse off. In this case, both people are better off.

But although the bargain at P_2 is Pareto-superior to P_1, there are still Pareto-superior bargains that Alf and Betty can make starting at P_2. The gains from trade have not been exhausted: so long as Pareto-superior moves are available, Alf and Betty can keep trading and at least one will benefit. When are the possible gains from trade exhausted? We can easily see that when they reach a bargain at which their indifference curves are tangent, Pareto-superior moves are exhausted.

Consider, for example, point P_x. At point P_x Alf can only move to a higher indifference curve if Betty moves to a lower indifference curve. But, by definition, that would make her worse off, and a move is only Pareto-superior if no one is made worse off. So, too, starting at point P_x, the only way that Betty can rise to a higher indifference curve is if Alf moves to a lower one—that is, he is worse off. Point P_x is thus a *Pareto-optimal* bargain since any departure from it would make either Alf or Betty worse off. Point P_x, therefore, is *efficient*: all the gains from possible exchanges have been exhausted.

But point P_x is not unique in this regard: any bargain that occupies a point on which Alf and Betty's indifference curves are tangent is Pareto-optimal. The line A-B (which is called the *contract curve*) represents all such possible efficient bargains—ones that use all the possible gains from trade. Along that line there are possibilities for efficient contracts or trades between individuals. Obviously, starting from point P_2, some of the efficient contracts favor Betty while others are better for Alf.[4]

Notice two things. First, the assumption of decreasing rates of substitution is crucial in explaining why economically rational people trade with each other. Because they each prefer varied to uniform bundles of goods, if Alf is pizza-rich he will want to exchange with Betty, who is chicken-wing-rich. This is a fundamental point that merits emphasis: given decreasing rates of marginal substitution (or decreasing marginal utility), everyone can become better off through market exchange without any increase in the total number of goods.

Second, taking part in such trades is simply another example of marginal costs equaling marginal benefits. We have essentially the same story in a different form here, rather than employing cardinal utility, we are analyzing the problem in terms of ordinal utility (i.e., preferences over bundles of goods). The marginal costs of Alf keeping those last two slices of pizza (his opportunity costs of foregoing acquiring four chicken wings) are greater than the marginal benefits that he gets from those two slices of pizza. Thus, as we have depicted the problem, it is irrational for Alf and Betty to refrain from trading: if they keep their bundles at P_2 they are satisfying lower- over higher-ranked preferences.

We are now in a position to understand the concept of Pareto, or allocative, superiority and efficiency.[5]

---

4. Of course, if we bring in endowment effects and Alf and Betty have a preference to keep what they already have, then they may not trade. We can now better see why endowment effects worry economists: they go to the very heart of efficiency.

5. Some distinguish allocative from Pareto efficiency; allocative efficiency is said to obtain when marginal benefits equal marginal costs, and this is distinguished from the Pareto criterion. There are other concepts of efficiency employed in economics. X-efficiency concerns getting

---

D_2 is *Strongly Pareto-superior* to (more efficient than) D_1 if and only if no person is on a lower indifference curve in D_2 than that person is in D_1, and at least one person is on a higher indifference curve in D_2 than she is in D_1.

D_1 is *Strongly Pareto optimal* (efficient) if there are no Strongly Pareto-superior distributions to it.

D_2 is *Weakly Pareto-superior* to (more efficient than) D_1 if and only if every person is on a higher curve in D_2 than that person is in D_1.

D_1 is *Weakly Pareto optimal* (efficient) if there are no distributions that make everyone better off.

Unless otherwise stated, by "Pareto superior" and Pareto efficient" we shall mean Strongly Pareto superior/efficient.

Put simply, some state of affairs is Pareto superior to another when at least one person in society is better off in that state of affairs and no one is worse off than they are in the status quo. A Pareto-optimal state of affairs exists when it is not possible to make any more Pareto-superior or dominant moves.

Pareto efficiency can be related to notions of contract and agreement. Since Pareto-superior moves are said to *dominate* all Pareto-inferior moves or deals, we can assume that someone would always agree to Pareto improvements and never agree to the opposite. Joint Pareto-dominant options will be options that it is possible for individuals to agree to or contract on.

If despite the possibility of a move to a Pareto-superior distribution we stay in D_1, there is at least one person who could achieve a higher level of preference satisfaction without lowering anyone else's. Thus, in figure 4.2, the distribution identified by P_x is Pareto-superior to the distribution of P_2. As in all the cases we have discussed thus far there is something irrational about maintaining Pareto-inferior distributions. In addition to being Pareto-superior to P_2, point P_x is also *Pareto-optimal* just because there is no alternative distribution that is Pareto-superior to it. That is, if Alf and Betty have arrived at P_x, there is no way in which one of them can be raised to a higher indifference curve without the other moving to a lower curve.

Problems with Pareto Efficiency

Now that we have some idea of what efficiency is and how powerful it is, we should turn to some of the main drawbacks or problems with using Pareto efficiency as the only standard for political or social evaluation.

---

maximum outputs for a given level of inputs; dynamic efficiency concerns maximizing growth; and technological efficiency concerns the use of the best technology.

Indeterminacy

The main drawback with efficiency as a standard is indeterminacy. Once we generate the Pareto frontier for a group or an indifference curve for an individual, we cannot say anything very interesting about the points on that frontier or curve. Since individuals are indifferent to the various allocations, by definition we can't rationally distinguish between any of the particular allocations. This is even more of an issue when we are dealing with groups and the Pareto frontier.

Imagine a world with three individuals: Alf, Betty, and Charlie. Imagine also that there is only one resource of value in this world and that currently the three only have 15 units of that resource divided evenly so that each person has 5. They have created a new technology that allows them to substantially increase their resources and move from their current Pareto frontier of 15 total units to one with 100 total units. They have three options for how that world will look, represented by the X, Y, and Z in table 4.1.

TABLE 4.1. Pareto Efficiency Table

	X	Y	Z
Alf	90	75	25
Betty	5	15	25
Charlie	5	10	50

Each option Pareto dominates their current state of affairs, so they should choose one of these options. But which one? From the point of view of efficiency, each is as good as the other. Pareto efficiency does not provide the resources to choose between any of the particular Pareto-optimal options. It tells us to choose from the Pareto frontier, but it doesn't tell us which point on the Pareto frontier to choose from. Obviously, Alf, Betty, and Charlie are not indifferent between these options, but the Pareto condition alone doesn't tell us which to pick. Put another way, efficiency alone doesn't tell us anything about how various efficient options should be distributed socially. We will return to this problem when we address social choice.

Path Dependence

Pareto optimality can also sometimes be path-dependent and restricted. That is, it may be impossible, in some cases, to make only Pareto-dominant moves in order to reach a Pareto-optimal option. Similarly, as Russell Hardin argues, some Pareto-permissible moves will close off further options to others in some exchanges, which can introduce more path dependence into the story and make some Pareto situations look less like mutual advantage.[6] How could this be possible? Figure 4.3 suggests an answer.

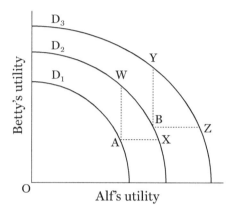

FIGURE 4.3. A Series of Paretian Moves

Suppose we start at point O and make the Pareto-superior move to point A, which is one possible distribution along D_1—the Pareto Frontier, which is the set of possible Pareto improvements from O. Once we are at A, the Pareto improvements to D_2 are limited to those between points W and X; other points on D_2 make either Alf or Betty worse off than in D_1, so are not Pareto improvements. Assume then that at some point distribution D_2 becomes a possibility: Alf and Betty make the Pareto move to point B on D_2.

Suppose now that in the future D_3 becomes possible; now the possible Pareto improvements are limited to those falling between Y and Z. We can see that successive applications of the Pareto criterion move distributions along a path that is increasingly beneficial to Alf and of less benefit to Betty. If we had been able to jump to D_3 all at once, everything on it would be a Pareto improvement over O, but once we have made the intermediate moves to A and B, most of D_3 is excluded by the Pareto criterion. Perhaps then Betty would have good reason to object to the initial Pareto move to point A. The Pareto principle allows a wide range of moves, and it may matter a lot which of those is actually made, and in what order.

This example shows that where you can go depends on where you have been when we are considering Pareto improvements. This also suggests, however, that

6. See Hardin, Indeterminacy and Society, 10–11.

it might be possible or even necessary to make Pareto-inefficient moves, which is to say move off the Pareto frontier, in order to move to even better mutually beneficial options. This, however, is somewhat paradoxical. Getting the most mutually beneficial and efficient outcome might require being inefficient in the short term to move to a higher Pareto frontier in the future. This introduces a number of complexities into efficiency analysis and, more important, undermines the plausibility of efficiency as the only standard of social evaluation.

Conflicts Between Efficiency and Rationality

Another serious problem, which we will explore in more depth in the next chapter, is that individual rationality and group efficiency can sometimes come apart. Throughout this chapter, we have argued that efficiency is merely an implication of economic rationality, which is correct as far as it goes, but in the case of the "prisoner's dilemma," we are confronted with a scenario where individual rationality and efficiency diverge. Again, we will examine this case in greater detail in the next chapter, but it is worth raising here as well.

Efficiency and Welfare

The Pareto criterion is often understood not simply as a requirement of *rationality* qua efficiency, but as a standard by which we can judge the *moral* desirability of a distribution or, in general, a social state. To many it seems clear that distribution D_2 is morally better than D_1 if (and, perhaps, only if) some person's welfare is "higher" in D_2 and no one's is lower than it was in D_1. Especially in politics, it is thought, what is good for people—their welfare—must be the (sole) criterion of a good policy. This view has definite roots in utilitarian moral theory, which identified promoting human happiness as the sole goal of morality and politics. The ultimate aim clearly was human happiness, though the proximate aim of economics was the growth of wealth.

Contemporary *welfare economics* typically understands a person's "welfare" to be measured by her utility function. If the utility of Betty is $U(x)$ in distribution D_1 and is greater than $U(x)$ in D_2, then it is said her welfare is higher in D_2 than in D_1, and D_2 is a better distribution than D_1. Here, however, things get complicated. The early utilitarians such as Jeremy Bentham and his followers believed that "utility" (pleasure) of different people could be measured along a metric, such that, when contemplating a move from D_1 to D_2 we could sensibly add the utility Alf received from the move from D_1 to D_2, to the utility Betty received, and then subtract the loss of utility to Charlie (who, let us say, was better off in D_1).

Having done our sums, we could then decide whether, overall, the move from D_1 to D_2 increases overall aggregate utility. But we have seen that there is no particularly good reason to add von Neumann–Morgenstern cardinal utilities of different people; unless there is a special case for some additive function, it is simply arbitrary to sum up or otherwise aggregate cardinal utilities. The contemporary welfarist appears to have a problem: how to compare social states without interpersonal comparisons of utilities.

The Pareto criterion seems to offer a way out of this problem: if *no one* is worse off in D_2 than she was in D_1, and at least one person is better off in D_2 than he was in D_1, then D_2 is Pareto-superior to D_1. And since the welfare economist has identified a person's welfare with her utility, it looks as if we can say that D_2 does better from the perspective of human welfare.

It is often thought that this cannot be a very useful criterion of "moral betterness" since it only yields a judgment that D_2 is better than D_1 if *no one* is worse off in D_2. But how often is it the case that no one is made worse off? On the Pareto test, if in D_2 one million people are made better off than they were in D_1, but one person is worse off, we cannot say that D_2 is Pareto-superior to D_1. Is there ever, we might well wonder, a Pareto-superior move to be made? We are now in a position to see the economist's deep attraction to market transactions. Under certain idealizing conditions, e.g., full information, no third-party effects, each market transaction moves us to a Pareto-superior distribution. When people trade, they prefer what the other person has to what they offer to give up, and so we move to a Pareto-superior distribution. As long as we have not exhausted the possibilities for exchange—as long as there are trades that people want to make—we have not exhausted the possibilities for Pareto-superior moves.

Markets and Efficiency

One of the great achievements of twentieth-century economics was the proof, by Kenneth Arrow and Gerard Debreu (who developed the idea independently, but at roughly the same time) that a market economy as a whole can be in an efficient and stable equilibrium, given certain basic assumptions.[7] Their respective models of general equilibrium built upon early models, most notably on the work of Leon Walras (1834–1910). The idea of general equilibrium is that a market clearing price can be found to match every producer with every consumer in a given economy. It is a representation of the supply and demand of the market as a whole. So far, we have looked at limited markets of one or two goods (e.g., wings and pizza) and two traders (Alf and Betty). This is what economists call a "partial equilibrium" model. General equilibrium

---

7. Arrow and Debreu, "Existence of an Equilibrium for a Competitive Economy."

models are, not surprisingly, a generalization of all the goods and consumers in a given market. What Arrow and Debreu showed is that there is a contract curve where optimal trades can occur across the entire economy given certain assumptions.

The main assumption is that the market must be perfectly competitive. What they mean by this is that nothing prevents optimal trades from occurring (e.g., transactions costs or lack of knowledge) and there are no unaccounted-for costs (i.e., externalities) in those trades. Firms or sellers must also be "price takers," which is to say no seller can "make the market" by determining the price monopolistically. If these conditions exist, the first fundamental theorem of welfare economics says that the market equilibrium will be Pareto-optimal, which is to say that the market will be maximally efficient. This can be considered a proof and generalization of Adam Smith's idea of the invisible hand that individuals acting in their own interest in the market will be led as if by an invisible hand to serve the common good, though it is not part of their intention.

If this is right, general equilibrium theory and the fundamental theorem of welfare economics provide a powerful standard for normative evaluation of the market order as a whole. If the market is competitive, we can assume it is Pareto-optimal and, therefore, that any intervention in the market would make someone worse off than they would be in the competitive market. Intervention in the market, and government more generally, could only be justified insofar as the market fails in some way by not being competitive. This is what is called the "market failure" approach to welfare economics. This approach is powerfully challenged by many of the "public choice" thinkers that we will meet in chapter 9, but on its own terms it has a distinctive allure since it seems to generate a normative standard of social evaluation from the ground, starting with preferences and rationality. If this is right, the market might constitute what David Gauthier called a "morality-free zone," where no moral or normative standards are needed besides efficiency.[8]

This approach to using welfare economics as a general social normative system faces two significant challenges. First, we might doubt that we should accept the identification of "preference satisfaction" with "welfare." We have seen that preferences need not be about one's own good or self-interest: any time one ranks an outcome above another, one has a preference. Recall our last-mango refuser from chapter 3. Her preference is not to take the last mango, though, as Sen notes, she would like that mango and would welcome someone forcing her to take the mango. In that case it seems doubtful that we should

---

8. See Gauthier, Morals by Agreement, chap. 4.

say that her welfare is enhanced by satisfying her preference not to take the last mango, since her moral preference instructs her not to do what would be good for her. Those who identify "welfare" with "preference satisfaction" often simply seem driven to stipulating that in this case one's welfare *must* be advanced because one is getting what one "prefers." Here, we think, is a perfect example of the way that the ambiguity between the technical and ordinary senses of "prefer" leads to serious confusion.

Second, we might doubt that the conditions of perfect conditions are likely to obtain. Technically, this is a case of "market failure," but we find that the existence of externalities, transactions costs, and rights all make perfect competition unlikely in most markets. This should not necessarily make us think that more intervention is necessary in the market to "correct" for these problems, rather the ubiquity of these features might also make us look for different normative standards to apply, beyond the basic market failure approach. We will review these in the rest of the chapter.

Externalities

We have looked at one type of inefficiency or waste in the form of underconsumption or underproduction, but there is another kind that concerns both economists and political philosophers in the form of what are called *externalities*. Externalities are results of some exchange, production, or consumption that are not captured by the parties to the exchange, production, or consumption. These can be positive (benefits) or negative (costs) that do not go to the direct parties involved but are instead foisted onto third parties.

Examples of typical negative externalities include:

- Pollution
- Offense
- Noise

Pollution and noise are noxious side effects of certain forms of production or trade. They are also, importantly, inefficient since they are waste that the producers or traders do not eliminate themselves, but instead send out into the community.

Offense of various sorts is also a negative externality that can highlight the complicated nature of externalities in general and some of the limitation of efficiency. A community of Catholics may find it noxious that a community of Protestants or atheists moves into their community. Similarly, a community of Muslims may find it offensive that non-Muslim women walk around their neighborhood uncovered. Even more important, there are various types of speech that offend some people (more on this below). We tend to be inclined to think that these externalities are not as politically important as, say, pollution, but it is nevertheless true that both have essentially the same form.

Examples of typical positive externalities include:

- Education
- Vaccines (herd immunity)
- Network effects

These externalities are cases where not all of the benefits of an exchange can be captured by those involved. There are many social benefits to education that neither the school nor the student can really capture and that flow to the community in general. The same is true of vaccines. Even those who are not vaccinated benefit from those who are.

Perhaps the most interesting case of positive externalities involves network effects. Network effects occur when some good or type of production becomes substantially more valuable the more people that use it. Think of telephones, the Internet, or social media. If Alf is the only person in his town with a telephone, it is not very valuable since he can only talk to himself (something he didn't need a phone for!). The more additional people that get telephones, however, make Alf's telephone exponentially more valuable. The same is true of the Internet and social media, among many other things. Much of the contemporary economy is based on network effects and their importance. Although we tend to think of positive externalities as good things, from the point of view of efficiency, they count as waste and so are inefficient.

Compensation and Kaldor-Hicks Efficiency

Because of the existence of externalities and the informational costs of coming to agreements, sometimes it is difficult or impossible to find Pareto superior ways to move to Pareto optimal outcomes. It is hard to think of any uniform policy that does not disadvantage someone. What if, though, the winners from any non-Pareto superior move could compensate the losers so as to bring them up to a place where they are at least as well off as before the change? Any generally welfare enhancing move can be made Pareto dominant if enough side-payments are made to those who are made worse off in the deal. This is the basis of what is known as Kaldor-Hicks efficiency based on compensation.[9]

More precisely, the move from distribution D_1 to D_2 can be efficient even when some lose by moving from D_1 to D_2 so as long as those who gain from

---

9. Named after Nicholas Kaldor and John Hicks, see Kaldor, "Welfare Propositions; Hicks, "The Foundations of Welfare Economics."

the move could compensate the losers out of their gains.[10] To grasp what it means to say that a person *could* be compensated for a loss, consider Alf, who is the sole person who has been made worse off by the move from D_1 to D_2 (to make the case simple, assume that everyone else is better off in D_2). To say that Alf has been made worse off means that he is on a lower indifference curve in D_2 than he was in D_1. Now imagine that after the move to D_2 the gainers transferred enough of their gains to Alf to raise him back to the indifference curve that he occupied in D_1: this would bring about a new distribution D_3, which is indeed Pareto-superior to D_1 because everyone except Alf is at a higher indifference curve in D_3 than they were in D_1, and Alf is on the same indifference curve.

Kaldor-Hicks Efficiency

D2 is Kaldor-Hicks Pareto-superior to D_1 if there is a distribution D_3 that

(1)   could be produced by redistributing the gains made by moving from D_1 to D_2, and
(2) D_3 is (in the normal sense) Pareto-superior to D_1.

Note the Kaldor-Hicks test says that given (1) and (2) D_2 is Pareto-superior to D_1 even though no actual compensation has been paid. Distribution D_3 is that in which compensation actually has been made, but Kaldor-Hicks does not say simply that D_3 is Pareto-superior to D_1; it says that D_2 is Pareto-superior to (more efficient than) D_1 even though some people have actually incurred losses by the move from D_1 to D_2. Because D_2 *could* give rise to D_3, and because D_3 would be Pareto-superior to D_1, D_2 is Kaldor-Hicks Pareto-superior to D_1.

For instance, virtually all economists agree that free trade between countries is mutually beneficial and creates long-run Pareto-superior states of affairs. Nevertheless, freer trade can, in the short term, put some low-marginal productivity workers out of business by making it impossible to sell the goods they produce at the same price as before. Since many other members of the society and business will see short-term gains from trade, it is possible for those who benefit to compensate those who lose in any given state of affairs that is genuinely a move to a more Pareto-optimal state of affairs.

This may seem pretty odd. The Pareto criterion, which was based on the denial that gains for some can outweigh losses for others, is now employed to justify policies that benefit some at the expense of others. The move from D_1 to D_2 makes some people worse off, yet it is justified as a Pareto-superior move! Kaldor-Hicks looks like a backdoor way of getting interpersonal comparisons of utility loss and gains within a Paretian framework.

---

10. This test is fundamental to much social cost-benefit analysis.

In practice there are substantial barriers to carrying out effective compensation. It is difficult to identify all the winners and losers in any situation, and if the possibility for compensation is involved, this can make it profitable for people to pretend to be losers or exaggerate their losses in order to get more compensation. This can lead to inefficient compensation. So, while this is a theoretical possibility, we should be somewhat wary of it in practice.

Welfare, Rights, and the Liberal Paradox

We have talked about some of the drawbacks of using efficiency as the sole standard of political evaluation, but we have only hinted at the most serious objection, namely that people should or do have moral rights to do certain things and not others. Preferences regarding others pose another problem for Paretian welfarism. This objection strikes at the heart of the approach to politics that only takes the welfare effects seriously—*welfarism*. Interestingly, one of the most sophisticated defenders of welfarism, Amartya Sen, also raised one of the most serious objections to welfarism in his *liberal paradox*.[11]

To demonstrate this point, Sen introduced a story about two friends, Prude and Lewd. Prude abhors anything indecent and, most of all, wants to keep indecent items out of the hands of lascivious Lewd. Not surprisingly, Lewd loves nothing more than an indecent book or magazine and thinks that Prude should expose himself more to this kind of thing to open his mind. Imagine that Prude and Lewd come upon an indecent book of some sort (in the original article Sen used *Lady Chatterley's Lover*, a book that, we suspect, would no longer shock) and are evaluating the states of affairs with respect to it.

Prude would rather that neither of them read the indecent book, but if someone must read it, he thinks that he will be less harmed by reading it than Lewd. Lewd would, of course, like to read the book himself, but would get even more pleasure from Prude reading it in the—likely vain—hope that it will open Prude's mind. If Prude won't read it, Lewd will get some pleasure out of reading it. These rankings are represented table 4.2.

TABLE 4.2. Prude and Lewd

Prude	Lewd
Neither reads the book (*o*)	Prude reads the book (*a*)
Prude reads the book (*a*)	Lewd reads the book (*b*)
Lewd reads book (*b*)	Neither reads the book (*o*)

---

11. Sen, "The Impossibility of a Paretian Liberal."

Sen conceives of a person having a right as having authority to decide the social preference over at least one pair of alternatives (x,y) such that if a person chooses $x > y$ that is the social preference (let us call this social preference xPy); and if the person chooses $y > x$ then yPx (i.e., the social preference is y over x). Sen shows that if there are just two persons, each with at least one right to determine the social order between two options and assuming all possible orderings of social states are permissible, the social outcome selected by the rights can conflict with a version of the Pareto principle according to which, if for everyone $x > y$, then xPy. That is, if everyone prefers x to y, then the social preference must be x over y. If everyone prefers x to y, then surely society should prefer x to y.

However, if we accept *both* the idea that individuals have *some* rights (surely not a wild thing to claim) and Paretian welfarism, we can always end up with intransitive social preferences. Notice in table 4.2 above that both Lewd and Prude prefer for Prude to read the book over Lewd ($a > b$ and so aPb). But, if we also assume that Lewd can use his right to read the book rather than let it go to waste, then we get $b > o$ and, since we are respecting liberal rights, bPo. But Prude also has rights and would prefer $o > a$ and so, with respect for Prude's rights, we get oPa. But these orderings taken together yield $bPoPaPb$, an intransitive social ordering.

We will explore cases likes these in more detail in chapter 8 on social choice theory, but the key idea here is that both individual rights and Pareto are two different ways of taking individual ordinal preference orderings and devising an overall social ranking, so the "society" of Lewd and Prude can make a social decision. Note that neither uses interpersonal comparisons of utility: *rights* say that one person makes the social decision between x and y, and Pareto says that if all agree that $w > z$, then society should prefer w. If using the two criteria produces an intransitive social ordering, then the overall social ordering violates one of the basic constraints on a rational ordering. Sen saw his proof showing the unacceptability of the Pareto principle as a universal rule compatible with liberalism.[12] Sometimes it seems that a commitment to Pareto efficiency can lead us astray.

One way to respond to this problem is to exclude some sorts of preferences from consideration: thus we might restrict our welfare Paretianism to self-regarding preferences (preferences over different states of one's own life) and so ignore preferences that other people do rather than not do certain things (or that they not read rather than read certain books). It is hard to see how this can work: many of our preferences concern the behavior of others. Surely we

---

12. Sen, "The Impossibility of a Paretian Liberal," 157.

do not wish to restrict the idea of human welfare to what promotes a rather narrow idea of a person's interests, where this takes no account of a person's interest in her social surroundings and how others behave. But if we do allow such preferences, and if we accept Pareto as a social criterion of what is the "better" social state, we cannot also consistently have a system of individual rights.

More important, the existence of liberal rights is a way to manage these types of preferences and to stop them from causing problems. But as we saw above, there is in principle no way that welfarism and Pareto evaluation rules these kinds of preferences out. It looks like any attempt to use only the Pareto criterion will require us to either beg certain questions about rights, freedom, and the nature of harm or to take these questions head-on.

Property Rights

As we have seen, externalities involve some inefficiency in a trade or production of a good. One way to minimize externalities is to get the parties engaged in trades or production that creates externalities to internalize them, i.e., to directly pay the cost of that externality rather than impose it on others. Only if Betty *fully internalizes* all the costs and benefits of her activity will she stop at just the point where social marginal benefits equal social marginal costs. And only if Alf and Betty fully internalize the costs and benefits of their trade can we say the trade necessarily moves us to a Pareto-superior state. If there are third-party costs (negative externalities), Alf and Betty might make trades where the social marginal costs exceed the social marginal benefits because they do not take account of the costs to Charlie. If third-party benefits exist, Alf and Betty may not trade even though the social marginal benefits exceed the social marginal costs.

Property rights are a way to induce agents to internalize possible externalities. Property rights accord agents the full benefits and force them to pay the full costs, of his activity, when they are allocated well. Consider the well-known case of the "tragedy of the commons" such as fisheries (more on these cases in the next section). Many fisheries around the world are overfished, resulting in a depletion of stocks. Now it would probably be to the benefit of fishermen for Alf to reduce his catch this year to secure a good yield next year if he could be confident of obtaining all the future benefits of his reduced yield this year. Without clear rights, however, he cannot. If Betty and Charlie fish anyway, the stocks will still be depleted. Alf will have paid a cost but will not gain the full benefits of his restraint. Conversely, Betty and Charlie do not pay the full costs of their overfishing, since the costs of depletion are transferred to other fishermen such as Alf. Thus, the fisheries are overfished, and the marginal social costs exceed the marginal benefits. A scheme of property rights that internalized all costs and benefits would solve the problem. Of course, we have this problem just because property rights over fish in the ocean are difficult to institutionalize, as fish tend to swim around a lot.

However, the ideal of a system of property rights that internalizes all benefits and costs is unrealizable unless we restrict what counts as an externality. Think about Sen's case of Prude and Lewd's preferences for reading *Lady Chatterley's Lover*. If Mr. Lewd exercises his right and reads the book, there is an externality. Prude is made worse off, since Prude prefers that no one reads it to Lewd reading it. Lewd has negatively impacted the utility function of Prude. If people have preferences over what others do or don't do, then externalities will be everywhere. Suppose Alf prefers that people shop at Target rather than Walmart; if so, every transaction at Walmart involves a negative externality. You can create externalities of others φ-ing simply by preferring that others did not φ!

Using Rights to Define Externalities

One possible solution to this difficulty might be called the *rights-based solution*, according to which Alf's action has a negative externality on Betty if and only if it violates a right of Betty's. Rights, we might say, protect a certain set of preferences: impinging on *those* preferences constitutes cost or harm to an individual. The rights-based solution is suggested by John Stuart Mill (1806–1873), who was especially concerned that people might be held accountable to others for every cost they impose upon them, including "costs" to others resulting from performing actions that their neighbors simply don't like. Mill argued that such "costs" should be ignored, and people should only be said to impose recognized social costs on others when they set back "certain interests, which . . . ought to be considered as rights."[13] Thus, says Mill,

> Encroachment on their rights; infliction on them of any loss or damage not justified by his own rights; falsehood or duplicity in dealing with them; unfair or ungenerous use of advantages over them; even selfish abstinence from defending them against injury—these are fit objects of moral reprobation, and, in grave cases, of moral retribution and punishment.[14]

The idea, then, is that we identify a crucial set of interests (or sets of preferences over certain aspects of our life) and hold that if an action or transaction

13. Mill, On Liberty, chap. 4, para 3.
14. Mill, On Liberty, chap. 4, para. 14.

imposes costs on other parties in terms of *these preferences,* the action or transaction has a social cost (i.e., rights have been infringed). That the action involves a social cost does not show that it should be prohibited, since the social benefits may still outweigh the costs.[15]

This results in a moralistic conception of efficiency. This means that we must first know which subsets of a person's preferences are protected by that person's rights before we can know what constitutes an efficient level of any activity. If, as Mill emphatically argued, no one has a right that others don't read (rather than read) books one finds offensive, Prude incurs no cost when Lewd reads *Lady Chatterley's Lover*—there is no externality because no right was violated.

There are, though, real worries about this moralistic view. For one, it does not make sense of a core argument of most liberal political economists, viz., that we should evaluate systems of property rights in terms of their efficiency-promoting characteristics. If we are to say that private property rights promote efficiency, we must be able to first identify what an efficient level of production would be, and then show that private property rights are apt to result in this level. But according to the rights-based solution, we must know what our property and other rights are *before* we can identify externalities, and so efficient outcomes. Say that Alf wants to build a tavern on his land and Betty objects. What is the efficient outcome? If Alf has the rights on his side, then the efficient outcome is that he builds it; if Betty has the rights on her side— she has a right not to have her property values lowered by living next to a tavern—then the efficient outcome is that the tavern is not built. If both have rights, then we must still somehow weigh the costs and benefits.

The Coase Theorem

Recognizing the problems that externalities and compensation pose, Ronald Coase (1910–2013) developed a theory of how it is possible to incentivize people to *internalize* their externalities by absorbing the costs of those externalities and to efficiently compensate those who are made worse off by some activity. The key insights that led to what is known as the Coase theorem are that:

- Bargaining, exchanging, and contracting are not costless but rather include what he calls *transaction costs.* These costs must be taken into account in any exchange.
- Externalities are not valued the same by everyone. One person may benefit from another by imposing externalities more than it costs that person to bear the externalities. This creates a possibility for exchange.

15. Mill, On Liberty, chap. 5, para. 3.

- Externalities are symmetrical. Without a background notion of rights or privileges, we cannot tell who is imposing externalities on whom.

Ronald Coase proposes an analysis that is almost the reverse of the rights-based view. On Coase's view, achieving an efficient outcome does not depend on the specific way that the initial rights are assigned.[16] Suppose that we live in a world free of transaction and bargaining costs, and in this world, Alf gets a lot of joy out of listening to his records at extremely high volumes. Betty, Alf's neighbor, gets less joy out of this. Without knowing who has a right to play loud music and who has a right to not be kept up all night, it is not clear who would be restricting whom since it looks like the interference can be construed from the point of view of either party. Another way to think of this is to think that there is no privileged perspective from which to view an externality.

Coase has an elegant solution to this problem. He argued that if there were no transactions cost, that is, if it were free to make deals and negotiate, any distribution of rights to impose externalities would be efficient because the parties involved would always contract with one another to compensate the other at the efficient level.

This is not meant to reflect the reality of our situation. Coase knew perfectly well that transactions costs are not zero and, indeed, are often substantial barriers to exchange and trade, which make these possibilities impossible or difficult to realize in practice. The important point that Coase noticed, however, is that the globally efficient level of externalities is not zero if we allow exchange. If there is a benefit to creating some kind of disturbance, people will be willing to pay those who are affected for the right to do it. This makes everyone better off in an efficient manner.

According to Coase, then, in the absence of transaction and bargaining costs, parties to activity with externalities will agree to some Pareto-efficient allocation of resources regardless of the initial distribution of property rights. Many read Coase's theorem as calling into question one of the main justifications for government activity. In the absence of a perfect scheme of property rights that internalizes both costs and benefits, it has been widely argued, government action is necessary to regulate the "market failure" that results from externalities. But Coase argues that market transactions could, in the absence of transaction and negotiation costs, solve the problem of externalities and get us to a Pareto-optimal outcome.

It is not clear, though, that this is the correct conclusion. In our world, where there are transaction and negotiation costs, who has the property right makes a huge difference. Perhaps the really basic lesson from Coase is that

16. See Coase, "The Problem of Social Cost."

whenever we assign a right to Alf against Betty, we are preventing Betty from harming Alf (which is the traditional view), but we *are also* allowing Alf to harm Betty in the sense that Alf can engage in the protected activity whether or not it sets back's Betty's interests.

The traditional approach has tended to obscure the nature of the choice that has to be made. The question is commonly thought of as one in which A inflicts harm on B and what has to be decided is how we should restrain A. But this is wrong. We are dealing with a problem of a reciprocal nature. To avoid the harm to B would inflict harm on A. The real question that has to be decided is, should A be allowed to harm B, or should B be allowed to harm A? The problem is to avoid the more serious harm.[17]

In the case of costless negotiation, we see that the parties both have an interest in whether the activity will be allowed or prohibited, and they would reach a Pareto-optimal solution through transferring resources. This alerts us to the fact that the parties have different interests, and that in instituting a system of property, society must decide whose are the more important interests. We can think of the job of property rights as being to decide which is the more valuable activity and to place the property right with the person engaging in it. Thus, a system of property rights might be seen to be guessing what the bargain—under zero-transaction costs—would be.

The other important aspect of Coase's theory is that he recognized that the logic of Pareto efficiency is that value will be attracted to the highest value producers. That is, without the friction from transaction costs, rights will tend to be held by those who are the highest valued users of those rights. More important, when we see a situation where we think the rights are not being held by the highest value producer, it is likely because transaction costs have become too high to allow efficient exchange.

The Coase theorem led to revolutions in economics, law, and policy. The field of law and economics extended and applied Coase's idea in a variety of ways and developed a new, sophisticated version of cost-benefit analysis. Similarly, institutional economics can be seen in some ways as the study of the relationship between rights and transaction costs in the real world.

Public Goods

Related to the question of externalities is the special case of public goods. Public goods are defined in terms of two characteristics. First, they are characterized by *non-rival consumption*. Consider clean air. If it is provided at all, it

---

17. Coase, "The Problem of Social Cost," 2.

can be provided to Alf without taking any of it away from Betty. Once the good is there, consumers do not compete for it; everyone can freely use it without diminishing the amount left for others.

Second, we cannot control the flow of benefits from public goods: they are *non-excludable*. If a public good is provided, it is provided for all to use. If we clean the air, everyone has clean air. We cannot exclude those who have not paid their share. A pure public good is one that perfectly meets these two conditions; a pure private good is one that does not meet either. Table 4.3 identifies four classes of goods based on these two characteristics.

TABLE 4.3. Types of Public Goods

	Excludable	Non-excludable
Rival	Private Goods	Common Pool Resources
Non-rival	Club Goods	(Pure) Public Goods

Private Goods—Private goods are the typical market good. If you go to the store to purchase milk, (1) the good is excludable—those who don't pay for it do not get it; (2) it is rival. If I consume that carton of milk, you cannot.

Club Goods—Some goods are non-rival within a group, but people can be excluded from the group (or "club"). Think of a movie theater with good stadium-style seats, so all can easily see the movie. Within the theater, consumption is non-rival. If I "consume" the movie, there is no less of a movie for the person next to me to "consume." One person's consumption does not detract from that of others. However, the theater can exclude those who enter and, hence, limit the number of people consuming the good.

Common Pool Resources—Elinor Ostrom (1933–2012), who won the Nobel Prize for economics in 2009 (the first woman to do so), studied common pool resources such as fisheries.[18] With such resources, one person's use of a resource detracts from the resources available to another. If Alf take a fish out of the ocean, Alf has consumed it and Betty cannot now consume it, thus their consumption is rivalrous, but in common pool resources, it is also very hard to exclude anyone. More on these cases in chapter 7.

Public Goods—These goods have both characteristics. First, the flow of benefits from public goods cannot be controlled since they are non-excludable. If a public good such as clean air is provided, everyone has clean air. We cannot

---

18. Ostrom, Governing the Commons.

exclude those who have not paid their share: if clean air is provided at all, it can be provided to one person without taking any of it away from another, and so consumption is non-rival.[19] Once the good exists, consumers do not compete for it; everyone can freely use it without diminishing the amount left for others. A *pure* public good is one that perfectly meets these two conditions. In most cases both conditions are not perfectly met, and this may matter a good deal for policy. Defense, law and order, regulation of air pollution, highways, ports, public works, and elementary education are usually cited as public goods, though economists have disputed the "publicness" of almost every item on this list.

All this is fairly standard. However, having stated the canonical definition according to which public goods are characterized by these two dimensions, in ensuing discussions it is often unclear just how each dimension enters into the "public goods problem"—why they are apt to be "undersupplied" in markets in which buyers and sellers seek to maximize only their own utility. Let us consider the problems of each dimension separately.

Non-Excludability and the Free-Rider Problem

The classic textbook example of a public good is a lighthouse. A lighthouse warns all ships away from danger and one ship does not "use up" the light so there is non-rival consumption and it is not possible to exclude the light from the ships who did not pay for the lighthouse, so non-excludability is met. As Coase points out, early discussions of lighthouses focused on non-excludability.[20] In the *Principles of Political Economy*, John Stuart Mill argued that his general case for laissez-faire did not apply to lighthouses:

> It is a proper office of government to build and maintain lighthouses, establish buoys, &c. for the security of navigation: for *since it is impossible that the ships at sea which are benefited by a lighthouse, should be made to pay a toll on the occasion of its use,* no one would build lighthouses from motives of personal interest, unless indemnified and rewarded from a compulsory levy made by the state.[21]

In the same vein, in his *Principles of Political Economy* (1901) Henry Sidgwick stressed that "it may easily happen that the benefits of a well-placed lighthouse

---

19. The second feature has been characterized variously in terms of joint supply, joint consumption, consumption externality, and non-rival consumption. Some consider these essentially equivalent, but on some interpretations they diverge.

20. Coase, "The Lighthouse in Economics."

21. Mill, Principles of Political Economy, Volume 3, 968.

must be largely enjoyed by ships on which no toll could be conveniently imposed."[22]

The idea is straightforward. In markets for normal private goods, one can obtain the benefits of the good only by paying for it: one internalizes both the costs and the benefits. With a public good such as a lighthouse, non-payers cannot be excluded from enjoyment of the good, so all users have incentives not to pay, as they can gain it for free if it is provided at all. Thus, Mill argues that the normal case for free markets fails, and the provision of such goods is properly within the prevue of the state, which can supply the good and tax all beneficiaries (or the general public).[23]

When we look at game theory in the next chapter, we shall explain more formally why public goods tend to be undersupplied, but the crux of the explanation appears, at least at first sight, clear. Even if everyone prefers having the public good to not having it, each of us will receive it for free if someone else pays for it. After all, the benefits are non-excludable: if anyone gets the good, everyone does. So, we typically have an incentive to *free-ride*: each, hoping the other pays, holds back from paying.

Non-Rival Consumption

Given the focus on strategic analysis in most discussions—especially in philosophy—one might think that the problem of non-excludability simply *is* the public goods problem. But what of our second feature, non-rival consumption? Suppose the operators of our "lighthouses" developed a technology that allowed them to control the flow of benefits such that those, and only those, who purchased a signal decoder could enjoy the benefits? This would make the lighthouse signal a club good, which is excludable but still has the feature of non-rival consumption. In this case, no one is tempted to free-ride or play chicken, and they need not worry about whether enough others will contribute since, if one buys the decoder, one gets the service.

The operators have solved the strategic problem, but they have not solved the public goods problem, for the solution is still apt to be inefficient.[24] Because of non-rivalness, the cost of supplying an additional ship the signal at any given time is zero. Since A's use of the signal does not detract from B's use,

22. Sidgwick, The Principles of Political Economy, 406.

23. Whether there really was no efficient way for bona fide private entrepreneurs to collect tolls from passing ships has been the subject of lively dispute. In addition to the above article by Coase, see van Zandt, "The Lessons of the Lighthouse"; Bertrand, "The Coasean Analysis of Lighthouse Financing."

24. Samuelson, Economics: An Introductory Analysis, 151.

A has not "used up any signal" so there is still enough and as good for *B*. Now suppose that the charge of the operators for the signal was $X, and *B* decided that he did not get $X worth of benefit, so *B* declined to purchase the decoder. As long as *B* would get *any* benefit at all from the signal, society is forgoing a gain that it could have at *zero* cost.

We can see the problem of efficiency from another angle; consider the question of how much of a public good a person has incentive to provide under the assumption that each only pays for the amount she wishes to consume. Suppose Betty can supply various units of a public good *p*—it is continuous in the sense that each increment she produces adds to the total public good. Within a large range at least, picking up litter is such a good; the more one picks up, the cleaner one's neighborhood. Now, in deciding whether to produce a particular unit *u* of *p*, person *i* will produce it only if the benefits to *her* exceed *her* costs. If she is thinking about whether to produce an additional unit of *p*, she will do so if the benefits to her $(b_i u)$ exceed the costs to her $(c_i u)$, so she will produce a unit *u* of *p* only if $b_i u > c_i u$.

Because *p* is non-rival, her production of *u* automatically makes *u* available at zero cost to others. In this context, this is what it means to say that the production of *p* has a *positive externality*. If we assume that there are *N* persons, the benefit of person *i*'s production of a given unit *u* is the sum $b_i u + \ldots + b_n u$. Now, because person *i* will only produce a unit of *p* if the benefits to her exceed the costs, there will come some unit u^* at which this is no longer the case: for u^*, b_i c_i, so our person *i* will not produce u^*. From her individual perspective this makes sense, but because the overall benefit of u^* is not just the benefit $b_i u^*$, but the sum $b_i u^* + \ldots + b_n u^*$, the overall benefits of the production of u^* are apt to far exceed $c_i u^*$. From the social perspective, more, perhaps much, much, more, of *p* should be supplied. Thus, even with no strategic behavior (seeking to free-ride), under these conditions the public good will be undersupplied. This is another instance where we see individual rationality and efficiency diverging.

Public Goods and State Action

Public goods confront us with "collective-action problems." Collectively, it would benefit everyone to supply the good, but each individual often does better by not cooperating to produce the good, instead letting others provide them and then enjoying the goods they provide. We will consider such a collective-action problem in more depth in chapter 5. Thus, the classic public good argument is for state action to fix the market's failure to generate efficient outcomes. In the interests of efficiency, it is often said, government must require everyone to contribute to the production of such goods. While powerful, the argument is not quite as simple as it seems. Several points must be kept in mind.

First, for an adequate public goods argument for state action, it must not only be the case that everyone wants the good, but that in everyone's preference, ordering {contributing to secure the good & paying my share} is preferred to {not paying my share & not having the good}. If supplying the good is to move us to a Pareto-superior condition, it is not enough that everyone wants the good; they must prefer having it *and* paying for it to not having it.

Second, it is not the case that markets never supply public goods, or never do so efficiently. Suppose Alf's goat wanders into Betty's garden and eats her veggies, and Betty's dog wanders over to Alf's property, scaring his goat so that it does not give milk.[25] A fence would be a public good. Assume that each would benefit by unilaterally building the fence—each would be better off building the fence alone than not having one—but, of course, each would prefer that the other build the fence. So, each has the following ordering: (i) the other builds, (ii) we split the cost, (iii) I build, (iv) neither builds. In such a case, since each would prefer to pay for the entire good rather than do without it, the public good will be provided.

Public goods do not constitute a market failure or a collective-action problem until we add further conditions, such as no one individual's utility function is such that it is rational for him to purchase the entire good at the efficient level, there are a large number of people (so each is tempted to free-ride, or we do not know how many people's cooperation is necessary to secure the good), etc.[26] As the number of individuals involved increases, the need for some sort of formal agreement about allocation of contributions becomes necessary. It is, then, not simply public goods per se, but public goods that require collective action of a large number of agents that are most likely not to be adequately supplied by the market.[27]

Third, inefficiency is not always a worry. If we consider a world in which it costs c to produce a non-rival good and a uniform price x is charged for access to it, there will be some who will not purchase the good for x who would get value from it; since these people can be offered the good without increasing the cost of producing it, it is Pareto-superior (it makes some better off and no one worse off) to supply p to these others at less than x. For full efficiency

---

25. See Mueller, Public Choice III, 16ff.

26. Because the purchase of public goods has a positive externality, they will not generally be supplied at the efficient level.

27. Mueller gives a nice overview of the extent to which individual voluntary choices will secure public goods, and how this results in undersupply. See *Public Choice III*, 18ff. The discussion that follows draws on this part of Mueller.

differential pricing would be necessary. But is such "inefficiency" really a worry? Perhaps sometimes, depending on the good, but in plenty of cases there is no problem with the good only going to those who are willing to pay $x. Satellite television is such a good. People pay for the signal, and this provides an incentive for an entrepreneur to provide the service, though it is true that, at least over a wide range, the marginal cost of providing the service to an additional consumer approaches zero. We see here an important lesson: while in many contexts seeking Pareto-efficient outcomes may be an important desideratum, in a large range of cases the uniform pricing of a good that brings it to market may lack Pareto efficiency yet be no cause for concern.

None of this is intended to undermine the basic idea that usually the state should tax everyone to secure public goods. The point is that we should be aware that the necessity and desirability of state action to secure universal contribution is by no means a quick and easy inference from the mere existence of a public good and the pursuit of efficiency.

Homo Economicus *or Voluntary Cooperation?*

The problems we have been canvassing presuppose that behavior can be adequately modeled as *Homo economicus*—each individual is concerned only with best promoting her own goals. But, of course, we always face the question whether this is the best model of human action in various contexts. There is good reason to doubt that *Homo economicus* is an adequate general model of human action. As Elinor Ostrom has shown us, groups of individuals often develop social (non-state) institutions and social norms that assign responsibility for doing one's share in securing collective goods; indeed, government policies can crowd out these social institutions, making cooperation in public goods contexts less likely.[28]

A great deal of experimental evidence indicates that people are often willing to contribute to public goods, even under conditions of anonymity; if they are allowed to punish those who do not do their part, voluntary contributions to public goods can be quite stable and robust.[29] In a typical public goods game, 10 participants might be given an endowment, say $20 each; each can choose either to pocket the entire $20, or contribute some or all of it to a common pool. The experimenter will then take the total contributions to the common

28. Ostrom, Governing the Commons; Schwab and Ostrom, "The Vital Role of Norms and Rules."

29. See Ledyard, "Public Goods: A Survey of Experimental Research"; Chaudhuri, "Sustaining Cooperation in Laboratory Public Goods Experiments."

pool and increase it by some factor, for example, by .5. If all 10 people contributed their endowment of $20, that would be a common pool of $200. The
experimenter would then increase that by .5, increasing the pool to $300.
Everyone in the group then gets an equal share of the $300, so $30 each.

However, while each benefits from universal contribution over universal
non-contribution, each also has an incentive to defect. If everyone else but Alf
contributes to the common pool, it will be $180; the experimenter will add
$90, giving a total pool of $270. Everyone, including Alf, gets an equal share of
the $270, or $27. But Alf has kept his $20, hence his holding is $47. So, there is
a temptation to free-ride.

In many experiments most people contribute about half their endowments
to the public good. However, over a series of plays, observing that some do not
contribute, contributions begin to break down. This breakdown can, usually,
be halted either by allowing punishment of free riders (people use some of
their endowment to pay to take some of the free riders' gains away), or if con-
tributors can reliably exclude non-contributors.

In an important cross-cultural study of subjects in market economies such as
the United States and the small-scale societies of the Machiguenga of the Peru-
vian Amazon and the Mapuche of Southern Chile, Joseph Henrich and Natalie
Smith found that Machiguenga are especially prone to free-riding, withdrawing
an average of 77% of the pooled money in the first round. While both the Americans and the Machiguenga have a number of free riders, the Machiguenga have
a consistent tendency to take more for themselves than do the Americans; the
key difference is that about a quarter of the Americans are fully cooperative,
withdrawing nothing in the first round, while the Machiguenga sample has no
full cooperators, and even relatively few who withdraw only 20%. This suggests
the fascinating hypothesis that market societies are *less* prone to act in public
goods contexts as economists typically predict.[30]

Conclusion

In the last three chapters, we looked at what it means for an individual to make
rational choices and how rationality can be modeled as a cardinal utility function. In this chapter, we complicated this story by introducing multiple rational agents, all of whom are looking for ways to jointly maximize utility. In this
context, we introduced the idea of Pareto efficiency as a way to make sense of
mutual benefit without introducing interpersonal comparisons of utility. From
this simple idea, we are able to generate models of optimal contracting using

---

30. For a summary, see Henrich et al., "In Search of *Homo Economicus*."

the Edgeworth box and to develop an idea of welfare. As we also saw, though, there are limitations to Pareto efficiency, most notably its indeterminacy and it path dependence. We also saw that the introduction of property rights, externalities, and compensation complicates the model as well. We saw that the Coase theorem connects efficiency and the allocation or distribution of property rights, while Sen's impossibility theorem suggests that efficiency can come into conflict with freedom.

Discussion Questions

(1) Does the indifference curve analysis presuppose that each care only about her own consumption bundle? Suppose that Alf is an altruist, and he cares only about maximizing Betty's enjoyment of her pizza and wings, and Betty is also an altruist, who seeks to ensure that Alf has the most enjoyable meal. Suppose Betty starts with all the pizza and Alf with all the chicken wings. Can you draw an Edgeworth box for them?

(2) Suppose that Alf has two moral commitments: "Give to charity" and "Improve my mind by reading Philosophy." And suppose that he has a utility function that meets the axioms of cardinal utility. Can you draw his indifference map? Do you need to bring in any assumptions from *Homo economicus* about the shape of his utility functions?

(3) If economics is based on the idea of Paretian efficiency, but the Pareto criterion is conservative because it starts with the status quo distribution, does this mean that economics is inherently a "conservative science"? Does that idea make any sense?

(4) If individual rights can conflict with the Pareto criterion, how should this dispute be resolved: in favor of rights or Pareto? Either way, does Sen show that you cannot have a liberal and efficient state?

(5) Identify: (i) a club good provided by non-state actors and one provided by state actors; (ii) a common pool resource regulated by non-state actors and one regulated by state actors; (iii) a public good provided by non-state actors and one provided by state actors. For each pair, are there features of the good that lend themselves to state or non-state provision?

(6) What type of good is at issue in the problem of global warming? Why is voluntary action ineffective in solving this problem? What is the problem faced by state action in solving this problem? Is there any efficient way to solve the problem?

5

Foundations of Game Theory

In our examination of utility theory in chapters 2 and 3, we focused on a rational agent as one who has preferences over outcomes and a set of fixed action-options, and who can correlate outcomes with action-options; her preferences over outcomes determined her preferences over action-options. In chapter 4, we began to consider how rational utility maximizers (who also are characterized by the additional features of *Homo economicus*) interact, and especially how rational economic agents will engage in efficient transactions. But the analysis of rational interaction in chapter 4 focused on Pareto-superior moves—roughly, cases in which agents concur on what are better outcomes. We largely ignored the possibility of conflict or strategy. We now move to the theory of games—general theory of what is rational when interacting with other rational agents, and especially when what is best for Betty may not be best for Alf. In this chapter we employ the general idea of individuals as utility maximizers: the specific, additional features that are required for *Homo economicus* are not central.

Strategic Rationality

Up to this point, we have only considered cases of individual or joint optimization. As we have seen, a number of complications arise from making sense of individual decision-making or optimization, especially when we include multiple goods and multiple agents. Decision theory is a theory of optimization against nature. The only unknown when we select actions is whether a given state of affairs will obtain or whether a given action will lead to a specific outcome. The answer to these questions is determined by nature or, if you prefer, by chance. But sometimes other people determine whether a particular action leads to a particular outcome through their actions. In these cases, we need to take into account what other people are likely to do in order to decide what we should do. Optimization requires strategy, which involves anticipating the likely choices of others.

To illustrate the difference between strategic rationality and the "paramet-ric" rationality of individual optimization with regard to nature, consider the case of Robinson Crusoe. In the novel by Defoe, Crusoe is shipwrecked on a desert island off the coast of Venezuela. At first, he is on his own and must figure out how to survive by making shelter, finding water, and gathering food. His choices at this point are classic optimization problems. He must make choices about how to survive given the conditions he finds on the island. Later he en-counters Friday, a captive of nearby natives that he helps to free. Once Friday enters the scene, Crusoe's choices move from parametric optimization to stra-tegic rationality since he must now consider what Friday will do when he makes his choices. They can jointly optimize in the search for food and water, but they may also need to coordinate their production and plan their encounters with the native cannibals. Once Friday arrives, it is no longer just the states of affairs that determine how action choices relate to outcomes, Friday's choices may also generate outcomes so Crusoe will need to take those into account.

The theory of games was developed to provide a method of analyzing op-timal choice in strategic circumstances. It was created in its modern form by John von Neumann (1903–1957), one of the greatest mathematicians of the twentieth century, and Oskar Morgenstern (1902–1977), an Austrian econo-mist. We encountered their method for generating utility functions from the choice of lotteries in chapter 2, but their integration of that framework into a general theory of strategic rationality is their primary contribution. This framework for strategic analysis is called "game theory," and von Neumann and Morgenstern spend a considerable amount of time analyzing what we would think of as games, most notably poker, but their framework generalizes to any problem of conflict or coordination. Indeed, they initially wanted to call their book *The General Theory of Rational Behavior* instead of the *Theory of Games and Economic Behavior*, but they eventually decided on the latter.[1]

Game theory is the extension of decision theory to decision-making in strategic contexts, that is, in cases where there are multiple agents and where the outcomes an agent's actions bring about depend upon the actions that other agents perform. It has the same basic building blocks as decision theory, *agents*, *actions*, *states of affairs*, and *outcomes*. The decisions of individual agents depend on their preferences over the outcomes their actions might bring about. But, crucially, they also depend on the actions of other agents.

Morgenstern's first presentation of the problem that motivated game theory was the Holmes-Moriarty problem. This problem is interesting because it in-

1. Morgenstern, "The Collaboration Between Oskar Morgenstern and John von Neumann on the Theory of Games."

cludes several aspects of game theory. In "The Final Problem" Sherlock Holmes is confronted with a strategic dilemma. Professor Moriarty, his arch-nemesis, is attempting to find and kill him. In the past, Holmes easily outsmarted his opponents, but not so with Moriarty. We know that Moriarty is a threat because Holmes is notoriously vain and unwilling to heap accolades on others, especially for intelligence, but he nevertheless says this about Moriarty:

> He is the Napoleon of crime, Watson . . . He is a genius, a philosopher, an abstract thinker. He has a brain of the first order. He sits motionless, like a spider in the centre of its web, but that web has a thousand radiations, and he knows well every quiver of each of them.[2]

Holmes, to escape Moriarty, plans to flee to the continent, but he knows that if he takes a train from London to Dover and then a ship to France, Moriarty will anticipate this move and be waiting for him in Dover. Instead, Holmes and Watson get off the Dover train at Canterbury and evade Moriarty as he travels on to Dover.

The obvious problem with this solution is that Moriarty—being just as smart as Holmes—would have anticipated it and would have also gone to Canterbury. But, if that is true, Holmes would have also anticipated that and so on. Morgenstern saw, in an early article, that there was no clear way to solve this problem:

> I showed in some detail in particular that the pursuit developing between these two could never be resolved on the basis of one of them out-thinking the other ("I think he thinks that I think!! . . ."), but that a resolution could only be achieved by an "arbitrary decision," and that it was a problem of strategy.[3]

The solution to this problem involves what Morgenstern called an "arbitrary decision" and what would later be called a "mixed strategy." As we will see in more detail below, a mixed strategy involves all the agents in the game randomizing over a probability distribution of actions. This randomization will make it maximally difficult for one's opponent to know what actual strategy one will choose, but the way the probability distribution is chosen will also ensure the choice is optimal.

We can represent one aspect of the Holmes-Moriarty problem in the matrix in table 5.1.[4] Each person, Holmes and Moriarty, have two actions available:

2. Doyle, "The Final Problem," 645.

3. Morgenstern, "The Collaboration Between Oskar Morgenstern and John von Neumann on the Theory of Games," 806.

4. Taken from von Neumann and Morgenstern, Theory of Games and Economic Behavior, 177.

go to Canterbury or go to Dover. Sherlock's actions are represented in the vertical columns, while Moriarty's are represented in the horizontal rows. Each cell of the matrix represents an outcome for a given action of each player. We can think of the numbers as utilities in the sense that we discussed them in previous chapters. By convention, the first number represents the value of the outcome for the row player, while the second number represents the outcome payoff for the column player.

TABLE 5.1. Holmes-Moriarty Game

		Sherlock Holmes	
		Dover	**Canterbury**
Dr. Moriarty	**Dover**	100, −100	0, 0
	Canterbury	−50, 50	100, −100

If Moriarty meets Holmes at either Canterbury or Dover, he will kill him, which is the best outcome for him and the worst for Holmes, so 100 for Moriarty and −100 for Holmes. If Holmes escapes to Dover while Moriarty is stuck in Canterbury, this is the best for Holmes (50) and the worst for Moriarty (−50). Holmes must still worry about Moriarty down the road, though, so he isn't totally off the hook. If Holmes misses Moriarty in Canterbury, he is safe for now, but he hasn't really escaped, so that appears to be a tie.

We will return to the solution of this game when we look at mixed strategies; the thing to note here is the nature of the strategic problem. There is no hope of "outsmarting" one's opponent since both are assumed to be equally smart and to know all the possibilities and payoffs of each player. We can also assume each player is trying to get the best possible outcome, which is to say that they are utility optimizers. As it turns out, these conditions will generalize to all games and we can characterize them in the following three conditions:

(1) All players are rational in the sense of being utility maximizers.
(2) There is common knowledge of rationality. Alf knows that Betty is rational, and Alf knows that Betty knows this, and Betty knows the same thing about Alf and he knows she knows that he knows she is rational, and so on.
(3) There is common knowledge of the payoffs and options of all the other.

With these conditions in mind as the background of all strategic encounters or "games," we can start to look at different types of games. One type are games of pure conflict like the Holmes-Moriarty game, and we look at those first.

Zero-Sum Games

We start by focusing on very simple games, in which the total gains always equal the total losses, so that the overall gains and losses always add up to zero. Winnings minus losses equals zero. Games such as poker are obvious examples of *zero-sum* games: the only way to win is to get the money from a fellow player.[5]

Consider a game involving a defender and an attacker.[6] The payoffs are for the attacker (row player); since it is a zero-sum game, the defenders' payoffs are the inverse (lowest is best for them). The game is depicted in table 5.2.

TABLE 5.2. Example of the Maximin Solution

		Defender			
		Reinforce Left	Reinforce Center	Reinforce Right	MIN
	Attack Left	−3	2	10	−3
Attacker	Attack Center	8	6	9	6
	Attack Right	5	4	−2	−2
	MAX	8	6	10	

This matrix represents a game in what is known as its *strategic* or *normal* form with the possible strategies of Defender arrayed across the top, the possible strategies of the Attacker along the left-hand side. We assume that the moves are made simultaneously, without either party knowing what the other has chosen. Thus, we can see how this is a strategic situation: my preferred outcomes partly depend on what you do, and your outcomes partly depend on what I do.

---

5. Notice that these games are most easily understood in terms of monetary payoffs rather than utilities. If we suppose that people only have preferences in these games over the monetary payoffs, and that their preferences are linear with money, then utility and monetary payoffs come to the same thing.

6. Here we are following Sandler, Economic Concepts for the Social Sciences, 43.

The solution to the game is center/center. The MIN column indicates the minimum that an attacker can get if the defender correctly anticipates the direction of attack. Attack on the center is the *maximin* choice for the attacker since it has the highest minimum—it maximizes the minimum payoff one can expect. The MAX row is the maximum that the defender has to give up for any given defensive posture. The minimax—minimizing the maximum cost—defense strategy is to defend the center. Center/center is, then, the solution where *minimax* equals *maximin*.

Minimax theorem

The unique solution to any finite, two-person zero-sum game is when maximin equals minimax.

The reasoning behind minimax looks conservative. The more you assume that your opponent knows your move in advance and then offers their best reply, the more minimax is attractive. If one thought one first chose the row, and one's enemy then selected the cell in the row, maximin would make perfect sense. On the other hand, if both parties are really uncertain about what will happen, and cannot assign probabilities, they might select different strategies. If both players gamble in this way we cannot predict the outcome of the game.

John von Neumann demonstrated that in every zero-sum finite game (a finite number of moves), between two persons, there is always at least one minimax solution: there is always some outcome that is rational for both parties to accept and that is not rational to defect from. However, this outcome need not always be a combination of "pure" strategies. A *pure strategy* is when one always makes the same response to a certain move by the other; a *mixed strategy* is when one may respond to the same move by the other in different ways. Mixed strategies can be a little difficult to calculate (and to understand!), but we will discuss those in greater detail below.

Extensive Form Zero-Sum Games

Consider a simple cake-cutting game. Suppose Alf and Betty are in a zero-sum game in which Alf cuts the cake and Betty chooses the first piece, with Alf getting what is left. Let us assume that Alf has two options: cut the pieces as equally as he can (he never gets it quite equal, so one piece is always a bit bigger) or very unequally. We depict the game in its *extensive* form in figure 5.1.

Alf chose at the square choice nodes, Betty at the circles. The dots are "terminal nodes" that constitute possible outcomes. The numbers at each terminal node represent Alf's ordinal utility for each outcome (4 = best, 1 = worst);

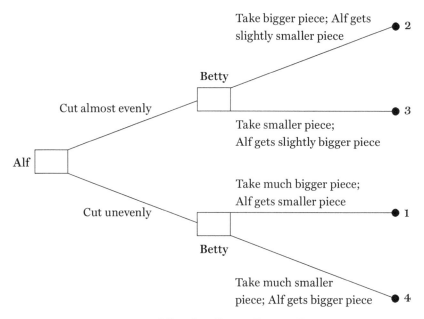

FIGURE 5.1. A Zero-Sum Game in Extensive Form

since this is a zero-sum game, Betty's ordering is precisely the reverse. Alf's best choice (where he gets 4 units of utility) is Betty's worst (she gets 1), and so on.

Remember, we are assuming that Alf and Betty are both rational agents, and each knows this. Therefore, Alf knows that Betty will make the best move for herself, so outcomes (4) and (3), his best outcomes and her worst, will not occur; the only way to get to those outcomes would be for Betty to select a less rather than a more preferred option. Alf's only choice, then, is between options (1) and (2). To maximize his share, Alf must cut evenly, so we end up with (2), which is the solution to the game.

We can put this game into the strategic or normal form, but it is a little more complicated than you might think. Normal form games typically do not include information about the order of the moves, since we assume the moves are simultaneous, but in the cake-cutting game Alf is the first mover. When that is so, by the time Betty moves she has information that Alf didn't have; he doesn't know what she will do, he has already moved, so she knows what happened.

That also means that she has more available strategies for she can condition her strategy on his. She can think to herself, "If Alf cuts almost equally, I'll take the smaller piece, but if he cuts really differently, I'll take the much larger piece." This gives her four distinct strategies, as represented in table 5.3.

TABLE 5.3. Strategies in Normal Form

		Betty			
		Always choose big	**Always choose small**	**Choose big when Alf cuts equal, choose small when Alf cuts unevenly**	**Choose small when Alf cuts equal, choose big when he cuts big and small**
Alf	**Cuts almost evenly**	(2) Betty gets slightly bigger piece	(3) Betty gets slightly smaller piece	(2) Betty gets slightly bigger piece	(3) Betty gets slightly smaller piece
	Cuts unevenly	(1) Betty gets big piece	(4) Betty gets smallest piece	(4) Betty gets smallest piece	(1) Betty gets big piece

Remember, these are Alf's outcomes—Betty's are the inverse. These four strategies are those available to her and she will pick the strategy that is the best response to Alf. The best response of Betty to Alf cutting almost equal is to play either "Always choose big" or "Choose big when Alf cuts almost equal, choose small when Alf cuts obviously big and small," since either will give her a second-best outcome, giving Alf his third-best outcome. If Alf's cuts are obviously big and small, Betty's best response is to play either her "Always choose big" strategy or her "Choose small when Alf cuts equal, choose big when he cuts big and small" strategy, giving Alf his worst outcome. Knowing this, the only rational option is for Alf to *maximize his minimum* by cutting almost evenly.

The Prisoner's Dilemma

Most interactions are not zero-sum; depending on what they do, Alf and Betty may find that their gains and losses vary. Thus, we usually play variable-sum games. Let's start with the most famous game of all, the Prisoner's Dilemma.[7] We took a look at this game briefly in the last chapter, but we didn't really have the resources then to go into detail.

7. The game was developed by Merrill Flood and Melvin Dresher of the RAND Corporation; the name "Prisoner's Dilemma" has been attributed to Albert Tucker. For a detailed treatment of the history of the problem and of game theory more generally, see Poundstone, Prisoner's Dilemma.

The familiar story behind the Prisoner's Dilemma goes like this. Two suspects, Alf and Betty, have been arrested by the police. The police have enough evidence to convict both on a relatively minor charge. If convicted of this charge—and the police can obtain a conviction—each will get two years in prison. The police, however, suspect that Alf and Betty acted together to pull off a bigger crime, but they have inadequate evidence. They make the following offer to Alf and the same offer to Betty simultaneously:

> If you, Alf, turn state's evidence against Betty, we'll let you go free; we'll demand the maximum penalty for Betty, so she will get 12 years. Of course, if Betty confesses too, we're not going to let you both go free and you'll each get 10 years. However, if you keep quiet and she confesses, we'll let her go free, and you will be the one to get 12 years. But if neither of you confess to the bank job, we won't have enough evidence to prosecute. We will then proceed with the lesser charge, and you'll get 2 years each. We've offered Betty the same deal and the clock is ticking. What do you want to do?

We can present this problem in the matrix shown in table 5.4 in terms of years in jail, so the higher number is worse for each person. Alf's "payoffs" (time in jail) are depicted on the left of each cell, Betty's on the right.

TABLE 5.4. Prisoner's Dilemma

		Betty	
		Keep Quiet	**Confess**
Alf	**Keep Quiet**	2, 2	0, 12
	Confess	12, 0	10, 10

In this game, rational optimizers, who know that each other are rational and have common knowledge of the payoffs will end up both confessing. Why? Isn't this a bad outcome for both? How could it be rational to end up in a bad outcome, when the better outcome of both keeping quiet is available? Let's look at Alf's reasoning.

> If Betty confesses, and I keep quiet, I'll get 12 years; if Betty confesses and I confess too, I'll get 10 years; so, I know one thing: if Betty confesses, I better confess too.

But what if Betty keeps quiet?

If Betty keeps quiet and I keep quiet too, I get 2 years; if Betty keeps quiet and I confess, I go free. So, if Betty keeps quiet, I do best by confessing.

Alf has shown that confessing is a (strictly) *dominant strategy*: no matter what Betty does; he does best if he confesses. Confessing is a dominant strategy for both players: no matter what Betty does, Alf does best if he confesses, and no matter what Alf does, Betty does best by confessing. It's rare for players to have a single dominant strategy. Even if there is one action that is best in most circumstances, there will typically be some circumstances in which other actions bring about better outcomes.

Dominance

A *strictly* dominant strategy is one's single best response regardless of the strategy of the other player.

A *weakly* dominant strategy is no worse than any other response regardless of the strategy of the other player.

Betty, who is in the same situation as Alf, will reason the same way. She will conclude that no matter what Alf does, she does best by confessing. So, they will both confess, and get 10 years. We call this the *equilibrium* outcome. Most games have more than one rational equilibrium, this one only has one. The (sole) equilibrium outcome is for both to confess.

The puzzle here is that, as we mentioned in the last chapter, the {confess, confess} equilibrium is Pareto-inferior to the non-equilibrium, dominated outcome of both staying silent.[8] Rational players should always snitch according to this game since it is the best option, whatever else your partner does. If Alf stays silent, it is best for Betty to snitch. Similarly, if Alf snitches, it is best for Betty to snitch. Snitch is the rational thing to do even though it will necessarily lead to a Pareto-dominated outcome. Both would be better off if no one talked, but the only rational outcome is for both to confess, which will make everyone worse off!

We have simply assumed that the players want to stay out of jail, which may not reflect their utility. In order to really get the result that the rational thing for them to do is to confess, we need to say something about their *preferences* over outcomes. We can generate an ordinal utility function for Alf in terms of his preference rankings for the different outcomes, if his rankings satisfy the standard axioms. Employing an ordinal scale where I is best and IV is worst, we get the results in table 5.5.

---

8. Joint outcomes are conventionally represented by strategies for each player within brackets.

TABLE 5.5. Prisoner's Dilemma Equilibrium

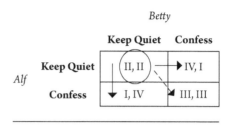

Here we can clearly see what is causing the problem. Keep quiet, which is circled, is the Pareto-dominant strategy—it is the option where each player gets the best option possible without making someone else worse off—but it is only the second most preferred option for each player. So, if Alf and Betty were at this outcome, each would be better off by confessing, securing their best outcome if the other kept quiet (indicated by the solid arrows). But, given that both will do this, they will be led to the second to worst outcome where they both confess (shaded).

The mutual confession outcome dominates all the other outcomes, not because it is the best outcome, but because it is the best option given the best option for the other players. In the case of the Prisoner's Dilemma (PD), there is one strictly dominant strategy for each player. This strategy {confess, confess} is, therefore, the sole *Nash equilibrium* of the game.

A Nash equilibrium, named after the mathematician John Nash (1928–2015), obtains when no player could be made better off by moving to a different strategy, given the strategy that the other players have also rationally chosen. It is a player's best response to the other player's best responses.

Nash Equilibrium
___

In a Nash equilibrium, each player makes her best response to the strategy of the other. Given this, no player can improve her payoffs by a unilateral change of strategy.

___

We call the Nash equilibrium a *solution concept*, which means that it is a method for determining what equilibrium outcome rational players should choose. There are a number of different solution concepts, but the Nash equilibrium is the simplest and most general. Most other solution concepts are refinements of the set of Nash equilibrium solutions.

John Nash's great contribution to game theory was to show that all finite competitive games (those in which there are no binding agreements) have at least one such Nash equilibrium (there may be many). Nash's result is a generalization of von Neumann's minimax theorem: minimax solutions are also Nash equilibria.

Given the standard von Neumann–Morgenstern axioms that we saw in an earlier chapter, we can convert ordinal utilities into cardinal utilities, which not only give the ordering of the payoffs but also the size of the differences in the payoffs for each or—strictly speaking—the ratios of the differences. Assuming the higher the number, the better the outcome, table 5.6 gives the general cardinal form of the Prisoner's Dilemma, while table 5.7 just below it gives a specific example of how the numbers might come out.

TABLE 5.6. The General Form of the Prisoner's Dilemma

		Betty	
		Keep Quiet	**Confess**
Alf	**Keep Quiet**	*x, x*	1, 0
	Confess	0, 1	*y, y*

$$(\text{where } 1 > x > y > 0)$$

TABLE 5.7. A Specific Example of a Prisoner's Dilemma with Cardinal Utility

		Betty	
		Keep Quiet	**Confess**
Alf	**Keep Quiet**	.85, .85	1, 0
	Confess	0, 1	.1, .1

In the second table, Alf and Betty reason themselves into an outcome that, on each of their cardinal scales, gives him/her .1 out of 1, whereas the {keep quiet/keep quiet} outcome would give each .85 out of 1.

Rationality and Efficiency

In the previous chapter, we argued that rationality and efficiency were intimately related: efficient transactions are just ones that raise both parties to higher indifference curves, so such transactions are part and parcel of rational utility optimization. In the Prisoner's Dilemma, though, what is rational to do leads to a Pareto-inferior result. Even if Alf and Betty are experts in game theory, the best move that each can make in response to the other is to confess. In fact, experts in game theory make this response more often than nonexperts. If one should "cooperate" (i.e., not confess), the other will get 1 out of 1 by confessing, while the cooperator will receive 0 out of 1. So, these perfectly rational agents can be certain that by being perfectly rational they will end up with a utility of .1 out of 1, where "less rational" agents—those who both cooperated—would receive .85 out of 1.

This is the lesson of the Prisoner's Dilemma: efficiency and rationality don't always work together. Economists from the time of Adam Smith until today have developed elaborate tools to show how voluntary interactions will always be Pareto-efficient and how properties of efficiencies lead "as if by an invisible hand" to make everyone better off. This is true enough in the market and in voluntary interactions, but in other types of interactions the invisible hand is substituted for what some have called the invisible fist, where rationality inevitably leads to sub-optimal outcomes. The Prisoner's Dilemma is a core example of what are called "social dilemmas" where rationality and efficiency diverge. They are, unfortunately, common and we find them especially in political situations and in situations that call for political institutions. For that reason, these cases especially concern the political philosopher. So tight is the connection between being rational and achieving your goals that many insist that there is a more comprehensive notion of rationality that would direct us to cooperate in the Prisoner's Dilemma.

Many believe that the Prisoner's Dilemma offers key insights about the relation of self-interested action to moral and political rules. The Prisoner's Dilemma models a number of real-life situations in which individual efforts to best pursue one's own goals lead to competitive situations that do not benefit anyone. Contemporary philosophers often use the Prisoner's Dilemma to model the relation between the sorts of self-interested agents that Thomas Hobbes (1588–1679) is widely held to analyze in *Leviathan*.[9]

In the absence of morality and law, many argue, almost all social life could be understood as a Prisoner's Dilemma. According to Hobbes, life without common rules followed by all would be a state of constant war of each against all others. For Hobbes, the basic problem is that humans are fundamentally equal in the crucial sense that anyone can kill anyone else. This equality gives rise to war, because each person is as hopeful as the next of obtaining her goals. But that means that if they both want something, neither is apt to give in, since

9. See Hobbes, *Leviathan*, edited by Edwin Curley. Curley's introduction considers the Prisoner's Dilemma–based interpretations of Hobbes.

neither considers herself inferior to the other. And thus, Hobbes tells us, they are apt to become enemies. We can depict Hobbes's state of nature as a sort of deadly Prisoner's Dilemma.

TABLE 5.8. Hobbes's Deadly Prisoner's Dilemma

		Betty	
		Don't Attack	Attack
Alf	Don't Attack	Peace	Betty conquers Alf, takes his property, kills or enslaves him
	Attack	Alf conquers Betty, takes her property, kills or enslaves her	War

The result is, as Hobbes said, a state of war:

> In such a condition, there is no place for industry; because the fruit thereof is uncertain: and consequently no culture of the earth; no navigation, nor use of the commodities that may be imported by sea; no commodious building; no instruments of moving, and removing, such things as require much force; no knowledge of the face of the earth; no account of time; no arts; no letters; no society; and which is worst of all, continual fear, and the danger of violent death; and the life of man, solitary, poor, nasty, brutish and short.[10]

In what Hobbes called a "state of nature" in which there was no law or morality, the rational utility optimizer would be driven to a condition of war for the same reason Alf and Betty were driven to mutual confession.

Now suppose that, in addition to a person's own goals, each individual has her own moral code. Some codes say, "You shouldn't kill," while others say, "Attack the weak." Will people with such codes avoid the state of war? Well, those who have a code that says "My personal morality is never to attack" will not see attacking the other as a real option, and so will soon find themselves in the loser's cells shown in table 5.8—they will be attacked by

10. Hobbes, Leviathan, chap. 13, para 9.

others, and so get their fourth choice ("You enslave me"). Those with a more warlike code will fare a little better. If they are lucky enough to meet someone who never attacks, they will win, getting their first choice ("I attack, you don't, so I enslave you"); if they encounter another warrior, they will find themselves in a state of war ("we both attack"). But, unless one is willing to run the risk of being killed or enslaved by an aggressive opponent, it will not do for a person to unilaterally adopt a cooperative stance. Instead, we need a common morality that we all follow, so I can be confident that you will see defection ("attack") as ineligible, and you can be confident that I will.

But, embracing the same code will not be enough since, as long as each gain most by violating the moral code, even if we all agree to abide by morality, it looks as if we will all "defect"—take the dominant strategy and break the moral rules. Hobbes himself apparently saw Prisoner's Dilemma–type reasoning not as a justification of a common moral code but as showing why even a common moral code available to everyone through reason would not be sufficient to avoid the war of all against all. Even if we know it is better to cooperate, we also know that everyone's incentive is to defect. Instead, he believed some powerful government that would enforce cooperative behavior by punishing those who followed the noncooperative, "attack" option was needed to institute a genuinely common morality. Caught in a Prisoner's Dilemma, individuals would see that they require "a common power to keep them in awe and to direct their actions to the common benefit."[11] If people are punished for noncooperative behavior, then we can escape the Prisoner's Dilemma since we will replace the Prisoner's Dilemma with a different game in which noncooperation is no longer the dominant strategy.

Although Hobbes assumes individuals are selfish utility maximizers, the general form of the Prisoner's Dilemma does not require us to assume that the players are selfish; as long as their orderings over the outcomes conform to the general form of the Prisoner's Dilemma, they are stuck. Consider, for example, two ideologically opposed countries, each of which thinks that the other is out to oppress the human race and so each believes that it is important for the future of humanity that their side is victorious. As table 5.9 shows, two such countries can be caught in a Prisoner's Dilemma. If the first choice of each is to free the world from the threat of the other, but each would prefer peace to a war that might kill millions since to let the other side dominate the world is worse than war. In this kind of situation, our two crusading countries are in a Prisoner's Dilemma.

11. Hobbes, Leviathan, chap. 17, para 12.

TABLE 5.9. A Prisoner's Dilemma with Crusading Countries

		Red	
		Don't Attack	**Attack**
Blue	**Don't Attack**	Peace	The world is saved from the threat of the Blues
	Attack	The world is saved from the threat of the Reds	War

Public Goods and the Prisoner's Dilemma

The Prisoner's Dilemma also provides a nice analysis of why public goods will not be voluntarily provided by individuals, even though everyone wants the good. This can be seen easily in the context of a multi-person Prisoner's Dilemma, in which each person (Alf in this case) is playing against "everyone else." The numbers in table 5.10 represent Alf's ordinal utilities (I = best).

TABLE 5.10. A Multi-Person Prisoner's Dilemma

		Everyone Else	
		Enough others cooperate so that public good is secured	**Not enough others cooperate, so that public good isn't secured**
Alf	**Contribute**	Alf gains the public good, but has to pay part of the cost for it (**II**)	Alf pays the cost, but since others don't cooperate, he doesn't get the public good (**IV**)
	Doesn't Contribute	Alf gets the public good for free (**I**)	Alf doesn't get the public good, but at least he doesn't pay anything (**III**)

Again, we see that not contributing is the dominant strategy since no matter what the rest of society does, Alf does best by not contributing. If everyone is rational and reasons just as Alf does, the public good will be undersupplied, even if everyone prefers having the public good to not having it.

Coordination Games

So far we have looked at games of pure conflict in the form of zero-sum games and a game where individual rationality leads to sub-optimal outcomes. In zero-sum games, there is no point in coordinating, and in the Prisoner's Dilemma, coordination is rationally impossible. These are interesting and instructive cases, but there is also a category of games where the solution to the game involves coordination.

Chicken

Our first example of a coordination problem actually involves anti-coordination in a way similar to the Holmes-Moriarty problem. Recall our public goods story from the last chapter about Alf's goat and Betty's garden and dog. His goat wanders into her vegetables while her dog wanders onto Alf's property, scaring his goat so that it does not give milk. We saw that in this case for the public (or, really, club) good, a fence would be provided since each would prefer to pay for the entire good rather than do without. We now can analyze the situation in terms of a game, as in table 5.11 (again, I > II > III > IV).

TABLE 5.11. An Assurance Game

		Betty	
		Builds	**Doesn't Build**
Alf	**Builds**	II, II	III, I
	Doesn't Build	I, III	IV, IV

This game has the same strategic representation as the game of "Chicken." It is named after a game that teenagers played in the movie *Rebel without a Cause*: two teenage boys—and, of course, it was boys—drive toward each other with the pedal to the metal, and the first one to swerve is "chicken."[12] So the best result is to keep driving straight while the other swerves: he chickened, you didn't. This is best for you but is the second worst outcome for the chicken. If both swerve, both reputations take a bit of a hit, but it is better to both chicken than for one to back down when the other doesn't; so, let's say

12. In fact, in the movie they do not drive toward each other, but toward a cliff—the first one to stop before the cliff is the "chicken."

this is the second-best outcome for each. If, on the other hand, neither swerve, they both take a much bigger hit and crash. This is represented in table 5.12.

TABLE 5.12. A Game of Chicken

		Betty	
		Swerve	**Don't Swerve**
Alf	**Swerve**	II, II Both Chicken	III, I Alf Chicken
	Don't Swerve	I, III Betty Chicken	IV, IV Crash

In the game of Chicken, only two outcomes are in equilibrium (Alf Chicken or Betty Chicken). Remember, an outcome is in (Nash) equilibrium when neither party can make himself/herself better off by unilaterally changing a move. If Alf and Betty find themselves in the Both Chicken outcome, either can gain utility by switching moves, assuming the other keeps playing the current move; so too with Crash outcome. But note that this is not the case in the outcomes where either swerves.

Chicken is often used as a way to model international confrontations generally and the Cuban Missile Crisis in particular. In October 1962, the United States discovered that the Soviet Union (USSR) was in the process of placing nuclear missiles in Cuba. This meant that Soviet missiles could reach American cities in a matter of a few minutes, giving the United States no time to launch a retaliatory strike. Because of this, President Kennedy and his advisors determined that the missiles destabilized nuclear deterrence and so it was absolutely imperative that they be removed. Some in the administration thought that it was best for the United States to accede to the new status quo—let the missiles stay. But that was a small minority, and for the most part Kennedy's team of advisors seriously considered two options: an air strike against the missiles (perhaps followed by an invasion) that would kill Soviet technicians as well as Cubans, and a blockade of Cuba that would stop any further shipments of missiles to Cuba. This blockade would not itself force the Soviet Union to withdraw the missiles it had already installed; some further measures to apply pressure to remove existing missiles might be necessary. The Soviets had the options of withdrawing the missiles or remaining in Cuba. It was thought that, if the United States launched an air strike and the Soviet Union refused to withdraw, there was a real chance of nuclear war.

Table 5.13 presents an analysis that explains the outcome in terms of Chicken.

TABLE 5.13. The Cuban Missile Crisis as a Game of Chicken

		USSR	
		Withdraw	**Maintain**
USA	**Back Down**	II, II	III, I
	Demand Removal	I, III	IV, IV

The standard representation is that the Soviet Union "chickened," that the United States got its first option—took public action and demanded that the Soviets withdraw their missiles—and that the Soviets got their third—public humiliation of backdown (the outcome in the south-east quadrant). This modeling, however, depends on the set of options we identify and how we think policymakers ranked them: some have disputed that this was a game of Chicken.[13] Consider another representation of this situation in table 5.14.

TABLE 5.14. A Game of Chicken Where No One Chickened?

		USSR	
		Withdraw	**Maintain**
USA	**Blockade**	II, II	III, I
	Air Strike	I, III	IV, IV

Here, the worst outcome is air strike/maintain because that may lead to nuclear war. Each side would prefer that the other backs down; again, the equilibrium solutions are for one or the other to back down. But note that the actual outcome was that the United States blockaded, and the USSR withdrew, which is the equivalent of both swerving. But if these were the orderings, then although we have a game of Chicken, the actual outcome was not an equilibrium solution.

Perhaps this should lead us to think that the Cuban Missile Crisis was not a game of Chicken after all. Steven Brams argues that rather than Chicken we had another game, represented in table 5.15.[14]

13. See Steven J. Brams, "Game Theory and the Cuban Missile Crisis," *Math Plus* 13 (January 2001). http://plus.maths.org/issue13/features/brams.
14. Brams, "Game Theory and the Cuban Missile Crisis."

TABLE 5.15. Bram's Model of the Cuban Missile Crisis

| | | USSR | |
		Withdraw	Maintain
USA	**Blockade**	II, II	IV, I
	Air Strike	III, III	I, IV

First, Brams argues that it would *not* have been best for the United States to take the aggressive action (air strikes) when the USSR backed down ("they swerved"), since the United States would be widely condemned for its overreaction and reckless action. On the other hand, Brams argues that the danger of nuclear war was not as highly estimated as in the Chicken representation. If the United States had attacked an obstinate Soviet Union, the world would have generally supported its action and the Soviet Union likely would have capitulated. Notice that in the ordinal form, this game does not have an equilibrium solution. Although Nash showed that all finite variable-sum games have at least one Nash equilibrium, this may require a *mixed strategy*, and for that we need cardinal utilities. More on these below.

The example of the Cuban Missile Crisis shows three limits of attempts to apply game theory to actual interactions. First, whether a game models an actual strategic interaction is highly sensitive to just how we describe the options and compare them in the eyes of the decision-makers. Second, if we only have ordinal utilities, some games do not have Nash equilibrium solutions.[15] Third, in the actual world, games are played under imperfect information in which players are in doubt about both the rationality and the utility functions of their opponents. Under these conditions it is not surprising that in one-play games, the outcome may not be a Nash equilibrium.

Stag Hunt

Jean-Jacques Rousseau presents a depiction of man's natural condition in which simple people's "love of [their own] well-being" leads them to cooperate with each other, but not always in the most far-sighted ways. According to him, such men would acquire:

15. Brams provides an interesting solution relying on "the theory of moves," which we cannot explore here.

some gross ideas of mutual undertakings, and of the advantages of fulfilling them: that is, just so far as their present and apparent interest was concerned: for they were perfect strangers to foresight and were so far from troubling themselves about the distant future, that they hardly thought of the morrow. If a deer was to be taken, every one saw that, in order to succeed, he must abide faithfully by his post: but if a hare happened to come within the reach of any one of them, it is not to be doubted that he pursued it without scruple, and, having seized his prey, cared very little, if by so doing he caused his companions to miss theirs.[16]

Rousseau's story can be formalized into a game called the Stag Hunt as presented in table 5.16 (I > II > III). Best for both is if they hunt a stag together and have lots of meat. But one person cannot catch a stag: both must cooperate. One, however, can hunt a hare alone. If the other hunts stag, you should hunt stag, but if the other hunts hare, you should hunt hare (both are Nash equilibria).

TABLE 5.16. A Stag Hunt

		Betty	
		Hunt Stag	**Hunt Hare**
Alf	**Hunt Stag**	I, I	III, II
	Hunt Hare	II, III	II, II

Though not as paradoxical as the Prisoner's Dilemma, the Stag Hunt may serve as a better model for understanding social life. Rather than the main issue being "should we try to outdo each other in or live in peace?" perhaps the really important question is whether we go it alone and get something (hunt hare), or cooperate (hunt stag) and get (much) more?[17]

As in Chicken, the Stag Hunt has no dominant strategy, and there are multiple equilibria. But what is more surprising about the Stag Hunt is that one equilibrium in pure strategies (Stag/Stag) is better for both parties, yet there is another equilibrium in pure strategies (Hare/Hare) that is also possible. Alf and Betty cannot be sure they will end up sharing a stag. Some students question this. If Alf and Betty have common knowledge of the payoffs and of their

16. Rousseau, "Discourse on the Origin of Inequality," 25–110.

17. For an analysis that focuses on the Stag Hunt, see Skyrms, The Stag Hunt and the Evolution of Social Structure.

own rationality, shouldn't Betty assume that Alf will hunt stag (and Alf assume that Betty will too)? After all, as rational agents they see that there is an equilibrium (Hunt Stag/Hunt Stag) that is strongly Pareto-superior to the other (Hunt Hare/Hunt Hare): why would either think the rational other would select the Pareto-inferior option? As Rousseau suggests in the passage quoted earlier, it would seem that only some sort of short-sightedness (imperfect rationality) could lead to hunting hare.

To understand why this worry is insightful, yet still not quite right, we need to grasp the distinction between *rationalizable* strategies and *common conjectures*. As some students rightly recognize, rational players can sometimes use their common knowledge to eliminate those strategies that are not "rationalizable." I can know that my rational opponent will not choose some strategy A if, for every move I might make, she has available a strategy B which is better for her. If B is always better for her than A no matter what I do, then we can say that for her B *dominates* A, and so as a rational player she will never play A. Dominated strategies are never rationalizable. As a rational player, then, we can suppose that she will never play such a dominated strategy; by successively eliminating dominated strategies, a complicated game may ultimately have a simple solution in pure strategies. We look at this in more detail in the next section.

In the Stag Hunt, however, both hunting stag and hunting hare are *rationalizable*. The problem is that, after all, Alf cannot be entirely confident that Betty will hunt stag. Why? Because it is rational for Betty to hunt stag only if she thinks Alf will. For Betty to certainly hunt stag, she would have to be sure that Alf will hunt stag too. So, then, does Betty *know* that Alf will hunt stag? No, because Alf will hunt stag only if he thinks Betty will hunt stag: he needs to know that she will hunt stag. So, she will hunt stag if she knows he will, and he will if he knows she will. We can see that the rationality of hunting stag is contingent on the other person hunting stag, but whether each will hunt stag is contingent on whether they think the other will, which is contingent on each thinking that the other will, and on and on.

What Alf and Betty require is a *common conjecture* about how the game is to be played that allows them to hit on the "hunt stag" equilibrium: they need to play in a way that both play the desirable equilibrium. Here communication would help. If Alf and Betty tell each other that they intend to hunt stag, then they should both hunt stag: neither would have any incentive to say one thing and do the other; neither could gain by "tricking" the other into hunting stag. If Alf does decide to hunt hare, it doesn't matter to him what Betty does, so why deceive her? That hunting stag strongly Pareto-dominates hunting hare is an excellent reason to settle on stag. Yet sometimes it may be difficult to settle even on a Pareto-dominant equilibrium.

Common conjecture via communication works less well in a very similar game, the Assurance Game.

TABLE 5.17. A Different Stag Hunt

		Betty	
		Cooperate (Stag)	Defect (Hare)
Alf	Cooperate (Stag)	I, I	IV, II
	Defect (Hare)	II, IV	III, III

Sometimes this game is also called Stag Hunt, but we can see that the payoffs differ from those in table 5.16. Unlike the true Stag, although the best option is for both to hunt stag, Betty's second-best option is to hunt hare when Alf hunts stag. Now the game has room for deception, and so communication may not provide for a common conjecture on how to play the game.

Suppose that Alf and Betty are in the hunt hare/hunt hare equilibrium and Betty tells Alf that she intends to switch to hunt stag. Regardless of what she intends to do, it makes sense for her to convince Alf to play Stag, so her verbal evidence makes sense of both a decision to change her move and a decision not to. Alf has a harder time taking her at her word: communication may help a lot less in establishing common conjectures about how the game is to be played.

Battle of the Sexes

A similar game to the Stag Hunt is the so-called Battle of the Sexes.[18] In this game, imagine that Alf and Betty want to spend the day together, but one would rather spend the day together at the beach, while the other would like to spend the day together at the Cricket Test Match (Alf and Betty are Aussies in this example). Alf would rather go to the cricket than the beach and Betty would rather spend the day at the beach than at the cricket. Both would rather do either than not spend the day together. Either coordination point—both go to the cricket or both go the beach—are Nash equilibria.

---

18. Luce and Raiffa, Games and Decisions, 90.

TABLE 5.18. Battle of the Sexes

		Betty	
		Cricket	**Beach**
Alf	**Cricket**	I, II	III, III
	Beach	III, III	II, I

Despite the fact that the game involves coordination, there is still room for conflict and strategy. For instance, Alf may simply leave a message on Betty's phone that he will meet her at the cricket and then turn his phone off. Or Betty could tell Alf that she has become agoraphobic and can't stand crowds. But they do not wish the conflict to get out of hand so long as they prefer both coordinated to both uncoordinated outcomes.

Jeremy Waldron believes that the Battles of the Sexes game is the key to understanding politics. As he writes, "the felt need among members of a certain group for a common framework or decision or course of action on some matter, even in the face of disagreement about what the framework, decision or action should be, are the circumstances of politics."[19] In politics, we need to settle on a common path, recognizing that not everyone agrees about which path is best.

As Waldron understands politics, we will debate and discuss the merits and demerits of each of the possible coordination points (policies); since it is an impure coordination game, I prefer a different coordination point (policy) than do you, so we have something to argue about. However, we each prefer any coordination point to lack of coordination. In essence, then, Waldron argues that we need to coordinate on some single policy, even if it is not the one that each of us sees as best. Politics is essentially an impure coordination game: we desire to coordinate but disagree about which coordination point is best.

It seems unlikely in the extreme, though, that every piece of legislation is an impure coordination problem: if anyone prefers even one uncoordinated outcome to even one way of acting together, we no longer have an impure coordination problem: somebody can be made better off by a unilateral defection from some ways of acting together. If, say, Alf is a Millian liberal who thinks that there should be no laws concerning self-regarding acts, then what legislation we should have concerning pornography cannot be a coordination

---

19. Waldron, *Law and Disagreement*, 104. Gaus considered Waldron's analysis in more depth in his *Contemporary Theories of Liberalism*, chap. 4.

problem. Alf may benefit by unilateral defection from any policy on this matter. It is more plausible to see, not each policy or act of legislation, but government itself, as an impure coordination problem. We all agree that we need some government, but we disagree about which one is best, and we cannot all go on our way. This, though, can only hold over some set of types of government. Although Hobbes may have thought that any government is better than no government, few agree. Oppressive governments that invade people's life, liberty, and property may well be worse than no government at all. So, we first need to find the set of governments that everyone sees as superior to "going it alone," and only in relation to selecting among them can we see political theory as based on an impure coordination game.

Dominance and Rationalizability

We have talked a lot about multiple equilibria, but how do we find the Nash equilibria when it isn't obvious in a nice 2 × 2 game? The basic way is to eliminate "dominated" strategies.

Alf's strategy S_1 *strictly dominates* his S_2 if for every strategy in Betty's strategy set, S_1 does better against it than does S_2. A rational player will never use S_2, a dominated strategy, since S_1 always does better.

Alf's strategy S_1 *weakly dominates* his S_2 if for every strategy in Betty's strategy set, S_1 never does worse against them than does S_2 and S_1 sometimes does better against all of Betty's strategies than does S_2.

Let's go through an example. Suppose that the basic game is in table 5.19. Alf and Betty each have three strategies available to them: up, middle, and down for Alf and left, center, and right for Betty.

TABLE 5.19. A Game Illustrating Rationalizability

		Betty		
		Left	**Center**	**Right**
	Up	73, 25	57, 42	66, 32
Alf	**Middle**	89, 26	35, 12	32, 54
	Down	28, 27	63, 31	54, 29

We can make the game simpler by eliminating dominated strategies, which cannot be used, since if a strategy is dominated, there is another of the player's strategies that is *always* better to use.

Let's look at Betty's strategies. Does Left dominate Center? Which is to say, does Betty do better playing Left rather than Center regardless of what Alf does? To answer this, we just compare Betty's payoffs in each row when Left and Center are played, not taking Right into account.

TABLE 5.20. Elimination of Dominated Strategies Stage 1

		Left	Center
			Betty
	Up	X, 25	X, 42✓
Alf	**Middle**	X, 26✓	X, 12
	Down	X, 27	X, 31✓

We can eliminate Alf's payoffs, since they don't matter when we are looking at which of Betty's strategies dominates the other, so we have replaced his payoffs with an X. As we see with the checkmarks, Center dominates Left when Alf plays Up or Down, but not Center. Because of this, we can't say that Left or Center dominates the other and, hence, we can't eliminate that strategy.

TABLE 5.21. Elimination of Dominated Strategies Stage 2

		Left	Right
			Betty
	Up	X, 25	X, 32 ✓
Alf	**Middle**	X, 26	X, 54 ✓
	Down	X, 27	X, 29 ✓

What about Left and Right? It looks like Right is better for better every case, so we can say that Right dominates Left. Because of this, we can eliminate Left since it can't be an equilibrium strategy for Betty. If we do this, we are left with a reduced form of the game as represented in table 5.22.

TABLE 5.22. Elimination of Dominated Strategies Stage 3

| | | Betty | |
		Center	Right
Alf	Up	57, 42	66, 32
	Middle	35, 12	32, 54
	Down	63, 31	54, 29

Once we eliminate this strategy for Betty, we need to look at Alf's strategies. This is why we call this method an *iterated* elimination of strategies, since we iterate between Alf's and Betty's strategies to eliminate dominated strategies. We can compare Up and Down—does either dominate the other?

TABLE 5.23. Elimination of Dominated Strategies Stage 4

| | | Betty | |
		Center	Right
Alf	Up	57, X	66, X ✓
	Down	63, X ✓	54, X

No. Down is better when Betty plays Center and Up is better when Betty plays right. What about Up and Middle?

TABLE 5.24. Elimination of Dominated Strategies Stage 5

| | | Betty | |
		Center	Right
Alf	Up	57, X ✓	66, X ✓
	Middle	35, X	32, X

Yes, Up is better than Middle whatever Betty does, so we can eliminate Middle since it is dominated by Up. We are left with the following reduced form of the game.

TABLE 5.25. Elimination of Dominated Strategies Stage 6

| | | Betty | |
		Center	Right
Alf	Up	57, 42	66, 32
	Down	63, 31	54, 29

Ok, back to Betty. Is either Center or Right a dominant strategy? Yes, it looks like Center dominates Right.

TABLE 5.26. Elimination of Dominated Strategies Stage 7

| | | Betty | |
		Center	Right
Alf	Up	X, 42 ✓	X, 32
	Down	X, 31 ✓	X, 29

Because of this, we can eliminate Right since it is dominated by Center, leaving the reduced-form game below.

TABLE 5.27. Elimination of Dominated Strategies Stage 8

| | | Betty |
		Right
Alf	Up	66, 32
	Down	54, 29

As we can easily see, Up dominated Down for Alf, leaving us with one Nash equilibrium, {Down, Right}.

TABLE 5.28. Identification of the Unique Equilibrium Strategy

		Betty
		Right
Alf	**Up**	66, 32

Eliminating strongly dominated strategies is uncontroversial because you never eliminate a Nash equilibrium. If you eliminate weakly dominate strategies, however, you may do so. So, however useful iterated elimination of strictly dominated strategies will be, it will miss Nash equilibria that include weakly dominated strategies.

Mixed Strategies

John Nash demonstrated that in every finite game (a finite number of moves), between two persons, there is always at least one Nash equilibrium. However, this equilibrium need not always be a combination of "pure" strategies. A *pure strategy* is when one always makes the same response to a certain move by the other; a *mixed strategy* is when one may respond to the same move by the other in different ways.

TABLE 5.29. Rock, Paper, Scissors

		Betty		
		Paper	**Rock**	**Scissors**
	Paper	0, 0	1, −1	−1, 1
Alf	**Rock**	−1, 1	0, 0	1, −1
	Scissors	1, −1	−1, 1	0, 0

An obvious case where a pure strategy won't do is a game of Paper, Rock, Scissors—a zero-sum game with no pure strategy equilibrium. Paper covers Rock, Rock crushes Scissors, Scissors cut Paper, so as strategies go, Paper > Rock > Scissors > Paper. You shouldn't always play Rock since, if you do, the other player will respond with Paper. You shouldn't always play Paper because the other player will respond with Scissors and you should not always play Scissors, because it will be crushed by Rock.

There is no one strategy that is always best whatever else your opponent plays. Another way to put this is that there is no strategy—Rock, Paper, or Scissors—that will win 100% of the time. This is what a pure strategy is, a strategy you should play 100% of the time. Given this, is there no equilibrium strategy to this game? No, the solution is to *mix* your strategies, playing Rock some of the time, Paper some of the time, and Scissors some of the time. This is what we call a mixed strategy, a probabilistic mix of strategies based on the best reply to the other player's best mixed strategy—in this case, a one-third chance of either Rock, Paper, or Scissors.

In Rock, Paper, Scissors, if Alf plays a pure strategy—say he always plays Rock—he can expect to lose 1 per game, since Betty will respond Paper, which will always beat it. Suppose Alf plays a mixed strategy of ½ Paper ½ Scissors. Betty will respond with a pure strategy of Scissors, ensuring she never loses, and she will win half the time. Alf's expected loss per game is ½ (since this is a zero-sum game, Betty's expected gain is also ½).

Suppose Alf plays a mixed strategy of playing each move 1/3 of the time. Betty's best move is the same mixed strategy, giving each an expected gain of 0. One-third of the time Alf will win, one-third of the time he will lose, and one-third of the time there will be a draw. Thus, there is an equilibrium in this game, as many young children know. The point of mixed strategies, then, is to neutralize the other player's choices of strategies.

However, if we are talking about a single-play game, it is not entirely clear what it means to say that a combination of mixed strategies is in equilibrium; clearly over a run of games the mixing strategy is best, but in a simultaneous one-play game, any strategy that is unannounced is as good as any other. Each pure strategy is part of the mixed strategy so in the single case, any pure strategy might be played. In the one-play case, mixed strategies can, perhaps, be seen as instructions to engage in a certain randomization process rather than a combination of strategies. Note, though, that the solution then does not involve a mix of strategies at all, but a new strategy involving a randomization device. We return to this point when we discuss correlated equilibria.

Mixed Strategy

In any game we must specify the set of *pure strategies* open to the players.

Call S the **strategy set**, with $S = \{s_1, s_2, \ldots s_n\}$ as possible strategies.

A **mixed strategy** is a probability distribution over pure strategies, i.e., the members of S.

Call M the mixed strategy set and let p_i equal the probability p of employing strategy i (read this as $p_i s_i$) in the strategy set. Remember that according to the basic principles of probability theory $p_1 + p_2 + \ldots p_n = 1$. That is, the sum of the probabilities must equal 1.

So, the mixed-strategy set $M = \{p_1 s_1, p_2 s_2 \ldots p_n s_n\}$

If for any strategy in $s_i \in S$, $p_i = 1$, then s_i is a **pure strategy**. In this way, we can think of pure strategies as special cases of a mixed strategy.

M is **strictly mixed** if it is not pure (if there is a probability of playing at least two strategies).

M is **completely mixed** if every strategy in M has a non-zero chance of being played.

The Nash Existence Theorem

Consider a game with just two pure strategies, s_1 and s_2. John Nash showed that if Alf's mixed strategy is in equilibrium it must be the case that the expected payoffs of $p_1 s_1$ must be equal to be expected payoffs of $p_2 s_2$. That is, M must mix the strategies in such a way that the expected payoffs of playing s_1 or s_2 are equal. If they weren't equal, some other mixture would outperform them, and each player would have reason to move to that mixture.

Nash Existence Theorem

If each player in a n-person game (a game with n persons playing) has a finite number of pure strategies in the strategy set, then the game has at least one and perhaps more than one Nash equilibrium.

However, although this is the result of a mixed Nash equilibrium, it is not the case that each player is seeking to equalize the payoffs of her pure strategies. There would be no point to doing so. Instead, each player is picking the best option given the best option the other player(s) are likely to choose. In zero-sum games, the best way to think of mixed strategies is that you are seeking to ensure that the other player cannot exploit you and get a higher payoff. Again, think of Paper, Rock, Scissors. If the other player has any strategy like play Paper, or play Rock, or play Scissors, that has a higher expected utility, then she can use that strategy to beat you. So, you must select a strategy that prevents you from being exploited by guaranteeing that the other player has no favored strategy; that each of her pure strategies has the same expected utility as the other. This can be a little hard to grasp, but you are trying to ensure that the other player's strategies have the same expected utility. Of course, in a mixed Nash equilibrium, this will be true for both players.

To see more clearly how this works, let's begin with a simple zero-sum game using cardinal utilities. Imagine Alf and Betty are coaching football teams—the Avalanche and the Bills—and Alf's team is on offense, while Betty's is on defense. Alf has two strategies. He can call either a run play or a pass play. Similarly, Betty can call for her team to either play a run or pass defense, depending on what she expects Alf to do. A running play that is not defended well can expect to gain 5 yards. With the Avalanche's excellent quarterback and receivers, a pass play that is undefended can expect to gain 10 yards.

Betty's defense is good too, and she believes that her pass rush can expect to sack Alf's quarterback and cost him 5 yards if she makes the right call. Her stout run defense will also likely stop any running back in his tracks behind the line of scrimmage, costing the offense 5 yards if she guesses a run play correctly. The strategies and expected payoff are given in table 5.30.

TABLE 5.30. Football Strategy

| | | Betty's Bills | |
		Run Defense	Pass Defense
Alf's Avalanche	Run	−5, 5	5, −5
	Pass	10, −10	−5, 5

There are no dominated strategies and there is no pure strategy that each should play, so we need to look for a mixed-strategy equilibrium. To do this we need to remember two things. First, each player's mixed-strategy set probability mixture should sum to 1. Second, the equilibrium should equalize the expected utility of each player's mixed-strategy set, otherwise one player would have the advantage by playing a different strategy set. We can start by assigning strategy a probability for Alf. In this case, there are two strategies p and $1-p$. And for Betty, we can use q and $1-q$. Our goal then is to solve for p and q. We can do this since we know that the expected utility of each player's strategy should be equal.[20]

TABLE 5.31. Finding Mixed-Strategy Solutions

| | | Betty's Bills | |
		Run Defense (q)	Pass Defense ($1-q$)
Alf's Avalanche	Run (p)	−5, 5	5, −5
	Pass ($1-p$)	10, −10	−5, 5

20. Although these fractions can be expressed with decimals, one should always use fractions when determining mixed strategies since they are exact, whereas decimals often aren't and because fractions are easier to work with.

So, to find what Betty's best probability distribution is, we need to find the mix where the expected utility of Run Defense is the same as the expected utility of Pass Defense. At the risk of being tedious, the steps for finding q and $(1-q)$ are listed in figure 5.2.

(1) Expected Utility (EU) of Run = EU of Pass
(2) EU Run = $-5q + 5(1-q)$
(3) EU Pass = $10q + -5(1-q)$
(4) So, $-5q + 5(1-q) = 10q + -5(1-q)$
(5) $-25q = -10$, by simplifying and subtracting from each side
(6) $q = 2/5$, by dividing each side by -25
(7) $q = 2/5$ and $(1-q) = 3/5$

FIGURE 5.2. Finding Mixed-Strategy Solutions Specified

We can do the same to find Alf's best mixture of strategies given that he guesses correctly about Betty's strategy. Given the way this game is set up, with the values the same and the signs reversed, Alf has the same probabilities, just in reverse, so $p = 3/5$ and $(1-p) = 3/5$. We can now look at what utilities each player can expect to gain if they play their mixed strategies.

TABLE 5.32. Football Strategy with Optimal Strategy Mixtures

		Betty's Bills	
		Run Defense (2/5)	Pass Defense (3/5)
Alf's Avalanche	Run (3/5)	−5, 5	5, −5
	Pass (2/5)	10, −10	−5, 5

Now we want to know what the expected utility of each player's mixed strategy is, and to do this, we need to know how likely each outcome is to occur, that is, how likely each player, playing their mixed strategies, will intersect in different outcomes. Let's start with Alf's expected utility. He will call Run with a probability of 3/5, and Betty will call Run Defense with a probability of 2/5. So, the probability of both of these things happening is 2/5 multiplied by 3/5, or 6/25. Then, the probability of Alf getting −5 yards when he calls Run and Betty calls Run Defense is 6/25. If we work out these probabilities, we get the results in table 5.33.

TABLE 5.33. Football Strategy with Optimal Strategy Mixtures and Expected Payoffs

		Betty's Bills	
		Run Defense $(2/5)$	**Pass Defense** $(3/5)$
Alf's Avalanche	**Run** $(3/5)$	$-5 * \dfrac{6}{25}$	$5 * \dfrac{9}{25}$
	Pass $(2/5)$	$10 * \dfrac{4}{25}$	$-5 * \dfrac{6}{25}$

Alf's expected value for the mixed strategy as a whole is all of these cells added together, which sums to 1. So, Alf can expect to gain a yard if he follows his mixed strategy. Not surprisingly, given that this is a zero-sum game, Betty can expect to lose a yard.

Mixed Strategies in a Coordination Game

Although the explanation of mixed strategies in zero-sum games is straight-forward since each player is trying to prevent their opponent from getting an advantage, in coordination games, the explanation is less clear. Consider the Battle of the Sexes game we looked at earlier.

TABLE 5.34. Impure Coordination Game

		Betty	
		Cricket	**Beach**
Alf	**Cricket**	2, 1	0, 0
	Beach	0, 0	1, 2

If we follow the same procedure that we used to find the mixed strategy in zero-sum games here, we will find that Alf should go to the cricket with a prob-ability of $1/3$ and the beach with a probability of $2/3$. Betty should go to the cricket with a probability of $2/3$ and the beach with a probability of $1/3$. Since Alf can expect to be at the cricket $2/3$ of the time and he knows, given her mixed strategy, that Betty will be at cricket $1/3$ of the time, he can discount his payoff by the expected probability that both will be there, which is $2/9$, When we work all of these out, we arrive at the results in table 5.35.

TABLE 5.35. Impure Coordination Game with Optimal Strategy Mixtures and Payoffs

	Betty	
	Cricket $(1/3)$	**Beach** $(2/3)$
Cricket $(2/3)$ (Alf)	$\left(2*\dfrac{2}{9}\right),\ \left(1*\dfrac{2}{9}\right)$	$\left(0*\dfrac{4}{9}\right),\ \left(0*\dfrac{4}{9}\right)$
Beach $(1/3)$	$\left(0*\dfrac{1}{9}\right),\ \left(0*\dfrac{1}{9}\right)$	$\left(1*\dfrac{2}{9}\right),\ \left(2*\dfrac{2}{9}\right)$

What we find if we add up all of the expected payoffs for each player is an expected utility of $2/3$ for each.

Recall that this game, in addition to the mixed strategy, has two pure strategy equilibria where both either go to the cricket or the beach. We can see the expected payoffs for each equilibrium strategy for each player in table 5.36.

TABLE 5.36. Impure Coordination Game Payoff Table

	Cricket	**Beach**	**Mixed Strategy**
Alf	2	1	$\dfrac{2}{3}$
Betty	1	2	$\dfrac{2}{3}$

Alf and Betty can expect to do better when they coordinate 100% of the time at either the cricket or the beach. This raises the question of why they would ever play a mixed strategy in this situation. This game is interesting precisely because it has three strategies, two of which dominate the other. How could picking the sub-optimal equilibrium be rational?

We have already seen one game where the equilibrium solution is sub-optimal—the Prisoner's Dilemma—but in that game the only equilibrium was sub-optimal, there wasn't any choice. In this game, there is a sub-optimal option that is also an equilibrium solution. But, by definition, Nash equilibria are rationalizable (though the reverse is not always true) and, in the sense we have been working with throughout this book, rational. But how could it be rational to play a mixed strategy in this game and do worse than you would have done in either of the pure strategy equilibria? We want a compelling reason to play an equilibrium strategy.

One answer comes from the symmetrical nature of the mixed-strategy pay-offs.[21] The Battle of the Sexes is what we call an "asymmetric" game in the sense that we cannot simply have Alf switch positions with Betty and expect to get the same result. In this case, this is because their preferences over outcomes differ. It is then perhaps no surprise that the pure strategy equilibria end up being asymmetrical as well then; Alf does better in one and Betty in the other. The mixed-strategy equilibrium is special in that it is symmetrical, each player can expect to do there as well as the other. So, one might prefer this solution on the grounds of fairness or, as we will see when we look at bargaining theory, as a technical feature of certain kinds of solutions. Fairness, though, is not the same thing as rationality, so even if fairness might give us a reason to select the symmetrical solution, it won't show that selecting the sub optimal solution is rational. We will return to this aspect of the problem in some detail in the next chapter.

Another possibility is that the mixed strategy represents the safest strategy if there is no way to communicate before choosing.[22] If Alf reasons that he should choose his best option and Betty should choose hers, they will miss one another and both get the worst outcome. Similarly, if Alf reasons that Betty is likely to select his best outcome and he is likely to select hers, they will also miss one another. So, there is a strong possibility that they will miss one another if they follow either of the pure strategy equilibria. If, however, they reason symmetrically, they can ensure a "safe" expected payoff of 2/3, which is more than zero. But, again, common knowledge of the game and rationality is not enough to show that each party will reason symmetrically, otherwise all games would privilege symmetrical solution. Indeed, common knowledge of symmetrical reasoning would produce perverse results, as we will see later.

As we can see, the rationale for playing a mixed strategy in this kind of co-ordination game is hard to come by, but this may be due, in part, to the nature of the game. A game like the Battle of the Sexes is what we can call a "conflic-tual coordination" game where the parties need to coordinate, but where their interests do not align. As we saw above, this makes games like this particularly interesting to political theorists, who are generally interested in cases of con-flictual coordination. One way to think about the game that will yield value fruits is as a cooperative rather than non-cooperative game. This will lead us

---

21. For a detailed discussion of symmetry with respect to coordination games and bargaining, see Thrasher, "Uniqueness and Symmetry in Bargaining Theories of Justice."

22. This is similar to the defense of the "maximin" solution given in Luce and Raiffa, Games and Decisions, 91–93.

into a discussion of bargaining and cooperative games more generally in the next chapter.

Do People Play Nash?

People usually have a hard time figuring out mixed strategies. Some seemingly simple games have a bewildering array of mixed strategies, which are typically far from intuitive. This raises the question of whether people are actually able to discern and play mixed strategies. If not, this might lead us to raise questions about how well traditional game theory, with its reliance on mixed strategies, represents actual strategic decision-making. It might also make us question the status of the Nash equilibrium as a cornerstone of our account of strategic rationality since, unlike dominance reasoning more generally, the Nash existence theorem requires mixed strategies for its proof.

The evidence here is mixed. Like in our football example from above, there is some evidence that opponents in sports often adopt strategies that look like mixed strategies, though the frequency varies within and between sports. Pitchers, at least on their first pitch, seem to select pitches in a way that largely conforms with the optimal mixed strategy.[23] That said, pitchers as a whole and football teams do not seem to be implementing optimal mixed strategies. Kenneth Kovash and Steven Levitt argue that many baseball teams would gain two wins over the course of the season and football teams would gain half a win if they switched to their optimal mixed strategy.[24] As David Romer explores, though, football teams predictably make sub-optimal decisions in a number of ways, most notably by punting on fourth down when they can expect to gain more by going for it.[25] It is hard to interpret what all of this means though, since football and baseball teams are large organizations and not all the incentives of each actors always align clearly. Coaches are likely to be blamed more for losing in a lot of cases than they will be rewarded for winning, so it might make sense for them to be a little more risk-averse. Tennis players, at least at the highest level, do approximate the optimal mixed strategy in their serve selections.[26]

In experimental settings, subjects regularly deviate from playing their optimal mixed strategies. Ido Erev and Alvin Roth have shown that subjects

23. Weinstein-Gould, "Keeping the Hitter Off Balance: Mixed Strategies in Baseball."

24. Kovash and Levitt, "Professionals Do Not Play Minimax."

25. Romer, "Do Firms Maximize?."

26. Walker and Wooders, "Minimax Play at Wimbledon"; Gauriot, Page, and Wooders, "Nash at Wimbledon."

deviate from optimal mixed strategies and that simple reinforcement learning techniques seem to better predict the behavior of subjects.[27] But, experiments show that chimps perform better than human subjects in many strategic contexts. In a fascinating recent series of experiments, Martin et al. had chimpanzee mother-child pairs playing competitive games that were all version of "matching pennies," which is similar to the Holmes-Moriarty game that we discussed at the start of the chapter.[28]

The equilibrium strategies to these games are not intuitive and difficult to solve for. Nevertheless, Martin et al. found that chimps are much better at finding the correct mixed response than are human subjects! Because the results were so striking, Martin and his coworkers set about testing two groups of human subjects, one receiving high, one receiving low, payoffs, in one of the games. Chimp play was much closer to the mixed Nash equilibrium than either human group. They conclude that

> these results suggest that the reason the chimpanzees converge more sharply to mutually best-responding (i.e., are closer to N[ash] E[quilibium]) is because they adjust to opponent behavior and to changes in incentives more strongly. This comparison does not depend on differences in the numbers of trials the chimpanzee and human groups faced (if anything, learning could be more evident in the shorter trial lengths of the human groups).[29]

What's going on here? Chimps seem to have evolved to have what has been called "Machiavellian Intelligence," that is, an ability to reason instrumentally for advantage and to assume others will do so as well.[30] Humans can also be Machiavellian, but we aren't as relentlessly instrumental and strategic in our reasoning as chimps. All of this raises a number of questions about the conception of rationality that we have established and whether it is an appropriate model of human reasoning. *Homo economicus* may be a better representation of chimps than humans. If so, we may need to complicate the picture presented so far to make sense of why. Norms, conventions, and more sophisticated solution concepts can explain this more fully. More on each of those in later chapters.

27. Erev and Roth, "Predicting How People Play Games."

28. Martin et al., "Chimpanzee Choice Rates in Competitive Games Match Equilibrium Game Theory Predictions."

29. Martin et al., "Chimpanzee Choice Rates in Competitive Games Match Equilibrium Game Theory Predictions," 3.

30. Byrne and Whiten, "Machiavellian Intelligence. "

Subgame Perfection and Backwards Induction

We have looked at two solution concepts—ways of finding equilibria in games—so far. The first we saw was *rationalizability*, which involves eliminating dominated strategies. The second was the *Nash equilibrium*, which involves finding best response strategies. All rationalizable equilibria are also Nash equilibria, but not vice versa, so they are not equivalent. They also have different rationales and methods. As we saw in the last section, the rationale and plausibility of Nash equilibria are not always clear. More important, though, most games have more than one Nash equilibrium. Some of these seem more reasonable or plausible than others, though, and this has led theorists to think about how to "refine" the Nash solution concept to pick out some equilibrium solutions and reject others by adding additional conditions or desiderata. We will look at two closely related versions of that approach in this section: subgame perfection and the rationale for it, backwards induction.

The Farmer's Game

Let's return to the Prisoner's Dilemma, but model it as a sequential game in extensive form. David Gauthier tells a tale adapted from David Hume:

> My crops will be ready for harvesting next week, yours a fortnight hence. Each of us will do better if we harvest together than if we harvest alone. You will help me next week if you expect help in return that I shall help you in a fortnight. Suppose you do help me. Consider my decision about helping you. I have gained what I wanted—your assistance. Absent other not directly relevant factors, helping you is a pure cost to me. To be sure, if I were to help you I should still be better off than had I harvested alone and not helped you, but I should be better off still if having received your help, I did not return it. This calculation may appear short sighted. What about next year? What about my reputation? If I do not help you, then surely I shall harvest alone in future years, and I shall be shunned by our neighbors. But as it happens I am selling my farm when the harvest is in and retiring to Florida, where I am unlikely to cross paths with anyone from our community.[31]

Being rational persons, we both know that the scenario I have sketched is plausible. It would be pointless of me to pretend otherwise. So, you know that I would not return your help, and being no sucker, that will therefore leave me to harvest my crops alone. Neither of us will assist the other, and so each of us

---

31. Gauthier, "Assure and Threaten."

will do worse than need be. If this is a correct representation of our situation, we will fail to gain the potential benefits of cooperation.[32] The problem is depicted in figure 5.3.

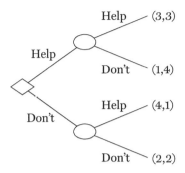

FIGURE 5.3. Farmer's Game

My neighbor chooses at the diamond, I choose at the ovals; payoffs are ordered from 4 (best) to 1 (worst), first my neighbor's, then mine. Now, in analyzing game trees of this sort we suppose that if we start at any node, we can think of that node as *subgames* in the larger game. The rational players should make the rational move at any subgame. So, we can split above as depicted in figure 5.4.

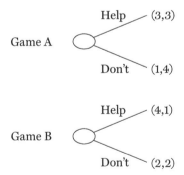

FIGURE 5.4. Decomposed Farmer's Game

Both these games start at the second node. So, if you are player 2, you must decide what you will do in each game. Rationally, your choice is easy. In Game A, helping gets you a worse payoff, so you will not help. And in Game B, you

32. Gauthier, "Assure and Threaten"; Hume, A Treatise of Human Nature, bk. III.ii.5.

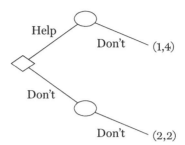

FIGURE 5.5. Sub-Game Perfect Strategies in the Farmer's Game

also do better by not helping, so you will not help again. Now we face the problem that since the other farmer knows all this, and knows you play the subgame perfect move, the farmer won't be inclined to help in the first place, knowing that you won't reciprocate. So now she looks at the original game, knowing what you (the second player) will do.

You neighbor has trimmed the "tree" of moves by you that are not *subgame perfect*, which is to say moves that are dominated in any subgame. So, the famer plays the only subgame perfect move and does not help. As in the familiar versions of Prisoners' Dilemma, we are both stuck at a Pareto-inferior outcome.

Two Kidnappers

Betty has kidnapped Alf.[33] Betty would like to get the ransom money, release Alf, and then walk away. She certainly wants the ransom money and to avoid jail. Alf wants to get away with his life! Figure 5.6 depicts the game, with Betty moving at the square and Alf at the circle, with cardinal utilities.

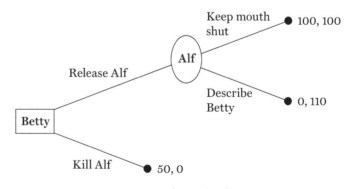

FIGURE 5.6. Kidnapper's Dilemma

---

33. See Ken Binmore, *Game Theory: A Very Short Introduction* (Oxford: Oxford University Press, 2007), 44–47.

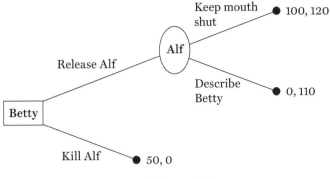

FIGURE 5.7. Kidnapper's Dilemma

Alas! Alf is rational and will play the subgame perfect move and will de-scribe Betty if he is set free. Betty knows this, and so will kill Alf—though both would prefer at the beginning of the game the "release/keep mouth shut" outcome.

Now suppose that Alf has grown attached to Betty during his long captivity. He now *wants* her to get away with it. So, for him the best option is for her to release him and for her not to get caught, his second-best option is to be re-leased and Betty gets caught because he ends up ratting, and the worst, not surprisingly, is to get killed by Betty. Now things look better for Alf and Betty, as the figure shows. Betty now will release Alf.

Backwards Induction

An outcome arrived at via subgame perfect moves will be a Nash equilibrium. "Backwards induction" is the typical method for solving a sequential game and is based on the crucial idea of *modular rationality*, which says that at each pos-sible point in the decision tree, a rational chooser always takes the best option. When trying to find the solution to a game, we start at terminal nodes; we know that if that node is a solution to the game, the last chooser got us to that node by taking the option that maximized his utility. Using this same assumption—that at every point in the tree the chooser took the course that maximized her utility—we can trace back through the trees the series of deci-sions that would lead to that outcome. Only a path along which, at every point, each chooser took the action that maximized her utility is consistent with the assumption of modular rationality. A utility maximizer would not choose an action that satisfied lower-ranked rather than higher-ranked preferences. The result of this path will always have eliminated dominated choices, and the re-sult will be a Nash equilibrium.

Subgame Perfect Equilibrium

In extensive games of perfect information where there is common knowledge of rationality, an equilibrium is subgame perfect when a Nash equilibrium is played at every node of the game and subgames are eliminated by backwards induction.

We can see how backwards induction works by looking at the centipede, represented in figure 5.8.

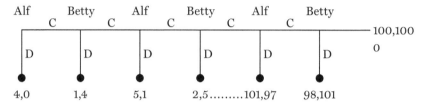

FIGURE 5.8. Centipede Game

In this Centipede game, players take turns. At node 1, Alf can either cooperate or defect. If he defects the game ends, with him getting 4 and Betty getting 0. Or else he can cooperate and send the money on to Betty. If there is a second node, Betty can then either cooperate or defect. If she defects the game ends, and she gets 4 and Alf gets 1; if she cooperates, she sends the money back to Alf. If Alf gets to make a choice at the third node, he can either end the game by defecting (in which case he gets 5 and Betty gets 2), or he can send the money on to Betty. If they keep the game going to its end, each ends up with 100.

But will they? At the final and last node, Betty has the option of either getting 101 (by defecting) or 100 (by sending the money to the end). Subgame perfection requires that she choose to end the game (101 > 100). But, since Alf knows that she will do this on her last move at his penultimate move—his choice is between 101 and 98—subgame perfection requires that he ends the game by defecting, getting 101. You should be able to see that the logic of backwards induction goes right back to the first move and indicates that Alf ought to defect at the first-choice node, and so the final payoffs are 4,0. Hardly an inviting result! We will look at a similar game in chapter 6, the trust game, and find that most real players don't do what subgame perfection requires.

Gauthier's Solution

Think again about the Farmer's Game. David Gauthier is convinced that an adequate conception of rationality cannot lead to this result (or to the 4,0 result in the Centipede game). The aim of rationality is that one's life goes "as well as possible," but in these games, subgame perfection instructs one to do what does not make one's life go well. He argues:

> If a person's reasons take their character from her aim, then it is surprising and troubling if acting successfully in accordance with her reasons, she must sometimes expect to do less well in relation to her aims than she might. If my aim is that my life go as well as possible, and I act successfully in accordance with the reasons determined by that aim, then should I not expect my life to go as well as possible? If the orthodox account of the connection between the aim and reasons were correct, then sometimes I should not expect success in acting on my reasons to lead to my life going as well as possible.[34]

Notice that Gauthier is invoking a version of rationality as effectiveness, which we discussed in chapter 1. For Gauthier, an action is "successful if and only if at the time of performance, it is part of a life that goes as well as possible for the agent." And he is clear that "an agent is primarily concerned with the outcome, and not the manner of her deliberations."[35] If someone follows what rationality requires and it is quite clear that in doing so she will not effectively achieve her goals, this shows that this was not truly the rational thing to do. He argues that "[D]eliberative procedures are rational if and only if the effect of employing them is maximally conducive to one's life going as well as possible."[36]

For Gauthier, then, rational people should pursue the Pareto-optimizing strategy if the other is willing to as well:

> [His] Pareto-optimizing theory . . . provides only a single set of directives to all the interacting agents, with the directive to each premised on the acceptance by the others of the directives to them. If the others are not prepared to cooperate, then an individual may have no way of reaching on his own an outcome that is optimal or, if optimal, that offers an acceptable division of the payoffs. In a Prisoner's Dilemma, a Pareto-optimizing analysis prescribes the dominated strategy for each, but if one agent can be expected to follow maximizing reasoning, were the other to attempt to optimize, he would have to choose his cooperative strategy, which would leave him with his worst possible outcome. It would be Pareto-optimal, because, being the other agent's best outcome, no alternative would be Pareto-superior to it.[37]

---

34. Gauthier, "Twenty-Five On."
35. Gauthier, "Twenty-Five On," 701.
36. Gauthier, "Twenty-Five On," 700.
37. Gauthier, "Twenty-Five On," 700.

Gauthier insists that the tie between rationality and optimality is so close that, when we see "fully rational" agents unable to secure mutually beneficial outcomes, we should reevaluate our very conception of rationality, and so eliminate subgame perfection as a basic requirement.

Nuclear Deterrence

Let's look at one more game. One with very high stakes.

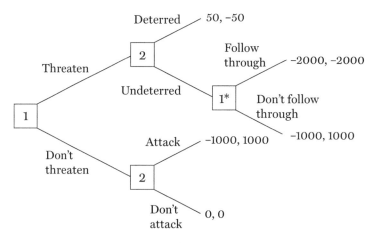

FIGURE 5.9. Nuclear Deterrence Game

This games models nuclear deterrence as it was understood during the Cold War. Player 1 seeks to deter an attack from Player 2, in which we assume Player 2 will be victorious (payoffs of −1000, 1000). So, Player 1 seeks to deter Player 2 with a nuclear threat. But by backwards induction, we know that at 1* the first player will not choose −2000 (nuclear war) over −1000 (i.e., being defeated in the attack). So, Player 2 will not believe the threat: it is not a credible threat. Therefore, a successful attack by Player 2 is the subgame perfect result. But can Player 2 count on Player 1 to abide by subgame perfection?

This leads us back to the definition of subgame perfection. Remember that the game must be one of perfect information and have common knowledge of rationality for subgame perfection to be an appropriate solution concept. To put it differently, we can only assume that both players will use backwards induction if they both believe the other is rational and they both share the same information about the game. In this case, it is plausible to assume that both conditions hold, though this won't always be the case. In this case, the credibility of Player 1's threat at the first node depends—because of backwards induction—on the rationality of carrying out the threat if Player 2 attacks. But, as we can see, doing so is worse for Player 1 than not retaliating. Given that Player 2 knows this, the credibility of Player 1's threat is undermined. Since the threat is incredible, though, this undermines deterrence. Paradoxically, both players in this situation would likely be better off if Player 1 could somehow credibly signal a commitment to carry out the less rational strategy if the threat were to fail.

Commitment

As in many of the games that we have seen, the conception of rationality used in game theory makes commitment to carry through on a sub-optimal strategy irrational and, hence, incredible. This is puzzling, as we have seen in numerous examples in this chapter, because it means that the only rational outcomes of several games are sub-optimal. In most of these games, the players could move to an optimal solution if they could credibly signal that they are committed to playing an off-equilibrium strategy at some point in the game. For instance, in the deterrence game, if Player 1 can credibly commit to playing the irrational strategy of retaliating after Player 2 initiates a first strike, this makes it less likely that Player 2 will strike first, thereby avoiding the war altogether. Similarly, in the Farmer and Kidnapper games, the problem is that since no one can make credible commitments to play strategies in later stages of the game that are ruled out by backwards induction, both parties are worse off.

In the Cold War, the United States was committed to a strategy of Mutually Assured Destruction (MAD). The idea was that the United States would not initiate a first strike against the Soviet Union, but would respond to any strike with overwhelming force, ensuring that both sides were completely destroyed. Given that the Soviets couldn't benefit from a first strike, the threat of retaliation would deter them from initiating conflict. Since the strategy relied on making the threat to retaliate credible, the United States put considerable resources into making it impossible for the Soviet Union to wipe out the retaliatory capacity in an effective first strike. This included dispersing and hardening command and control, diversifying the retaliation options, and improving the ability to detect a first strike. Nuclear capability was effectively a three-legged stool of land-based missiles, submarine-based missiles, and nuclear bombers. The last of these were always deployed and would likely withstand a missile-based first strike. The Soviets engaged in the same strategy, which led to a massive build-up of nuclear weapons and capability since any advantage would undermine the credibility of deterrence.

The weak point of this strategy was the so-called trembling hand of retaliation. If, for instance, an American president was told that the Soviets had launched a first strike against the United States, would the president really be willing to retaliate knowing that doing so would cause the deaths of at least hundreds of millions of lives, while also not saving the lives of any Americans? Maybe, maybe not. Fortunately, we haven't had to test this proposition, at least not yet.

MAD, from the point of backwards induction, seems like an obviously mistaken strategy. Given that there is no rational point in retaliating, the threat of deterrence is incredible and, hence, it makes sense for each side to strike first before the other does. The uniquely subgame equilibrium is to strike first! This conclusion could be avoided if either side were to credibly commit to retaliating, though. The movie *Dr. Strangelove* (1964) introduces a clever solution to this problem in the form of a "Doomsday Machine" that will automatically destroy the world if it detects a nuclear launch, thereby eliminating the trembling hand problem and ensuring that deterrence is effective.[38] The problem, in real life and in the movie, is that any device credible enough to ensure deterrence would also be prone to false positives, cases where an accident or rogue actor triggered the deterrence device. This is what happens in the film and the possibility of accidents leading to retaliation were very real—there were several cases that almost led to a full-scale nuclear war.

The real reason that MAD can work as a strategy is that neither of the conditions of subgame perfection is fulfilled in the real-life case of nuclear deterrence. As we can see from the cases of accidents, the game is not one of perfect information. Both the Soviets and the Americans used extensive espionage networks to learn as much about the capabilities of the other and their strategies as possible. Regardless, both sides were always partially in the dark about the other. Common knowledge of rationality could also not be assumed. Remember that "rationality" here means not playing dominated strategies at each node. But player error and irrationality are possible with actual agents and, hence, it is not obvious that either side would definitely not retaliate.

The larger point is that commitment is necessary in all sorts of human behavior, but largely shown to be irrational by game theory. As we will see in the next two chapters, to explain human behavior and institutions that do involve commitment, we need to introduce some important complications to the story of individual and strategic rationality that we have developed so far.

Conclusion

In this chapter we developed basic building blocks of game theory, which is an extension of individual rationality to strategic situations. Strategic—as opposed to parametric—rationality requires agents to take into account what

---

38. Such a device was proposed by American researchers at the RAND Corporation, and something similar was built but was probably not deployed by the Soviets.

other rational agents will do. We looked at several central solution concepts in game theory. The first, the Minimax theorem, applies in zero-sum games. The second, rationalizability, is applicable in solving games with only pure strategy solutions, while the third and most general, the Nash equilibrium, applies to any game with mixed strategies. We looked at the Prisoner's Dilemma, which has fascinated philosophers and social scientists because it suggests that there is at least one, possibly widespread case, where individual rationality and efficiency diverge. This challenges the normative attractiveness of the idea of welfare based on efficiency that we looked at in the last chapter. Coordination games raise the possibility of multiple equilibrium solutions, which introduces the "equilibrium selection" and equilibrium refinement problem. We looked at one such refinement, subgame perfection, and how it is connected to commitment. In the next chapter, we expand the complications and refinements of the basic game theoretic concepts we have developed here.

Discussion Questions

(1) Do we confront many zero-sum games? Would you say they are more common in the market or in politics? What do you think an economist would say?

(2) It is often said that the problem with the PD is that the parties cannot trust each other. If you absolutely know that the other party trusts you, what is your best strategy?

(3) Provide the matrix to show that your generation is caught in a PD, with each having to seek a university degree for jobs that previously did not require it. Do you think that is an accurate characterization?

(4) Experimental studies of people's behavior in the Prisoner's Dilemmas (where the payoffs are monetary) show that they cooperate much more than game theory would predict. Interestingly, humanities students seem to cooperate more than economics students. Does this show that (a) humanities students do not understand the game (as some economists have suggested); (b) that humanities students are irrational; or (c) that humanities students care less about money than economics students? If humanities students do not care as much about money, can they still be caught in a PD, where the rational thing would be to defect?

(5) Is Chicken a zero-sum game?

(6) Do you think games of Chicken are more common in politics or business? Can we talk of a zero-sum game in expected utility? How

could we do this without being able to interpersonally compare utility? (There is not a simple answer to this question!)

(7) Can war be rational?

(8) Provide two examples from politics where a rational person's best option is to play a Mixed Nash Strategy.

(9) Give a simultaneous Prisoner's Dilemma an extensive form (game tree). Solve it. Give a simultaneous game of chicken in an extensive form and solve it.

6

Advanced Topics in
Game Theory

In the last chapter we saw that individual rationality can be understood in strategic settings using game theory. We also saw that the rationality assumption at the heart of game theory seems to make commitment, cooperation, and reciprocity appear irrational. This is not the end of the story, though. In some contexts, the assumptions at the heart of traditional game theory and its solution concepts make sense and are excellent models of strategic rationality. For those that don't, it is possible that by expanding the notion of the strategic environment, the agents, or both, we can get a richer toolbox of game theoretic models. We look at some of those possibilities in this chapter.

Repeated Games

So far we have only looked at what are called "one-shot" games, that is, games that are only played once. In these games, the rational solution to the game is narrowly constrained since what happened in the past and what is likely to happen in the future doesn't matter. When games are repeated, however, each game becomes part of a larger game and this changes the rationality of playing certain strategies.

Most of the situations we face in real life are in essence some version of a repeated game, and often what looks like a one-shot game is actually a part of a larger repeated game. Think back to the football zero-sum game we looked at in the last chapter. In a real football game, coaches know that what play they call early in the game will affect what strategy they can expect their opponents to use later in the game. For instance, it is a common strategy to "establish the run" early in the game by repeatedly calling run plays in order to make it easier to complete big pass plays later in the game. A family of strategies known collectively as the "west coast offense" does the opposite and uses short and intermediate passing plays to open up running lanes.

This is not unique to football or to zero-sum games. When games are re-peated, new strategies open up. It is even possible for strategies that are not equilibrium strategies in a one-shot game to become equilibrium strategies in repeated games. Perhaps the most striking result here is with regard to one of the most troubling games we looked at in the previous chapter, the Prisoner's Dilemma.

Tit-for-Tat and the Evolution of Cooperation

Robert Axelrod, a contemporary political scientist, shows how rational indi-viduals may be able to cooperate in a Prisoner's Dilemma if they face an in-definite series of Prisoner's Dilemmas.[1] Table 6.1 presents his specification of the PD.

TABLE 6.1. Repeated Prisoner's Dilemma

		Betty	
		Cooperate	Defect
Alf	Cooperate	R, R	S, T
	Defect	T, S	P, P

$$\text{where } T > R > P > S \quad \text{and} \quad R > (S + T)/2,$$

Axelrod adds that $R > (S + T)/2$ to ensure that the cooperation payoff is greater than a payoff that could obtained by alternating being a sucker (S) and Taking (T) (defection).

An iterated PD is a series of Prisoner's Dilemmas. Alf and Betty will con-front each other repeatedly in such games. Thus, each game can be seen as part of a larger game. The critical idea in such a series is what has been called "the shadow of the future." Alf's play in this game is not simply determined by the payoffs in this game but also includes his expatiations with regard to the play in future games. If his play in this game can affect Betty's behavior in future games, then his concern is not simply this game's payoffs but a possible stream of payoffs going into the future.

Now, given what we know about backwards induction, we can see imme-diately why a finite series of Prisoner's Dilemmas played in a subgame perfect

1. Axelrod, "An Evolutionary Approach to Norms."

way leads to defection from the very first game. The reasoning here is the same as in the Centipede game we looked at in the last chapter. Suppose we have a series of 100 PDs of the form of the game represented above. Take the last one. In that game, Alf and Betty know that this will be their last game, and so there is no "shadow of the future." They will thus both play their dominant strategy and defect. Ah, but that means in game 99, they know that nothing they do in that game can affect future behavior, since it has already been determined that in game 100 they will both play the subgame perfect move and defect. Thus, as far as they are concerned, there is no "shadow of the future" in game 99 either, so they will play their dominant "defect" (T) strategy. This reasoning goes all the way back to the first move and, as in the Centipede game, they should defect in the first game.

To avoid this result, let us introduce the idea of an indefinitely long series of Prisoner's Dilemmas. To be more precise, Axelrod introduces a discount parameter, w, which reflects the fact the players are always uncertain whether there will be another game after this one. The parameter w is a discounting of the future—if the existence of a future allows future payoffs to cast a shadow over present decisions. The parameter w indicates that this future fades as the future gets further away. Thus, for Axelrod, the payoff for a string of defections (P), would be $P + w(P) + w_2(P) + w_3(P) + w_4(P) \ldots$, which equals $P/1 - w$. If the future is discounted at too high a rate, a person will play the current PD as a single-play game, since the future matters so little.

Axelrod has shown, using a computer simulation, that one of the best strategies is a very simple one, namely, tit-for-tat. According to tit-for-tat, your first move is the cooperative move. But if you're caught out and Alf defects rather than cooperates, the next time around you will be uncooperative too. In short, except for the first move of the game, you decide whether to cooperate or act aggressively with respect to any person by a simple rule: Do to the other what was done to me in the last round. Essentially, a tit-for-tat player says to others:

> If you defect on me in this game, you will get away with it, but I guarantee that in the next game I will defect, so that we will both be losers. But I am forgiving: if you start cooperating again, I'll begin cooperating again on the move after your cooperative move.

Axelrod constructed a computer program specifying a game with hundreds of moves, and a variety of actors employing different strategies. Some always act cooperatively no matter what others do, while some always defect. Each strategy played a 200-move game with each other strategy, thus creating more than 100,000 moves. In this strategy tournament, tit-for-tat won.

For a while people tended to think that tit-for-tat was *the* solution in iterated Prisoner's Dilemmas. It seemed "cooperative" (it started off by cooperating), it refused to be "suckered" more than once before punishing, and yet was "forgiving" (after one retaliation for defection, it would return to cooperation). However, tit-for-tat can lose against some strategies, and it has its own distinctive problems. If two tit-for-tatters are playing and Alf makes a mistake like accidentally defecting, Betty will punish him on the next round; so, he will then punish Betty on the round after that, to which Betty will respond by another round of punishment. They can go on and on, alternating punishments forever. A more forgiving strategy such as "it takes two defections in a row before I punish" can be more stable in the face of some errors. Perhaps even better is a strategy that randomly decides to be forgiving and then waits to see what happens.[2]

We can build into repeated game theory the possibility of learning, so that the players' responses change as they learn from interacting with other players. In this vein, Peter Vanderschraaf models a Hobbesian state of nature in which some players have more cooperative Assurance Game orderings while other players have less cooperative Prisoner's Dilemma ordering.[3] Vanderschraaf shows that if players tend to anticipate each other's strategies and learn from experience by changing their anticipations throughout the course of a game, even a population with a small number of noncooperators easily ends up at an equilibrium of a Hobbesian war of all against all.

Brian Skyrms has argued that because of the shadow of the future, we should focus more on assurance games like the stag hunt when thinking about social interaction than the Prisoner's Dilemma.[4] If we do, one thing we will learn is that the puzzle or rational cooperation is not, as Gauthier thought, about the tension between rationality and optimality, but rather about how to credibly signal to one's partner that one is likely to cooperate.[5] In general, it is important to distinguish between social dilemma problems like the PD and assurance problems like stag hunts or public goods provisions.[6] We will return to this topic in the next chapter.

2. Nowak and Highfield, SuperCooperators, chap. 1.

3. Assurance games, like the Stag Hunt, allow for rational cooperation insofar as each player can "assure" the other that they will play the cooperative equilibrium. See Vanderschraaf, "War or Peace?"

4. Skyrms, "The Stag Hunt"; Skyrms, The Stag Hunt and the Evolution of Social Structure.

5. Gauthier did see elements of this possibility, but it is not the core of his argument. See Gauthier, Morals by Agreement, chap. 6.

6. For a mechanism that distinguishes between the two, see Schmidtz, The Limits of Government.

The Folk Theorem

Another strategy in Axelrod's tournament was the "the Grim strategy." Grim cooperates on the first move, but if its opponent defects, Grim will punish for every move after that—forever. Two Grim players are also in a cooperative Nash equilibrium since neither would benefit from defection. The important thing is that *punishing* strategies can also achieve equilibrium. If Alf can punish Betty for defecting from a cooperative interaction, repeated Prisoners' Dilemmas allow what are essentially "self-policing contracts" to cooperate. Since we are playing indefinitely many games, Alf can afford to punish Betty to force her back to the cooperating table, and seeing that, Betty will not unilaterally defect.

The real insight here, though, is that *any* cooperative outcome that gives each player more (or, more formally, at least as much) as the minimum the player would get if the other player acted in the most punishing way can be an equilibrium. If we are each above this minimum point, then one party still has room to inflict punishment on the other for a deviation from the "contract." Thus the "minimax payoff" is the baseline since it is the payoff a person could obtain if her opponent treated the game as a zero-sum game in which he was intent on making sure she got as little as possible. As long as the agreement— the coordinated payoffs—is above this minimum there is room for punishment, and so unilateral defection will not pay. Thus, there will be a Nash equilibrium. This result is known as "the folk theorem."

This folk theorem is important since it shows that there are numerous pathways for cooperation in repeated games. It also shows, however, the crucial problem that repeated game introduce. Since any cooperative strategy that is at least as good as what one would get if one's partner defected can be a long-run equilibrium strategy, the possible solution space of a repeated game opens up considerably. This means that there will be a number of possible equilibriums in such games, with none being rationally required. This leads us back to the program of equilibrium refinement that we saw in the last chapter. As we will see again and again, introducing repetition and learning into game theory raises the problem of equilibrium selection.

The Evolution of Direct Reciprocity

On the model of "reciprocal altruism" or "direct reciprocity," evolutionary and rational actor analyses manifest a striking convergence. In his classical article on the "Evolution of Reciprocal Altruism," the biologist Robert L. Trivers argued that "the relationship between two individuals [organisms] repeatedly exposed to symmetrical reciprocal situations is exactly analogous to the

Prisoner's Dilemma."[7] Axelrod is a political scientist, but he also worked with the biologist William D. Hamilton in developing his ideas. In principle, the same analysis applies to cooperation between groupers and cleaner fish (Trivers) and trench warfare in the First World War (Axelrod). Robert Trivers also supposed that it was sequential, in which one player moved first. In strategic form, that would give us a game as depicted in table 6.2.

TABLE 6.2. Repeated Prisoner's Dilemma Conditional Strategies

		Betty			
		Do what A does	Do the opposite of what A does	Always cooperate	Always defect
Alf	Cooperate	R, R	S, T	R, R	S, T
	Defect	P, P	T, S	T, S	P, P

Trivers's examples included food sharing in humans and warning calls in birds. Suppose Alf shares food with Betty at time t_1; this increases the fitness of B, but A gives up some of his food. It is rational/fitness enhancing for "selfish" A to so act only if B returns the favor at time t_2 since otherwise Alf gets the "sucker" S payoff. But why would B refrain from suckering A? Clearly, if doing so secures yet more—future—assistance from A. We can also think of this in terms of punishment (as in the folk theorem): A can essentially "punish" the lack of reciprocity (defection) from B at t_2 by withholding future assistance at t_3. And, critically, the fitness of both is increased by the $\{R, R\}$ outcome over the $\{P, P\}$ outcome, so both are better off by assisting each other than mutually defecting.[8]

Evolutionary Games

In the last section, we noted the similarity of Axelrod's and Trivers's analysis of reciprocity in iterated PDs. Yet Axelrod's basic approach is radically different from Trivers's. In his book, *The Evolution of Cooperation*, Axelrod applied his

7. Robert L. Trivers, "The Evolution of Reciprocal Altruism."

8. Remember $\{R, R\}$ is also better than taking turns playing each other for a sucker, as specified by Axelrod's $(R > (S + T)/2)$.

analysis of tit-for-tat to trench warfare in the First World War.[9] That war was characterized by the combatants facing each other across small distances in opposing trenches; the lines tended to be stable for a long period, and the soldiers on each side could communicate with the other. On Axelrod's account, the ordering of the soldiers was typically:

1st I shoot, you don't
2nd No one shoots
3rd We both shoot
4th You shoot at me and I don't return fire

These, of course, are PD orderings. In a one-shot—no pun intended—game, the equilibrium is to shoot, and the implication is a long, drawn-out war. But, in the conditions of trench warfare, not only were the lines stable, but the same soldiers tended to face each other for long periods, and new soldiers were informed of the arrangement. And the arrangement was, Axelrod argues, tit-for-tat. "If you don't shoot to kill (shoot at me), then I won't shoot at you. If you do shoot, I'll shoot back, but then see what happens." Axelrod, drawing on the diaries of the soldiers, reports one incident in which a German soldier shouted to the British after an artillery shot, "We are very sorry about that; we hope no one was hurt. It is not our fault; it is the damned Prussian artillery."[10]

On the other hand, Axelrod also applies the PD to evolution, as did Trivers, of course. But here we confront a fundamental distinction between two types of game theory. In Axelrod's account of the soldiers, they rationally arrived at the tit-for-tat strategy, and if conditions changed, they would change the strategy. It seems that the tit-for-tat strategy came to an end when the High Command in the armies enforced fighting by making the troops charge each other. But in natural selection an organism does not "change" its behavior to adapt; rather, an individual organism acts out its "program," and those with less successful, less adaptive programs die out and are replaced by more adaptive types. What changes here is not the individual behavior but the "species behavior" in the sense that the average member of the species ends up acting differently.

Evolutionary game theory models typically employ "replicator dynamics." In games of this type, players encounter each other for a period, using different strategies. As play goes on, some strategies do less well than others. The replicator dynamic—say, at the end of a period—will adjust the relative representation of the types in the population, increasing the percentage of the more

9. Axelrod, Evolution of Cooperation.
10. Axelrod, Evolution of Cooperation, 85.

successful and decreasing the less successful. Then another period of play, and then another adjustment. This can continue for thousands of periods, modeling an evolutionary dynamic. No organism changes its behavior; but overall, the population can, because the types have changed. Notice there is no rationality involved here at all. Bacteria or, in the case of Axelrod's tournament, fixed computer programs, can compete and "evolve," but they aren't acting rationally in the traditional sense.

We can think of each strategy as "hard-wired" with the "players" simply acting on the instructions of their strategy, never modifying or abandoning their strategy. The typical replicator dynamic has strategies replacing other strategies over time in the population. We can suppose that strategies that do better are more *fit* in that environment; we might suppose that the number of players following a strategy is positively correlated with how fit that strategy is. So, the fitter the strategy, the faster it grows within a population. Notice, then, that we can thus remove reason and choice from game theory. Indeed, we can even remove the players, and simply think of the strategies playing each other. Because this approach to game theory is based in rational choice, it is unpopular among economists and it raises distinctive philosophical problems. We can see some of these by looking at some classic examples of evolutionary game theory in action.

Hawk-Dove Game

Think of a population that is divided between Hawks and Doves.[11] When they come into conflict over who will occupy a territory, Hawks act aggressively, while Doves back off. When a Hawk meets a Dove, the Dove quickly retreats; when a Hawk meets another Hawk there is combat, in which one Hawk will win, but the other will be defeated and injured in a fight. Let's say that any Hawk will win half the time against another Hawk. When two Doves meet, they might engage in some bluffing, one randomly will back down, and no fight results. Suppose Hawks and Doves are types of individuals in the population. A hawk always battles for a territory until either it is injured or its opponent retreats. A Dove engages in display battle and if it meets a Hawk, it quickly retreats without injury; if it meets another Dove, half the time it will retreat—in no case does it sustain injury. Let v be the value of the territory (and suppose it is positive); and c be the cost of injury from fighting over a territory; then when two hawks encounter one another they can expect $\frac{1}{2}(v - c)$. The general form of the game is represented in table 6.3.

---

11. This game is explored in detail in Maynard Smith, Evolution and the Theory of Games.

TABLE 6.3. Hawk-Dove Game

	Hawk	Dove
Hawk	$\frac{1}{2}(v-c)$	v
Dove	0	$\frac{1}{2}v$

This is an evolutionary game. Again, players do not change strategies, but play their strategy against whomever they meet. So "Hawk" always plays hawk and "Dove" always plays dove—they never vary their response.

If we assume the value of the territory is less than the cost of fighting ($v<c$), when a Hawk meets another Hawk, they will get caught in a destructive battle. Think of this as {don't swerve/don't swerve} in a game of Chicken from the last chapter. When a Hawk meets a Dove, the expected payoff is the value of the territory for the Hawk. Again, in the game of Chicken this is the payoff for not swerving when the other swerves; the Dove (or we might say chicken) runs away and the Hawk wins. Let's denote the expected Hawk payoff against a Dove as $E(H|D) = v$, i.e., the expected payoff of Hawk playing against Dove is v. When two Doves play each other, each gets a payoff of $E(D|D) = \frac{1}{2}v$. They have a small ritual fight, one flees and the other stays—assume that this is random, so 50% of the time each Dove gets the territory in a conflict with another Dove. In the game of Chicken, this is like {swerve/swerve}; both take the cautious option.

The form of the payoffs in Hawk-Dove are the same as the payoffs of Chicken. But again, it needs be stressed that row and column are no longer individual players who can vary their strategies; when a Hawk meets another Hawk, it will still play Hawk. In the game of Chicken this will not happen since, if Alf knows that Betty will not swerve, he certainly will swerve. And in the Hawk/Dove game, if two Doves meet, they will both "swerve," but this will not happen in Chicken; if Betty knows that Alf is a "chicken" she will not also "chicken." Because the Hawks and Doves do not adjust their moves to the anticipated moves of the other players, we cannot say that off-diagonal cells are in equilibrium in the Hawk/Dove game, though they are in Chicken.

So, if the Hawks and Doves do not vary their strategy, what constitutes "playing" or "winning" the game? In evolutionary game theory, your strategy "wins" if, compared to the opponents, those following your strategy have greater reproductive fitness, which is to say roughly that they reproduce at a greater rate such that, over many generations, they tend to dominate the population. We can assume that reproductive fitness is correlated with how many points the strategy accumulates in each generation so that the more points the strategy accumulates—we can think of this as the more food and other goods it gets—the more able it is to reproduce.[12] So as the Hawks and Doves play each other again and again, the percentage of Hawks and Doves in the population from generation to generation will vary with how many points they gather in our Hawk/Dove game.

Whether it pays to be a Hawk (or a Dove) depends on the composition of the rest of the population and the respective costs of conflict and the value of territory. Suppose that we have a population of all Hawks, for every interaction the expected payoff is the conflictual payoff. Imagine we introduce a Dove. Now its average payoff will be 0; although the average payoff of the Hawks will go up a tiny bit—when a Hawk does find the Dove the Hawk gets v, which is greater than 0—overall, the Dove will still do better than the average Hawk. Every time a Dove meets a Hawk, it gets 0, whereas the Hawks are caught in serious fights with an expected payoff of less than zero. So, a mutant Dove will thrive in a population of all Hawks. If we invert the story and start with a homogeneous Dove population, it is even clearer how a mutant Hawk will thrive. The Dove population will have an average payoff of ½ v, but the mutant Hawk will get v in all its interactions with the Doves.

Evolutionary Stable Strategies

There are different proposals for a solution or equilibrium concept applicable to these games, but the most common is when the population achieves a mix in which neither strategy can increase its share in the population at the expense of the other. This idea can be formalized in terms of an *evolutionary stable strategy* (ESS). The basic idea of the ESS is that a strategy can't be invaded by a mutant strategy. So, if the population is made up of one strategy S, it is evolutionarily stable if any S does better by playing against any other S than a mutant S* would do playing against an S. In cases where the expected value of S playing against another S is the same as S playing against S*, the population can still be in an ESS if S playing against the mutant S* does better than the mutants do playing against each other

Evolutionary Stable Strategy (ESS)

Let us say that S is an evolutionary stable strategy if and only if, with respect to a mutant strategy S* that might arise, where E(S|S) means the expected payoff of strategy S when it plays another S:

---

12. Strictly speaking, fitness and replication are not the same, but it is an ongoing debate among philosophers of biology exactly how they are related.

Either:

$$\text{(i) } E(S|S) > E(S^*|S)$$

Or

$$\text{(ii) } [E(S|S) = E(S^*|S)] \text{ \& } [E(S|S^*) > E(S^*|S^*)]$$

The idea is this. Suppose that we have an S population in which one or a few S* types are introduced. Because of the predominance of S types, both S and S* will play most of their games against S. According to the first rule, if S does better against S than S* does against S, S* will not get a foothold in the population. Suppose instead that S* does just as well against S as S does against itself. Then S* will begin to grow in the population, until there are enough S* so that both S and S* play against S* reasonably often. According to the second rule, once this happens, if S does better against S* than S* does against itself, S will again grow at a more rapid rate. To say, then, that S is an ESS is to say that an invading strategy will, over time, do less well than will S.

In our Hawk-Dove case, the evolutionary stable strategy is a "mixed strategy" where this does not mean that players mix their strategies, but that the population contains a mix of strategies, in this case of Hawks and Doves. If we call the entire population P, we can see that in this case the ESS will occur when the expected payoff of Hawks playing the rest of the population is the same as the expected payoff of Doves playing the rest of the population, which is the same as the expected (average) payoff of the population playing against itself. Hawks and Doves do as well against the mixed population as the entire population on average does playing against itself.

More intuitively, we can see that the Hawks and Doves are in equilibrium: if any imbalance is introduced (suddenly more Hawks are born), the population will return to the evolutionary stable mix. The actual mix depends on the values of v and c. When the value of the territory is greater than the cost of conflict ($v \geq c$), Hawk is the unique ESS and Hawk can successfully invade a population of Doves and, in turn, resist invasion from mutant Doves. In this variant, the Hawk-Dove game is actually a Prisoner's Dilemma. If, as is more likely, the cost of conflict is greater than the value of the territory so that $v > c > 0$, then the mixed strategy equilibrium is v/c

Asymmetries and the Origin of Property Rights

All this assumes a rather simple, symmetrical model, in which the strategies meet each other randomly and they choose what to do independently of what the other does. The simple Hawk-Dove game is symmetrical in that both strategies treat the territory the same in the sense that neither the Hawk nor the Dove strategy can behave conditionally with respect to the territory. What if there were another strategy, though, that could vary whether it played Hawk or Dove based on whether it was on the territory in question? So, for instance, this strategy would play Hawk in defense of its territory and Dove if it is invading another territory. John Maynard Smith introduced a strategy into the simple Hawk-Dove game that he called "Bourgeois" since it has the middle-class virtue of respecting property.[13] If we add this strategy, we get the game represented in table 6.4.

TABLE 6.4. Hawk-Dove with Bourgeois Strategy

	Hawk	Dove	Bourgeois
Hawk	$\frac{1}{2}\,(v-c)$	v	$\frac{3}{4}\,v - \frac{1}{4}\,c$
Dove	0	$\frac{1}{2}\,v$	$\frac{1}{4}\,v$
Bourgeois	$\frac{1}{4}\,(v-c)$	$\frac{3}{4}\,v$	$\frac{1}{2}\,v$

The payoff here may be a little hard to parse, but the upshot is that Bourgeois has found a way to get the best of both worlds of Hawk-Dove, by introducing a territorial asymmetry. Bourgeois can be seen as a "first possession" strategy, which acts like a Hawk on its own territory but a Dove off its territory. As Brian Skyrms has shown, this territorial asymmetry is an example of a correlated convention mechanism.[14] Two Bourgeois will not fight over a territory since the Bourgeois already in possession will act like a Hawk, and the one who is off his territory will act like a Dove. In the table of this game, we assume that Bourgeois is "at home" half of the time.

Suppose that Bourgeois conducts half its confrontations with other Bourgeois on its own territory. We can see that Bourgeois does better against Hawk than Hawk does against itself. That is, when Hawk meets another Hawk their average payoff is $\frac{1}{2}\,(v-c)$, but Bourgeois will only fight half the time—when it is on its own territory—so it only gets the Hawk-Hawk payoff half of the time, which is $\frac{1}{4}\,(v-c)$. This is less costly than what Hawk can expect. Bourgeois also does better against Dove than Dove does against itself. When two Doves come together, their expected payoff is $\frac{1}{2}\,v$, while Bourgeois will win

13. One of the authors calls the same type of strategy "Lockean" in Gaus, The Order of Public Reason.

14. Skyrms, The Stag Hunt and the Evolution of Social Structure, 76–79.

against Dove half of the time that Bourgeois is in its own territory and will draw with Dove the other half of the time, which is ¾ v.

So, since Bourgeois does better against each than each does against itself, Bourgeois can invade both the Hawk and Dove populations. Moreover, once it takes over, we can see that, according to ESS, it will be stable vis-à-vis Hawks and Doves. Recall that when it plays itself its expected payoff is ½ v. Thus, Bourgeois does better against itself than either Hawk or Dove does against it and they could not invade a Bourgeois population.

Ownership can be understood as a common asymmetry in real Hawk-Dove type encounters.[15] Many have seen in this example what Herbert Gintis calls the "property equilibrium."[16] Introducing an asymmetry in terms of property helps us avoid fights over resources and allows cooperation.[17] Over the long term, many have thought, we can expect to see social convergence on some Bourgeois (in our broad sense) conception of property rights. This is largely what we do see across most societies. There is, however, a puzzle here since Bourgeois is not the only possible asymmetrical strategy. There are actually many more, but one interesting strategy introduced by John Maynard Smith that we can call the Anti-Bourgeois strategy does the opposite of Bourgeois by playing Dove when it is "at home" and "Hawk" when it is away.[18]

TABLE 6.5. Hawk-Dove with Bourgeois and Anti-Bourgeois Strategy

	Hawk	Dove	Bourgeois	Anti-Bourgeois
Hawk	½ $(v-c)$	v	¾ $v - $¼ c	¾ $v - $¼ c
Dove	0	½ v	¼ v	¼ v
Bourgeois	¼ $(v-c)$	¾ v	½ v	½ $v - $¼ c
Anti-Bourgeois	¼ $(v-c)$	¾ v	½ $v - $¼ c	½ v

Although this strategy is somewhat paradoxical in that it leads to an infinite regress, anti-bourgeois is also an ESS in this game. This means that the common story that labeling asymmetries can lead to stable property (or quasi-property) regimes is not so straightforward.[19]

15. Maynard Smith, Evolution and the Theory of Games, chap. 8.
16. Gintis, "The Evolution of Private Property."
17. Schotter, The Economic Theory of Social Institutions.
18. Maynard Smith, Evolution and the Theory of Games, 96–97.
19. Sherratt and Mesterton-Gibbons, "The Evolution of Respect for Property."

Nevertheless, there are several insights to be gained by looking at this game in the way that we have. The first is that the symmetrical game is wasteful compared to the asymmetrical one. Introducing labeling asymmetries in the case of "ownership" here helps avoid wasteful conflict. The lesson may be that it is often beneficial to take advantage of asymmetries in natural and social situations. As we saw in the example of the Battle of the Sexes from the last chapter, both parties are better off adopting either asymmetric solution rather than playing the symmetric mixed-strategy solution. The second lesson is that arbitrary asymmetries can be ESS, but the puzzle is why the "property" equilibrium seems to be more common than the "anti-property" ESS.[20] There are several reasons why the property equilibrium seems to outperform the anti-property one in most environments, but the larger lesson is that in evolutionary game theory—as in all game theory—game theoretic models need to be carefully considered in the ecological context that they are modeling.

Polymorphic Equilibria

ESS may be either be monomorphic, in which a single strategy takes over, or polymorphic, where more than one strategy is in equilibrium. Insofar as our interest is often with morality and related social concerns, we may worry about polymorphic outcomes, in which the population settles into an equilibrium where people have, say, different "strategies" concerning what is right or just.

Consider a very simple case drawn from Brian Skyrms's work.[21] Suppose we are playing a cake-cutting game in which each party makes a claim for a fraction of the cake. If their total claims are not greater than 100% of the cake, both players get their claim; if the total claims exceed the whole cake, neither player gets any cake. Suppose that there are three strategies: demand ⅓, demand ½, demand ⅔. It is possible for a population to end up in what Skyrms calls a "polymorphic trap"—a mixed equilibrium in which people have different demands. The population might divide into a mix of the Greedy (always demanding ⅔) and the Meek (always demanding ⅓). Whether they do so, or whether one strategy such as "demand ½" takes over the entire population, depends on the relative size of each strategy in the initial population *and* also on whether strategies can find the right players to play against. If "demand ½ players" have a better than random chance of meeting, it becomes far easier for them to take over the population, so that the entire population moves toward a ½ monomorphic equilibrium.

20. Herbert Gintis discusses this at length in The Bounds of Reason, chap. 11.
21. Skyrms, Evolution of the Social Contract, 14ff.

Skyrms has also employed evolutionary game theory to examine the conditions under which in the Stag Hunt the equilibrium will be on hunting stag rather than hunting hare, that is, when we find cooperative practices that make us all better off rather than each going our own way.[22] What is interesting is that for large groups hunting hare can easily take over; indeed, even in small groups in which players have a modest chance of being wrong in their conjectures about how their neighbors will play, hare hunting can quickly take over. An interesting aspect of Skyrms's analysis is that he distinguishes two different types of dynamics: best response and imitate the best. Best response is the crux of game theory: we consider the moves of others and respond to them in a way that maximizes our payoffs. But since evolutionary game theory is not really about rational choice, we can analyze a very different type of dynamic: look around, see which of the neighbors is doing well, and imitate that behavior. In evolutionary games of the Stag Hunt, best response and imitate the best dynamics can lead to very different outcomes.

ESS and Nash

While it should be clear that all ESS are Nash Equilibria, the reverse is not true. Some Nash equilibria are not ESS. Let's return to a game we looked at in the last chapter, Rock, Paper, Scissors, changed slightly to make it more amenable to evolutionary analysis.[23] In the new version, each strategy replicates at the rate of its payoff below, where the replication of the strategies is indicated by their payoffs with $a > 1$.[24]

TABLE 6.6. Rock-Paper-Scissors

	Paper	Rock	Scissors
Paper	1, 1	$a, 0$	$0, a$
Rock	$0, a$	1,1	$a, 0$
Scissors	$a, 0$	$0, a$	1,1

22. Skyrms, The Stag Hunt and the Evolution of Social Structure.

23. The representation of this game follows Zhijian Wang, Bin Xu, and Hai-Jun Zhou, "Social Cycling and Conditional Responses in the Rock-Paper-Scissors Game." 5830, https://doi.org/10.1038/srep05830.

24. If $a < 2$, the Nash equilibrium of each strategy at $1/3$ of the population is unstable. If $a > 2$, it is stable but it still exhibits cycling dynamics. See Wang et al., "Social Cycling and Conditional Responses in the Rock-Paper-Scissors Game."

The game involves an intransitive cycle whereby Rock beats Scissors, which beats Paper, which beats Rock. The mixed-strategy Nash equilibrium involves playing each strategy one-third of the time, so we might expect the population to stabilize with each strategy represented as one-third of the population, but this is not what we find. Instead, the population cycles between various polymorphic mixes of the population.[25] The Nash Equilibrium is not an evolutionary stable strategy.

Scientists have found cycling behavior that matches what we see in the Rock, Paper, Scissors model in nature. One is male side-blotched lizards (*Uta stansburiana*).[26] The males of this species have a coloration on their throats that—as in the asymmetry in the Hawk-Dove game that we saw above—indicates how likely they are to defend their territory. Blue-throated lizards are very aggressive and defend a large territory, orange-throated lizards are somewhat aggressive and defend a smaller territory, while lizards with yellow stripes on their throats are not aggressive at all and don't defend any territory. Reproduction rates depend on how much territory (and hence females) each lizard can defend. The types cycle over time, with no stable distribution ever emerging in exactly the same way that we see in the Rock, Paper, Scissors game. The scientists who discovered this dynamic explain:

> As in the game where paper beats rock, scissors beat paper, and rock beats scissors, the wide-ranging "ultra-dominant" strategy of orange males is defeated by the "sneaker" strategy of yellow males, which is in turn defeated by the mate-guarding strategy of blue males; the orange strategy defeats the blue strategy to complete the dynamic cycle. Frequency-dependent selection maintains substantial genetic variation in alternative male strategies, while at the same time prohibiting a stable equilibrium in morph frequency.

Similar phenomena have been studied in other species, including in E. coli bacteria populations.[27]

Evolutionary Game Theory and Rationality

At this point it is not clear whether further exploration of evolutionary game theory will enlighten us about our main concern—rationality. Evolutionary game theory might be understood as reviving Rationality as Effectiveness: our

---

25. The free agent-based modeling tool Net-Logo (http://ccl.northwestern.edu/netlogo /index.shtml) includes Rock, Paper, Scissors as one of its demo models so you can download the program and see how the population cycles given how you set a variety of parameters in the game.

26. Sinervo and Lively, "The Rock–Paper–Scissors Game."

27. Kerr et al., "Local Dispersal Promotes Biodiversity."

model of a "rational" agent is simply a being that engages in instrumentally effective behavior. We saw, though, that effective action can be divorced from
rationality, thus evolutionary game theory can devote itself simply to the study
of effective behavior, be it in bacteria, birds, or humans. In an important sense,
this vindicates our rejection of Rationality as Effectiveness since if we adopted
it, our "theory of rationality" can apply to genes or bacteria, but that clearly
must mean it is not a theory of rational action at all. As we suspected at the
outset, even instrumental rationality must involve more than effective action.

Signaling

Closely related to evolutionary games are signaling games, where parties in the
game try to indicate what they intend to do or who they are to other players.
These are games of imperfect information where at least one of the parties
doesn't know the type of player or the payoffs of the other party. In the basic
signaling game, there are two players, the sender and the receiver. The sender
is able to send a message to the receiver and the receiver must use that information to decide what to do. The sender is one of several types, which is unknown
to the receiver. The sender sends a message to convince the receiver that the
sender is one type rather than another.

   This kind of game is best illustrated by an example. Imagine that Alf is a
fisherman who has done well for himself and his family over the summer and
has salted enough fish to keep his family fed throughout the winter. In the
surrounding town, however, there has been a bad harvest and the rest of the
townsfolk have not been able to source sufficient provisions to feed them and
their families through the winter. In a town meeting, Betty remembers that Alf
mentioned that he has a surplus of fish. Betty implores the other townsfolk to
go seize the fish that Alf, she claims, has so selfishly hoarded. She reasons that
since he knows that he cannot withstand the combined force of the entire
town, he will give up immediately and hand over his food without a fight. So,
merely by threatening to seize his food, Alf will give it up.

   Betty is using backwards induction to determine that a rational actor, seeing
that the situation is hopeless, will acquiesce to the demands of the mob at the
outset. The paradoxical implication is that, if Alf is rational, he can expect his
food to be seized anytime the mob gets hungry. But this conclusion assumes
that Alf is rational in the strict sense that backwards induction requires. It also
assumes that Alf's rationality is common knowledge. This scenario is one more
example of the deterrence problem that we looked at in the last chapter. As in
that game, if Alf can commit himself and credibly signal that he will play an
off-equilibrium strategy in the later part of the game, he can potentially deter
attack.

If he is unable to do this, the implications are pretty dire. Since Alf will know any time the mob wants his food and that they can take it whenever they want, he will be less likely to spend the time and energy finding the surplus food in the first place. This will mean less surplus for trade and fewer opportunities for specialization. As Kim Sterelny has argued, deterring potential expropriators was a crucial problem in the evolution of large-scale cooperation for precisely this reason.[28] Thomas Hobbes makes a similar point in *Leviathan*, arguing that there is no possibility for trade and cooperation in the state of nature.[29]

What Alf needs to do is to signal that he is committed to defending his property and, hence, is not rational in the sense of always playing equilibrium strategies. He needs to show that he is a hawk rather than a dove and that even though he may not be able to successfully defend his resources against the mob, he will inflict enough damage on them in the process to make the prospect seem less attractive. This is where signals come in since he needs to communicate somehow that he is the type of person who will irrationally defend his property regardless of the odds of his success. How would he go about doing this?

One possibility is that he could just send a message to the town meeting telling them that he will defend himself in the case of an attack. Since this message would cost him nothing to send, it is an example of "cheap talk." There is nothing that Alf is communicating by sending the message other than the words of the message itself. Let's say, in this example, that Alf is actually prepared to defend his resources with a fanatical ferocity. If, instead, Alf was bluffing, there would be no way to tell from the message. There is nothing about the message that helps Betty and her mob distinguish between a bluff and a true threat from Alf. This shows an important part of signaling theory—signals that anyone can causelessly send can't help with distinguishing between types since they could just as easily be sent by anyone, regardless of type. This is why talk is "cheap"–since anyone can do it, it doesn't mean anything. The signal, in the case of cheap talk, is indistinguishable from noise.

What Alf needs to do is make his signal costly, distinguishing it from cheap talk. One way he could do this is by having established a reputation over time of responding to aggression with violent retaliation, showing that he is the type of person likely to defend his property with fanatical zeal. This signal is costly since Alf will have had to pay a cost in these previous encounters to demonstrate his toughness. He might also show that he is erratic in some other way, thereby undermining the confidence that Betty should have in his rationality and, by extension his likelihood of playing equilibrium strategies. In the

28. See Sterelny, "Cooperation, Culture, and Conflict."
29. Hobbes, Thomas Hobbes, chap. 13.

context of the Cold War deterrence problem that we looked at in the last chapter, Richard Nixon adopted a "madman theory" in his foreign policy to lead the adversaries of the United States to suspect that he might act irrationally in the case of aggression against the United States.

Costly signaling is a common way of showing commitment and, thereby, of creating assurance that one is the type of person who will play certain types of ways. We can see this clearly by looking at prisoners, who are constantly under threat of violence from their fellow inmates. As Diego Gambetta explains, prisoners are at pains to "display features that testify to past fighting 'achievements' that leave observable traces such as scars. They also choose to cultivate activities that generally signal their fitness."[30] Weightlifting and visible scars show that one is capable of defending one's self and that there is a past history of having done so. As Gambetta points out, "Scars are not signs that one is a loser . . . They are rather signs that one has been through many fights and has survived."[31]

Tattoos also act as costly signals showing that one is able to withstand a certain amount of pain to get the tattoo, as well as demonstrating that one isn't likely to be able to pass easily in "polite society." Tattoos also often include information about what other prisons one has been in and what crimes one has committed. Face tattoos are especially effective, not only because they are the most visible, but also because they are impossible to hide. The same goes for tattoos with extreme messages. Gambetta quotes the description of the tattoos of an inmate in a South African prison:

[His] face is covered in tattoos. "Spit on my grave" is tattooed across his forehead; "I hate you, Mum" etched on his left cheek. The tattoos are an expression of loyalty . . . Facial tattoos are the ultimate abandonment of all hope of a life outside.[32]

New inmates are immediately tested with aggression. As Gambetta argues, the initiation of aggression is a test of type, and the new inmate must credibly signal that they are of the "tough" type to get along in prison.

The man is on trial, and he is fatefully examined. The penalty for failure is accelerated victimisation. If a man acquits himself fully, he ensures his immunity to attack. The test is manliness. The criterion is courage. Courage is evidenced by willingness to fight and by the capacity for doing so.[33]

30. Gambetta, Codes of the Underworld, 85.
31. Gambetta, Codes of the Underworld, 85–86.
32. Quoted in Gambetta, Codes of the Underworld, 41.
33. Gambetta, Codes of the Underworld, 99.

This signaling is crucial since prison seems to be a generalized game of deterrence, "The prison hierarchy seems to sort prisoners initially into two main types—not so much winners and losers, but fighters and passive victims."[34]

Prisons provide a stark example of the importance of signaling, but we can find other examples of it throughout nature and human society. The classic example is the male peacock, who invests considerable resources into developing impressive plumage to attract females. This is costly in terms of resources needed to make the tail as well as in handicapping the bird when it is flying. Because of this, the tail posed something of an evolutionary puzzle: why would such an expensive display be adaptive, given its costs? One explanation was sexual selection; peahens, for whatever reason, happened to like large tails, leading them to be selected for over time.[35] This explanation, however, has been outcompeted—so to speak—by another explanation using costly signaling. This theory, known as the *handicap principle*, argues that since only relatively healthy and strong males can afford to invest the resources and bear the costs related to having an elaborate tailfeather display, plumage of that sort reliably communicates relative health and strength.[36] The handicap is a costly signal. This principle has been generalized to show that even traits that are costly to everyone can be selected for insofar as they benefit "high" types more than "lower" types in a population.[37]

Signaling theory has been deployed to explain a number of puzzling phenomena in human society as well. One of the most important is job-market signaling theory.[38] In the job market, potential employers are not able to directly observe the type of potential employees, so they have to rely on indirect signals to distinguish "higher" from "lower" types. One kind of costly signal is one's education. Going to a "fancy" college and completing a degree signals that one not only values their skills and education enough to pay the price of going to college in terms of time and money, but also that the college in question already judged the applicant to be worthy enough to admit them.[39] Signaling is also important in reputation-based businesses like restaurants, hotels, transportation, car-dealers, doctors, and basically any indus-

---

34. Gambetta, Codes of the Underworld, 100.

35. For a general account of sexual selection, see Ridley, The Red Queen.

36. Zahavi, "Mate Selection—a Selection for a Handicap"; Grafen, "Biological Signals as Handicaps."

37. Hutteffer et al., "The Handicap Principle Is an Artifact."

38. Spence, "Job Market Signaling."

39. Taken to its limit, this line of argument can be used to show that higher education's primary value is in the costly signal it sends. On this, see Caplan, The Case against Education.

try where one party in the exchange is likely to have more information about the quality of the good or service than the other. Used-car dealers, where this problem is acute, have developed elaborate mechanisms for signaling that they are honest dealers.[40] Further afield, feuds and honor can be seen as signaling mechanisms.[41]

What signaling games and signaling theory show us, in a different way, is something we learned by looking at evolutionary game theory, namely that we can't assume that a given population is uniform in its composition. We also can't assume that all the agents have perfect knowledge or that there is common knowledge of rationality. This is an important part of explaining why many of the games that we looked at in the last chapter are instructive but only tell part of the story about the questions that motivate us in PPE. Much of the behavior in real political and economic environments is involved in developing signaling systems to solve the puzzles that Prisoner's Dilemmas and Assurance problems introduce. In this sense, the basic game forms that we saw there are only the beginning of the story; one needs to look more closely at what is happening in the actual world to learn how people find ways to overcome strategic problems of rationality. We look at more systematic strategies in the next chapter.

Bargaining Theory

All of the games we have looked at so far are what are called noncooperative games. This is true even in the games where cooperation seems to be the goal, such as in coordination games. In the games we have looked at, pre-play communication is either not possible or it is pointless since it is "cheap talk."[42] More important, the players in these games are not able to form binding agreements. Recall the Prisoner's Dilemma, if the two prisoners could make a binding agreement with each other not to confess, they could achieve the optimal outcome, which eludes them. Cooperative game theory changes these two assumptions, allowing players to send credible communication and to make binding agreements. Doing so opens up a huge range of possibilities that are important to PPE. We will look at two classes of cooperative games here. The first are two-person bargaining problems and the second are multi-person coalitional games.

---

40. Akerlof, "The Market for 'Lemons.'"

41. Thrasher and Handfield, "Honor and Violence: An Account of Feuds, Dueling, and Honor Killing."

42. The exception was in signaling games where it is possible to send costly signals.

The most extensively studied cooperative game and the most relevant to PPE is the bargaining game. In this situation, we can assume there are two parties who are trying to decide how to divide up some benefit to them both. Like in the coordination games we looked at, they are both better off by making an agreement, though they will not necessarily benefit equally from the agreement. The classic economic analogy is an agreement between a labor union and an industry. We can also think of the problem as representing the rational division of the benefits and burdens of social life more generally or the cooperative surplus of the economy as a whole. In this sense, it can serve as a general model of distributive justice. David Gauthier goes further and uses the bargaining problem as a model of the costs and benefit of morality.[43] Gauthier thinks of moral rules as imposing differential costs so that even if everyone benefits from having a morality, any specific morality may benefit some more than others. These differential costs and benefits need to be justified according to Gauthier for rational individuals to have reason to endorse and comply with the rules of morality.

In its general form, the bargaining problem seeks to understand which of the several potential contracts two rational individuals would choose, given that both parties' benefits form agreement, but do not share the same interests. Recall the idea of a Pareto frontier and contract curve from chapter 3. Basic economic theory can show that, given some basic assumptions, a series of potential Pareto-optimal contracts exist but, as we saw, it cannot distinguish between the relative rationality of those feasible options. Bargaining theory understood as solutions to the bargaining problem attempts to show that some of those agreements or contracts are more rational than others, ideally by showing that there is one uniquely rational agreement point that rational agents should settle on.

To do this, we need to model the bargaining problem. We start by assuming that any agreement will be costlessly enforced. We also assume that there is a set of bargainers N, which we will specify as Alf and Betty for our purposes. Not all of the results from two-person bargaining situations are easily extended, so we will focus on two people unless otherwise noted. There are two general approaches to modeling the bargaining problem, what Ariel Rubinstein calls the *axiomatic* and the *strategic* approaches.[44] The first abstracts the bargaining solution away from any process of bargaining and asks, as John Nash put it, what are the properties that "any reasonable solution" to the prob-

43. Gauthier, Morals by Agreement.

44. John Nash describes these as the axiomatic and negotiation approaches, but they mean roughly the same thing. See Nash, "Two-Person Cooperative Games."

lem should have.[45] The strategic approach looks at what solutions would come out of a reasonable process of bargaining. Ideally, these two methods will agree, but they are different in approach and so we will start with the more straightforward axiomatic approach.

The idea in the axiomatic approach is to show that, given a set of reasonable axioms, there is one solution to the bargaining problem that uniquely meets those conditions. To be a little more precise, we will need to characterize the problem and the solution more formally. Given two parties, say Alf and Betty, the bargaining problem is an attempt to find a unique point in two-dimensional real number space $(\mathbb{R}^2)$, which we call the bargaining "solution." We can think of every point in this space as being the Cartesian product of Alf's and Betty's respective proposals for agreement. These proposals are the payoffs—represented in von Neumann–Morgenstern utility functions for each player. Remember, these scales are not absolute values and are only unique with respect to linear transformations, which is to say we still can't make a direct utility comparison between the two players so that a payoff of 2 for Alf may not be equivalent to a payoff of 2 for Betty. If we say Alf's possible proposals are listed on the x axis and Betty's on the y axis, a proposal of $(1,1)$ would mean each proposed 1. We can limit this space by assuming there is a set of feasible agreements S that is also compact and convex.[46] There is also some disagreement point $d \in S$ that both parties can expect to reach if there is no agreement. The bargaining solution is a function that assigns a specific proposal based on its expected payoff to Alf and Betty within the feasible set S, given their disagreement points d.

The first and still most significant solution to the bargaining problem is the Nash solution. It proposes four seemingly straightforward axioms and shows that there is only one solution that satisfies all of them.

The first axiom is *linear invariance* and follows from the assumption that each player has vNM utility functions. The bargaining problem is rescaled to make the disagreement point d the common zero point of the utility scale for each player, making the feasible set S the whole of the bargaining set. Given the utility assumptions for each player, this axiom is uncontroversial, though this model of utility is not the only one that a bargaining problem could have. For instance, transferable or utility scales with interpersonal comparisons are, in principle, possible as well.

---

45. Nash, "Two-Person Cooperative Games," 136.

46. A set is compact if it is closed and it is bounded. It is strictly convex if a line drawn between every x and y value of the set in Euclidean space is within the interior of the set.

The second axiom, *Pareto optimality*, moves the feasible set of bargaining outcomes to the Pareto frontier of S. This assumes that neither player would be willing to take a worse outcome if a better one is available to them without making the other player worse off. This seems to be a requirement of rationality and common knowledge.

The third axiom, *symmetry*, says that if the bargaining space is symmetric such that the joint outcome for Alf and Betty doesn't depend on who is who, then the solution should also be symmetric. This assumption is a little trickier to make sense of than the others, though many take it to be trivial. Assume that when Alf and Betty come to an agreement, some third party gives them their respective payoffs in envelopes marked "Alf" and "Betty." This assumption says that, when every payoff in the bargaining space is reversible between Alf and Betty, the bargaining solution shouldn't depend on whose name is on the payout envelope in the end since, in effect, both are getting equivalent payouts. This assumption is needed to pick out a unique point in a narrowly constrained, symmetrical bargaining space. Once this is done, we can generalize this result with the conjunction of the next axiom and the first to generalize the result and guarantee that there will always be a unique solution to the bargaining problem.

The final axiom is called *Independence of Irrelevant Alternatives* (IIA). This axiom, which should not be confused either with the version that we have already encountered or that we will see in chapter 8, states that any bargaining solution should be consistent with regard to a contraction of the overall bargaining set so long as it remains within the feasible set. This may seem obscure, but the idea is that if certain options are taken off the table, as long as that option was not chosen in the original solution, it shouldn't make a difference to the outcome.

Given these four assumptions, John Nash showed that there was one and only one bargaining solution that is available, which has come to be called the Nash bargaining solution.

Nash Bargaining Solution

For a bargaining problem (S,d) with the feasible outcome space S and disagreement point d, there is only one solution $f(S,d)$ that meets the following four conditions:

1. Utility Invariance to Linear Transformation
2. Pareto Optimality
3. Symmetry
4. Independence of Irrelevant Alternative (IIA)

$$f(S,d) = \max_{s_{Alf}, s_{Betty} \in S} (s_{Alf} - d_{Alf})(s_{Betty} - d_{Betty})$$

The Nash solution maximizes the joint product of cooperation.

The Nash bargaining solution has proved to be incredibly popular as a bargaining solution concept among theorists. One reason is the simplicity of its result and the plausibility of its axioms. Under closer examination, though, the axioms are not as straightforward as they may seem. In a one-shot bargain, for instance, the Pareto assumption may seem like an implication of rationality, but if a bargain is part of a series, it may make sense to accept or propose non-optimal agreements for the benefit of future outcomes or to signal one's type.

Even more interesting, non–Pareto optimal outside options in a game can induce the other player to choose options that wouldn't otherwise be equilibria.[47] This is sometimes known as "money burning," where Alf's option to "burn money" and make a sub-optimal move can, even if Alf doesn't exercise this option, induce Betty to adopt a strategy that she wouldn't have otherwise. Imagine a very young child and a parent in public. The very fact that the child could throw a loud, unpleasant, and embarrassing tantrum if displeased can change the way that the parent will act, precisely to avoid this mutually destructive outcome. Anticipating the possibility of a destructive outside option and using past behavior as evidence of player type is called "forward induction."[48] This phenomenon is a combination of signaling and a result of the structure of the game being able to change the optimal set of strategies. This phenomenon makes more sense in the context of noncooperative representations of bargaining games (more on that below), but the larger point is that the rationality of behavior in bargaining scenarios will be pretty sensitive to the representation of the available and perceived outside options and beliefs about future encounters.

The symmetry assumption is also not as straightforward as it may seem. We can see this by looking at the changing justification that is given for it over time. In his original 1950 article on the bargaining problem, John Nash defends it by saying that it is a representation of the "equality of bargaining skill" of the parties.[49] Nash backs off from this justification in 1953, though, when he argues that it is not equal skill, but equal intelligence, that justifies symmetry.[50] Since the bargaining game is a game of complete information, there is no question of being able to fool or dupe one's partner. John Harsanyi (1920–2000) in 1961 gives a clearer justification for symmetry when he argues that the "symmetry postulate has to be satisfied, as a matter of sheer logical necessity, by any theory

47. Avery and Zemsky, "Money Burning and Multiple Equilibria in Bargaining."
48. Cooper et al., "Forward Induction in the Battle-of-the-Sexes Games."
49. Nash, "The Bargaining Problem."
50. Nash, "Two-Person Cooperative Games."

whatever that assigns a unique out-come to the bargaining process."[51] He means this literally. Without having the model apply equally to both players, it will be impossible to generate a unique solution to the bargaining problem.

John Harsanyi argues that the need for uniqueness creates two problems with regard to symmetry, one internal to the bargaining problem itself and the other external. The first is how to justify symmetry by appealing only to rationality.[52] Symmetry is a feature of structure of the model, not the rationality of the players. But this response leads to the question of the external validity of the bargaining problem in general and the Nash solution in particular. Thomas Schelling (1921–2016) raised this point early on when he argued that in no interesting cases of actual bargains or divisions would it be likely that agents would be situated symmetrically.[53] Schelling argued that this should lead us away from symmetrical models of game theory and bargaining toward more realistic and asymmetric models of conflict and cooperation. Harsanyi disagreed, and this dispute over how we should think about game theory still rages.

The most controversial assumption is IIA. We can easily see why by looking back to our earlier discussion of independence. There are any number of cases where independence doesn't seem to hold, when changing our options can rationally change our choice. The classic example is the case of the traveler who ends up at a restaurant he has never been to before.[54] On the menu he sees sushi and fried chicken. He prefers good sushi to good fried chicken but is wary of bad sushi. Given that he doesn't know anything about the restaurant, he decides to maximin and pick the fried chicken. After he has given his order, the waiter returns and says that he forgot to mention that hamachi kama (grilled yellowfin collars) and soba noodles are also on the menu. As it happens, he likes both of these options less than either fried chicken on sushi, but upon hearing this, he changes his original order to sushi. Why? Shouldn't the addition of these third and fourth dominated options be irrelevant to the choice at hand? Not necessarily. Restaurants that have hamachi kama and soba noodles on the menu are more likely to also serve decent sushi, either because they cater to customers who appreciate Japanese cuisine or because the chef

51. Harsanyi, "On the Rationality Postulates Underlying the Theory of Cooperative Games," 188.

52. One of the authors has made this case in relation to social contract theories that rely on a bargaining model; see Thrasher, "Uniqueness and Symmetry in Bargaining Theories of Justice."

53. Schelling, "For the Abandonment of Symmetry in Game Theory"; Schelling, The Strategy of Conflict.

54. This is a version of the example from Luce and Raiffa, Games and Decisions, 288.

has a specialty in Japanese cuisine. So, learning about a new option tells us something about the choice situation that we didn't initially know. Although it is irrelevant in our rankings, it is not irrelevant to our choice.

Although this is an example of expansion rather than contraction consistency, it is easy to see how the same type of case could apply with the removal of options as well. The larger point—aside from showing, again, how signaling and learning are important—is that while IIA may make sense in a number of contexts, it probably shouldn't be considered a stricture of rationality. Violations of IIA are not necessarily irrational, though they may be in some contexts.

In response to questions about the assumptions behind the Nash solution, other bargaining solutions have also been advanced. One, used in the two-person version by David Gauthier in *Morals by Agreement*, is the Kalai–Smorodinsky solution, or what Gauthier calls minimax relative concession.[55] This solution rejects the IIA assumption and instead proposes a resource monotonicity assumption that as the "pie" of resources to be divided by the bargain increases, both parties should benefit. In Gauthier's description, this solution seeks to minimize how much each party has to give up in relation to their maximum offer in order to reach agreement.[56] This solution relies on the parties making maximal proposals and the solution depends on what those offers are in relation to each other and their respective disagreement point.

Another alternative is the egalitarian solution proposed Ehud Kalai.[57] This solution is explicitly compared to Rawls's analysis of choice behind the veil of ignorance and, like Rawls's theory, but unlike the other two bargaining solutions, it requires some interpersonal comparisons of utility. In Rawls's theory, this interpersonal comparison is achieved by normalizing the perspective so that the agents are all symmetrically situated, effectively eliminating the distinctions between them. Again, we see the importance of symmetry. This is done through normalizing their information through the use of the veil of ignorance and by unifying their utility functions through the use of primary goods as the single outcome scale.[58] In some ways, the great interest of the egalitarian solution is that it makes explicit some of the assumptions that

55. Kalai and Smorodinsky, "Other Solutions to Nash's Bargaining Problem."

56. Gauthier later rejected this solution in favor of the Nash solution, in Gauthier, "Uniting Separate Persons." He then later introduced another bargaining solution called "maximin relative benefit" in Gauthier, "Twenty-Five On." This is not exactly a solution to the bargaining problem, but rather a representation of the ideas underlying the social contract itself, see Moehler, "Orthodox Rational Choice Contractarianism."

57. Kalai, "Proportional Solutions to Bargaining Situations."

58. Gaus and Thrasher, "Rational Choice in the Original Position."

Rawls's theory must rely on. This solution, like the Nash solution, also relies on an IIA assumption and, as we have seen, a symmetry assumption.

One of the common objections against the Nash solution, especially understood as a principle of fairness or as a component of a principle of justice, is that the Nash solution is sensitive to the disagreement points of the parties. Disagreement points were initially called one's "threat advantage" and Rawls notes in *A Theory of Justice* that "to each according to his threat advantage is not a conception of justice."[59] Gauthier makes a similar argument against the use of the Nash solution in *Morals by Agreement*. There is also a concern that if the parties to the bargain have radically unequal disagreement points, the resulting bargains will be unstable. To solve these problems, Michael Moehler introduces what he calls the "stabilized Nash Bargaining Solution."[60] This solution adds a baseline to the original Nash solution so that the disparities between each threat advantage do not grow too large.

The problem with bargaining solutions is not that there are too few, but that there are too many. In fact, we have only mentioned some of the most prominent here. We face the same problems that we saw with the folk theorem in repeated games and in evolutionary games, namely, how to select from many possible solutions. One possibility, for bargaining solutions at least, might be to see if any of the bargaining solutions would survive the move from cooperative to noncooperative game theory. Put differently, which of these solutions would be stable Nash equilibria in a noncooperative bargaining game?

Ariel Rubinstein famously proved that the Nash solution would be the unique solution in a bargaining game of alternating offers.[61] In this game, one party makes an initial offer about how to divide some set resources and the second party can either accept or make a counter-offer. This continues until an offer is accepted by both parties. Rubinstein's surprising result is that there is a unique, subgame perfect equilibrium in this game, even when the game has no time limit and can, in principle, go on infinitely. This solution coheres with the axiomatic Nash solution, but does not require any of the other underlying assumptions. There are a number of complications here that are important, but the basic idea is that a more realistic bargaining model that doesn't need to make all of the assumptions that are made in the axiomatic models generates a unique and plausible solution. Because of this, economists have tended to use noncooperative models of bargaining since Rubinstein.

59. Rawls, A Theory of Justice, 116.
60. Moehler, Minimal Morality, 86–88.
61. Rubinstein, "Perfect Equilibrium in a Bargaining Model."

The move to noncooperative models of bargaining also makes it easier to test bargaining solutions in the lab with real people. The results from these experiments are mixed with regard to the Rubinstein solution. Much depends on the time discounting, the time limit, and what each player thinks the other will do. As we have already seen, real agents do not always use backwards induction in the way that traditional game theory suggests that they should. One game where this clear is the "ultimatum game."[62] This is an asymmetric bargaining game with two players, a proposer and a decider. Both players are given some fixed sum of resources (c) that they must divide. The proposer can propose any amount (x) between 0 and c to the decider as a "take it or leave it offer." If the decider accepts, the proposer gets c-x and if the decider rejects the offer, neither gets anything. This is represented in the game tree shown in figure 6.1.

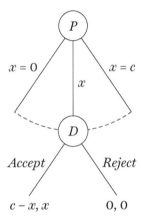

FIGURE 6.1. Ultimatum Game

Since the decider stands to get nothing, any offer $x > 0$ should be accepted. Given backwards induction, though, this implies that the only subgame-perfect equilibrium of this game is for the proposer to offer the minimum offer above zero. So, if the game involves dividing $10, the proposer should always be expected to offer only one dollar and the decider should always accept this offer. But in what is surely one of the most replicated findings in social science, virtually no one offers the minimum and very few accept it. Most offers cluster around 50%–40% of the whole amount in the basic game, and these are mostly accepted. The exact offers depends on how the proposers and deciders are chosen, whether dummy players are introduced, and a host of other features.

62. Güth et al., "An Experimental Analysis of Ultimatum Bargaining."

Regardless of the changing focal points, though, virtually no one plays the unique subgame perfect equilibrium strategy.

This result is even more stark when we look at a variant of the ultimatum game, the "dictator game." This is exactly like the original ultimatum game except the second party has no option to reject the offer. Knowing this, the only equilibrium strategy is for the first player to take as much as they can. But again, this is not what people do; most give something to the second party, though not as much as is offered in the ultimatum game.[63]

Given these results, we might ask whether this is good evidence against the *Homo economicus* model of rationality. We will return to this question in chapter 9 when we look at trust games and voting behavior, but we can say at this point that the model of rationality that comes from classical decision and game theory, embodied in the idea of *Homo economicus*, should be questioned in light of this evidence. As we saw, however, some of this is complicated once we introduce signaling and learning into our strategic models. As we will see in the next chapter, players seem to have views about various conventions and norms that may guide their predictions about what other players are likely to expect in these games. This may drive at least some of their behavior. We will study this possibility in greater detail in the next chapter.

Conclusion

In this chapter we went beyond analyzing the one-shot strategic encounters that we introduced in the last chapter and looked at games that include repeated encounters, incomplete information, population dynamics, as well as cooperative bargaining games. Simply repeating a game introduces the shadow of the future and changes the strategies we can expect rational agents to play—so much so that it is even possible to generate cooperation out of repeated Prisoner's Dilemmas in the right circumstances. Evolutionary game theory models the possible strategies of a game as a population and the payoffs in terms of the replication of that strategy. This approach models strategic dynamics without assuming rationality, which makes it excellent for looking at population dynamics. We saw that the basic Hawk-Dove game can be used to show how property rights can be a stable evolutionary equilibrium. If we think of evolutionary games as game theory without rational agents, we can think of signaling games as strategic environments where rational agents face incomplete information. These types of games are important in economics and politics since it is likely that economic and political actors lack crucial information

---

63. Forsythe et al., "Fairness in Simple Bargaining Experiments."

about the game or the players. Cooperative or bargaining games are games of full information with rational players who are looking for a mutually acceptable way to divide some surplus. As such, these games can be used to model fair or acceptable division.

Discussion Questions

(1) Can you think of a case where you have played tit-for-tat with someone?

(2) The Chaldeans are a non-Arabic, Christian ethnic group who emigrated from Iraq to the Detroit metropolitan area. The Chaldeans are a fairly large group—about 100,000 Chaldeans live in the Detroit area in the United States. Research indicates that intragroup cooperation is sustained partly by direct reciprocity. Funeral expenses, for example, are paid for by mourners leaving money in envelopes with their names on them. Chaldeans keep records of these contributions; when the mourner herself dies, families will consult their records to determine how much she has contributed to funerals in their family, and leave the equivalent amount at her funeral. Why is such bookkeeping so important? What might happen if precise records were not kept?

(3) Solving which game is most important for leaving Hobbes's state of nature: the iterated PD, Hawk-Dove, or Stag Hunt?

(4) Can you think of common behavior that might seem puzzling if we disregard the signaling role they play?

(5) A lot of behavior online, especially on social media, is related to signaling. Can you think of some examples?

(6) Given that there are multiple plausible bargaining solutions, does this mean that there is no rational solution to the bargaining problem or that there are many?

(7) If Alf and Betty are bargaining and Alf thinks that the Nash solution is the best while Betty thinks that equal division is the only rational solution, what should they do?

(8) Does the bargaining solution seem like a conception of fairness or equity? Why or why not?

7

Conventions, Norms, and Institutions

In the last two chapters we have looked at a number of methods of modeling strategic interactions and strategic rationality by using game theory. As we have seen, game theory is a powerful tool for understanding social life. We looked at one-shot, repeated, and evolutionary games and we saw that the time horizon of the game can powerfully affect the rationality of different strategies. The same is true for how much information is available about the game, as we saw when we looked at signaling games.

Most of the time, though, we don't approach situations as if we are encountering them for the first time, without any information about what other people are likely to do. Instead, we take for granted that there are stable behavioral regularities that we can expect other people to follow and that we, in turn, are expected to follow. When we leave our driveways, there are stable rules of the road that we expect others to follow. We don't treat every encounter as a new strategic interaction and optimize our strategy accordingly. Instead, we generally look to the conventions and norms that hold in our circumstances to determine what we should do. In this chapter we examine what conventions are and how they arise, how norms emerge and stabilize, and how institutions organize individual and collective choice.

Conventions

Why do the Japanese bow when greeting one another while Americans shake hands? Why do people tend to say "bless you" or "Gesundheit" after someone sneezes? Why do some cultures bury their dead, while some expose or cremate them? The answer to all of these and many other similar questions is *convention*. A convention is a behavioral regularity that exists when what one does depends on what you expect others to do and vice versa.

Conventions are distinct from both explicit agreements and from individual rational choice. For instance, Europeans tend to keep their fork in their left hand while eating and to use the fork and knife to move food from the plate to the mouth. Americans tend to keep their fork in their left hand when cutting with the knife, but then switch it to the right hand to move food into the mouth (assuming they are right-handed). There was never any "congress of cutlery" where the Europeans decided on one method and the Americans on another—there was never an explicit agreement that each side of the Atlantic would eat in one way rather than another. Most people also probably don't have strong views on which method they independently prefer.[1] Europeans do it one way and Americans another because it has become a convention to do so.

Why do some ways of doing things stick, while others don't? Can it be rational to follow conventions? How does the idea of a convention fit in with the ideas of strategic rationality that we developed in the last two chapters? The answers to these questions get to the core importance of conventions for PPE.

Conventions and Coordination

The philosopher David Lewis argued that conventions are stable solutions to coordination problems.[2] Recall that coordination games are games where all the parties involved want to coordinate on the same equilibrium, but where there are multiple equilibriums available. Consider a simple case (adapted from David Lewis) where Alf and Betty want to meet at either the Beach, the Park, or the Game and they don't care which, so long as they do it together.

TABLE 7.1. Meeting Game

| | | Betty | | |
		Beach	Park	Game
	Beach	1,1	0,0	0,0
Alf	Park	0,0	1,1	0,0
	Game	0,0	0,0	1,1

1. As it happens, one of the authors does prefer the European method for ease of use and efficiency over the American method, despite being raised in the American method.

2. Lewis, Convention: A Philosophical Study.

In this game, there are three pure strategy equilibria where Alf and Betty go to the same place. Perhaps surprisingly, there are also four mixed-strategy equilibria, one where each goes to each place with a 1/3 probability and three where each goes to two of the options with a probability of ½. But, as we have seen, mixed strategies don't typically make sense in pure coordination games since the expected payoff is typically less than any of the pure strategy equilibria.

To make this game more realistic, we can imagine that Alf and Betty originally decided where to go, but both have forgotten what they decided. One solution to this problem is to have a preexisting convention that says where one should go in cases when there is some confusion or when both are lost. Maybe the convention is to meet at the park, in which case, assuming both parties know the convention, they can expect the other to also go there, which in turn gives them a reason to go to the park too.

This case highlights a couple of key features of conventions. The first is that one's preferences in cases of conventions are conditional on what one expects the others to do. In this case, Alf and Betty are indifferent between all of the options (a point we will return to below) so there is, by stipulation, no reason for them to prefer one option over another. The only reason they might prefer the park to the beach is because they expect the other to be there. So, while coordination conventions are cases of strategic rationality, they are special cases that rely on conjectures about what others are likely to do. When there is a stable convention, it is common knowledge what one expects others to do and vice versa (more on this below).

How Do Conventions Emerge?

Conventions can arise for any number of reasons. The economist Thomas Schelling developed an account of coordination conventions that relies on conventions emerging because of "salience," which can lead some options rather than others to become focal points. In one classic example, Schelling asks us to imagine two people parachute into an unknown territory and need to meet on another but are separated during the jump.[3] The only thing each knows about the other is that they each have the same map. On that map there is a stream with one bridge crossing the stream, several buildings, a pond, and several roads. Where should they meet? It is likely that they will both expect the other to see the bridge as the salient focal point and meet there.

---

3. Schelling, The Strategy of Conflict, 55.

Where would meet if you and a friend got separated in Paris? New York? Los Angeles? Sydney? Do any of these cities have places that you would be confident would be salient meeting places? Imagine you and a partner will win a prize if you independently pick the same number from one to ten. Which number would you pick? What about if the numbers are 2,4,6,8,9? You can try these examples with others and see if you coordinate.

The idea is that there is usually something in the context of the situation or in the structure of the game that makes it salient as a possible coordinating point. Often this won't be obvious from the payoffs of the game alone. So, in the many real-world bargaining games like the ultimatum game that we looked at in the last chapter, it is common to split the pie 50–50. One reason might be that, as in this case, that is the only symmetrical solution to the game and, as such, it is naturally salient. In other cases, there might be some other feature that is likely to stand out to the participants.

> Most situations—perhaps every situation for people who are practiced at this kind of game—provide some clue for coordinating behavior, some focal point for each person's expectation of what the other expects him to expect to be expected to do. Finding the key, or rather finding *a* key—any key that is recognized as the key becomes *the* key—may depend on imagination more than logic.[4]

Schelling's argument here has fairly broad-ranging implications since he is suggesting that to understand most strategic situations where some coordination is involved, we need to think about more than just the payoffs in the game and equilibrium strategies. We sometimes need to know what the other people are bringing to the table in terms of their larger expectations and predictions to know what they are likely to do. This raises a whole host of issues that complicates traditional game theory and bargaining theory, some of which is explored by experimental and behavioral economists.

Common Knowledge

Consider a case where Alf and Betty want to coordinate, but they only do so when they don't do the same thing. In this case, Alf and Betty are out to dinner and they need to decide who should pay; if either both agree to pay or neither do, then they will either overpay or underpay. The only pure equilibriums exist when one allows the other to pay. But let's assume that each wants to be generous and pick up the check, how do they settle on a coordination equilibrium? We have all been in

---

4. Schelling, The Strategy of Conflict, 57.

situations like this and there are a number of ways it could play out. Maybe Alf is quicker than Betty in picking up the check or paying the bill, maybe Alf paid last time, so Betty offers to pay, or maybe they flip a coin. All of these are possible solutions to the coordination problem. To be a convention, though, there needs to be a solution to the coordination problem that is common knowledge.

TABLE 7.2. Picking Up the Tab Game

		Betty	
		Pay for Dinner	Don't Pay
Alf	Pay for Dinner	0,0	1,1
	Don't Pay	1,1	0,0

So, if Alf and Betty always let the person who showed up first to dinner pay, and they know that each other also knows that this is the rule, they will have solved the coordination problem with a convention.

For Lewis, a convention is a coordination equilibrium where each party would be worse off if they didn't coordinate. In the language of game theory, a convention is a Nash equilibrium of a coordination problem. We see that when either pays and the other defers, we have a Nash equilibrium where each player would be strictly worse off by deviating from that coordination solution.

Another important condition of Lewis's account of convention is that the solution be common knowledge, which is to say not only that each party knows that the coordination solution obtains, but also knows that each knows that they know that it obtains. Common knowledge has the somewhat confusing nested property that Alf must know that Betty knows that Alf knows that Betty knows and so on. In this sense, common knowledge goes beyond everyone knowing something. For instance, in the classroom a teacher may ask the class if anyone can name the sixteenth president of the United States. As it happens, everyone knows that Abraham Lincoln was the sixteenth president of the United States, but if no one or only a couple of the students raise their hands, not everyone will know that everyone knows that Abraham Lincoln was the sixteenth president and so, despite everyone knowing that fact, it won't be common knowledge.

Conventions function to aid coordination and they can't do their job unless everyone knows what the right coordination point is, and everyone knows that everyone knows that each knows the right coordination point. Put differently, conventions require *mutual expectations* of the form that "everyone knows that φ is the done thing around here" and everyone knows that everyone knows.

Lewis's definition of convention includes several elements: a population of people P, a recurring situation or context S, and a behavioral regularity R. The people within P are assumed to be rational in the sense we have developed it throughout this book, and the expectation is that others are rational as well. We need the situation S to be recurring rather than a one-off to generate the mutual expectations for coordination that a convention requires. Within that, R is a convention if it is established as an actual coordination point, everyone prefers to coordinate on that solution so long as everyone else does, and everyone knows that everyone knows that.

Lewis Convention

Given a population P, some context of a recurring situation S, and a behavioral regularity R, R is a convention if:

(1) Almost everyone conforms to R in S (Existence)
(2) Almost everyone expects everyone else to conform to R in S (Mutual Expectations)
(3) Almost everyone prefers to coordinate on R in S rather than some alternative, so long as they expect others to do so as well (Coordination Solution)

Some aspects of this definition of convention are controversial, especially the requirement of common knowledge and the existence convention. There are a number of complicated issues related to common knowledge that later philosophers and economists have explored. We will return to one of them when we discuss correlated equilibria below.

Conventions and Arbitrariness

One of the key features of the definition of convention that Lewis proposed is that conventions involve alternatives. If there is only one possible coordination solution, that can't be a convention according to Lewis. Indeed, one of the core aspects of conventions for Lewis is their arbitrariness. We drive on the right side of the road in the United States, but we might have driven on the left; which one happened to be chosen seems arbitrary. In what sense are conventions arbitrary, though?

Peter Vanderschraaf distinguishes between two kinds of arbitrariness in conventions.[5] The first is the *indifference* sense of arbitrariness where the

---

5. Vanderschraaf, Strategic Justice, chap. 2.2.

parties to the convention are indifferent to this or that coordination solution becoming the convention. In the meeting game above with Alf and Betty, neither wants to go to any of the places any more than any other, so each possible coordination convention is as good as any other. Where conventions solve pure coordination problems, we are likely to find conventions that are arbitrary in the indifference sense.

The second kind of arbitrariness is what Vanderschraaf calls the *discretionary* sense. In an impure coordination problem, represented in table 7.3, either going to the beach or going on a hike could be a solution to the coordination problem and, hence, could be a convention. Alf would prefer the beach convention and Betty would prefer the hike convention, though, and because of this, it would be wrong to say that Alf and Betty are indifferent to possible conventions that could solve their coordination problem. Nevertheless, there isn't one uniquely rational equilibrium here, so there is discretion in which equilibrium they end up settling on as a convention.

TABLE 7.3. Impure Coordination Game

		Betty	
		Beach	**Hike**
Alf	**Beach**	3,1	0,0
	Hike	0,0	1,3

As Vanderschraaf argues, all conventions are arbitrary in the discretionary sense, but only a subset are also arbitrary in the indifference sense.[6] So, all conventions are arbitrary, but this does not mean that most people who follow the convention will be indifferent between the existing convention and an alternative.

Convention and Contract

One distinctive aspect of conventions is that they do not require explicit agreement. David Hume uses the example of two men rowing a boat together as being an example of a convention that doesn't require explicit agreement.[7] Although conventions do not require explicit agreement, there is a sense in which they are still agreements. The Latin root of convention is *conventio*,

6. Vanderschraaf, Strategic Justice, 67.
7. Hume, A Treatise of Human Nature, bk. 3.2.2.10.

which can mean an agreement or a compact. The larger goal of David Lewis's *Convention* was to show that language could arise conventionally without explicit agreement. Similarly, Hume argues that justice can arise from a convention that doesn't require explicit consent in the form of a promise. Rather, justice arises, according to Hume, out of common interest, in a manner that roughly aligns with Lewis's treatment of conventions.

> It is only a general sense of common interest; which sense all the members of the society express to one another, and which induces them to regulate their conduct by certain rules. I observe, that it will be for my interest to leave another in the possession of his goods, *provided* he will act in the same manner with regard to me. He is sensible of a like interest in the regulation of his conduct. When this common sense of interest is mutually express'd, and is known to both, it produces a suitable resolution and behaviour. And this may properly enough be call'd a convention or agreement betwixt us, tho' without the interposition of a promise; since the actions of each of us have a reference to those of the other, and are perform'd upon the supposition, that something is to be perform'd on the other part.[8]

Hume thinks that justice can't be the result of an explicit agreement or promise because he argues that promising itself is a convention based on justice.

Hume is taking aim at the social contract tradition of Thomas Hobbes and John Locke, who argued that governments are established by the consent of the governed through an agreement. Hume is arguing that since justice is a convention, it needn't (and couldn't) be based on explicit promise or contract. Many have followed Hume on this point and have argued that conventional theories of politics and social contract theories are thereby at odds.[9]

David Lewis's account of convention, however, shows that the strict dichotomy between convention and contract is unnecessary in political philosophy. Everyone has reason to follow a convention once it has been established—it is a Nash equilibrium—and so there is a sense in which they consent to the convention without explicitly agreeing to it. Or, if not consent in the strong sense, at least a good reason for following the convention. Social contract devices, insofar as they use conventions, can function as models of political systems that rational people have good reason to endorse and comply

---

8. Hume, A Treatise of Human Nature, bk. 3.2.2.10.

9. Although at least one prominent philosopher has argued that Hume himself should be understood as having a contractual theory of justice; see Gauthier, "David Hume, Contractarian."

with.[10] Lewis adds an additional condition to social contracts as distinct from conventions, namely that social contracts are always evaluated against a baseline of general non-conformity with any convention, which he calls the *state of nature*.[11] While this distinction may make sense when we are thinking about the Hobbesian social contract, it is less compelling when we think about the social contract that Locke or many contemporary theorists like Rawls, Harsanyi, or Gauthier have in mind since they don't need to assume a state of nature without any stable conventions.

Social Norms

Many of the informal rules that we use to coordinate our behavior go beyond the idea of the conventions that we have so far developed here. The cost of not following a convention is the foregone benefit of coordination. As we saw when we looked at repeated games in the last chapter, this cost can be very high in some circumstances. But sometimes the failure to regulate our behavior in accordance with the prevailing convention can trigger actual punishment. When these conventions are codified in the form of formal rules and explicit formal punishment, we are usually dealing with legal or institutional rules (more on these below). But when the rules and the punishment are informal, ranging from "gossip to open censure, ostracism, or dishonor for the transgressor," we are dealing with social norms.[12] Sometimes this punishment is internal in the form of guilt or shame that we feel from violating the norm, sometimes it is the expectation of informal punishment from others.

In Cristina Bicchieri's terminology, what distinguishes social norms from mere conventions is the addition of normative expectations about what one expects others expect that you should do and what, in turn, it is expected that one should do.[13] This "should" goes beyond the normative claims of rationality that we have been exploring throughout this book, and while it may seem somewhat circular to define norms in terms of normative expectations, the point is just that when one violates a norm, one is not merely acting imprudently but is also breaking a rule that matters in some way.

For instance, if you are looking for a parking spot and you see someone—who doesn't have a handicapped placard and who doesn't seem to be handicapped—

10. For more detail of this understanding of social contracts as models, see D'Agostino et al., "Contemporary Approaches to the Social Contract."

11. Lewis, Convention: A Philosophical Study, 89.

12. Bicchieri, The Grammar of Society, 8.

13. Throughout, unless otherwise noted, we follow the account of norms developed in Bicchieri, The Grammar of Society.

park in a handicapped spot, how would you respond? If all you cared about was finding a parking spot, you might be happy. After all, if this person hadn't parked in the handicapped spot, they would have likely parked in a spot that you might also want to park in. If not parking in handicapped spots (when you aren't handicapped) was merely a convention, you should actually feel bad for parking scofflaw since they are—by stipulation—deviating from a coordination convention and therefore should be worse off by doing so. Instead, you are likely to be angry since the expectation is that the non-handicapped shouldn't park in handicapped spots. Is it immoral to do so? Maybe, but whatever the normative basis of its wrongness, the expectation that one shouldn't do it goes beyond either straightforward self-interest or the expectations that come from conventions.

According to Bicchieri, social norms are behavioral regularities that, like conventions, involve empirical expectation that almost everyone in the population will conform to the convention, as well as the *normative expectation* that almost everyone thinks you should conform to the convention, either because they have some normative belief that violating the norm is wrong (in some way) or because they expect to be punished if they break the norm. Sometimes they have both, which is to say they may believe violating the norm is wrong and they expect sanction for breaking it.

Further, *social* norms are distinguished from other types of norms depending on whether one's preference to follow the norm is conditional on other people following the norm. Some norms, what Bicchieri calls *personal norms*, aren't sensitive to the expectations of others and our preference to follow the norm isn't conditional on whether other people are following it as well. An example might be a rule that one reads a certain amount each day or exercises every day. One doesn't do these things because it is expected that they do, and they don't care whether other people are also doing them.

Moral norms are similar in that our preferences to follow moral norms aren't conditional on what other people do. Unlike personal norms, though, we care whether others conform with what we take to be the moral rules and we expect, in a normative sense at least, others to follow the rule. This category is a little tricky since what we call "morality" in ordinary life is usually a combination of a set of moral norms that we affirm and expect (to a certain extent) others to follow as well as the *social morality* that actually exists in one's society. The latter is composed of social norms that do typically involve mutual empirical and normative expectations and render one liable for socially approved sanction and punishment in cases of non-compliance.[14] As Bicchieri allows,

---

14. The connection between moral and social norms is a central part of the work of one of the authors; see Gaus, The Open Society and Its Complexities, sec. 9.3.

most moral norms are actually personal norms, so these categories will often bleed into one another.[15]

If one's preferences to follow the rule are conditional on whether other people are following the rule, but there is no expectation that others will also follow the rule, we have what Bicchieri calls a *descriptive norm*. As Bicchieri puts it:

> in the case of a descriptive norm, people do not prefer to engage in a particular behavior irrespective of what others do. Instead, their preference for conformity is *conditional* upon observing (or believing) how others act.[16]

The classic example is a fashion or fad. In the mid-'90s the "Rachel," a hairstyle named after Jennifer Aniston's character on the TV show *Friends*, became extremely popular. Millions of women got Rachels, not because they wanted to look like one another, but because they liked the way Jennifer Aniston looked on the show and wanted to look like her.

When one's preferences to conform to the rule are conditional on what other people are doing, and when one has normative expectations that others will follow the rule, we have a *social norm*. Many of the rules that we are concerned with in social life are social norms. Bicchieri explains:

> Social norms prescribe or proscribe behavior; they entail obligations and are supported by normative expectations. Not only do we expect others to conform to a social norm; we are also aware that we are expected to conform, and both these expectations are necessary reasons to comply with the norm.[17]

One of the key aspects of a social norm is that those who follow it need not either (a) agree with the norm or (b) find the normative expectations of others with regard to the norm legitimate. This means that even those in the norm community may continue to follow the norm even when they would prefer a different norm to be established. We return to this phenomenon below when we look at bad norms. Nevertheless, some do follow the norm because they endorse it and find the expectations legitimate. Many social norms of etiquette work this way.

Bicchieri distinguishes between social norms, descriptive norms, and *conventions*. Conventions here differ slightly from David Lewis's analysis that we saw above. The easiest way to think of Bicchieri's account of convention is to think of it as a descriptive norm that is actually being followed. Conventions don't have their normative properties unless they actually exist as social regularities. It doesn't make sense to talk about a convention that no one follows. This distin-

15. Bicchieri, The Grammar of Society, 20–21.
16. Bicchieri, Norms in the Wild, 19. Emphasis in the original.
17. Bicchieri, The Grammar of Society, 42.

guishes them from social norms as well, but the other crucial difference is that conventions do not involve normative expectations. As Bicchieri puts it, "Because conventions do not run counter to selfish motives, but social norms often do, if only empirical expectations were fulfilled, one would have a reason to follow a convention, but he would be seriously tempted *not* to conform to a social norm."[18]

Social Norm

Given a population *P* and a social situation or context *S*, a behavioral rule *R* is a social norm if for some person (e.g., Alf) of a sufficiently large subset of *S*:

(1) Alf knows that *R* applies in situation or context *S* (Contingency)

(2) Alf prefers to follow *R* in *S* on the condition that: (Conditional Preference)

    (a) Alf believes that a sufficiently large subset of *P* will follow *R* in *S* (Empirical Expectation)

    and either

    (b) Alf believes that a sufficiently large subset of *P* expects Alf to follow *R* in *S* (Normative Expectation)

    or

    (c) Alf believes that a sufficiently large subset of *P* expects Alf to follow *R* in *S*, prefers Alf to follow *R* in *S*, and may sanction Alf if he doesn't follow *R* in *S* (Normative Expectations with Sanction).

What Norms Do

For Bicchieri, social norms are solutions to mixed-motive games where players have some reason to deviate from the coordination solution. Following Bicchieri, we can think of social norms as transforming social dilemmas into coordination problems, by changing the payoffs and expectations of those in the original social dilemma so that cooperation rather than defection becomes the most attractive option.

TABLE 7.4. Norms Transform Social Dilemmas into Coordination Games

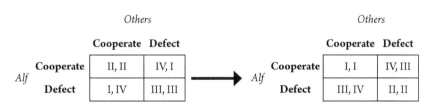

---

18. Bicchieri, *The Grammar of Society*, 38.

Recognizing that the actual distinctions between these categories are blurry in real life, it is helpful to conceptualize these type of norms categorically as in table 7.5.

TABLE 7.5. A Taxonomy of Norms

		Conditional Preferences?			
		No	Yes		
Mutual Expectations?	No	Personal Norm	Descriptive Norm		
	Yes	Moral Norm	Convention	No	**Normative Expectations?**
			Social Norm	Yes	

Again, these categories bleed into one another and in practice it is likely that a given behavioral rule may have more or fewer of the features of a given category. That said, one of the goals and—in the minds of the authors at least—benefits of the Bicchieri approach is that it is operationalizable and testable in behavioral experiments.

To be able to test whether there is a norm in play (and what kind) requires that we have a norm-based utility function that predicts the equilibrium behavior of agents who are acting on the basis of different norms. Bicchieri does this by adding a norm weighting to a traditional utility function. She includes a parameter k, which represents an individual's sensitivity to the rule R in question. Simplifying a bit from her original presentation, Alf's utility function involves the payoff he gets from following his strategy minus the maximum cost he would have to pay for norm violation, discounted by his sensitivity to the norm k, where $k \geq 0$. [19] Alf will follow a given norm if the expected utility of following the norm is greater than the utility of violating it. Erik Kimbrough and Alexander Vostroknutov call their version of a similar utility function, norm-dependent utility.[20] Kimbrough and Vostroknutov show, in a series of experiments, that the level of norm sensitivity differs from persons to person with predictable effects and, more important, they have developed a method for measuring general norm sensitivity.[21]

---

19. For a more detailed discussion the norm-based utility function and its applications, see Bicchieri, The Grammar of Society, 52–55, 219–22.

20. Kimbrough and Vostroknutov, "Norms Make Preferences Social."

21. Kimbrough and Vostroknutov, "Norms Make Preferences Social."

Bicchieri's account of norms, and other similar theories of norms, model norms as strategic equilibria based on conditional preferences. Norms are explicable in terms of rationality, given the empirical and normative beliefs and expectations that a community of people have. Her theory doesn't reference any irreducibly normative elements over and above the beliefs and preferences of the agents. To some, this type of approach misses what is distinctive about norm following, namely that when we follow a norm, we act on the basis of that norm directly. The most philosophically sophisticated and comprehensive theory that poses an alternative to Bicchieri along these lines was developed by four philosophers (one of which is also an economist) who were based at the Australian National University in Canberra, Australia.[22] The goal of the Canberra theory is to give a general account of norms that makes sense of how norms can be both composed of normative principles and make general demands on the behavior of individuals within the norm community. The Canberrans propose a non-reductive account that puts normative attitudes at the center of the theory or norms. They argue that norms require some cluster of normative attitude or judgment that doesn't reduce entirely to one's preferences. One implication is that norms are tied closely to accountability. Following and endorsing a norm entails that:

> We must judge that one *must* do as the principles prescribe, or *expect* others to do so, or *disapprove* of those who don't, and so on. In doing so, we necessarily regard ourselves as accountable to others so far as complying with the principles is concerned.[23]

As they argue, "creating accountability is simply what norms do."[24] Norms create accountability partly because, on their account, norms contain and express meaning based on their normative content.[25] We define ourselves, our social roles, and our community in large part based on how we identify with and signal our allegiance to different norms.

Norms and Cooperation

We have seen how norms, like conventions, play an important role in organizing and stabilizing coordination. In many cases, norms make cooperation possible by reducing the incentive to defect from or free-ride on the cooperative

---

22. Brennan et al., Explaining Norms.
23. Brennan et al., Explaining Norms, 37.
24. Brennan et al., Explaining Norms, 39.
25. Brennan et al., Explaining Norms, 156–58.

solution. As we saw in the last chapter, the pessimistic logic of the Prisoner's Dilemma can be changed by repeating the game indefinitely. Doing so, as Brian Skyrms argues, introduces the "shadow of the future" into the game and can turn it from a game with one, noncooperative equilibrium to a stag hunt game with one payoff-dominant cooperative and one risk-dominant noncooperative equilibrium.[26] Anticipating future interaction, the problem of the social dilemma becomes one of *assurance* that each will pursue the higher payoff rather than pursue the less risky strategy. This is not the case in the Prisoner's Dilemma since no amount of assurance or trust can make it rational to deviate from the equilibrium strategy of mutual defection.

Norms do something similar by changing the payoffs of the underlying base game in a way that often encourages cooperation. But, crucially, they do so without requiring indefinite repetition by making the impersonal norm and not predictions about the beliefs of other agents the center of gravity. Knowing that there is a norm to, say, pay for our food after we eat at a restaurant means that, as diners, we don't need to strategize about whether we can effectively signal that we will pay and thereby induce the restaurant to serve us food. Similarly, the employees of the restaurant do not need to size us up or inquire about our reputation to determine whether they should serve us. Instead, it is common knowledge that we will pay after we have been served and everyone acts in accordance with that expectation.[27]

Most important, this norm does not require repeated interaction since it is likely that most of the customers of any given restaurant are strangers to each other and the staff. This is even more obvious when one is dining at a roadside café while traveling cross-country or as a tourist in another country. In those cases, it is very unlikely that the customer has been to the restaurant before or that they will ever return and, crucially, this fact is usually common knowledge. In those cases, personal reputation and the likelihood of future cooperative encounters can't be playing any role in generating incentives to behave cooperatively. Cooperation here is supported by the mutual expectations that come from the common knowledge of the relevant norm.

If you think about it carefully, you will realize that many, if not most, of our daily commercial and social encounters share many of the features of the restaurant case from above. We are often interacting with strangers that we don't expect to interact with again and who don't have any personal knowledge of

26. Skyrms, The Stag Hunt and the Evolution of Social Structure, 5.
27. Some restaurants do have customers pay before they receive their food, and in some places, like many parts of Australia and the UK, this is the norm in many casual restaurants and pubs as it is in many casual or counter-service spots in the United States.

our values or reputation. Our daily lives are made up of many iterations of the "farmer's dilemma" that we looked at in the last two chapters and, as we saw there, rational cooperation is not easy in those kinds of situations. We have seen that social norms can make it rational to coordinate by changing the expectations and incentives of the individuals in the norm community. This creates an expectation that others will cooperate, changing the rational incentives for cooperation generally. This is a big deal since it means that many of the cooperative puzzles that game theory exposed, which pit rationality and mutual benefit at odds, may often be solved by norms.

This is one of the great lessons taught by Elinor Ostrom and her collaborators, who showed that many problems with common pool resources such as access to common grazing land or the management of water for irrigation can and often are solved by the creation and maintenance of informal norms that limit access to the resource to punish those who violate the norm.[28] She showed, both theoretically and empirically—from the air, on the ground, and in the lab—that neither Leviathan in the sense of the heavy hand of state enforcement, nor complete freedom of access were the only solution in common pool resource cases. Instead, norms and the individuals who endorsed and complied with those norms could provide their own governance, often in the absence of government. This insight highlights an important point. Although we live in societies that have governments that claim authority over their territories, this claim is often more aspirational than actual. Most of the actual *governance* we encounter on a day-to-day level comes in the form of norms that are enforced by mutual expectations of compliance and some threat of internal or external punishment if they are violated. The implications of the ubiquity that norms play in our lives is profound.

Norms and Nash

A different approach to norms agrees with Bicchieri that norms are solutions to coordination problems and that they depend on mutual normative and empirical expectations, but rejects the claim that norms are Nash equilibria within an existing coordination game. Coordination games, recall, typically have many Nash equilibrium solutions, and Bicchieri and others argue that norms solve the equilibrium selection problem by settling on this rather than that coordination solution. Herbert Gintis argues, however, that many of these Nash equilibria solutions would be difficult for agents to identify and coordinate

28. Ostrom, Governing the Commons.

on, making it implausible that they would stabilize into norms.[29] He also argues, similar to the Canberra approach, that norms require some shared normative attitudes to maintain their stability; most Nash equilibrium solutions would be fragile in the face of mixed motives. But norms do seem to be relatively stable most of the time, at least more stable than Gintis thinks would be plausible if they really were Nash equilibria.

To explain this, Gintis develops an account of norms as *correlated equilibria*. A correlated equilibrium (CE) is a solution to a game that uses a signaling device—Gintis calls it a choreographer—that sends a signal to the other players in the game. These players then use that signal to coordinate on a coordination solution. The CE creates a super game, within which the original game is nested where the choreographer sends a public signal that is common knowledge, and the other players use this signal to jointly adopt the strategy that is associated with the signal. Following Gintis we can see stoplights as an example of CE.[30] Drivers could play a game of chicken with other drivers every time they approached an intersection, and it is possible that conventions and norms would develop to reduce the number of crashes. We see this in action in places without many traffic signals. But we could also solve this problem by putting a light at intersections that would tell drivers when to stop and go. Drivers can reference the signal directly to determine what other drivers will do, rather than make conjectures about their likely behavior by using other cues.

Norms as correlated equilibria has several advantages over norms as Nash equilibria, but also some serious drawbacks. One advantage is that *any* public signaling device can play the role of choreographer and, hence, there are vastly more possible CE than Nash equilibrium solutions to the game. This could potentially explain the diversity of norms that we see in different times and places, but it also means that it is very difficult to test and make predictions about CE. Even so, CE allow solutions to games that have unique but suboptimal Nash equilibria, like the PD, opening up the possibility that signaling and social cues might be able to solve problems that individual rationality alone cannot.

Another advantage, cited by the economist Robert Aumann, is that CE link Bayesian and game-theoretic rationality.[31] Bayesian reasoners should be able to assign probabilities to every aspect of a game, including to the probability that an agent will select a given strategy in a game. The assumptions at the

29. Gintis, "Social Norms as Choreography."
30. Gintis, "Social Norms as Choreography."
31. Aumann, "Correlated Equilibrium."

heart of traditional solution concepts, such as Nash's, require that there be common knowledge of the game including all of the strategies available to each player and their payoffs. This information, recall, is crucial (as we showed in chapter 4) for determining mixed-strategy Nash equilibrium strategies. This is a high epistemic bar to meet. Aumann showed, however, that if players have subjective probability assessments over all relevant states of the world in accordance with Bayesian rationality and it is common knowledge that they will maximize their utility, it is assured that they will coordinate on a CE. While Bayesian equilibrium concepts are important and common in signaling games, CE rely on very few additional assumptions and, according to Aumann, are more generally applicable than the Nash solution.

Peter Vanderschraaf develops a CE account of conventions and shows that his approach explains how justice can be understood as a high-level convention.[32] His theory shows how powerful the CE approach can be when it is used to explain social conventions and political questions more generally.

Bad Norms

Norms are important for understanding cooperation, but we shouldn't assume that all norms help generate and stabilize cooperation. Many norms are bad, and in these cases, the power of norms to induce an equilibrium solution can stabilize bad solutions to problems, making them very difficult to change over time. What amounts to a "good" or "bad" norm is likely to be the subject of considerable debate and it is difficult to determine precise criteria for distinguishing the two.[33] A norm that looks perverse to outsiders may play a crucial role in the functioning of a community or reflect the different values that members of the community hold dear. Nevertheless, some norms seem prima facie bad. These include female genital mutilation, child marriage, honor killing, and norms of revenge.

Female genital mutilation is a case of a persistent, troubling, and dangerous practice that resists change. Gerry Mackie argues that in many African contexts, FGM is a kind of coordination convention that has settled onto an inferior, though nevertheless stable, equilibrium.[34] The puzzle of FGM is why families would allow and even coerce their daughters, who they presumably love, to be subjected to such a painful and dangerous practice. Even more puzzling is the fact that most of the mothers who support FGM were themselves

---

32. Vanderschraaf, Strategic Justice.
33. On this point, see Thrasher, "Evaluating Bad Norms."
34. Mackie, "Ending Footbinding and Infibulation."

cut when they were young. We might explain this away by postulating that these mothers and fathers are under the sway of an especially perverse set of values or beliefs that drive them to abuse their own daughters, but there is little evidence to suggest that people who practice FGM love their children any less than people elsewhere, and FGM is not the cultural property of one group or culture. Some have argued that it is an outgrowth of Islamic religious belief, but though FGM is practiced exclusively in Islamic or neighboring countries, most Islamic countries do not engage in the practice.[35]

Mackie argues that in the parts of North Africa where FGM is common, the practice arose as a solution to a problem of assurance that polygynous societies create. Although it is usually clear who a child's mother is, the same is not true of the father. In societies where a man takes many wives, he wants to ensure that the children he has by those wives are his and not someone else's. In polygynous societies where resources are highly unequal, the families of unmarried daughters need to signal to high-status, rich potential marriage partners that their daughters are chaste and will remain reliable once they are married. This creates a problem of assurance in the "marriage market," where there is high demand for a relatively low number of male marriage partners among a large pool of potential wives. FGM is one of several conventional "solutions" to this problem. Others include honor killing and foot binding.[36]

On Mackie's account, for contingent historical reasons, certain communities settled on FGM as an especially effective way to signal chastity by either making it impossible for women to engage in sex outside of marriage or by making it painful to do so. The initial cost of the painful procedure is also a powerful signal that the family of the girl is committed to the norm of female chastity. Once the convention is established, it forms the basis of mutual expectations and any girl who isn't cut will suffer a disadvantage in relation to other girls who are. If all the girls in the community resisted FGM, then none would be at a disadvantage relative to one another in the marriage market. This is an equilibrium solution, but there is an advantage to any family that does have their daughter cut in this environment since that girl would gain a marriage premium relative to the other girls. Knowing this and not wanting to be at a disadvantage on the marriage market, families will be incentivized to have their daughters cut. This leads to

---

35. As Mackie notes, some Christian communities that overlap with Islamic communities do practice it.

36. Interestingly, the territorial areas where honor killing and FGM are practiced largely do not overlap, suggesting that they likely fulfill similar roles. For an analysis of honor killing and honor violence more generally as a norm-based solution to a series of related coordination problems, see Thrasher and Handfield, "Honor and Violence: An Account of Feuds, Dueling, and Honor Killing."

the stabilization of the equilibrium where everyone practices FGM in the community. The situation is represented in table 7.6.

TABLE 7.6. FGM Dilemma

		Other Girls	
		FGM	**No FGM**
Girl's Family	**FGM**	Cost of FGM, neither has Marriage Premium	Marriage Premium and Cost of FGM
	No FGM	Marriage Cost, No Cost of FGM	No Cost of FGM, neither has Marriage Premium

The important thing to note here is that none of the families that have their daughters cut need to endorse the FGM practice on its own for the FGM convention to be established and to remain stable. Since it is common knowledge that each family has an incentive to seek a marriage premium, though, they will likely be drawn to the mutual FGM equilibrium. Indeed, Mackie argues that most families dislike FGM since they love their daughters and are largely aware of the dangers of the practice and the pain it causes. They engage in the practice because not engaging in it would disadvantage one's daughter in terms of marriage opportunities.

Drawing on evidence from the successful anti–foot binding campaigns in China, Mackie argues that the key to moving from the general FGM to the No FGM equilibrium is to make it common knowledge that everyone in the community wants to move away from the FGM equilibrium and to create ways for the members of the community to assure one another that they will not defect from the No FGM equilibrium once it is established in order to gain a marriage premium. Doing so in practice is difficult and requires public declarations from the members of the community that they are opposed to and will no longer engage in the practice. In 1999, Gerry Mackie began working with Tostan, an NGO that had developed a similar approach, in Senegal, to encourage the abandonment of FGM. Over time, they were successful in helping several communities change the practice, and their method has since been adopted by other groups.[37] Their method puts an emphasis on public deliberation and reason-giving as a way not only to change beliefs but also to establish common knowledge and create assurance that the new equilibrium will be stable.

---

37. Mackie, "Social Norms Change: Believing Makes It So."

Mackie's analysis of FGM relies on seeing it as a social convention, and we might ask whether this puts it in conflict with a potentially competing explanation that FGM is a social norm rather than a convention. Mackie sees his account of convention as continuous with the account of social norms given by Bicchieri (though he argues both are at odds with the Canberra view).[38] The question, he argues, is whether the convention or norm in question is primarily a solution to a problem of coordination or whether it is a solution to a social dilemma that allows for cooperation. Norms of cooperation require more of a change to underlying payoffs from normative expectations and punishment than norms of coordination. In any particular case, it is an open question whether FGM is a coordination or cooperation norm. Mackie argues that the norm arose as a solution to a coordination problem, but some communities have internalized and moralized the equilibrium such that they believe it is not only necessary but "honorable" or "just" for their daughters to be cut. In those communities, families with uncut daughters may also face additional punishments from the community in the form of ostracism or censure if they don't follow the norm. These will create powerful additional incentives to follow the norm.

Robert Boyd and Peter Richerson have shown, using a simple model of cultural evolution, that the existence of punishment can stabilize *any* norm or convention. In the case of norms, punishment can take the form of external sanction from others in the community or internal sanction in the form of guilt or shame and can allow the existence and stabilization of cooperative as well as noncooperative norms in a community.[39] This has also been demonstrated in the lab in an experiment where punishment stabilizes a socially destructive norm.[40]

Norms create the conditions that allow for cooperation and trust, but the dark side is that they also create the conditions for socially destructive and unattractive practices as well. Understanding how norms and conventions form an important part of social and strategic rationality is crucial to the theoretical as well as the applied side of PPE going forward.

Institutions

Conventions and norms tend to be informal, which is to say that although the norms may be common knowledge, they generally are not written down anywhere. More precisely, their status as norms doesn't depend on their having

38. Mackie, "Social Norms of Coordination and Cooperation."
39. Boyd and Richerson, "Punishment Allows the Evolution of Cooperation (or Anything Else) in Sizable Groups."
40. Abbink et al., "Peer Punishment Promotes Enforcement of Bad Social Norms."

any official authorization. We might consult Miss Manners or some similar manual to find out how to behave properly in polite society, but these books are summaries of the rules and norms that already exist—they don't make the rules. Not so with many other kinds of rules. Legal rules, for instance, are binding because they are part of an explicit legal code. Most sports leagues also have formal rules. The "Laws of Cricket" and the "Official Baseball Rules" govern international cricket (ICC) and Major League Baseball (MLB) respectively. The rules of those games count as rules insofar as they are adopted by the bodies that keep those rules. In 2020, for instance, MLB imposed a universal Designated Hitter (DH) Rule—which allowed every team to use a player, who is not required to play in the field, to bat for the pitcher in the lineup—for one season. The DH, though already allowed in the American League, was neither a convention or a norm in the National League, but it was the general practice throughout the 2020 season because of the rule change.

Both cricket and baseball have a number of informal rules, norms, and conventions, which are sometimes called "unwritten rules." In 1981, during the last game of the cricket World-Series Cup between New Zealand and Australia, New Zealand needed six runs to tie the match. In cricket, a batsman can score six runs by hitting the ball over the boundary: the equivalent of a home run in baseball. The World-Series Cup was a One-Day International, limited over format where each team has fifty overs (each over consists of six balls bowled by an individual bowler) and in this game New Zealand was on its last over and its last ball. To ensure that the batsman, Brian McKechnie, would not be able to score the needed runs on the last ball, the Australian captain, Greg Chappell told the bowler, his brother Trevor Chappell, to bowl the last ball underhand, rolling it on the ground so that it would be impossible to hit. At the time, this was technically a legal move according to the Laws of Cricket (later changed), but most viewers and commentators were horrified by this breach of the informal norms of the game. They were horrified because Chappell broke the norms, but not the explicit rules of the game.

When we are thinking about the "rules of the game" in general, be it in an actual game like baseball or a more general strategic, social setting, we call this collection of rules an *institution*. The most commonly cited general definition of an institution is provided by Douglass North:

> Institutions are the rules of the game of a society or more formally are the humanly devised constraints that structure human interaction. They are composed of formal rules (statute law, common law, regulations), informal constraints (conventions, norms of behavior, and self-imposed rules of behavior); and the enforcement characteristics of both.[41]

---

41. North, Institutions, Institutional Change and Economic Performance, 4.

Institutions, according to North, are composed of three elements: formal rules, informal norms, and enforcement. Cricket or baseball as an institution consists not only of the official rules of the game, but also the unwritten norms and conventions of the game, and the mechanisms for enforcing deviation from those rules and norms. Congress, as an institution, is not only made up of the official rules of procedures, but also the norms that have developed over the last several hundred years, and the mechanisms of censure, impeachment, and relegation that are used to enforce those rules.

Although we can think of both norms and formal rules as being in some sense "rules," here we will distinguish the two for ease of exposition. Within the institutional context, we can think of some rules as being formal and codified in some rulebook, constitution, bylaws, or contract. But there are also informal rules that are as real as the formal rules. The rules of the English Common Law were (and to some extent are still) unwritten but nonetheless legal rules. Norms, though mostly informal, can also be formal. Examples include some academic honor codes and Article 133 of the Uniform Code of Military Justice in the United States, which states that any officer, cadet, or midshipman can be subject to Court Martial for behavior "unbecoming an officer and a gentleman."

Enforcement of these rules can also be formal or informal. Formal enforcement involves some external agency or body judging violations of the norms and rules and imposing penalties on the rule- or norm-violating parties. These include not only legal punishment for criminal behavior, but also civil adjudication and penalties. It may also include nongovernmental organizations like credit agencies or international trade bodies like the World Trade Organization (WTO). Informal punishment is typically applied by parties within the practice itself. Typical examples include ostracism, censure, gossip, and withdrawal of cooperation. Sometimes informal norms can be violent, as in the cases of feuds or vendettas.[42]

TABLE 7.7. Formal and Informal Rule and Norms

	Formal	Informal
Rule	Codified Rule	Customary Rule
Norm	Open-ended Codified Rules	Social Norms, Conventions
Enforcement	External, Impersonal Punishment	Internal, Personal Punishment

42. Boehm, Blood Revenge.

Two Types of Institutions

The idea of an institution is easy enough to make sense of; institutions are just the "rules of the game" that govern our social life. Even this simple idea, though, raises the question of how we are meant to view those rules or, put differently, how we are supposed to interpret or model institutions. There are two broad classes of views.[43] The first follows North's famous articulation of institutions as the "humanly devised" rules of the game and interprets institutions as structures of constraints that are exogenously given to agents.[44] Call this view the *institutions as rules* view.[45] When a baseball game starts, there is no question what the rules are or, more important, that there is any ability to change the rules in the game. Instead, the players treat the rules of baseball as a constraint that they need to take into account as they play the game.

A second view almost inverts the first. Rather than seeing institutions as a constraint on the way the game is played, this view sees institutions as the rules of the game that emerge in the playing of it. Call this the *institutions as equilibrium* view. Here the institution is whatever the players of the game decide the rules are. Andrew Schotter describes institutions, along these lines, as "adaptive tools" that we devise to structure social interaction. On this interpretation, institutions share many of the features of conventions and social norms, since all are behavioral regularities in equilibrium. For an example, consider the US Congress. It is established by the constitutions, but virtually all of the rules that govern its operation are rules voted on and approved by the Congress itself. At any time, it can change those rules if it so chooses and, crucially, everyone in the Congress knows that they can change the rules with enough votes. At any given moment within the "game," senators or representatives will treat the existing rules as constraints, but they also recognize that those rules are subject to change.

These two conceptions of institutions are different, but they are not necessarily at odds.[46] Indeed, the examples that we used above suggest how the two types of institutions might work together and overlap. The US government as a whole is established and constrained by the US Constitution. We can see the Constitution as an institution of the first sort, which constrains the players in

43. For a nice articulation of these two views, see Shepsle, "Rational Choice Institutionalism." Shepsle also includes a third view, which we ignore here.

44. North, Institutions, Institutional Change and Economic Performance, 3.

45. Schotter, The Economic Theory of Social Institutions, 2.

46. Hindriks and Guala develop a hybrid view that they call "rules-in-equilibrium" in some detail, see "Institutions, Rules, and Equilibria: A Unified Theory." Guala develops a comprehensive philosophical account of institutions in his Understanding Institutions.

the game. Within the constitutional order, though, there are many areas where the rules are silent, e.g., the rules of the Congress. Those rules are developed as an equilibrium among the players—past and present—in the game. So, the two types of institutions can exist together and interact with one another. Of course, the Constitution itself can be changed through amendment or judicial review, but these changes are not properly seen as the players changing the rules, rather we should think of these rules as different in kind.

Institutions and Transaction Costs

The economists Douglass North and Oliver Williamson emphasized that institutions determine the transaction costs of making agreements or trades.[47] Transaction costs are all the costs or anticipated costs of finding trading partners, making agreements, and keeping or adjudicated disputes related to those agreements. That is, admittedly, a pretty broad notion, but we can think of transaction costs as generally being the "cost of doing business," construed very broadly, whatever that business happens to be.

In the economic theory that we looked at in chapter 4, transaction costs play a very minor role. We never discussed or factored in the cost of coming to an agreement or bargaining in our Edgeworth box models or in the general theory of bargaining that we looked at in the last chapter. In traditional economic theory, buyers and sellers are assumed to be able to find one another effortlessly and contracts are assumed to be effortlessly enforced. Obviously, these assumptions are false, but sometimes false assumptions can create useful models. To see why ignoring transaction costs can lead us astray, we should look an instructive example.

Ronald Coase (of the Coase theorem from chapter 4) posed an interesting puzzle in his classic paper "The Nature of the Firm" that illustrates the problem.[48] In the neoclassical economic theory (of the sort that we examined in chapter 4), the existence of hierarchical firms is somewhat mysterious. Why not just outsource every activity of the firm to independent contractors? Why go to all the trouble of hiring employees on indefinite contracts with open-ended job descriptions? Why spend money on managers to make sure they know what to do, and why have fixed capital costs rather than just renting equipment when the firm needs it? In short, why do firms exist at all? Why don't we just see individuals contracting with one another for services as our

47. Williamson, "The Economics of Organization: The Transaction Cost Approach"; North, Institutions, Institutional Change and Economic Performance.

48. Coase, "The Nature of the Firm."

models of exchange suggest they should? The answer is that transaction costs make doing so very difficult and expensive. It is easier and cheaper to hire people on open-ended contracts to do lots of things that the employer doesn't need to specify directly rather than make spot contracts for every task a business needs.

There is an analogy between goods and services too. Why do you own a car rather than renting one or calling a taxi or Uber every time you need a ride? Why do you own a home or pay rent to a landlord on a long-term lease rather than renting Airbnb's or hotel rooms on a short-term basis wherever you need them? Usually, the answer is that you want the flexibility that comes from owning a car, for instance, rather than having to call a car or find a rental option every time you need one. In one sense, though, this is inefficient, since most of the time your car is sitting in your driveway and not being used. It would be more efficient in the sense of being less wasteful to just have a car when you need one, but it is difficult and expensive to find a car when you need one if you tend to need one a lot. You have, in effect, an open-ended long-term relationship with your car. If, however, the cost of getting transportation whenever you needed it was much cheaper in terms of search time, direct cost, and reliability—which is to say the transaction costs—it might be less attractive to own a car.[49]

The Internet and app-based rating and payment systems have radically reduced transaction costs for both goods and services, changing the economy in important ways. It is now possible to get transportation when you need it on a spot market through rideshare apps like Uber and Lyft. Not only does the app match drivers and riders easily (reducing search costs), the apps also have a rating system, relatively transparent price structures, and other safety features that reduce the possibilities that there will be a dispute about the arrangement after the fact (reducing enforcement costs). Airbnb, VRBO, and other apps do something similar for lodging. The idea of spending the night in a stranger's house or getting in their car for a ride would have been incomprehensible not too many years ago, but now it is commonplace. On the service side, the drivers for these rideshare businesses (and others like them) don't have long-term open-ended contracts with the companies. Instead, they work whenever they like for as long as they like. As technology continues to decrease transaction costs, it is possible that we will see more and more flexibility and efficiency in the economy.

49. For an account of how important reducing transaction costs is to the sharing economy, see Munger, Tomorrow 3.0: Transaction Costs and the Sharing Economy.

Conclusion

One of the central puzzles of basic economics and game theory is how long-term cooperative behavior is possible. As we saw in chapter 5, the rationality of *Homo economicus* lends itself neither to commitment nor to the disposition necessary to signal assurance to cooperative partners. In the last chapter we saw that this problem is attenuated considerably once we introduce the idea of repeated games and signaling, but even if we can show, using some combination of repetition and signaling, that cooperation is *possible*, we don't thereby show that it is likely to be common or that, once established, it will be stable. Enter conventions. David Lewis, in his groundbreaking account of conventions, showed how rational agents can establish stable conventions through interaction and common expectations. Norms go further by introducing expectations that one *should* follow the norm in question or that others expect that one should. Institutions go further still, introducing structures of rules and norms that govern behavior. All of this introduces ways of understanding how rational agents can see themselves as bound by conventions, norms, and rules and how they can credibly signal their commitment to those rules, norms, and conventions. The introduction of conventions, norms, and institutions into our toolbox should change the way we think about the possibilities open to *Homo economicus* as a cooperative agent. They should also change the way we think about economics more generally since institutions and norms add structure to economic interactions that should not be ignored.

Discussion Questions

(1) What is the difference between a convention and a norm?
(2) Is the requirement that conventions have common knowledge too strong? What does it imply in ordinary life?
(3) Can you think of examples of:
  a. Conventions
  b. Personal Norms
  c. Social Norms
  d. Descriptive Norms
  e. Moral Norms
(4) What are some bad norms? How do you know that they are bad?
(5) There is a phenomenon called "pluralistic ignorance" that occurs when everyone believes one thing but thinks (wrongly) that everyone else believes something else. A classic example is when a teacher, after a difficult lecture, asks if there are any questions. Each student

looks around and assumes that the other students understand what is going on since no one has raised their hand to ask a question. This leads everyone to assume that they are confused while everyone else is following the material. Can you think of other examples of pluralistic ignorance? How might bad norms sometimes be examples of pluralistic ignorance?

(6) What does it mean to say that some rules are formal while others are informal?

(7) Explain the idea of transaction costs. Can you think of some institutions that are clearly related to transaction costs?

8

Social Choice Theory

In the previous chapters, we have focused on how individuals make rational and strategic decisions. Now it's time for us to shift our focus to how individuals with different preferences can (or should) make decisions together. This is an area of mathematics, philosophy, economics, and political science known as social choice theory. At the most general level, there are two main aspects of social choice theory. The first involves theories of preference aggregation, that is, how the preferences that govern the rationality of individual choice can be combined to construct a rational collective or social choice. The second involves theories of collective decision rules, that is, how groups make decisions together. These two topics are related, though distinct, as we will see.

The Problem of Social Choice

Individual rationality, we have seen, can either lead us to efficient outcomes (chapters 2–3) or get us stuck in Pareto-inferior outcomes such as the Prisoner's Dilemma (chapter 5). We also saw that efficiency can sometimes conflict with rights and other values as well as problems of externalities and public goods (chapter 4). All of these considerations have led political theorists to justify government as a coercive organization that can move society to valuable or worthy social states that cannot be brought about by market transactions. Sometimes the problem is that the market has failed to yield efficient results—government, it is said, is necessary to move us to social states in which we enjoy public goods and regulate negative externalities (given non–zero transaction costs). At other times government pursues values in addition to efficiency; it seeks a fairer distribution of resources. Governments also define and enforce rights, including property rights, which are essential for markets.

This raises the question of what values governments should pursue. If we all agreed that government is to supply exactly the same set of public goods and the precise amounts, there would be no great problem. If we look at a 2×2 matrix of the Prisoner's Dilemma, it is obvious what we would want government to do—get us to the cooperate/cooperate payoff, by changing the game so that defection is no longer the dominant strategy. Clearly, though, this is to ignore the very fact on which economic analysis builds: our orderings of outcomes, which is to say our preferences, usually differ. In market transactions we benefit from the diversity of preferences. It is because you order the outcomes differently than I do that we can engage in mutually beneficial trade—Alf prefers a chicken wing to another slice of pizza, and Betty prefers a slice of pizza to a chicken wing, so they trade. But diversity of preferences is much more of a challenge in the political context since, in most cases, when the government acts, we must all do the same thing regardless of our underlying preferences.

There are two very different responses to this problem. We can call them—very broadly—*preference respecting* and *preference transforming* views of the collective choice. On a *preference respecting view*, we suppose that each person has an ordering over possible political outcomes that expresses their overall set of normative criteria. As we have seen, utility functions can accommodate all the normative criteria relevant to choice; we have been at pains to argue that they need not be about what promotes your self-interest, or wealth, or whatever. So long as the preference orderings fit certain requirements, they can be over anything. On this view, the basic data of politics should be the same as the basic data of economics since people's orderings of the outcomes capture all that they see as normatively important for making a choice. The difference between the market and the political forum is that in the market each person makes her own choice based on her preferences and option set, while in the political setting we come together with our individual preference orderings and seek to make a uniform collective choice. If this is true, there is no reason, in principle, why we can't establish criteria of rational collective choice as we did for individual choice.

The *preference transformative* view, however, insists that this is the wrong conception of the political. As Jon Elster understands it, the preference respecting view embodies a confusion between the kind of behavior that is appropriate in the marketplace and that which is appropriate in the forum.

> [In the market] the notion of consumer sovereignty is acceptable because, and to the extent that, the consumer chooses between courses of action that differ only in the ways it affects him. In political choice situations, however, the citizen is asked to express his preference over states that also differ in the way that they affect other people. . . . [T]he task of politics is not only to eliminate inefficiency but also create justice.[1]

1. Elster, "The Market and the Forum: Three Varieties of Political Theory," 111.

We should clearly distinguish two lines of criticism of the preference re-specting approach suggested by Elster's remarks. First, Elster insists that po-litical choice is not simply about efficiency but about justice, which is why aggregating individual preferences into a social choice is inappropriate. While this may be true if we suppose that political agents are simply *Homo eco-nomicus*, we have seen that utility functions can include the entire range of normative considerations, including notions of justice. So, the mere idea of starting out with individual preference orderings to determine a social choice about what is just is not, as Elster puts it, "incongruous."[2]

The second criticism, though, has considerably more bite. This is the idea that once we are concerned with collective choice, we can't simply rest, content with the idea that a person's preferences are his own business. Re-call Prude and Lewd from chapter 4. Each has a preference about what books the other is to read: should collective political choice take these pref-erences over what other people do—external preferences—into account? The fact that politics seems to require some people having a say over what other people do, it looks like external preferences of this sort will be a cen-tral concern of collective, political choice. This is a clear difference between social choice and market choice, though, since one's choice over what goods to buy or sell doesn't directly concern the actions or choices of other people.

In response to these worries, preference transformative views see politics as a way of coming together in the public forum, arguing, and changing each other's minds. It is not enough to simply assert that one prefers this to that in the public sphere—preferences that were not formed by a properly reflective process, or that include some sorts of external preferences, or preferences that could not be publicly revealed (say, racist preferences), should be transformed or eliminated in reasoned political discussion.

There is clearly some truth in the transformative view since we do not think that discriminatory external preferences should be the basis of a rational social choice. Still, the contrast between the market and the forum is not quite so sharp as advocates of the transformative view suggest. For one thing, we have seen that all desires or goals can be criticized as not sufficiently reflective or formed by non-autonomous processes. There is no reason intrinsic to market analysis to prevent arguing that some desires, say those for especially dangerous or noxious activities, should not be met by the market. Indeed, Cass Sunstein, an influential legal theorist, has offered a criticism of many market outcomes

---

2. Elster, "The Market and the Forum: Three Varieties of Political Theory," 111.

because they satisfy preferences that ought not to be respected.[3] Even in the market, some sorts of external preferences are a worry.

Another reason that the contrast between preference respecting and preference transformative views of politics is not as clear-cut as one might think is that, even after debate and transformation in the forum, we can still expect an extremely wide range of preference orderings about what is the best social choice. To be sure, some contemporary political theorists, known as "deliberative democrats," seem to hope for significant consensus on political issues, but this does not look terribly plausible in extensive and diverse societies that make up virtually all democratic nations. Even after deliberation and discussion we are apt to be left with a diverse set of preferences which, presumably, the social choice mechanism then will have to respect, thus leading us back to the preference respecting view of the forum.

In this chapter, we explore political choice on the preference respecting view. If one upholds the pure preference respecting view of politics—Elster's "market" view—then the following analysis should be of great interest. Insofar as one endorses the transformative view of the political, some of the problems explored in this chapter will be of less concern, as some of the worries about collective choice will stem from allowing citizens to hold any ordering over outcomes that their normative criteria recommend and respecting these orderings in the social choice process. However, even for the transformative theorist, many of the problems we discuss—such as path dependency and strategic voting—must remain a deep concern. As will questions about voting systems, generally.

Social Choice Theory

According to Thomas Jefferson, self-government requires following a collection of wills expressed by the majority, usually through voting.[4] Thinking of democracy as taking a collection of wills (individual preference orderings) and generating a social will (social preference ordering) is a long-standing and, in many ways, attractive idea. We might think of this "democratic collecting of wills" in two ways.

The most ambitious approach is to aim at a *social preference ordering*. It seems safe to suppose that we would want our social preference ordering to conform to the axioms of ordinal utility such as: asymmetry of strict (social) preference, symmetry of (social) indifference, reflexivity, transitivity, and

3. Sunstein, Free Markets and Social Justice, 18ff.
4. Padover, Thomas Jefferson on Democracy, 15.

completeness all seem as important for a social ordering as they were for an individual ordering. Let us call a social outcome with these properties a *social ordering*. We can call such social ordering a social welfare function (SWF). A social welfare function aggregates individual rational ordering into a collected social ordering. We can think of a social ordering as a construction of a social will out of a collection of individual wills.

Social Choice

A *social welfare function* (SWF) takes as *inputs* individual preference orderings and yields as *outputs* a social ordering.

A *collective choice rule* (CCR) takes as inputs individual preferences and yields a best option as an *output*.

Less ambitiously, we might aim only at a *collective choice rule* (CCR) that, from a set of options, selects the best or optimal choice. A CCR takes as inputs people's individual preference orderings and yields a socially best option. This is more akin to a formal conception of voting wherein there is some set of social options, some way of representing preferences over those outcomes (such as voting), and a rule (or set of rules) for determining how those preferences determine the optimal option. So, each individual will be able to order all of the available options according to the traditional preference binary relations, and some rule will transform those orderings into a collective decision on the "best" option as an output.

In either case, social choice theory has three basic building blocks:

1. Some set of individuals $\{i, j, \ldots\}$
2. Some set of options $\{x, y, z \ldots\}$
3. Binary social ordering relations R, I, P

Individual and Social Orderings Notation

Individual Orderings

For some individual i ($\exists i$)

- $x \geqslant y$ x is at least as good as y
- $x \succ y$ x is strictly preferred to y
- $x \sim y$ x is indifferent to y

Social Orderings

- xRy x is socially at least as good as y
- xPy x is socially strictly preferred to y
- xIy x is socially indifferent to y

$x \rightarrow y$ x implies y
$x \& y$ x and y
$\neg x$ not x

We will use the binary relations ($\geqslant, >, \sim$) for individual orderings of preference, strict preference, and indifference respectively and the binary relations (R,P,I) for the same orderings at the social level.

Collective Rationality

The idea of a social welfare function raises a fundamental question: does it make sense to think of *rational* social choice at all? That is, can we combine individual rational preferences—orderings that meet the conditions of reflexivity, symmetry of indifference, asymmetry of strict preference, and transitivity—and combine them in ways that lead to a rational social preference?

If so, then just as we might be able to identify a rational individual with a consistent chooser who can be represented by a utility function, we can think of a rational society as an agent that makes consistent choices and has a utility function that it maximizes. In that sense we can say that a society can be represented as making rational choices. If not, then we might have to face the possibility that while we make collective choices, these choices cannot or need not meet the standards of rationality. Either way we go has implications for how much normative weight we should give to the output of these procedures and how we should interpret their meaning.

Some famous and thoughtful economists find the very idea of collective choice and collective rationality a philosophically objectionable notion. According to James Buchanan:

> Rationality or irrationality as an attribute of the social group implies the imputation to that group of an organic existence apart from that of its individual components. If the social group is so considered, questions may be raised relative to the wisdom or unwisdom of this organic being.[5]

According to Buchanan, we should not expect society to display a notion of rationality akin to individuals, so the idea of social choice theory is in many ways misconceived. Buchanan was wary of any conception of social choice for this reason. There is no "social" choice as such. Instead, individuals decide in groups what to do. Democracy is not a representation of a "general will" but a

---

5. Buchanan, "Social Choice, Democracy, and Free Markets."

type of group decision that needs to be studied and understood as the representation of individual wills, not a construction of a social one. We will look more carefully at Buchanan's positive views along these lines in the next chapter.

May's Theorem and Majority Rule

One of the enduring questions for political philosophy is whether there is anything special about majority rule. Is choice by a rule "50% + 1 wins" arbitrary? Would 51% + 1 do just as well? How about 55%? Many are deeply attracted to what Brian Barry called "majority principle" as a fundamental aspect of democratic theory with some seeing it as the sine qua non of democratic governance.[6]

An important 1952 theorem by Kenneth May showed that majority rule is indeed special.[7] The power of May's proof, which concerns a collective choice rule (CCR) between two options (x,y), depends on the acceptability or reasonableness of the conditions that he imposes on any acceptable CCR.[8]

A word on this method of axiomatic social choice theory. When we are trying to decide on whether some social choice procedure C is desirable, we might pursue two different methods. *Output* evaluation would try to determine the sorts of decisions C yields, and then evaluate whether we approve of these decisions, and so approve of C. So, for example, a group of friends might decide that Alf makes the best decisions about where to go for pizza and so they endorse the rule, "When we are trying to decide where to go for pizza, Alf makes the decision." So here they are reverse engineering their evaluation: if they approve of the outputs, they approve of the procedure.

Another way is to independently evaluate the features of the procedure. Call this a *direct procedural evaluation*. This method asks, "what features would we like our procedure to have?" We then list the characteristics that we think are necessary in a procedure and try to determine whether there are any procedures that meet these criteria, and if there are, what they look like. This is the method of social choice theory: first determine the features that are required in a procedure to aggregate individual preferences into a social preference, and then see what procedures these yield.

---

6. Barry, "Is Democracy Special."

7. May, "A Set of Independent Necessary and Sufficient Conditions."

8. We could also see this as a SWF over two options. The distinction between a social welfare function and a collective choice rule only becomes important when we have three or more options in our option set.

May's Conditions

What, then, are some features that would be desirable in a procedure to take individual preferences and yield social preference? Since our interest is in majority rule, we assume that we are designing a voting procedure. May proposes four conditions that must be met for an acceptable voting rule.

(1) **Decisiveness**—The CCR must yield a decision between x and y for all possible configurations of individual preferences, such that xPy, yPx, or xIy. All possible permutations of x and y in the individual preference orderings must yield a single definite social choice. We cannot have $[(xPy)$ & $(yPx)]$ or $[(xPy)$ & $(xIy)]$ or $[(yPx)$ & $(yIx)]$.[9]

(2) **Anonymity**—The identity of the voters must have no effect whether xPy, yPx, or xIy. For a given preference profile among all voters, that preference profile will always yield the same decision when the identities of the voters are permutated. If the social choice mechanism is anonymous, it doesn't matter what names are attached to the votes: the CCR counts the votes without paying attention to the voter's identities. So, from the social perspective, when [Alf holds $x \geqslant y$ and Betty holds $y \geqslant x$] it is the same as when [Alf holds $y \geqslant x$ and Betty holds $x \geqslant y$]. In both cases, there is one vote for x and one vote for y.

(3) **Neutrality**—Here is a somewhat more complicated condition. We'll first state it, and then try to explain it and its rationale. If for a given profile of individual preferences, xPy and, keeping that profile, if x is relabeled as w, and y is relabeled as z, then it must be the case that wPz.

This condition is effectively anonymity for options. The idea is that a collective choice rule should be neutral between alternatives insofar as neither alternative has a built-in advantage, so the labels attached to the proposal don't matter. For example, a rule that a 2/3 decision is required to pass a proposal, otherwise it fails, violates neutrality: it is biased in favor of the status quo. Say that there are two proposals:

x = "Change the constitution: abolish the electoral college and elect the president by popular vote by majority vote"

y = "Do not change the constitution: keep the electoral college and do not elect the president by popular vote by majority vote"

---

9. This, of course, follows if we are aiming at a social ordering.

Say *x* gets 51% of the vote; even so, it would not pass. This is because a supermajority is required to change the US Constitution, so *yPx*. Now relabel *x* as *w*, where *w* = "abolish the electoral college and elect the president by majority vote" and relabel *y* as *z*, where *z* = "keep the electoral college and do not elect the president by majority vote." Having eliminated the label in *x* that the proposal changes the Constitution, *w* now wins (51%–49%), and so we have *wPz*, and neutrality is violated.

The rationale behind neutrality is that we do not want our social decision-making procedure to work to the advantage of some options ("no change from the status quo") and to the disadvantage of others ("change the status quo"). Under many voting rules, the decision-making rule favors those people with conservative preferences and places an extra obstacle in front of those with reformist preferences. Neutrality forbids this.

(4) **Strong Monotonicity**—This includes two conditions: *non-negative responsiveness and positive responsiveness*. According to *non-negative responsiveness*, if already *xPy*, and one or more voters change their previous vote for *y* to a vote for *x*, then still *xPy*. A social choice mechanism is weakly monotonic if it always is the case that if some individual changes her preferences such that she is *more favorable* to *x* than previously; then if there is any change at all in the social choice, it is an outcome more favorable to *x*. Non-negative responsiveness seems a minimum requirement for an acceptable CCR (or SWF). If we were deciding on what mechanism to adopt to produce a social choice out of individual preference orderings, we would insist that whatever social choice mechanism we adopt, it will never be the case that someone's becoming more favorable to an alternative itself, with no other changes on anyone else's part, causes that alternative to be rejected.

According to *positive responsiveness*, ties can be broken by just one voter changing her mind. If *xIy* and one *y* voter changes to *x*, then *xPy*. That is, the social choice mechanism positively responds to the decision of a single voter in the case of a tie. The rule used by most juries is not positively responsive. Say that a jury is deadlocked six for conviction, six for acquittal. This might be called a tie: 6(*xPy*) and 6(*yPx*). Now say that one person changes his mind such that five jurors are for conviction and seven for acquittal. In a jury this doesn't usually break the tie. If a system fails to be positively responsive, it says that there is nothing to choose between two alternatives even though some individual changes his preferences to support one while everyone else's preferences remain the same. In effect, such a system ignores this person's change of preference.

May's Argument

These, then, are the conditions that May believes any reasonable CCR should meet. May's theorem shows that one—and only one—CCR satisfies all four conditions when deciding between two options: *simple majority voting*.

The reasoning runs like this. The first three conditions imply that if the number of votes for y equals the number of votes for x, then $x I y$. To see why this is so, suppose that it was false, and so even though x and y had the same number of votes, $x P y$. We now appeal to Neutrality, and relabel x as w, and y as z. We then appeal to Anonymity and change the identity of the voters, so that everyone who voted for x becomes a z voter, and everyone who was a y voter becomes a w voter. Anonymity requires that the identity of the voters doesn't matter, just the number of votes, so it must be the case that if previously $x P y$, now $z P w$. But we have defined z as a relabel of y; so on the same set of preference profiles, the rule has selected both x and y, and that violates Decisiveness. Therefore, it is not consistent with our first three axioms to suppose that if x and y have the same number of voters, $x P y$. We can see that this reasoning will lead us to conclude that if the number of votes for y equals the number of votes for x, then $x I y$.

The next step is to invoke positive responsiveness. If one voter changes to x, then positive responsiveness requires that $x P y$. At this point we have arrived at the simple majority rule. 50% + 1 generates a winner. We also can show that non-negative responsiveness is satisfied by simple majority rule. Suppose that x beat y by k votes; then suppose that one y voter changes to x, so that x now wins by $k + 1$ votes. This change cannot reverse the outcome of $x P y$.

May's Theorem

Given two options x, y majority rule is the only CCR that meets the following four conditions:

1. Decisiveness
2. Anonymity
3. Neutrality
4. Strong Monotonicity

May's theorem, though limited to choices between two options, is still important. At some point we are apt to wonder. "What is so special about making decisions by a vote where over 50% wins? Why over 50% and not over 45% or 60%?" May provides an answer: out of every conceivable CCR, majority voting between two alternatives alone satisfies these four reasonable conditions. Tom Christiano, for instance, argues that majority rule is "intrinsically just," albeit only under "highly simplified circumstances."[10]

It also shows that majority rule is the unique way to settle questions between two options *only* if these four conditions hold. Which is not to say that majoritarianism may not have other virtues, but the claim to be the uniquely acceptable CCR only follows if these conditions hold. This raises a series of questions about how likely these conditions are likely to hold in most electoral settings. The first problem is that May's theorem only holds when there are two options. This, however, is not always the case. Even in most US presidential elections, there are more than two candidates. This restriction may not be as strong as was once thought, though. Recently, Robert Goodin and Christian List have offered a version of May's theorem that extends it to instances involving three or more options, where it provides a case for plurality voting in single ballot cases.[11]

The second problem is that May's theorem doesn't include any strong rationality condition like transitivity. Nor does it generate a complete social ordering. Instead, it delivers a verdict between two options given a set of individuals and their orderings. This is not, in itself, a drawback but it does show how limited CCRs are in relation to SWF. All they can do is generate a decision given certain input, they don't construct a rational social preference structure.

More seriously, anonymity and neutrality are very strong conditions. Neutrality in particular is a very strong restriction. Most bills introduced into a legislature are attempting to change the status quo in some way and sometimes the status quo has built-in advantages. Whether this will technically violate anonymity depends on the specific case, but we have already noted that any super-majority conditions (i.e., greater than 50% + 1 required to win) will violate neutrality. Anonymity is also violated in some cases where certain voters may have certain privileges, such as the ability to break ties.

Arrow's Theorem

Condorcet Voting and Its Paradox

May's theorem shows that majority rule uniquely satisfies his conditions when choosing among two options. Let's now consider choices among three or more options. Of all the ways of choosing between three or more policies,

10. Christiano, The Constitution of Equality, 290.
11. Goodin and List, "A Conditional Defense of Plurality Rule."

candidates, etc., the *Condorcet method* seems the most direct extension of simple democracy between two choices (x,y). Simple majority vote handles pairwise choices very nicely; it puts a question to the voters "x or y"? Things get complicated by the introduction of a third alternative, z. We often use plurality, or "first past the post," asking "which do you want, x, y, or z?" But plurality need not give us a majority winner: x can win a plurality contest with 40% of the vote (with y and z both getting 30%). The Condorcet method stays truer to the core idea of simple majority rule by taking a vote between each pair of alternatives: now we have three questions rather than just one: x or y?, y or z?, x or z? In each case the winner will be by simple majority: if one option beats every other alternative, then we can say that the majority prefers this option to every other; it is always preferred by a majority when compared against each other alternative, one at a time.

Condorcet voting gives rise to the Condorcet Paradox, as in profile of preferences shown in table 8.1.

TABLE 8.1. Condorcet Paradox Preferences

Alf	Betty	Charlie
x	y	z
y	z	x
z	x	y

If we take a series of pairwise votes, we get: xPy, yPz, and zPx—an intransitive result. Thus, out of a set of individual preferences that meets all axioms of a rational ordering, we generate an intransitive social "ordering." And what if we insist on transitivity? Then note that Alf alone is decisive over the (x,z) choice, for he is the only voter who holds that $x \gtrless z$. This line of reasoning will be critical to Arrow's theorem. In some ways Arrow's theorem can be understood as a generalization of the Condorcet Paradox. As we shall see, in one stage of the proof the Condorcet Paradox orderings are invoked.

Arrow's Conditions

Again, we employ the method of *direct procedural evaluation*. We list the characteristics that we think are necessary in a procedure, and then try to determine whether there are any procedures that meet these criteria, and if there are, what they look like. Alas, what Arrow will show is that once we do that, there is no procedure that meets them all!

Kenneth Arrow's argument, fully set out in his 1960 book, *Social Choice and Individual Values*, asked whether any system of social choice that didn't rely on an individual chooser—a dictator as he calls it—can produce a rational social ordering.[12] Specifically, he sought to determine whether his set of conditions is consistent with the social choice constituting a complete, transitive ordering of the options, that is, whether it will produce a social welfare function, an SWF. So, the requirement that the outcome must be a transitive ordering is entailed by the fact that his concern is whether the conditions he specifies are consistent with yielding a SWF. Some statements of his proof list transitivity as a condition, but that is somewhat misleading. So, Arrow's conditions are:

(1) **Universal Domain (U)**—The SWF must yield a social ordering for a set of options for all logically possible individual orderings of the options. This does *not* mean that there is no limit on the option set (this mistaken view is common). Rather, it means that once we specify an option set (x, y, z) that individuals are ordering, then we allow every possible ordering (permutation) of that option set. We cannot, for example, say that the ordering "$x \succcurlyeq z \succcurlyeq y$" is impermissible.

(2) **Weak Pareto Principle (WP)**—For any pair of options (x,y), if for all individuals $x \succ y$, then xPy. If every individual prefers x to y, then the social preference is x over y. We have already encountered this principle in Sen's story of Lewd and Prude in chapter 4.

(3) **Pairwise Independence of Irrelevant Alternatives (IIA)**—The basic idea here is that the social choice between x and y cannot depend on the presence or absence of a third—irrelevant for this pairwise choice—alternative, z. One way to formalize this idea is to suppose that we have a SWF, and we apply it to two different sets of individual preference orderings—by the same people—over the same option set, e.g., $\{w,x,y,z\}$, if x and y are in both sets and every individual orders x and y the same in both sets, then Condition IIA requires that the social preference between x and y cannot be different in the two sets. An individual might vary all the orderings of other preferences over other options between the two profiles, and the set of options in the two profiles may otherwise differ. Condition IIA requires that whatever social preference our SWF yields between x and y in the first profile must be the same in the second. Put slightly differently, if an individual prefers x to y when z is available, adding another option w or removing z should not change the fact that $x \succ y$.

---

12. Arrow, Social Choice and Individual Values.

Pairwise choice should be invariant to expansion or contraction of the set of options.

(4) **Non-dictatorship (D)**—There is no individual i such that for every option, whatever i prefers is the social preference. That is, it cannot be the case that there is some i, such that for every option in the option set, if $i{:}x \succ y$, then xPy.

The idea of a "Dictator" is easily misunderstood. Arrow will show that if the other conditions are met, there will always be a Dictator. But this does not mean that if we first specify a complete array of preferences—a complete preference profile for a group—we can inspect it at the outset and will find there is one-person i's preference profile such that their profile is equivalent to the entire social preference ordering. In other words, that there is a Dictator in Arrow's sense does not say that we begin with a certain snapshot of all the preferences at time t_1, and that snapshot will always reveal there is some person i, whose preferences are always at the outset the same as the social preference.[13] Dictatorship is a *power* such that there is a person i who can always change her preferences in such a way that she will have control over the social choice between any x and y regardless of what others prefer.

The First Stage of the Theorem: From Local Semi-Decisiveness to Global Decisiveness

One way to understand Arrow's proof is as a two-stage argument.[14] First it is shown that *if* an individual has the *power* to decide between any one ordered pair of options, i.e., that individual's preference is the social preference even if no one else agrees, that individual becomes the overall dictator. Second, it shows that there *really is* such a person; hence both steps together establish a

---

13. There are versions of Arrow's proof that provide a similar result for this "snapshot" case, where preferences are held fixed. The conditions, however, are different. In these versions of the proof, it is indeed the case that, looking at the preference profile, there is one person whose ordering is equivalent to the social ordering. It is interesting that there can be trivial dictators in this sense: if there is a person who is indifferent among all alternatives, then the social preference will imply her preference. She holds $x \succeq y$ and $y \succeq x$. If the social preference is xPy, that is consistent with her preference $x \succeq y$. If the social preference is yPx, that is consistent with her preference $y \succeq x$. And of course, if the social preference is for indifference, that is consistent with her preferences too. So, she always gets her preference satisfied. Even more obviously, on this "snapshot" view, if everyone happens to have the same preferences, then everyone is a Dictator (by virtue of Weak Pareto)! For an accessible fixed-profile proof, see Felman and Serrano, "Arrow's Impossibility Theorem."

14. The explication here follows Sen's in Collective Choice and Social Welfare, chap. 3.

dictator. The first stage of the argument, then, is to show how—roughly—if some individual has the sole power to make the social choice between two ordered options, this can give him the power to decide between all other pairs.

We must first introduce two more definitions:

(a) **Semi-decisiveness**—A set of individuals S is *semi-decisive* for x over y if xPy when for every individual in S $x \succ y$, and $y \succ x$ for every individual not in S. Note two things. First, that the set S is semi-decisive for x over y does not entail that S is semi-decisive for y over x. Second, we can see that semi-decisiveness is rather odd since S determines the social preferences only when everyone in it prefers x to y *and* everyone not in S has the opposite preference, y over x.

(b) **Decisiveness**—A set of individuals S is decisive for x over y if xPy when for every individual in S, $x \succ y$. So, if S is decisive, when it agrees that $x \succ y$, then xPy regardless of what those outside of S prefer. Decisiveness is a stronger condition than semi-decisiveness, so if S is decisive for x over y, S is *semi-decisive* for x over y.

We first can show that if there is some individual Alf, who is semi-decisive between any pair (x,y), then Alf must be a dictator. Starting with Alf's semi-decisiveness over just one pair, he becomes decisive over every pair and is, hence, a dictator.

So, our supposition is that Alf is semi-decisive for x over y. Let z be any other alternative. Suppose that Alf's preference ordering is $(x \succ y)$ and $(y \succ z)$, and for everyone else in society—call these "The Others"—$(y \succ x)$ and $(y \succ z)$. Remember, given the unlimited domain condition, we can specify any preferences we like. Note that the preference relation between x and z is only specified (via transitivity) for Alf (for whom $x \succ z$). For Alf, then, we have $x \succ y$, and for The Others, $y \succ x$; Alf's semi-decisive power over the (x,y) pair implies that xPy.

The Weak Pareto principle now can be invoked to determine the social preference between y and z; since for Alf $y \succ z$, and for The Others $y \succ z$, then by the Weak Pareto principle yPz. We also know that a SWF must yield a transitive social preference, thus given (xPy) and (yPz), it must follow that xPz. Again, we know that xPz even though we have not supposed anything about any non-decisive individual's preference between x and z. We have only assumed that for The Others, $y \succ z$ and $y \succ x$. Here the IIA condition comes in: by pairwise independence of irrelevant alternatives, we know that the preferences of The Others over y and z, and over y and x, cannot affect their preferences over x and z.

So, nothing in the assumptions we have made about the preferences of The Others has any implications for their preferences of x and z; it is only Alf for whom we have specified $x \succ z$. Hence for Alf $x \succ z$ implies that xPz regardless of how The Others order x and z. Alf's semi-decisive power for x over y has led to his decisive power for x over z. So now he is decisive over (x,z) too. His original semi-decisiveness has spread to decisiveness over a new pair. So, we have our fist conclusion:

(1) If Alf is semi-decisive over (x,y), he is decisive over (x,z).

And we can see that his decisiveness will spread even further. Suppose Alf's preferences are $(z \succ x)$ and $(x \succ y)$; that of The Others is $(z \succ x)$ and $(y \succ x)$. The Weak Pareto condition implies that, since for everyone $z \succ x$, it must be zPx. And since Alf is semi-decisive over (x,y), his preference $x \succ y$ implies xPy. Since we have (zPx) and (xPy), transitivity entails zPy. Again, note that we have no information about what The Others think about the preference relation between z and y; all we know is that Alf holds $z \succ y$ (by transitivity); so now Alf's semi-decisiveness over (x,y) has given him decisiveness over (z,y). So:

(2) If Alf is semi-decisive over (x,y), he is decisive over (z,y).

Now let's use our result from step (1). Recall that we discovered: (1) if Alf is decisive over (x,y), he is decisive over (x,z). Given definitions (a) and (b), if Alf is decisive over (x,z) he is also semi-decisive over that ordered pair. Let's now see how the semi-decisiveness over (x,z) spreads. Suppose next that Alf's preferences are $(y \succ x)$ and $(x \succ z)$, while for all The Others $(y \succ x)$ and $(z \succ x)$. Since Alf is semi-decisive over (x,z), it must be xPz. Again, since everyone holds $(y \succ x)$, the Pareto principle implies yPx. Invoking transitivity, if (yPx) and (xPz), then yPz. We again see that we have no information about the preference of The Others between (y,z), but we do know that (by transitivity) Alf holds $y \succ z$. So, the mere fact that Alf holds $y \succ z$ implies yPz. Thus:

(3) If Alf is semi-decisive over (x,z), he is decisive over (y,z).

By the close of the third step, Alf's semi-decisiveness over (x,y) has spread to decisiveness over the ordered pairs (x,z), (z,y), and (y,z). The same general reasoning can be repeatedly invoked to show that Alf's decisiveness keeps on spreading until he is decisive over every ordered pair among (x,y,z): (x,y), (y,x), (x,z), (z,x), (y,z), and (z,y). Table 8.2 summarizes the necessary steps.

TABLE 8.2. The First Step of the Proof

If Alf Is Semi-Decisive Over	Alf	The Others	Social Preferences	Alf Is Then Decisive Over
1. (x,y); assumption	$(x \succ y) \, \& \, (y \succ z)$	$(y \succ x) \, \& \, (y \succ z)$	$(xPy) \, \& \, (yPz),$ so (xPz)	(x,z)
2. (x,y); assumption	$(z \succ x) \, \& \, (x \succ y)$	$(z \succ x) \, \& \, (y \succ x)$	$(zPx) \, \& \, (xPy),$ so (zPy)	(z,y)
3. (x,z); from (1)*	$(y \succ x) \, \& \, (x \succ z)$	$(y \succ x) \, \& \, (z \succ x)$	$(yPx) \, \& \, (xPz),$ so (yPz)	(y,z)
4. (y,z); from (3)*	$(y \succ z) \, \& \, (z \succ x)$	$(z \succ y) \, \& \, (z \succ x)$	$(yPz) \, \& \, (zPx),$ so (yPx)	(y,x)
5. (y,x); from (4)*	$(z \succ y) \, \& \, (y \succ x)$	$(z \succ y) \, \& \, (x \succ y)$	$(zPy) \, \& \, (yPx),$ so (zPx)	(z,x)
6. (x,z); from (1)*	$(x \succ z) \, \& \, (z \succ y)$	$(z \succ x) \, \& \, (z \succ y)$	$(xPz) \, \& \, (zPy),$ so (xPy)	(x,y)

Once Alf is decisive over all combinations of (x,y,z), we can see that he will be decisive over *all alternatives from the full set of options* (that is, he is a dictator). To see this, take two options out of the larger set at random and call them (v,w). If (v,w) happened to be our original (x,y) alternatives, then we have already shown that Alf is decisive over them. Suppose that one of them was y, but the other was different, so we have a triple $\{x,y,w\}$. But we have already shown that if Alf is semi-decisive for x over y, he is decisive for all pairs in the triple containing x and y, so again Alf is decisive overall.

Last, suppose that v and w are different from x and y. Take just v; we have the triple $\{x,y,v\}$. We have already shown that Alf is decisive over every pair in a triple containing x and y, so Alf will be decisive for x over v. Now add to the $\{x,v\}$ set w, giving us the triple $\{x,v,w\}$. We have already shown that if Alf is semi-decisive over two options in a triple, he is decisive over all the options; since we have said that he is decisive for x and v—and so he must be semi-decisive between them too—he must be decisive for all ordered pairs of $\{x,v,w\}$. But now we have shown that Alf's semi-decisiveness over two options leads to an "epidemic" since if he is semi-decisive over one pair, he is decisive over all pairs.[15] That makes him a dictator.

15. See Craven, Social Choice, 36ff.

The Second Stage of the Theorem: Finding the Dictator

The first stage was hypothetical. It holds that *if* there is a person like Alf who has semi-decisive power over one pair (x,y), he will be a dictator. We now have to show that there is at least one pair over which Alf is semi-decisive; if we do that, given the first part of the proof, we will show he is a dictator. We know that there has to be some decisive set for every ordered pair, even if that S is the entire society. It follows by Definition (b), remember, that any set which is decisive is also semi-decisive. So let us examine all the decisive sets over all pairs, and choose the smallest such set (the smallest decisive set over *any* pairwise choice), and call it V. Assume that V is decisive for (x,y). We have said that V is the smallest decisive set; either it contains one person or more than one. If it contains one, we have found our dictator.

Suppose, then, that it contains more than one person. Divide V into two groups, Alf and "V minus Alf" (*V-Alf*). Call those outside of V, The Others, *O*. Unrestricted domain allows us to suppose any possible preference ordering, so we choose our Condorcet Paradox orderings, as they appear in table 8.3.

TABLE 8.3. Condorcet Paradox Ordering in Arrow's Theorem

Alf	V-Alf	O
x	z	y
y	x	z
z	y	x

Since for all members of V $x \succ y$, it must be that xPy: this follows from the definition of V being the decisive set over (x,y). What about y and z? We see from table 8.3 that only *V-Alf* holds $z \succ y$; if zPy, then *V-Alf* would be the decisive set for z over y. But we have supposed that V is the smallest decisive set; since *V-Alf* is a proper subset of V, it cannot be a decisive set. So, we know $\neg(zPy)$. By completeness, then, it must be that y is socially at least as preferred (strictly preferred, or indifferent) to z, so yRz. If, though, xPy and yRz, transitivity implies xPz. If x is preferred to y, and y is at least as good as z, then x must be preferred to z.

However, Alf is the only person who holds $x \succ z$, so Alf is semi-decisive for x over z. Therefore, we have located a single person who is semi-decisive over one pair. But, by the first part of the proof, that shows him to be decisive over all options, so he is a dictator. But we have assumed

Non-dictatorship: hence we have contradicted our original assumptions. All the conditions cannot be met.

Arrow's Theorem

Given more than two options and more than two individuals, there is no SWF that can generate a social ordering that meets the following conditions:

1.   Unlimited Domain
2.   Weak Pareto
3.   Independence of Irrelevant Alternatives
4.   Non-Dictatorship

Given conditions 1–3, the social outcome is either an ordering (transitive) or non-dictatorial, but not both.

Representation and Coherence

Arrow's proof is sometimes said to reveal a conflict between "representation" and "coherence." We can obtain coherent social preferences if we are willing to abandon the requirement that the social preference reflects the preferences of the body of citizens—we can accept a dictator or abandon the Weak Pareto principle—or we can ensure that the social preference reflects the preferences of the citizens, but then, as the Condorcet Paradox shows, we can end up with an incoherent social preference. One can easily see why Arrow's theorem is seen as a challenge to the rationality of democracy. If the aim of democracy is to generate a social decision that (1) represents the preferences of the citizens no matter what their preferences, and yet (2) is coherent, it seems that democracy aims at the impossible. Not all the conditions can be met; the set is contradictory.

The Importance of Arrow's Theorem

Does Arrow's Theorem Challenge Democracy?

Arrow's theorem shows that there is no way to construct a Social Welfare Function that is guaranteed to meet his conditions. Democracy can be seen as a way of aggregative preferences (notions of betterness) into a social decision. So then does Arrow's theorem undermine the rationality of democracy? Interestingly, some insist that it must cause us to question whether democracy can be said to be a way to generate a reasonable social choice, while others dismiss the theorem as interesting, but not crucial. There are four important ways to challenge it.

First, we might dispute whether Arrow's conditions are really intuitively compelling; to the extent that we do not mind dropping one of the conditions, the proof should not cause concern. The pairwise independence and unrestricted domain conditions both have been subject to considerable debate.

Second, it is sometimes argued that Arrow's theorem is concerned with mere "preferences," but democratic decision-making pertains to rational judgments about what is in the common good; so, it is said, Arrow's problem of how to aggregate individual preferences into a social preference is irrelevant to democratic decision- making. This challenge is, we think, misguided, for at least two reasons.

(a) As we have stressed throughout, a "preference" is simply a ranking of one option over another—it does not necessarily involve a liking, any sort of selfishness, etc. If democratic politics is about asking people to choose among candidates or policies (for whatever reasons), the idea of a preference is entirely appropriate.

(b) Christian List and Philip Pettit have presented an Arrow-like impossibility theorem that concerns the aggregation of judgments based on several reasons. So even if we understand democratic politics as a "forum" in which people debate (and vote on) the reasons for their political judgments rather than simply reporting their conclusions (rankings), a result very much like Arrow's obtains.[16]

Third, some insist that in democratic politics we do not aim at a social ordering, but only a social choice, that is, we should see democracy as a CCR (Collective Choice Rule), not a SWF, and thus, again, we need not worry about the theorem. We consider that reply in the next section.

Fourth, it can be argued that Arrow's theorem relies on the Condorcet Paradox preference orderings in finding the dictator, but if this pattern of orderings does not, as a matter of fact, often arise, then we won't actually confront the inconsistency at the heart of the proof. Indeed, it is important to realize that unrestricted domain does a lot of work in the theorem.

---

16. See List and Pettit, "Aggregating Sets of Judgments." The List-Pettit result is relevant to contexts in which the several reasons are relevant to a conclusion. Suppose a legal doctrine says that a person is responsible for his action ϕ at law if and only if conditions A, B, and C all hold. Instead of taking a vote among jurors and asking each for their final decision ("Do conditions A, B, and C all hold?"), we might take a series of votes: "Does condition A hold?," "Does condition B hold?," and "Does Condition C hold?" After taking a series of votes on these three questions, we might say that the person is liable if and only if a majority of jurors have answered "yes" to all three questions. The answer generated by this procedure can differ radically from the answer that would be generated by asking each juror, "Do all three conditions hold?"

Dimensionality

So, are Condorcet Paradox orderings a problem in politics? There is a nice answer to when we can expect Condorcet Paradox sorts of orderings to arise. Let us call a *dimension* an option space along which each person has some ideal point, and in each direction, the further you get from the person's ideal point, the less preferred is the option. Right to Left in politics; Dove to Hawk on war issues; pro to con on civil rights—all these are examples of an option dimension.

Consider a voter, Alf. Say he sees the options (x, y, z) as arranged along the Left/Right dimension in politics. Alf is a middle-of-the-road independent, so he prefers y as the best; x and z are worse than y. But let us say he thinks that z is better than x. Betty too sees the options in terms of a Left/Right dimension, but being a Leftist, she ranks x as the best, Alf's middle-of-the-road y as the second best, and z as the worst. Charlie also sees the options along this dimension, but as a conservative he orders them $z > y > x$. We thus obtain figure 8.1.

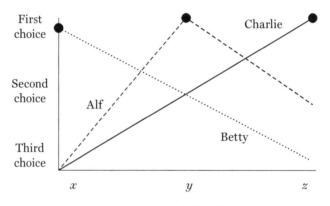

FIGURE 8.1. Single-Peaked Preferences

In this case, although Alf, Betty, and Charlie disagree on the best option, because they order their options along the same dimension, all their preference curves are *single-peaked*. If all the preferences are single-peaked, Condorcet Paradox preference orderings cannot arise.

Assume, though, that Betty no longer sees the options in terms of Left/Right, but in terms of for or against free markets, and she rejects free markets. And suppose that she sees x as the best option (the most left and the most restrictive in terms of markets) but her second choice is z, the proposal of the right, since she thinks that conservatives at least appreciate the limits of the market—the conservatives too have doubts about "liberal economics" characteristic of *y*. She thus changes her ordering, and we get figure 8.2.

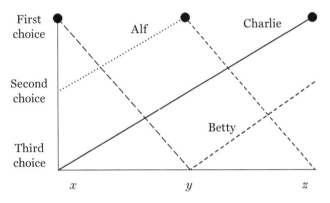

FIGURE 8.2. Double-Peaked Preferences

Betty no longer orders her preferences along the *x-y-z* dimension; we can see that her preference curve is *double-peaked*: this is not the relevant dimension along which she orders her options. Even though *y* is closer to her ideal point than is *z*, she prefers *z* to *y*. And now we have a Condorcet Paradox ordering. Thus, when voters do not agree on the relevant dimension of the option space, Condorcet Paradox orderings can arise.

How often do cycles actually arise? There is spirited debate about this in the literature on democracy: some think that uncontrived cycles are rare, while others believe they are more common. As we will see, however, the main importance of Condorcet Paradox type cycles may be the way they lend themselves to various sorts of contrived manipulation.

Collective Choice Rules

It is hard to have faith in any SWF in the light of Arrow's theorem. To be sure, as we have stressed, SWFs can, under some profile of preferences, satisfy the Pareto principle, non-dictatorship, and the independence of irrelevant alternatives. But when the preference profiles of the citizens display considerable multidimensionality, Arrow-type problems come to the fore. Moreover, as we shall see, minorities can generate voting cycles by misrepresenting their true preferences, thus magnifying the problems to which Arrow points.

At this juncture, though, students of democracy may insist that social welfare functions are not really of much interest. After all, we do not want a social ordering, just a social *choice*: for any set of options, we only want to pick out the *best*. Our interest should be in collective choice rules, not social welfare functions. At first blush this looks inviting since some CCRs meet all of Arrow's conditions, so the proof does not preclude all Collective Choice Rules. The difference between a SWF and a CCR is, of course, the transitivity requirement—Arrow requires strict transitivity of the social ordering of all options.

What does a CCR require? Let us follow Sen in requiring of any collective choice rule that, for any set of options $\{w,x,y,z\}$, the CCR can select one option as best. Now Sen shows that, so understood, such a CCR requires social preferences that are reflexive, complete, and *acyclical* over the entire set of preferences.[17] Social preferences are acyclical if $\{wPx, xPy, yPz\}$ then wRz, that is, w must be, socially, at least as good as z. We can easily see how cyclical preferences mean that there may be no best choice from some sets. Consider the Condorcet Paradox preferences and consider what is the best choice from the set $\{x,y,z\}$. There is, of course, no best choice from the entire set: we get xPy, yPz, zPx, so we cannot choose. So, if we are going to guarantee that a choice can always be made, we must ensure that we do not have cycles; thus, we require that the results be *acyclical*. To get a better idea of a Collective Choice Rule, consider an example of a rule that Sen discusses:

> *Pareto Choice or Indifference*—if for everyone $x > y$, then xPy; if it is not the case that for everyone $y > x$, then xRy (that is, x is socially at least as good as y).

So, on this rule, x is socially preferred to y only if everyone prefers it; and, of course, the same goes for y vis-à-vis x. If there is any disagreement in people's strict preference profiles about x and y (for some $x > y$, for others $y > x$), then (xRy) and (yRx)—x is socially at least as good as y, and y is socially at least as good as x. And that means that socially $\{x$ and $y\}$ are indifferent (xIy).

Using this Collective Choice Rule, our Condorcet Paradox orderings yield a "choice" of xIy, yIz, xIz. But in this case the rule satisfies all of Arrow's requirements. Suppose instead we just consider Alf's and Betty's preferences. For Alf $(x > y > z)$ and for Betty $(y > z > x)$. Since for both $y > z$, the CCR yields yPz; since they disagree on the other pairings, we get social indifference—xIy, yIz. Now, however, transitivity is violated. Given (xIy) and (yPz), we should get (xPz): if society is indifferent between x and y, but y is better than z, transitivity would hold that x is better than z. Instead, our CCR says xIz.

However, acyclicity does still hold: we get a "best" (even if it is a tie) from every possible set. We also can see that Pareto choice or indifference satisfies

---

17. Sen, Collective Choice and Social Welfare, 14–18.

all the rest of Arrow's conditions. It obviously satisfies the Pareto condition, since it is defined never to yield a choice against it. It does not violate the independence of irrelevant alternatives, since we can see that in deciding between x and y, it is only concerned with people's preferences over x and y; we have a good inkling that unrestricted domain will not cause trouble, since we have used Condorcet Paradox orderings; and we can never have a dictator, since xPy only if everyone agrees.

Problems of Collective Choice Rules

However, while Arrow's theorem does not apply to CCRs (since they do not require transitivity), they have their own Arrow-like problems. Arrow, it will be recalled, showed that a SWF meeting the pairwise independence condition (IIA), unrestricted domain (U), and the Pareto principle (P) always has a dictator; it has been shown that any CCR that meets *IIA, U,* and *P* will always have something very much like an *oligarchy* (a subgroup) that can always veto a social choice.[18] That is, the dynamic of Arrow's theorem, in which decision-making power becomes concentrated in one person, also obtains for CCR, though in a somewhat mitigated form. Instead of a dictator, we find subgroups that are able to impose their will by blocking whatever others want or (given slightly different conditions) actually imposing their will.

Transitivity can be seen as a condition of consistent choice in Social Welfare Functions. When we consider Collective Choice Rules, we still need some conditions of consistent choice. Two properties seem attractive: the *contraction* and *expansion* properties. According to the *contraction* property, if x is chosen from the entire set S, it must be chosen from all subsets of S in which x is included. Our polite mango refuser from chapter 2 violates this by selecting a mango from the set {mango, mango, apple} but an apple from the subset {mango, apple}. Our chooser will also violate the weak expansion principle: if an option is chosen from each of two subsets, it must still be chosen when the sets are combined. Suppose our person is confronted with two sets {apple, apple, mango} and {apple, mango}. Because she will not take the last mango, she will choose {apple} from the first set and {apple} from the second. But if

18. We are simplifying a bit here. If one adopts a condition slightly stronger than acyclicity, called "quasi-transitivity" (transitivity of strict preference only), then there will always be an oligarchic group who can impose their preferences; if one adds positive responsiveness to the conditions, then such a CCR will have a dictator. The results for a CCR that only meets acyclicity are weaker, uncovering a vetoer, who is very similar to an oligarch group. See Riker, *Liberalism Against Populism*, 131.

we combine the two sets to get {apple, apple, apple, mango, mango} she will choose a mango, thus violating the weak expansion property. So according to the *contraction principle*, if from a set {x,y,z} a person chooses x, he must choose x from the other subsets in which it enters {x,y}, {x,z}. If it is the best in the entire set, it must be best in every subset it is in. It would be odd indeed if, thinking that x is the best choice when confronted by three options, one no longer thinks that x is best if one considers it in relation to just one of those options.

According to the *expansion principle* (roughly), if x is chosen as best in the set {x,y,z}, and if there is a set {w,x,y,z}, y or z cannot be the social choice from the larger set; if x is better than y and z in the small set, it must be better than they are in the larger set. This expansion principle implies the *weak expansion principle*: if x is chosen from the set {x,y,z} and x is chosen from the set {v,w,x}, it must be chosen from the union of those two sets.

These seem to be reasonable conditions of consistent choice since collective choice rules that violate them yield inconsistent choices about what is the best depending on how we divide the options. If we violate these principles, then an option that is best in a large set may not be best in a smaller set; an option that beats another in a small set may lose to that same option in a larger set. However, it can be shown that the expansion property applied to CCRs essentially turns them into SWFs, and so Arrow's theorem then applies to such CCRs. Thus, if we wish to avoid Arrow's theorem by adopting a CCR, we must abandon the expansion principle as a principle of rational choice. And that involves a considerable cost. But if we do not abandon it, Arrow's theorem applies to our collective choice rule.

Extending Social Choice Rules

We know from May's theorem that simple majority decision-making over two alternatives is uniquely characterized by universal domain, anonymity, neutrality, and strong monotonicity. The problem—and this is at the heart of Arrow's theorem—is that we seldom have only two alternatives since usually there are a number of possibilities among which we are trying to decide. Is there any way to extend the wonders of majority decision-making to these cases with three or more alternatives? Although there are indeed methods—some of which are widely used—that seek to extend majority decision-making to three or more alternatives, each of them has flaws.

Remember that a social choice mechanism is some way of taking all the preference orderings of individuals and generating out of these a Collective Choice. If a full social ordering is produced, we have a Social Welfare Function; if only a best choice is made, we have a Collective Choice Rule.

Condorcet Method

We have considered the Condorcet method in our explication of the Condorcet Paradox. It seems the most direct extension to majority vote between two alternatives to a vote among more than two alternatives: it splits the choices into pairs, and then makes pairwise majority decisions. We have seen from the Condorcet Paradox that the Condorcet method violates transitivity. This also means that it violates May's Decisiveness condition, since it cannot identify a best from the set.

A Weakly Positional Method: Plurality

Let's distinguish two sorts of positional methods, Weakly Positional and Strongly Positional methods.

A *weakly positional* method uses a categorical (yes/no; best choice) ballot, and then determines the outcome based upon tallying the categorical ballots. A categorical ballot doesn't ask you to order the candidates. Instead, it simply asks you which one do you like the best? You ignore all the other options and vote for the one that you think is the best.

Plurality is employed in most elections in the UK and the United States. These systems are based on a categorical ballot. When a Republican, a Democrat, and an Independent are running against each other, voters are not asked to rank them in order of preference. All they are asked to do is report their first preference. The plurality method then allows society to order the candidates by the number of votes they get: the candidate that is at the top of the list wins. Plurality is probably best conceived of as a Collective Choice Rule, since it seldom cares about anything but the candidate who gets the most votes. Yet it can also function as a SWF, when it makes a difference which party came in second (perhaps they will form the official opposition).

We call this a *weakly* positional method because (1) the voters do not order the candidates but (2) all the candidates run against each other at the same time, and (3) the candidate who comes out on top—has the top position—wins.

Plurality is a simple method. Unlike the Condorcet method or the Borda method (see below), we do not have to do a great deal of work in order to find the plurality winner. The problem is that plurality is able to select what is, in a fairly clear sense, the most unpopular option, as shown in table 8.4.[19]

---

19. Table take from Riker, Liberalism Against Populism, 50.

TABLE 8.4. Plurality Voting Example

Voters	1st	2nd	3rd	4th
9	w	z	x	y
6	x	y	z	w
2	y	x	z	w
4	y	z	x	w
5	z	x	y	w

Note that w gets the most first-place votes (9) but everyone else (17) places it last. William Riker argued that this has occurred in actual American elections, such as the US 1912 presidential election, and perhaps the critical 1860 election that elected Abraham Lincoln.

Viewed as a Collective Choice Rule, plurality violates the expansion condition. It can beat an option in a small set but loses to that same option in a larger set. Suppose that we have a five-member electorate, choosing between only x and y, and the results are as presented in table 8.5, where x gets three first-place votes and y gets two, so xPy. Now z enters, and two voters (Betty and Charlie) prefer it to x, giving us the results in table 8.6.

TABLE 8.5. Plurality Voting with Two Options

Alf	Betty	Charlie	Doris	Eugene
x	x	x	y	y
y	y	y	x	x

TABLE 8.6. Expanded Plurality Voting with Three Options

Alf	Betty	Charlie	Doris	Eugene
x	z	z	y	y
y	x	x	x	x
z	y	y	z	z

Notice that no one changes their relative orderings of x and y in the two pro-files; all that changes is that they now must insert z into their orderings. But we see with the addition of z, which is not relevant to the social preference between x and y, the social ordering goes from xPy to yPx (we have a tie for first place, zIy). This violates the expansion consistency condition: you can defeat a victor, x, without changing *anyone's* preference, simply by adding an-other option. Thus, "splitting the opposition" by introducing a third alternative is a typical strategy in systems that use plurality.

A Strongly Positional Method: Borda Count

A strongly positional method presents the voters with an ordinal (rather than categorical) ballot, and then compares all the candidates at the same time to get a social ordering. A strongly positional method is the Borda count. The Borda count tallies the ranks that each voter assigns to each candidate. The candidate with the lowest score wins. Table 8.7 calculates the Borda winner (and ordering) from the plurality profile from above.

TABLE 8.7. Borda Count Example

	1st	2nd	3rd	4th	Total
w	9 (×1)	0	0	17 (×4)	77
x	6 (×1)	7 (×2)	13 (×3)	0	59
y	6 (×1)	6 (×2)	5 (×3)	1 (×4)	37
z	5 (×1)	13 (×2)	8 (×3)	0	55

So, we get $yPzPxPw$—a different result from the plurality rule. Borda has many attractive qualities. It has, for example, a high tendency to track the Condorcet winner when there is one: when Condorcet yields cycles, Borda will usually yield a tie.

Yet, it has drawbacks. As a positional method it violates Independence (IIA). We can actually identify two Independence conditions. Recall the char-acterization that I employed in Arrow's theorem: suppose we have an SWF, and we apply it to two different sets of individual preferences orderings over the same option set. Suppose that x and y are in both sets, and every individual orders x and y the same in both sets. That is, whatever individual i's preference is between x and y in the first profile, he has the same pairwise preference in the second profile.

To see how Borda violates this condition, compare tables 8.8 and 8.9.

TABLE 8.8. Borda Count Basic Case

Voters	1st	2nd	3rd	4th
9	w	z	x	y
6	x	y	z	w
2	y	x	z	w
4	y	z	x	w
5	z	x	y	w

TABLE 8.9. Borda Count with Preferences that Violate IIA

Voters	1st	2nd	3rd	4th
9	w	z	x	y
6	x	y	w	z
2	y	x	w	z
4	y	z	x	w
5	z	x	y	w

Two groups of voters have changed their relative evaluation of z and w—they have decided that w is better than z—but no one has changed their relative evaluations of x and z. Yet, because z now gets additional points by those voters who have relegated it to their fourth position, society goes from zPx to xPz, a violation of pairwise independence.

The Independence condition can also be understood as an *expansion or contraction consistency* condition. On this interpretation, we take option set $\{x,y,z\}$ and we either expand it to include w, or contract it to omit z. According to this interpretation, if everyone's ordering between x and y is the same in both profiles, the social ordering of x and y should be the same in both profiles. Consider table 8.10, which is simply a contraction of our initial profile with y omitted, and no one has changed *any* orderings of the remaining w, x, or z.

TABLE 8.10. Borda Count Contraction Inconsistency

Voters	1st	2nd	3rd
9	w	z	x
6	x	z	w
2	x	z	w
4	z	x	w
5	z	x	w

Again, society goes from zPx to xPz,[20] violation of this understanding of pairwise independence.

Cardinal Methods

A positional method such as Borda counts "aheadness"—it counts how many places ahead one option is to another. To say that w ended up three places behind y in the social ordering is not to say that anyone, or society, preferred y three times as much as w, or even that it far more intensely prefers y to w. However, a number of democratic theorists—especially, we think, economists—have felt that we should measure how *much* you prefer an option. We thus may seek to measure the utility an option gives a voter—say, using von Neumann–Morgenstern utilities—and then aggregate them.[21] But wait! We also need full interpersonal comparisons, so that we can say that if for Alf $\mu(y) = 1$, that is the same utility as Betty $= \mu(y) = 1$. We have already looked at a bit of the debate surrounding interpersonal comparisons of utility in chapter 2. To use the cardinal method of voting, there must be a good argument for comparing people's utilities in a certain way.

A simpler method—one that does not seek to account for attitudes toward risk—is just to ask each person to place each option on a cardinal scale, and again we assume that the top and bottom of these scales are in some sense "equivalent" for each voter. At this point we could either simply add the utilities (this is sometimes called the "Bentham method") or, alternatively, we

20. x now gets 30 points and z gets 43.

21. In order to say society preferred y three times as much, we would need a ratio scale with a non-arbitrary zero point, but we can set that aside for now.

perform some other aggregation method such as multiplying the utilities (this is sometimes called the "Nash method"). Cardinal methods violate Independence for much the same reason as Borda does.

Elimination Methods

Given that majority vote over two options has the wonderful qualities May demonstrated, perhaps what we should be doing is trying to get down to a binary choice. Elimination procedures seek to do this through a series of votes (or stages) in which a large set of options is reduced to two. Runoff elections and primary systems are examples of elimination procedures.

Some elimination procedures are built into the way the voters are counted. Consider for example, a system along the lines of that used in elections to the Senate in Australia—the single transferable vote (STV). Elections to Australia's Senate (the upper chamber of the legislature) combine the single transferable vote with proportional representation. Voters have to order all the candidates running from first to last (or at least some minimum number).[22]

TABLE 8.11. Single Transferable Vote (STV) Example

Voters	1st	2nd	3rd	4th
9	w	z	x	y
6	x	y	z	w
2	y	x	z	w
4	y	z	x	w
5	z	x	y	w

The single transferable vote works by rounds. If a round does not produce an option that has more than 50% of the vote, the option with the least number of votes in that round is eliminated, and its votes are *transferred to* the voter's

22. Technically, in Senate elections in Australia, voters can vote "above the line" or "below the line." The second option involves ranking at least twelve candidates and as many as all of them. Voting "above" the line involves ranking at least six parties. The preference rankings (not necessarily the candidates) of each party are then used instead of the direct ranking of candidates. Before the election, the parties make deals with one another, "trading preferences" to include other parties' candidates higher in their rankings.

next preference. If no majoritarian winner yet appears, the procedure is repeated until one option gets a majority. So, at the end of the process, some option does get a majority of support.

In table 8.11, no option receives a majority in the first round, so the option with the least votes in that round is eliminated: in this case z, which has five first-place votes. So, we now have the profile presented in table 8.12.

TABLE 8.12. Second Stage of the STV

Voters	1st	2nd	3rd
9	w	x	y
6	x	y	w
2	y	x	w
4	y	x	w
5	x	y	w

There is still no majority winner, so y (the remaining option with the lowest first-place votes), and its votes are transferred to the voter's next choice, as in table 8.13.

TABLE 8.13. Third Stage of the STV

Voters	1st	2nd
9	w	x
6	x	w
2	x	w
4	x	w
5	x	w

At this point x emerges as the majoritarian winner. Alas, elimination procedures violate May's condition of non-negative responsiveness (which is implied by Arrow's Weak Pareto Condition). To see this, let's go back to the original figure, shown in table 8.14.

TABLE 8.14. STV with Monotonicity Violation

Voters	1st	2nd	3rd	4th
9	w	z	x	y
6	x	y	z	w
2	y	x	z	w
4	y	z	x	w
5	z	x	y	w

Recall that on the single transferable vote system, x is the winner. Now non-negative responsiveness (monotonicity) requires that it is impossible for x to be hurt by being *more* preferred: someone voting for x cannot cause x to lose!

To see how the single-transferable vote violates this condition, suppose that the two voters who rank the options $y \succ x \succ z \succ w$, decide they prefer x to y, so they switch their order to $x \succ y \succ z \succ w$. So, let's go through the elimination procedure again. Note that y is now the weakest option in the first round, so it is eliminated, and its votes transferred to the voter's next choice, producing the second-round tally in table 8.15.

TABLE 8.15. STV Winner after Vote Switching

Voters	1st	2nd	3rd
9	w	z	x
6	x	z	w
2	x	z	w
4	z	x	w
5	z	x	w

Now x is eliminated (having 8 votes to z's 9), and z goes on to win. Thus, because two voters became more favorable to x, it lost. Many, including Riker, believe this is a serious flaw in a voting system. It also, we shall see, makes elimination systems subject to manipulation.

What to Choose?

So where are we in deciding how to extend majority voting to three or more options? In our core example, Plurality chooses w, the Condorcet method chooses z (check this for yourself), Borda selects y, and the Single Transferable vote gets us x. We have managed to select all four possibilities through commonly used voting systems. In this case, pick your favorite way of extending majoritarianism to three options, and you can also pick your favorite option. As we will see, this is a generalizable feature of voting systems.

Path Dependency and Agenda Manipulation

Arrow stressed the importance of a final choice being *independent of the path to it.*[23] The crux of *path independency* is that the best choice from the set $\{w,x,y,z\}$ should not vary depending on the order in which we take up the options, or the subsets we first consider in our path to a final choice. Path *inde*pendency assures us that when our CCR (Collective Choice Rule) selects a "best option" from a set, this selection is not an artifact of the order in which we considered the options—the path by which the final choice was reached. If we considered the same options in a different order, we would have arrived at the same choice from the same set.

If we aim at a CCR that really uncovers what is the best social choice given a profile of individual preferences, we will insist on a path-independent choice rule. When we employ a path-*de*pendent choice rule, we must accept that while our CCR selected y as best from the set, it could have selected some other option from the same set if we had considered the options in another order. In that case our choice is an artifact of the path. However, it turns out that path independence requires the *contraction* and *weak expansion principles*; thus, any path-independent CCR is subject to Arrow-like problems of concentration of decision-making power in some oligarchic-like group.[24]

If we want to avoid Arrow-like concentration of power problems, we must embrace path-*de*pendent CCRs. Well, we might ask, what is so bad about path-dependent Collective Choice Rules? Why not avoid Arrow-like problems by simply rejecting the contraction and weak expansion principles?

Consider more closely what follows from path dependency, such as the procedure used to decide on bills in the US Congress. First a proposal (call it x) is brought before Congress; amendments (call one y) are then proposed,

23. See Sen, Collective Choice and Social Welfare, 48n.

24. See Riker, Liberalism Against Populism, 135.

and a vote is taken between x and y. Finally, there is a vote between no bill at all (call it z) and whatever bill won the x versus y contest. This means that one of the pairs—either (x,z) or (y,z)—is never voted on. Since the outcome depends on the order in which the options are considered—or, we might say, the way the total option set is divided up in decision-making), those who control the agenda—the order in which the options are considered—have great power in determining the outcome. A committee chair who sets the agenda may well be able to determine the outcome! Path-dependent CCRs thus allow for *manipulation of the agenda.*

Path Dependency in Legislation

Again, there is lively dispute about how pervasive path dependency and agenda manipulation are. William Riker famously argued that they were the stuff of politics. Consider, for example, Riker's account of the aid to education bill in the late 1950s and early 1960s.[25] The Democratic leadership in the US House of Representatives put forward a bill that would provide the states with federal funds for building schools. The Democrats were generally in favor of such aid while the Republicans opposed it. However, each time the bill was proposed, Adam Clayton Powell, an African American member from Harlem, offered an amendment, requiring that aid would only be given to states whose schools were "open to all children without regard to race." This was called the Powell Amendment.

Southern Democrats—who supported federal aid to education, since they would be net recipients—opposed the amendment, since under the amendment the South would not receive aid, having segregated school systems. In contrast, urban Democrats from the North supported the amendment; but the Democratic leadership opposed the amendment, primarily because it would make the school aid bill harder to pass. The Republicans, who were generally against the expansion of the federal government, opposed federal aid to education. To analyze the voting, let:

x = the bill with the Powell amendment
y = the original, unamended bill
z = the status quo (no federal aid to education)

Let us distinguish four groups in Congress:

---

25. This account comes from Riker, The Art of Political Manipulation, chap. 11. All quotes are from this chapter.

The Powellians $(x > y > z)$—These members preferred the amended bill to the original bill and preferred both to no bill at all. Northern Democrats would form the core of this group.

The School Aiders $(y > x > z)$—This group preferred school aid to anything else. This included Democrats following the Democratic party leadership—who saw the Powell amendment as killing school aid—and some Republicans.

The Southerners $(y > z > x)$—As the story indicates, they were segregationist Democrats who supported school aid, but strongly opposed the Powell amendment.

Republicans Against Aid $(z > x > y)$—This probably is not quite right; Riker argues that the Republicans split into two groups, as we will see later on. But for now, we will treat them as one group with this preference order.

Riker advances the following estimate of the relative strengths of the groups:

The Powellians $(x > y > z)$: 132
The School Aiders $(y > x > z)$: 67
The Southerners $(y > z > x)$: 130
Republicans against Aid $(z > x > y)$: 97

Given this estimate, the result of Condorcet voting would be xPy (229 to 197), yPz (329 to 97), zPx (227 to 199)—a cycle. Note that the original bill (y) easily defeats no bill (z) by a large margin of 329 to 97. But because of path dependency, z was actually selected. Recall that given the path-dependent process followed by Congress, once y was defeated by x it was eliminated from consideration, leaving only x to survive and confront z, with x losing to z. We see, though, that y would have defeated z, since we are in a cycle.

Gerry Mackie has investigated Riker's examples (including the case just presented) and has argued that careful investigation does not support Riker's conclusions. He makes two distinct claims.[26]

First, he challenges Riker's estimations of the voting strength of these groups. If y (the original bill) met z (no bill), Mackie argues that, based on another similar vote, z would have defeated y, hence there would have been no cycle.[27] Whereas Riker holds that y would have beaten z by a large margin, Mackie argues that z would have beaten y by a smaller one. So, there is dispute about the true strengths of the groups, and whether there was a cycle—Riker

26. Mackie, Democracy Defended.
27. Mackie, Democracy Defended, 201.

himself suggests that there may not have been a "real" cycle, but that some of the Republicans voted "strategically."

Second, Mackie argues that even if Riker's estimates of the strength of the groups are correct, Riker's conclusion that there is no coherent way to combine preferences still does not follow. "Does an alleged cycle," Mackie asks, "show once again that the aggregation of preferences is incoherent?" "No," he answers, because there would be other ways to choose among these preferences that would not result in a cycle. "If there was a cycle, then the problem is not with the preference rankings, the problem is with the voting procedure."[28] We are not sure what Mackie means by this. Consider again our Condorcet preference orderings.

TABLE 8.16. Condorcet Preference Ordering

Alf	Betty	Charlie
x	y	z
y	z	x
z	x	y

We know that pairwise voting yields a cycle, xPy, yPz, zPx. But, as Mackie suggests, we might employ another procedure such as the Borda count that will avoid a cycle. In this case, the result is a three-way tie. In some cases, the Borda method can yield a strict social preference even when pairwise voting yields a cycle.

This seems the basis of Mackie's claim that the problem is pairwise voting, not the preference rankings—some other system of voting would yield an answer. Yes, but recall Arrow's theorem: the problem is that every system of voting violates one of the conditions. Borda does have the nice advantage that it gives us a social preference in these cases that is path-independent: there is no ordering of the voting process. Pairwise voting violates transitivity in the case above—to avoid that result, use of Condorcet voting typically imposes an order on the way the pairs are taken up, and that leads to path dependence. But if we use Borda, as we have seen in the previous sections, we then violate pairwise independence of irrelevant alternatives (IIA).

28. Riker, The Art of Political Manipulation, 200. Mackie also disputes this claim of Riker's (and just about every other claim Riker ever made!). See Mackie, Democracy Defended, 201ff.

The lesson of Arrow's theorem is that, as it were, we must choose our poison—will it be intransitivity, violation of the pairwise independence condition, the Pareto principle, unrestricted domain, or non-dictatorship? We can always avoid cycles, but then we must violate some other condition. The "incoherence" of aggregation systems is not that they must yield cycles—that is clearly not the case, and Riker never thought it was—but that they must violate some basic axiom.

Agenda Control in the Flying Club

Michael Levine, a professor of law at USC, went to Charles Plott, a professor of economics at Cal Tech, and said, "Charlie, I'm chairman of an agenda committee of my flying club.[29] We're going to decide on a new fleet. They made me chairman because I'm the only lawyer in the club. But you know more about voting than I do. What's the fair way to do this?" Plott replied that there is no true aggregation of individual preferences into a social preference; lots of reasonably fair rules will yield lots of different results. So, we might as well get the one you want. Let's arrange things that way.

The flying club had sixty-five members who, in 1973, paid $1800 each to join, plus $30 a month, and $25 per hour for the plane rental. They had a fleet of six single-engine planes: three five-year-old Beechcraft E33As, one three-year-old Beechcraft F33A, one three-year-old Beechcraft V35, and one new Cessna 210. The members preferred roomy, fast aircraft, which tend to be expensive. They were dissatisfied with the current fleet because:

- It was not uniform (the V35 and the Cessna 210 had different operating characteristics from the rest of the fleet, a safety concern).
- The older planes were shabby and disliked. They wanted better avionics equipment.
- The planes were not always available when people wanted them.

Members had a clear preference for eliminating the one V35. But, given the club's resources, they were limited to a fleet of four Beechcraft E33A and F33A and possibly one or two six-seated airplanes, either a Beechcraft A36 or Cessna 210. Table 8.17 provides the options.

29. We follow the presentation of this classic example from Riker, The Art of Political Manipulation. You can get the example firsthand from the principles involved, however, in Levine and Plott, "Agenda Influence and Its Implications."

TABLE 8.17. Flight Club Options

Make and Model	Abbreviation Used	Number of Seats	Estimated Rental Per Hour
Beechcraft A36	A	6	$31.50
Beechcraft F33A	F	4	$30.00
Beechcraft E33A (refurbished)	E	4	$24.00
Cessna 210	C	6	$27.00

Most members prefer Beechcraft, while members of the governing board preferred Cessnas because of their new Cessna dealership. A few highly influential members wanted Beechcraft A36s, the most luxurious and expensive single-engine Beechcraft. On the other hand, many members seemed concerned about expenses; they expected to refurbish three E33As but didn't want to buy additional E33As.

Levine's Preferences:

(1) Include in the fleet some six-seated aircraft for family trips. He preferred the cheaper Cessna 210s to the more expensive Beechcraft.
(2) If the 210 was bought, he would like two.
(3) If the A36 was bought, he would want one.
(4) He was indifferent about buying new F33As or E33As to refurbish.

So, his overall fleet preferences were:

1. (5E, 2C) or (3E, 2F, 2C)
2. (5E,1C) or (3E, 2F, 1C)
3. (6E, 1A) or (3E, 3F, 1A)
4. (5E, 2A) or (3E, 2F, 2A)
5. and lower (all E and F)

Levine believed this differed from the rest of the club, who might have preferred all Es, and if the rest of the club did accept a secondary fleet of six-seat planes, they probably preferred As to Cs.

The problem he and Plott confronted was how to devise an agenda that would produce a fleet with one or two Cs against a possible majority for Es and maybe As. The way they would do this is to devise an *agenda* to decide the following questions sequentially:

1. **What type of aircraft should be in the primary fleet?**

    This question was to be decided by Borda count, not because they had any doubt about the outcome, but to ease the concerns of those members who feared being stuck with an expensive fleet, i.e., one that was foisted on them by the influential members who wanted As, and make them agreeable to a seven-plane fleet, which would be more likely to include Cs than a six-plane fleet.

2. **How many planes do you want?**

    This was the crucial question. They believed a plurality wanted a fleet of six four-seat planes. It was important to pose this question in a way to isolate this plurality. They wanted to produce a majority coalition for seven planes, consisting of those who wanted seven four-seaters and those who wanted a fleet with some six-seaters, either As or Cs—the odds of getting a six-seater were better in a seven-plane fleet.

3a. **Do we want a mixed fleet?**

    The third question was intended to pit all those who wanted any kind of six-seat plane—either A or C—against those who wanted a fleet of all Es and Fs. Note here that Plott and Levine were seeking to use the supporters of A to reach a point on the agenda where C could defeat A.

3b. **Should the secondary fleet be one or two planes?**

    In the course of the meeting this question was added to the agenda.

4. **What type of aircraft should be in our secondary fleet?**

    This was intended to finally pit the As against the Cs. Given their expectation that a seven-plane fleet would be adopted, those who were concerned with expenses would side with those who favor the cheaper planes, the Cs.

5. **How elaborately should we equip our aircraft?**

    Levine and Plott saved this for last to make sure that expensive outfitting wouldn't preclude a seven-plane fleet.

The results of this elaborate agenda went in line with their expectations. First, the club tied on the fleets of (3E, 2F, 2C) and (3E, 2F, 2A), but since the governing board preferred Cessnas (they owned the dealership!), this ensured Levine's s favorite outcome of (3E, 2F, 2C). Second, a questionnaire was sent to all members after the meeting asking them to rank the alternatives. If all the main alternatives had confronted each other in a round robin tournament, the winner would have been (3E, 3F, 1A). That would be the Condorcet winner. Levine's preference would have come in second.

The chairman of the club, however, sought to impose his own agenda; he tried to change the opening question to "should we have a fleet of all Beechcraft?" This probably would have been passed and would have precluded Levine's favored fleet. He also tried to introduce before Levine's second question: "If we have a secondary fleet, do we want Beechcraft or Cessena?"

Finally, after question 2 but before 3a, he tried to introduce the question, "Do we want at least one A?" An affirmative answer to any of these questions would have ruled out a fleet with C.

On all these points he was ruled out of order, preserving Levin's agenda.

The result is that Plott and Levine were effectively able to manipulate the Flying Club into selecting their preferred alternatives and to outmaneuver the attempts by the chairman to do something similar. The lesson, according to Riker, is that this type of manipulation is the essence of politics, what he calls "Heresthetics." This is the art of structuring the choice situation in order to win. Agenda manipulation is at the heart of this skill, which Riker argues that all genuinely good political actors must possess.

Riker's lesson goes deeper, though, since the possibility of Heresthetical techniques arises because of the underlying instability of results that Arrow's theorem and similar results show. Agenda manipulation is the result of disequilibrium, such as we find in a Condorcet cycle. In that there is no equilibrium, we can expect a wide variety of results from the same set of preferences; we can go down a wide array of paths, each one yielding a different outcome. And disequilibrium occurs when voters employ different dimensions of evaluation.

Strategic Voting

The problems we have thus far been exploring all have assumed that each individual is reporting their "true" preferences. Of course, on revealed preference theory it does not make any sense to distinguish what a person truly prefers from their behavior; but even so, there is a sense in which a person might order options not because they want the outcome as such, but in order to induce a further outcome. So, we suppose that people can indeed misreport their preferences; by doing so they often can obtain their favored outcome. The most obvious case of strategic voting involves multi-stage votes—such as votes on amendments and bills in Congress—and runoff elections.

For example, in the Aid to Education bill discussed previously, Riker notes that the Democratic leadership in the House was convinced that the Republicans were not really in favor of the Powell amendment, but were voting strategically just to help kill the aid to education bill.[30] That is, the Democratic leadership was convinced that the Republicans' true preference ordering was: $z > y > x$ (no bill, original bill, amended bill). If that was the true preference ordering of even half the Republicans, the amendment would have failed, and Congress would have voted on the unamended bill, which would have passed. By misreporting their true preferences—voting for their third choice over the second choice when the amendment was initially proposed—these Republicans helped to secure their first choice.

Now, what amounts to "true" preference here is a little misleading. The Republicans, for instance, may have preferred $y > x$ if they alone were able to select from that pair, but of course this was not the situation in which they found themselves. The objection or even identification of strategic voting seems to presume that voting is more akin to a parametric decision problem, where the voter acts to bring about an outcome directly, rather than a strategic problem, where the voter acts—in conjunction with other voters—to bring about an outcome. To ignore the strategic nature of any voting situation is to misrepresent the choice problem, though. Unless we assume that voters are primarily concerned with the act of voting rather than with the outcome voting is meant to bring about, we shouldn't be surprised that they will respond to the strategic situation they find themselves in.

Other Examples of Strategic Voting

The Borda count discussed above is clearly subject to strategic voting. Consider table 8.18.

TABLE 8.18. Example of Strategic Voting

Alf	Betty	Charlie	Doris	Eugene
x	x	x	y	y
y	y	y	x	x
z	z	z	z	z

If we use the Borda count, we get $x = 7$ points; $y = 8$ points, $z = 15$ points, so xPy. Suppose that Doris, who wants y to win and knowing that z will win

---

otherwise, strategically reports that x is her third, not her second choice. The outcome would then be 8 points for both x and y, producing a tie (xIy).

Elimination procedures and runoffs are also clearly subject to strategic voting. Think again of our example of a single-transferable vote.

TABLE 8.19. Strategic Voting with the STV

Voters	1st	2nd	3rd
9	w	x	y
6	x	y	w
2	y	x	w
4	y	x	w
5	x	y	w

Suppose the w voters realize that w simply can't win and that if they report their true preferences, the result, we have seen, is x winning, their third choice. If they vote for z rather than w in the first round, however, we have seen that z will go on to beat x if it can survive the first round, so they get their second rather than their third choice by voting against their first choice. In elimination procedures it is often the case that, if one opponent who would have defeated your candidate in the final round can be eliminated early on, your candidate can go on to win.

Logrolling: Vote Trading in Legislatures

Another case of voting strategically occurs when legislators vote against their preferences on Issue 1 (which they care less about) to achieve their preferred outcome on Issue 2 (which they care more about). Sometimes this is called "logrolling" or "vote trading."[31] Assume that we have two issues to be decided in a legislature split into three factions.

> x: whether to provide increased federal funds for urban renewal projects, which will mostly benefit the Rustbelt Areas. Someone *against* this we can say is for not-x, which will be designated $\neg x$.
> y: whether to increase expenditure for defense. Those in the Sunbelt Areas will primarily benefit. Someone against this is for $\neg y$.

---

31. On the ethics of this practice, see Thrasher, "The Ethics of Legislative Vote Trading."

Our three groups are, then: Rustbelters, Sunbelters, and Others. Each has 100 votes in our imaginary legislature. Their preferences are ordered in table 8.20.

TABLE 8.20. Logrolling Preferences

Rustbelters	Sunbelters	Others
$x \& \neg y$	$\neg x \& y$	$\neg x \& \neg y$
$x \& y$	$x \& y$	$\neg x \& y$
$\neg x \& \neg y$	$\neg x \& \neg y$	$x \& \neg y$
$\neg x \& y$	$x \& \neg y$	$x \& y$

According to the *Rustbelters'* preferences, they want urban aid (x), but they don't want to also incur the costs of increased defense spending (y). Perhaps they hope to fund the aid to urban areas with defense cuts. But they would prefer both the urban aid and increased defense spending $(x \& y)$ to no urban aid at all $(\neg x)$. If they can't get their urban aid, they want to at least hold the line on federal spending so that their economies might improve. The last thing they want is increased federal spending and no urban aid $(\neg x \& y)$.

According to the *Sunbelters'* preferences, they not only want to resist defense cuts, but also want some increases in defense spending to spur growth in their states, many of which rely on defense contractors. They don't want to increase the federal deficit with urban renewal expenditure (x); however, they would prefer to have both urban renewal and increased defense spending to no increase in defense spending $(x \& y)$. But if they can't get the increase they want in defense spending, they certainly want to at least hold the line on other new expenditures, so they can go back to their districts arguing that they were in favor of keeping the lid on federal expenditure $(\neg x \& \neg y)$. The worst thing that could happen for them is for the Rustbelters to get their urban renewal aid, thus increasing the deficit but leaving them empty-handed $(x \& \neg y)$.

The *Others* are not enamored of either project; they are worried about the deficit and see no pressing need for either expenditure $(\neg x \& \neg y)$. But if there has to be an expenditure, it always sits better with their constituents if it is for defense $(\neg x \& y)$. They don't, however, want to fund both projects at the same time—that would lead to terrible strains on the budget; so they prefer to fund the Rustbelters alone rather than to pay for both projects.

If we suppose sincere voting on the issues separately, both x and y are defeated, leaving us with $(\neg x \& \neg y)$. However, there is a clear possibility here for vote trading since the Rustbelters will agree to vote for the defense spending when that vote comes up (even though they prefer $\neg y$ to y), and the Sunbelters will agree to vote for urban aid when that vote comes up (even though they prefer $\neg x$ to x) in order to get the conjunction of both bills rather than neither. If they do so, the decision in favor of neither program $(\neg x \ \& \ \neg y)$ is changed to $(x \ \& \ y)$ with both succeeding. They each get their second preference instead of their third. Here, as in the case of the w voters in the STV case, the strategic vote against their first preference gained them their second choice. Yet in one sense, society ends up with a result that would be clearly rejected if the votes were not linked. As we shall see next, this dynamic might lead to the society making choices that are worse for everyone.

The Gibbard-Satterthwaite Theorem

These, of course, are just examples. However, Allan Gibbard and Mark Allen Satterthwaite, using versions of Arrow's theorem, have shown elsewhere that, roughly, all nonrandom, nondictatorial voting procedures that are sensitive to the voter's full statement of preferences are subject to strategic manipulation.[32] Thus, to vote over three options is to open the door to strategic manipulation.

Conclusion

In this chapter we looked at the logic of collective choice. We saw that there are important differences between social choice that aims at generating a complete representation of a social welfare function compared to one that aims only at generating a determinate social choice. The first approach runs afoul of Arrow's theorem, which shows that a social welfare function can only be socially rational if it is dictatorial. This poses problems for certain conceptions of collective choice and for populist theories of democracy. Collective choice rules have their own set of challenges. We saw that there is no generally acceptable voting rule that satisfies all of our notions of what collective choice should be. Further, collective choice rules are manipulatable, susceptible to strategic voting and agenda manipulation. Although many have argued that the results of social choice theory challenge the very idea of democracy, the pure logic of collective choice is too formal and lacking in substance to allow us to draw

---

32. Gibbard, "Manipulation of Voting Schemes: A General Result"; Satterthwaite, "Strategy-Proofness and Arrow's Conditions."

such sweeping conclusions. In the next chapter, we add substance to this model and show some of the implications for political theory.

Discussion Questions

(1) What is most important to democracy: that it is preference trans-forming or preference respecting?

(2) Does it make sense to talk of "collective rationality"? Was Buchanan right?

(3) Is May's theorem important for democracy? Do you have doubts about any of his conditions?

(4) What do you find confusing about Arrow's Theorem?

(5) Provide three examples of political disputes which you think are critically multi-dimensional.

(6) Do you think voters ought to vote strategically?

(7) Is vote trading in a legislature ethical? Is it efficient?

(8) Defend what you think is the best rule for deciding among three or more options against what you think are the three most serious objections.

(9) Did Levine and Plott do anything wrong? Is there an ethical way to set an agenda that is not biased?

9

Public Choice and Democracy

Social choice theory can be described as the basic logic of collective choice. After all, social choice theory developed out of applied mathematics and economic theory, rather than the direct study of politics. Understanding it is essential, but as with formal logic, what one gains in generality one loses in specificity and applicability to actual political systems. However, by adding a few plausible assumptions about political agents to the basic picture developed in social choice theory, we can develop tools that will allow us to model and study real political organizations and their dynamics.

In the postwar period, a number of thinkers began to do just that. By applying the logic of social choice theory and economic analysis to politics, these thinkers developed a distinctive approach to understanding politics, based on modeling individuals as rational economic choosers in a political context and by viewing collective choice as the result of individual choices. Although this approach is now part of the mainstream of political science and parts of economics, it was originally described as "public choice" theory.

We began the last chapter with Jon Elster's distinction between the market and the forum. Social choice theory, Elster maintained, employs an economic model based on fixed preferences and wrongly applies it to politics, which he argues is really about deliberation and preference change. We looked at the substance of Elster's claim in the last chapter, but it is worth noting that social choice theory is only "economic" in a very weak sense: it employs utility theory based on given preference orderings and analyzes ways to aggregate these preferences. Social choice theory does not, however, rely on a *Homo economicus* model of human behavior since, as we have stressed, *Homo economicus* makes specific assumptions about utility functions, not about the nature of rationality.

Public choice theory models politics on a much more robustly economic conception of rationality by adding many of the assumptions of *Homo economicus*. This chapter begins with some core modeling assumptions used by public choice theory about individual rationality in politics. We then look at how rationality can be used to model voting, before turning to Down's simple "economic model" of democracy, in which he depicts politicians as entrepreneurs and voters as consumers. We then consider a basic problem for any economic conception of politics.

Basic Spatial Model of Democracy

Although political science has subsequently developed much more sophisticated "spatial" theories of voting,[1] Anthony Downs's classic *An Economic Theory of Democracy* is still the best introduction to the public choice approach to politics.[2] Downs offers a formal theory of democracy that models voters as self-interested consumers of policies and politicians as self-interested producers, seeking to maximize election outcomes and influence. As with the general model of *Homo economicus*, Downs goes beyond the basic model of rational instrumental behavior to further specify the nature of voters' and politicians' aims. Downs's conception of political rationality has three main elements.

First, he assumes the basic model of rationality and assumes that preferences can, in principle, be represented in cardinal utility functions.

Second, Downs assumes that political rationality is concerned with producing favored outcomes. This specifies a general end of political choice and action. Although a person might vote just to vote, Downs is *not* concerned with voting as an act of pure consumption. For him political activity is always a way to bring about results that one wants.

Third, Downs adopts the view that *Homo economicus* is self-interested. According to what Downs calls the "self-interest maxim," a rational political act always aims at "selfish ends."[3] Downs is aware that this is false; not everyone in politics is selfish—there are public spirited voters and politicians. But, like those who endorse the self-interest axiom for *Homo economicus* in general, Downs holds that this simplifying assumption allows more determinate applications of the model. We will look more closely at the general plausibility of this assumption in the next section.

Many reject the economic theory of democracy because they reject the idea that people are generally selfish in politics. This, they argue, is false. Perhaps, but Downs doesn't really need to assume that all political actors are selfish.

1. For a good overview, see Enelow and Hinich, The Spatial Theory of Voting.
2. Downs, An Economic Theory of Democracy.
3. Downs, An Economic Theory of Democracy, 27.

Instead, he can rely on two, more narrow and modest assumptions about the specific motivation of politicians and voters respectively.

Downs assumes that the main aim of politicians is to seek to win elections. Their goals are power, income, glory, and the thrill of political office. As Downs argues, "Parties formulate policies in order to win elections, rather than win elections in order to promote policies."[4] The basic idea is that politicians act to gain and maintain their offices. This may or may not be strictly selfish. In a democracy, winning elections is a necessary condition of achieving any larger political end. This does not mean that politicians will do anything necessary to win elections. Going beyond the bounds of sense and propriety, to say nothing of law, will endanger their future prospects. Richard Nixon used underhanded means in the pursuit of his reelection in 1972, which ultimately led to his downfall once the Watergate scandal came to light. Even committed Machiavellians will be wary of pushing the envelope too far.

The second group that Downs considers is the voters. Voters are also, he says, selfish, but it is not clear that he needs to rely on such a strong assumption. Rather, the Downsian model supposes simply that voters are utility maximizers—hardly anything needs to be supposed about the content of their preferences. Alf's aims may center on world peace, Betty's on high income, and Charlie's on good sanitation and each can act to satisfy their own preferences, but it doesn't follow that these are thereby selfish. All that Downs actually supposes is that these voters have *non-tuistic preferences*. Recall that if one is non-tuistic, one acts to satisfy one's own set of preferences rather than the preferences of others. Alf may have the preferences of a saint, and still be non-tuistic; all that non-tuism requires is that our saint, Alf, acts to further his own preferences, and not the preferences of Betty. His preferences may concern the well-being of Betty as he understands it, but they can't be *her* preferences. If non-tuism holds, Alf's actions can always be explained as an attempt to maximize his own preferences, which are independent of Betty's. If so, then we would never explain why Alf did something by saying that doing this satisfies Betty's preferences; Alf's actions always are based on what Alf prefers, though he may prefer to be a generous saint. Non-tuism in no way whatsoever assumes selfishness; all it assumes is that each satisfies their own preferences, however selfish or selfless those preferences may be. We can follow Downs in putting this in cardinal rather than ordinal terms so that each voter has a cardinal utility function that sums up the utility he receives from each of the policy options offered.

In the basic model of democracy given these assumptions, politicians and parties offer packages of policies and positions and voters vote for them on the

4. Downs, An Economic Theory of Democracy, 28.

basis of the expected benefit or cost of those policies. The analogy between economic choice in the market and political choice here is thereby pretty clear. The main difference is that voters do not choose for themselves, they choose for everyone affected. That is, they neither bear the full cost of their choice, nor can expect to reap the full benefit. This creates significant differences with the market analogy and the economic theory of choice. To make sense of these differences, we will need to develop the model further.

Uncertainty and Ideology

Given these assumptions about the ends and rationality of the voters and politicians, if we suppose that voters can compute the benefits and costs of all the policies on offer, they will simply tally the total utility they would receive from Party A's package of policies, compare it to the utility they would receive from Party B's package, and vote for the party that gives them higher utility. There are some complications even here—voters have to make expected utility calculations about likely policies each party will pursue in the *future* (after the election) using the best information available, i.e., what sort of policies the current government has offered in the *past* (during its last term in office). But the real interest in Downs's theory is when he brings into the analysis of democratic politics costs and ignorance. Voters may be uncertain about what party gives them the most utility because:

1. Voters may be aware that they benefited (or the opposite) from a given politician or party, but be unsure whether that party or politician was actually responsible for the benefit (or the opposite).
2. Voters may not know how some proposed government policy will benefit or cost them.
3. Voters may be unaware that the government has adopted some policies that affect them (positively or negatively).
4. Voters may not know the extent to which their own views and votes affect public policy.
5. Voters may be uncertain as to how other citizens plan to vote.[5]

As Downs sums it up, "In short, voters are not always aware of what the government is or could be doing, and often they do not know the relationship between government actions and their own utility."[6] The model of democratic politics is transformed when uncertainty enters the scene. Perhaps the

---

5. Downs, An Economic Theory of Democracy, 80.
6. Downs, An Economic Theory of Democracy, 80.

most important new element is the rise of *ideologies*. Ideologies are more or less coherent sets of principles, policies, and associated rationales. They link various policies and politicians into packages with brand identifications in terms of political parties and political ideologies.[7]

In a world of complete certainty—where the voters knew just what they wanted and whether the party or politician in question has given it to them—there would be little room for ideologies. To be sure, political parties would still compete, but this competition would be only on the level of packages of policies. Each party would simply frame its overall package of policies to attract the most votes. But ideology enters into the picture once we include voters' uncertainty.

> Voters do not know in great detail what the decisions of government are, and they cannot find out except at significant cost. Even if they did know, they could not always predict where a given decision would lead.[8]

Under these conditions of uncertainty, voters will find political ideologies to be a useful guide. Party ideologies free the voter from having to evaluate the detailed policy packages since a party's ideology gives the voter useful evidence of the general way in which the party's aims relate to general political preferences. They are shortcuts that save voters time and energy; by identifying a certain party as having the ideology closest to yours, you can end your investigations and vote for it.

The Simple Spatial Model

Ideologies are shortcuts for voters. Of course, they are also ways for parties to try to win over voters; parties wish to depict their ideologies in a way that will attract the maximum number of voters. Remember that in Downs's model, politicians only wish to maximize their share of votes so they can attain or retain office. Offering a party ideology, then, is simply a way to attract voters—they will shift their ideology in order to maximize their share of the vote. If the politicians want to attract enough voters so that they can win, how should they pitch their ideology?

To answer this question, let us suppose that political preferences are all single-peaked on a left-right dimension. Consider figure 9.1.

7. Sometimes parties are explicitly ideological, in which case the party and ideology will overlap completely, but usually parties and ideologies only partially overlap.
8. Downs, An Economic Theory of Democracy, 98.

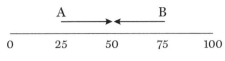

FIGURE 9.1. Simple Spatial Model

Suppose there is one citizen at each point along a political spectrum from 1 to 100. There are two parties, A and B. Initially, Party A adopts an ideology that conforms to the position 25, whereas Party B adopts an ideology that can be placed at 75. What will happen?

The hypothesis of Harold Hotelling, an economist who first explored spatial theory in economics in the 1920s, was that parties A and B would converge at the center.[9] Why? Because Party A knows that none of its extreme voters—those, say, in the 0–10 range—will vote for B as long as it is to the left of Party B, it will get those votes. And Party B knows that as long as it remains to the right of Party A, it will keep its extreme voters. The battle is over the voters between 25 and 75. So, each party will move toward the middle ground, trying to pick up votes in the middle while ensuring it will keep its extreme voters.

To see this better, assume that Party A moves to the 45 position, while Party B moves to 50. Party A would be assured of support from the population in positions 0–45, while B would get 50–100; those between 45 and 50 would—given the assumption of single-peaked preferences—vote for the party that is nearer to their preferred position; so (roughly) A and B will split these voters equally (46 and 47 will vote for A, 48 and 49 will vote for B). So, B wins with more than 50% of the vote. Party A must also move toward the center, getting as close as possible to B without, of course, "jumping" over it and becoming the right-wing party. Hence, it was suggested by the Hotelling analysis that parties' ideologies would converge at the middle in their quest for votes.

This reasoning underlies the *median voter theorem* in political science, according to which if *I* is a single-dimensional issue, and all voters have single-peaked preferences defined over issue *I*, then the *m* voter, the median voter, cannot be outvoted under majority rule. We have already seen what it means for voter preferences to be single-peaked, which is to say that an issue can be arrayed along a single dimension, such as the left-right scale.

To see this, consider any voter *z* who is not *m*, and suppose first that *z* is to the left of *m*. By definition, all voters to the right of *m* prefer *m* to *z* (*m is nearer their ideal points*), and the number of voters to the right of *m* (including *m*) is at least N/2; so, *m* could not lose to *z*. Now suppose instead that *z* is a point

---

9. See Hotelling, "Stability in Competition."

to the right of m. By definition, all voters to the left of m prefer m to z, and the number of voters to the left of m (including m) is at least $N/2$; so, m could not lose to z. Thus, under majority rule the median voter's position cannot lose to ideal points either to the right or left of it. Thus, the median voter cannot lose under majority rule.

Median Voter Theorem

Given the following assumptions:

1.   Majority Rule
2.   Single Dimension for Voting
3.   Single-Peaked Voter Preferences

The outcome of the election will be determined by the median voter.

Complicating the Basic Spatial Model

The simple spatial model is about convergence of two parties in the middle of the ideological spectrum. The median voter theorem supports this, showing that the party that captures the median voter cannot lose. However, the *median voter* only occupies the median ideological position under special circumstances, such as when voters are equally distributed along the ideological dimension. We also have been assuming that everyone votes—the median voter theorem is, of course, explicitly about *voters*. As the economist Arthur Smithies showed, the spatial model becomes more complicated if we allow that the extreme "voters" might become disenchanted with this movement toward the center and so abstain.[10] Although the extreme followers of A will never vote for B, they may decide not to vote at all since they may no longer see the choice between A and B as one that makes any difference.

Now, if every movement toward the center—which, we have seen, gains new centrist voters—causes an equal loss of voters at the extremes, the convergence toward the center of the *ideological spectrum* would stop. But, as Downs shows, even with abstentions, the movement toward the center of the ideological spectrum will continue if the voters are normally distributed along the line as in figure 9.2.[11]

---

10. Arthur Smithies, "Optimum Location in Spatial Competition," *Journal of Political Economy* 49 (1941): 423–39.

11. A normal distribution is also known as a Gaussian distribution.

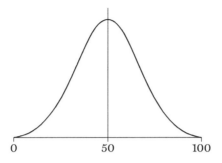

FIGURE 9.2. Simple Spatial Model with a
Normal Distribution of Voters

If political views approach a normal distribution, there will be many more people in the center than at the extremes. If political opinions are distributed in this way, political parties will converge toward the center once again. The pickings in the center are so good that even if you lose extremists, you stand to pick up a lot more voters by occupying the middle ground. So, under a two-party system, the political parties will converge and present very nearly identical ideologies. Both ideologies will stress the satisfaction of the broad middle ground, although they will be different in that they will make some appeals to different extremes.

Consequently, if the political opinions of voters are distributed in the way indicated above, the party platforms will be almost identical—hence the complaint in two-party systems that the voters have no real choice, since the parties are offering essentially the same policies. But it is not inevitable that in a two-party system the ideologies will converge; as we have just seen, it all depends on the distribution of voters. Figure 9.3 presents a different distribution, one that, Downs conjectures, encourages the growth of multi-party systems rather than two-party systems.

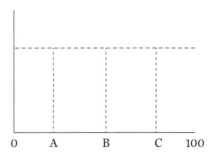

FIGURE 9.3. A Distribution of Voters that
Encourages a Multi-Party System

In this figure, A, B, and C occupy a position on the spectrum—A caters to those voters on the left, B to voters in the middle, and C to voters on the right. Now assume that B tries to move toward C; whatever it takes away from C, it will lose to A. Here there is no strong pull to occupy the center because movement toward the center is likely to lose as many votes as it gains; in this case it makes sense for each party to occupy a clear position on the ideological spectrum and not converge with its opponents.

The Plurality Rule and the Two-Party System

As it happens, there are two major parties in the United States and the United Kingdom.[12] This basic spatial model suggests that the "two-party system" is no accident, given the voting rule and distribution of votes. Both democracies—for most elections—use a plurality or "first past the post" voting rule that decides the election in favor of the candidate or proposal that wins the most votes. The United States and the United Kingdom also tend to elect representatives by districts in winner-take-all voting. In this system of politics, there is no prize for second place, one either wins or goes home. Because of this, there is no point in voting for a candidate or a party that one likes, but that is unlikely to get a plurality of votes. The French political scientist Maurice Duverger argued that because of the nature of winner-take-all elections and first past the post voting, political systems with those features would tend toward having two major parties.[13] This is known as *Duverger's Law*. It is, however a sociological and not a logical "law" since it relies on voters wanting to avoid wasting their votes on candidates with no chance of winning and avoid "spoiling the election" and inadvertently electing their least favored candidate. In countries with two parties, like the United States, proponents of third parties try to combat this phenomenon by convincing voters to vote their conscience despite having little chance of winning.

The fact that Duverger's law predicts that there will be two parties in plurality systems does not mean that other points of view are eliminated. Rather than being represented by distinct parties, these points of view and positions tend to be represented within each party as a faction. Ideological battles are fought within as well as between parties.

12. In both cases, there are notable "third parties"; the libertarian party in the United States and the Liberal Democrats in the UK, but neither seriously challenge the dominance of either of the two major parties.

13. Duverger and Brogan, Political Parties.

The inverse of Duverger's law is that systems with other forms of voting systems tend to be more amenable to multiple political parties. We have already seen how the single transferable vote and the Borda count make it so that votes are wasted (whatever their other drawbacks). Moving from winner-take-all multi-district elections to multiple winner elections also encourages multiple parties. One way to do this is through *proportional representation*. In a proportional representation system, the number of seats in the legislative body is determined by the proportion of the votes that candidates or parties receive.

In the United States, the state of Washington currently (2020) has ten House members. In the district-based system, as it currently stands, each representative is assigned to a district and the election in those districts is winner take all. As of 2020, Washington has seven Democrat and three Republican representatives. Although there are many ways to design a proportional system, imagine Washington state introduces a proportional system whereby each party puts up a ranked slate of candidates and the voters vote for whichever slate they like. In the 2020 presidential election, roughly 60% of the state voted for the Democratic candidate Joe Biden and a little fewer than 40% voted for the candidate running under the Republican banner, Donald Trump. Around 2% voted Libertarian and around ½ % voted Green. Extrapolating from these numbers—if voters voted along these party lines—six reps would be assigned to the Democrats under the proportion system and four to the Republicans, a pickup of one representative for the Republicans. But the logic of Duverger's law suggests that moving to a proportional system would make it more attractive for some people to vote for other parties and have a reasonable expectation that they might pick up a representative or two. It is certainly plausible that more people would vote for Libertarians and Greens under a proportional system and likely that other parties would emerge to meet the new demand. Coupling proportional voting with a voting method other than plurality would amplify this effect.

Choosing the Rules

Recall that market exchange, at least under some conditions, is mutually beneficial since both parties can expect to gain. Many find this hard to believe; we often think of the world in terms of zero-sum games—every winning must come out of someone's pocket. The importance of the Edgeworth box that we looked at in chapter 4 is in clearly showing how two parties can both benefit from exchanging, even assuming a fixed stock of goods. If the total stock of goods is increasing, it is obvious how all can benefit, but even under static conditions, exchange can make each person better off. Market efficiency is an attractive idea: rational economic agents, caring only about their own aims, can produce conditions that are an improvement from everyone's point of view.

However, in the political sphere, mutual gain isn't guaranteed even in ideal conditions. Political actors—especially coolly rational ones like *Homo economicus*—can often gain by taking away from others. It is in the sphere of politics that we are apt to witness real zero-sum and, even worse, negative-sum games. In politics, individuals and groups can seek "rents," i.e., group-specific payoffs that do not contribute to efficiency. Often these payoffs are extracted from others and are created explicitly by political actors to be distributed. This is not because people in politics are nastier than they are in the market, but because the mechanism of politics provides incentives for *Homo economicus* to gain by exploiting others rather than by benefiting them. This tendency for politics to create opportunities for conflictual rather than cooperative encounters is what led William Riker to label political science and not economics "the truly dismal science."

One feature of politics that public choice theory highlights is the ability of political actors to choose and change the rules that govern them. In economic analysis, we typically assume the background rules of the market are fixed. This makes it easier to identify Pareto efficiency and mutual gain in market exchanges. Participation in markets is also generally assumed to be voluntary, so no one will trade if they don't see the benefit of doing so. This is not always or even usually true in politics. Consequently, if we want to make Pareto efficiency our guide in politics, we can't only look at how political actors choose outcomes, but also how they choose the rules that generate those outcomes. Recall from the last chapter that because no decision rule eliminates the possibility of manipulation, choosing the rules will often be extremely important. This applies at every level, but we can start our analysis of rules by looking at the broad collective choice rules.

Unanimity

The Swedish political economist Knut Wicksell (1851–1926) proposed a method for evaluating collective decisions that is meant to be the political equivalent of a Pareto mutual benefit standard. Wicksell proposed a kind of unanimity principle for legislature that, in order for the state to supply some public good G, there must be unanimous consent to its provision, including the tax that will pay for it.[14] Voting to provide a benefit in the form of a public

---

14. Here we are following the discussion in Mueller, Public Choice III, chap. 4.

good also requires voting for the cost of that good in terms of the taxes needed to pay for it. By linking expenditures and taxation, James Buchanan argued that the Wicksellian unanimity principle "provides the institutional analogue to two-person trade in strictly private or partitionable goods."[15]

To see how the unanimity rules relate to efficiency, think back to the diagram of a contract curve from chapter 3. Each point on the contract curve is Pareto-efficient; at each point the indifference curves are tangent—there is no eye, and so there is no way for one party to gain without the other losing. With a unanimity rule (just between Alf and Betty right now), public good tax proposals for G will be accepted until the line A-B is reached—i.e., until a proposal somewhere on that line is accepted. Until that point is reached, Pareto gains can be achieved so new proposals can be devised. Once a proposal on this "contract curve" is accepted, no further agreements will be accepted by both parties, since the opportunity for Pareto-superior moves has been exhausted. So, unanimity rules can in principle mimic market transactions and get us to the Pareto Frontier—the place where no further Pareto improvements are possible.

However, given non-zero transaction costs—cost of reaching agreement— and lack of full information about other people's preferences, decision-making via unanimity is costly and may well not lead to Pareto-optimal results. With this in mind, James Buchanan and Gordon Tullock, in *The Calculus of Consent*, used the unanimity rule to analyze the relative costs of different, non-unanimous voting rules.[16] Their idea was to see what non-unanimous voting rules rational actors would be willing to unanimously endorse.

Why would rational political actors agree to non-unanimous rules? One reason is the cost of decision-making under a strict unanimity rule. The Paretian, unanimity standard is thus merely a representation of voluntary or consensual choice: if all would agree to move from constitution (or rule) A to B, then B is Pareto-superior. Recall from chapter 3 that one of the reasons we might want to engage in politics and collective choice in the first place is because markets can create externalities; costs that are not internalized. But political decisions can also generate externalities in the form of unchosen costs. In a non-unanimity rule—say majority rule—the majority can impose costs on the minority. The minority may have to pay taxes for goods that they don't want and can't use, as people without children are forced to pay for public education.

Knowing this, a rational actor would choose to minimize the external costs that can be expected to be generated by a given collective choice rule. We would

15. Buchanan, *The Limits of Liberty: Between Anarchy and Leviathan*, vol. 7, 40.
16. Buchanan and Tullock, *The Calculus of Consent*.

want a decision-making rule to minimize these externalities of collective decision-making, which are depicted by the external cost curve in figure 9.4.

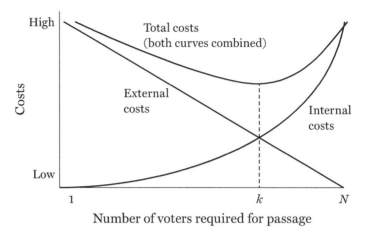

FIGURE 9.4. Buchanan and Tullock Cost Curve

If only one person's vote is required for passage, the external costs—the costs that one group of voters can impose on the rest—are extremely high. If, on the other hand, in an N-person population, all N votes are required and so we have the unanimity rule, no one can impose uncompensated costs on anyone else.

Of course, as the number of voters required for passage rises, so too do the decision-making costs. Call these the "internal costs" of decision-making: the time necessary for passage, bargaining, bluffing, and so on. As the internal cost curve shows, these costs are greatest under unanimity since one holdout can veto an agreement and least where one person is dictator and decides for all. The optimal set of rules would be one that minimizes the combined costs, as depicted in the total cost curve.

What Buchanan and Tullock showed with the analysis represented in this figure is that rational political actors would unanimously choose a non-unanimous decision rule in order to minimize the combined external and internal cost of collective choice. The k rule—requiring less than the entire population—is the most efficient. Buchanan and Tullock argue that there is no reason to think that $k = N/2 + 1$ (i.e., majority rule). The way the cost curves are drawn, the k rule is between simple majority and unanimity. According to their modeling, the efficient rule is a super-majoritarian.[17]

17. For a more detailed analysis of this conclusion and the argumentation that led to it, see Thrasher and Gaus, "On the Calculus of Consent."

This all depends on the shape of the curves, though. If there is a kink in one of the curves (either the internal or external cost curves) at $N/2+1$, then there may well be a case for majority rule as uniquely optimal. Here is one reason for a kink: for any rule where the required number is less than a majority, there is the possibility that inconsistent collective decisions will be made by the group. If only 20% is required for passage, different fifths might pass laws that contradict each other. So, we would expect the internal decision-making costs to be quite high until we get to $N/2+1$ (i.e., majority rule). Figure 9.5 depicts Dennis Mueller's revision of Buchanan and Tullock's cost curves, a revision that provides a case for majority rule because the overall costs are minimized at majority rule.[18]

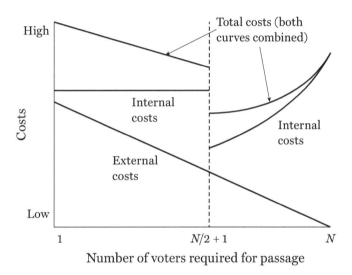

FIGURE 9.5. Mueller's Revision of the Buchanan and Tullock Cost Curve

Regardless of which model of costs is the correct one, the enduring importance of the argument from *The Calculus of Consent* is to apply the logic of contract by using unanimity as a stand-in for efficiency to show that rational actors would be able to unanimously select non-unanimous decision rules. This type of analysis raised a number of possibilities that continued to be explored in the comparative evaluation of different political and collective choice rules.

18. Adapted from Mueller, Public Choice III, 77.

Bicameralism

Modern public choice theorists were by no means the first to worry about the imposition of "external costs" in politics. The prevention of "factional legislation," in which one group imposes costs on others, is the dominant theme of *The Federalist Papers*, written by Alexander Hamilton, John Jay, and James Madison in support of the US Constitution. One of the devices employed in the US Constitution to minimize external costs is bicameralism (a two-part legislature). According to James Madison, writing in *Federalist* 62, bicameralism is an "impediment . . . against improper acts of legislation."

> No law or resolution can now be passed without the concurrence, first, of a majority of the people, and then of the majority of the States. It must be acknowledged that this complicated check on legislation may in some instances be injurious as well as beneficial . . . [but] as the facility and excess of lawmaking seem to be the diseases to which our governments are most liable, it is not impossible that this part of the Constitution may be more convenient in practice than it appears to many in contemplation.[19]

Publius—the pen name under which James Madison, Alexander Hamilton, and John Jay published the papers—is clear that requiring two chambers to concur in order to pass legislation makes it more difficult to enact legislation. This will prevent some good legislation from getting passed, but it will also protect the people from bad legislation:

> a senate, as a second branch of the legislative assembly distinct from and dividing the powers with a first, must be in all cases a salutatory check on the government. It doubles the security to the people by requiring the concurrence of two distinct bodies in schemes of usurpation or perfidy, where the ambition or corruption would otherwise be sufficient.[20]

Buchanan and Tullock provide a public choice defense of bicameralism in *The Calculus of Consent*. A bicameral legislature with each house employing majority rule is equivalent to a unicameral legislature operating under a supermajority rule. Consider a unicameral, or one-house, legislature. Assume that we have forty-nine voters divided into seven districts, each of which elects one member to a single-house, seven-seat legislature. We thus have a distribution of voters as in table 9.1.[21]

---

19. Madison, "Federalist No. 62."
20. Madison, "Federalist No. 62."
21. Adapted from Buchanan and Tullock, *The Calculus of Consent*, 237.

TABLE 9.1. Minority Control of a Unicameral Legislature

District

Rep 1	V1	V2	V3	V4	V5	V6	V7
Rep 2	V1	V2	V3	V4	V5	V6	V7
Rep 3	*V1	*V2	*V3	*V4	V5	V6	V7
Rep 4	*V1	*V2	*V3	*V4	V5	V6	V7
Rep 5	V1	V2	V3	V4	V5	V6	V7
Rep 6	*V1	*V2	*V3	*V4	V5	V6	V7
Rep 7	*V1	*V2	*V3	*V4	V5	V6	V7

In this case sixteen voters can form a winning coalition. Four voters can form a majority in four districts (in this case, the voters with asterisks in districts 3, 4, 6, 7), thus electing four representatives; and four representatives are a majority in our seven-house legislature. So, sixteen out of forty-nine voters can form a faction that enacts legislation.

Now suppose that we introduce a second house, as in table 9.2.[22] We have deleted the voters with whom we are not concerned—but they haven't died; they are still there.

TABLE 9.2. Difficulty of Maintaining a Minimum Coalition in a Bicameral Legislature

District	Sen 1	Sen 2	Sen 3	Sen 4	Sen 5	Sen 6	Sen 7
Rep 1							
Rep 2							
Rep 3	*V1	*V2	*V3	*V4			
Rep 4	*V1	*V2	*V3	*V4			
Rep 5			V3 (Sue) ⟵				
Rep 6	*V1	*V2	*V3 (Alf)	*V4		V6 (Joe) ⟵	
Rep 7	*V1	*V2	*V3	*V4			

22. Adapted from Buchanan and Tullock, The Calculus of Consent, 238.

In the two-house legislature, our winning coalition stays the same; our original sixteen voters can control both houses. So, on the face of it, we haven't provided any block to a minority faction controlling the legislature. But things are more complicated than this. In this coalition, each member is hard to replace. For example, in the single-house case, even if Alf (voter 3 in the sixth district) were to drop out, voters 5, 6, or 7 could take his place. But in this new coalition no one voter can replace Alf, because he is uniquely placed as being in both the sixth representative district and the third senate district. No other single voter could replace him if he chooses to defect. Indeed, if Alf drops out of the coalition, and the faction wants to stay as small as possible, it will have to construct a very different coalition, for now either the third senate or the sixth representative district will have to be dropped, thus dropping some of the underlined voters along with Alf.

There is no hope of capturing both of these districts with a minimum coalition without Alf. This may lead Alf to increase his claims on the coalition— since he is so valuable to the coalition, he may insist that the faction do more for him. The remaining faction members will either have to give in to Alf or try to form a new and very different coalition. This provides an incentive for all the coalition members to bargain for as much as they can possibly get, making the maintenance of the minimum faction of sixteen a difficult affair indeed.

There is, though, another option, namely, to replace Alf with two different voters, Sue and Joe. If the coalition takes on Sue and Joe to replace Alf, it can keep all the shaded coalition members; the faction does not have to start a radical rebuilding. The problem, of course, is that now it is a seventeen-member coalition rather than a sixteen-member coalition. In addition, there are now two classes of members of the coalition: those who are necessary to win in both the house and the senate, and those (Sue and Joe) who are only necessary to winning in one or the other. Other members will demand more payoffs than Sue or Joe receive.

Suppose the coalition says that, regardless of how important anyone is to win, everyone will have equal payoffs (in terms of getting the legislation that is most desired). That is, Sue and Joe get as much from the coalition as anyone else. But then some original member, needed to win in both the house and the senate, will say: "Look, to replace me you will have to recruit two new members to the coalition. And these two new members will each demand an equal payoff. So, the coalition is better off giving me 1.99 times what Joe gets because my replacements will each get the payoffs Joe gets, $1 + 1$."

But if the leaders of the coalition are stuck with demands for extra payoffs from the old coalition members, there will not be a significant difference between keeping one old member or replacing her with two new members. The result, argue Buchanan and Tullock (and we have only sketched their argument here), is that the winning coalition will increase in size. It could go as high as thirty-two in this instance, in which case it would be more than a majority of voters. But it is likely that at least some voters will be required for the coalition in both houses, so the coalition will probably be less than twice that necessary to control a single house.

Bicameralism greatly increases the minimum size that a faction must obtain in order to pass its favored legislation. For example, Buchanan and Tullock calculate that assuming a total population of 39,601 split into 199 districts, 10,000 voters could form a winning coalition in a unicameral legislature. But if there are two houses, each with 199 seats, and if voters are distributed randomly, it would require 17,500 voters to form a minimum coalition.[23]

Interestingly, if a unicameral legislature operated under a rule that legislation required the assent of seven-eighths of the representatives, the minimum coalition in this case would be the same—17,500 voters. And if a three-fourths majority were required of each house in a bicameral legislature, the minimum coalition in this case would be 24,000 voters—which is a larger minimum coalition than a unicameral legislature operating under an unanimity rule.

Logrolling and Making Everyone Worse Off

We have been assuming that the obvious problem in democratic politics is to prevent a majority from extracting resources from a minority. Or, what comes to essentially the same thing, when the majority passes legislation that benefits only it (say, funding for public universities), but makes everyone pay (including those who already pay tuition for private universities), some gain and others lose. Wealth is being transferred from the minority to the majority to fund the majority's consumption of public university education.[24] These are zero-sum interactions; some people's gains are other people's losses.

But sometimes the game can be negative-sum for all when everyone's costs can exceed their benefits. As Buchanan and Tullock showed in *The Calculus of Consent*, majority decisions can make *everyone* worse off, including the majority itself.[25] Interestingly, such a case involves vote trading (which we looked at briefly in the last chapter), and people often think that vote trading is a way

---

23. This concerns Buchanan and Tullock's "complete diversity" assumption which we haven't considered here. See Buchanan and Tullock, The Calculus of Consent, 242.

24. It has been argued that a liberal arts education is a public good, since it helps produce an informed citizenry. There are certainly positive externalities that come from public education (and some negative ones), but education—especially university education—is largely a private good that benefits an individual's human capital.

25. Buchanan and Tullock, The Calculus of Consent, chap. 10.

to ensure everyone benefits from legislation. "You want *x*, I want *y*; let's vote for each other's proposals, and we'll both be better off." We might think that if everyone participates in the trade, then it must be the case that everyone benefits. Not so.

To see this, consider a small town of 1,000 that meets to democratically decide on expenditures. Say the town is composed of five equal-sized groups (each has 200 voters):

> **Young Families** (YF)—who want to spend money to improve the primary schools. They would pay $600 each if they had to purchase the improvements themselves.
> **Older and Wealthier** (OW)—citizens who want to improve the local golf course. They too would pay $600 each if they had to purchase the improvements themselves.
> **Yuppies** (YP)—who want to close off the main street and pave it with cobblestones. Again, it is worth $600 to each Yuppy to do this.
> **Teenage Children** (TC)—Parents with teenage children who support improved facilities at the town recreation center. These improvements are worth $600 to each member of this group.
> **Outlying Residents** (OR)—who want to have some side roads paved. These improvements are worth $600 to each Outlying Resident.

Suppose the Young Families put forward their proposal. They need the support of two other groups if the proposal is to pass. Say they agree to trade votes with OW and YP. The Young Families agree to support the proposals of those other two groups in exchange for their support of school improvements. Each of the families knows that the school improvements are worth $600 to them, but they also know that they will have to support the OW and YP groups when they propose their own plans; they do not wish their total tax bill for all three projects to exceed $600, since that is what their own project is worth to them.

Say, then, that they are willing to bear $200 in tax in support of their own project, $200 to support golf course improvements, and $200 to pay for the Yuppies' paving of the pedestrian mall, for a total of $600. But if everyone in the community is taxed $200 to support school improvements, the community can raise $200 × 1,000, or $200,000 for school improvements. By themselves the 200 in this group were willing to pay $600, for a total of $120,000. So, they seem to get an additional $80,000 worth of improvements for free. They agree, the coalition is formed, and the measure passes.

At the next meeting the Older and Wealthier group (who favor golf courses) put forward their proposal. The Young Families are committed to supporting it, so it already has 400 votes. But they need additional votes. The pro–golf course adults decide to trade votes with the Outlying Residents since good roads are always a good idea. The calculations are precisely the same as with the YF. The pro–golfing adults are willing to bear $200 in tax in support of their own project, $200 in tax to support the school improvement they already have voted for, and the $200 they are expecting to pay for paving roads as part of their vote trading with the Outlying Residents. But if everyone in the community is taxed $200 to support the golf course, the community can raise $200 × 1000, or $200,000 for the improvements. By themselves the 200 in this group were willing to pay $600, or only $120,000. So, they seem also to get an additional $80,000 worth of improvements for free. They too agree.

Now the Yuppies come forward. They want their paved pedestrian mall. They have the promise of the Young Families, but they need another group's support, so they enlist those with Teenage Children. Another deal is done. Again, if everyone is taxed $200, the Yuppies can get $200,000 for their project, even though they would only pay $120,000 if they purchased it privately.

Now the families with Teenage Children (TC) come forward. They have the promise of the Yuppies, but they need another group's support, so they enlist the Outlying Residents. Another deal is done. Again, if everyone is taxed $200, the TC can get $200,000 for their project, even though they would only pay $120,000.

Finally, the Outlying Residents come forward. They already have the promises of the golf course group (OW) and the teenage parent's group (TC), so their measure also passes.

Table 9.3 sums up the bargains and total tax rates. Notice that each ends up paying $1,000 even though, if each had purchased the good themselves, they only would have spent $600 each. Because some of the cost could be pushed onto the dissenting minority, each group bought more improvements than they thought worthwhile, ending up with a too-expensive package of improvements. Insofar as each person had more preferred ways to spend the additional $400, each is worse off under this form of collective provision.

TABLE 9.3. Tax Coalition

	Coalition Partners	Tax
Young Families (YF)	OW, YP	$200
Older and Wealthier (OW)	YF, OR	$200
Yuppies (YP)	YF, TC	$200
Families with Teenage Children (TC)	YP, OR	$200
Outlying Residents (OR)	OW, TC	$200
Total Tax		$1,000

Intertemporal Coalitions

The problem in the above case is shifting coalitions: as coalitions are reformed, adding new members, vote-trading deals proliferate and ever more projects, with ever more taxation, get approved. Geoffrey Brennan and James Buchanan showed that this problem, which concerns serial logrolling with coalitions existing at roughly the same time, also arises with what we might call intertemporal coalitions.[26]

Suppose that we are worried about the US federal budget deficit and would like to vote for strong budgetary constraints. This is essentially a decision to forego present consumption and invest in the future—i.e., pay off debt so that future governments can tax less and leave more funds available for investment. But for the benefits of this policy to exceed the opportunity costs—in terms of foregone consumption—requires constraint over a relatively long period of time. If the budget is constrained only this year, there will be no significant overall decrease in the deficit, and I will have lost an opportunity to consume. Now say that in election e_1 there is a coalition in favor of severe restraint that needs an additional member.

Should we join? Well, only if we can be confident that the coalition will stay together at elections e_2 and e_3. But it is very hard to be confident. Some members of the coalition at e_1 may be simply rabid Party A members who will constrain the current Party B government; but should Party A win government, they will then wish to spend a great deal on Party A policies. Since coalitions are not permanent and contain members with different ultimate ends, we probably should not expect the coalition to stay together at elections e_2 and e_3. So even though we take a long-term view and prefer savings to present consumption, we have strong grounds to vote for present consumption, since it is doubtful that the coalition will stay together long enough to obtain the savings. Because of this, majority rule tends to be focused on short-term rather than longer-term policies, and so is biased in favor of present consumption over long-term savings and investment.

We can see, then, how public choice analysis leads to a project of constitutional design that seeks to identify rules and procedures that minimize the ability of some voters to extract resources and impose costs on others and, instead, channel politics to efficient, mutually beneficial policies. Of course, this project is "conservative" insofar as it is trying to find rules that prevent coercive redistribution from some to others. Those who believe that distributive justice requires redistribution balk at constitutional devices to push us toward mutual

26. Brennan and Buchanan, *The Reason of Rules*, 75ff.

benefit. In politics, they say, it is appropriate to take from the rich to give to the poor. Issues of distributive justice are outside the scope of this book. We need, though, to remember Buchanan's insistence that *Homo politicus* is simply *Homo economicus* operating in politics. Buchanan insists that *Homo economicus* will use politics for personal or group benefit, rather than on the public good.

Homo Economicus and the Symmetry Assumption

One of the key modeling assumptions that drives public choice theory is the idea that we should view choice in politics and choice in the market as symmetrical. More generally, as Geoffrey Brennan and James Buchanan argue, the same behavioral model should be applied across institutions unless there is some good reason for thinking otherwise.[27] Brennan and Buchanan defend a number of reasons for making this *symmetry assumption* as they call it.

The first goes back to the model of rational choice itself, pointing out that rational individuals act for reasons and rationality should be construed generally along the lines that we have developed it here. The *Homo economicus* model of human action holds that the main reason for choosing one thing over another in the market is relative price. Prices tend to be invariant between institutions, though, and we shouldn't expect individuals to make different choices when prices are the same across institutional contexts. So, if all things are equal, one prefers a cheaper car to a more expensive one, it shouldn't matter whether one buys the car through an auction or from a neighbor; one should always prefer the cheaper to the more expensive car. Changing institutions may matter for behavior when incentives differ, but the assumption here is that a *mere* change in context without a corresponding change in incentives should not matter.

We need to be careful here, though, since all things are rarely equal. We might be willing to pay double or triple at a high-end restaurant for the same bottle of wine that we could buy at the store. It also might make sense to pay more for a car if the process of buying it is easier than it might be elsewhere. In these cases, though, the context matters, and it changes the relative values of certain features of the goods in question. We have to be very careful how we think about contextual differences that might account for differences in choice since it is very easy to miss the relevant features of the case or context that are important.

Another reason for the symmetry assumption is that the diversity and conflict of actual interests in politics rule out making any other unified behavioral

---

27. Brennan and Buchanan, *The Reason of Rules*, 56.

assumption. Brennan and Buchanan argue that the same is true in economics. Mixed motives abound in politics as well as in the market and if we are interested in understanding how political as well as economic institutions can be structured in order to direct *Homo economicus* to act on behalf of the society as a whole, we cannot, as Brennan and Buchanan argue, "simply assume that persons who operate within those rules are naturally cooperative."[28]

As we can see from this argument, though, the symmetry assumption is not an empirical argument at all. Instead, it is a modeling assumption. The soundness of this assumption becomes a question of external rather than internal validity—that is, how well the model explains the data—and there will certainly be cases where the assumption will be misleading. Nevertheless, though it may be odd that the symmetry assumption "should be true in politics, which is false in fact," like many such false assumptions in our models, many interesting things can be learned on the basis of the analytic simplicity and uniformity of the assumption.[29]

It is important to understand both the power and flexibility, as well as the potential dangers, of this modeling assumption for understanding politics and social institutions more generally. The power is obvious and implicit in many of the models that we have discussed in this chapter, but public choice is often derided as a narrow conception of politics that focuses only on the sordid and self-interested aspects of politics. This charge, though sometimes true of particular theorists, is unfair to the field as a whole. The goal of public choice theory, according to James Buchanan, was a scientific understanding of politics. Developing such an approach, he argues, requires "politics without romance."[30] We should be as clear-eyed about our political institutions and the actors within them as we are about our economic institutions.

There are some cases, though, where the change in context will change the incentives for individuals. In a classic paper, economists Uri Gneezy and Aldo Rustichini found that parents picking up children from a Tel Aviv daycare were more likely to be late picking up their children if the daycare fined them for being late.[31] The explanation is that, as the title of the paper says, "a fine is a price," and once a price was put on their tardiness, some parents were willing to pay more to be a little late. Before there was a fine for being late, the parents felt guilty about making the daycare workers stay later with their children, but

---

28. Brennan and Buchanan, The Reason of Rules, 61.

29. Quote from Hume, "Of the Independency of Parliament," 3.

30. James Buchanan, "Politics without Romance."

31. Gneezy and Rustichini, "A Fine Is a Price."

once they saw themselves as paying for being late, many became comfortable with that trade-off.

Another example comes from experimental economics, where results in trust games aren't easily explained by the *Homo economicus* model. In the basic trust game (depicted in figure 9.6), there are two players.[32] Player 1 is given an endowment, in this case $20, and can decide to either keep that money for both players or send it to Player 2. If the money is sent, Player 2 can decide to reward Player 1's trust and settle for a payoff of $25 for each or take $30 and send $15 back to Player 1.

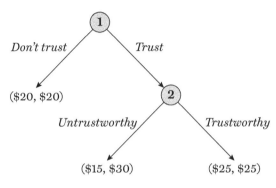

FIGURE 9.6. Trust Game

If we assume that Player 2 is *Homo economicus*, we should expect untrustworthy behavior at the second node. Knowing this, if Player 1 is also *Homo economicus*, we should expect Player 1 not to trust Player 2 and settle with the initial endowment. This is the assumption of backwards induction and subgame perfection that we saw earlier. Assuming that both players are *Homo economicus* we would expect the Don't Trust to be the only rational choice.

In experiment after experiment, however, it is common to find that usually more than half of the Player 1s decide to trust and a little more than half of Player 2s are trustworthy. When trusting and trustworthy are paired together, the trustworthy outcome can be achieved and sustained at high levels.[33] A bewildering number of other versions of this game have been tried but, except in a very narrow range of circumstances, it is rare to reliably generate the Don't Trust outcome.

Does this mean that the *Homo economicus* assumption has been falsified by experiment? Not exactly. The most straightforward response is to argue that

32. Berg et al., "Trust, Reciprocity, and Social History"; McCabe et al., "Reciprocity, Trust, and Payoff Privacy."

33. Rigdon et al., "Sustaining Cooperation in Trust Games."

trusting and trustworthiness in the trust game, like cooperation in the Prisoner's Dilemma, is strictly speaking irrational and that when subjects engage in such behavior, they are making a mistake. Although usually applied in the context of individual decision problems, this is basically the position of the program in behavioral economics of discovering biases and fallacies in reasoning, which shows that experimental subjects do not reason in the way that the *Homo economicus* model predicts.[34]

This approach has led some behavioral economists to develop sophisticated social preference models of decision-making that introduce preferences for fairness, reciprocity, or equality into the basic *Homo economicus* model.[35] Some have argued that social preferences of the sort used in these models are not really preferences at all, though, since they are not strictly speaking about different objective states of the world but rather about the process that brought those states about.[36] Robert Sugden has argued that social preference models assume a hidden "true self" that makes such theories liable to paternalistic tendencies.[37] The main issue with these theories, however, is that they lack the elegance and parsimony of the original *Homo economicus* model.

Another approach is to endorse contextualism of one sort or another. The original symmetry argument for politics argued that symmetry should be the default assumption, unless there is evidence that context does matter. Perhaps the trust game is a place where the difference in context should make us mistrust the application of *Homo economicus* to it. Vernon Smith and Bart Wilson argue *Homo economicus* is what we might call *a special theory* of rationality that applies in market contexts, but not generally. In most settings, various norms of fairness, reciprocity, and propriety (rights) constrain and prescribe the appropriate action.[38] Nevertheless, as Vernon Smith's numerous market experiments have shown, and as a recent massive replication of those results show,

---

34. This program was arguably initiated by Kahneman and Tversky, "Prospect Theory: An Analysis of Decision under Risk."

35. Good examples include Charness and Rabin, "Understanding Social Preferences with Simple Tests"; Fehr and Fischbacher, "Why Social Preferences Matter—the Impact of Non-Selfish Motives on Competition, Cooperation and Incentives"; Bernheim and Rangel, "Toward Choice-Theoretic Foundations for Behavioral Welfare Economics"; Camerer, Behavioral Game Theory.

36. Wilson, "Social Preferences Aren't Preferences."

37. Sugden, The Community of Advantage.

38. Smith and Wilson, Humanomics.

the *Homo economicus* model is extremely accurate in predicting market behavior in the lab.[39]

What should we make of the *Homo economicus* assumption in politics and of the symmetry argument more generally given all this? *Homo economicus* predicts behavior well in a specific context. These conditions are:

1. **Shared Value Metric**—the metric of value is relatively simple, objective, and shared.
2. **Similarity**—most of the actors are playing similar roles with regard to one another.
3. **Strong Incentives**—there are ecological or institutional forces that make non-equilibrium behavior costly and discipline non-rational behavior.

The metric in markets is typically money or, more precisely, opportunity cost. Politics has a shared metric in some cases, but not in others. In elections, the metric is votes. In bureaucratic battles, it is influence with budget size, etc., serving as proxies for influence.

Similarity means that nobody in a normal market can "make the market," which is to say that they can't unilaterally set prices. The same is usually true with regard to both voters and politicians. There are unusual cases where this condition isn't true in economics and politics, but they are rare.

The third claim is that it is unambiguously costly to ignore the shared metric. In the case of the market, one's business will fail, or they will no longer be able to trade in the market, if costs exceed revenue. In politics, losing an election or not being on a committee means that one no longer gets to play the political game. This plays the role of disciplining players in this "game" to play to win in the same way that *Homo economicus* is disciplined by the market to choose rationally.

The application of *Homo economicus* to politics has been extremely fruitful to our understanding of politics, but this does not mean that it is a useful assumption in all cases. The symmetry argument was more accurate than we might have thought since the assumption will tend to be fruitful when the political institution is more similar in the conditions outlined above to market institutions. One thing we should look for in our analysis of politics is when these conditions tend to hold and when they don't.

39. Lin et al., "Evidence of General Economic Principles of Bargaining and Trade from 2,000 Classroom Experiments."

Voting and Rationality

Recall Downs's notion of political rationality: people vote as a way to secure their favored outcomes. If this is so, an act of voting is rational only if the benefits exceed the costs, otherwise it is a waste of effort.

Now if it costs Alf nothing at all to vote, and if all Alf cares about is whether his own goals are advanced, then Alf will vote for the party that he expects to better advance his goals. If he expects precisely the same utility from both parties, Alf will abstain. But time is scarce, and so it is costly to vote.

At first sight these costs may appear so small that they could not possibly make a difference; how much cost is involved in missing fifteen minutes of TV, getting into the car, and going out to vote? Although these costs are very low, so is the expected return from voting. Some are surprised at this. A committed Democrat or Republican will say that it matters very much to her who wins: a great deal is at stake, so the expected returns must be high. Perhaps this is true in some sense, but in the narrow sense that concerns *Homo economicus*, this is not so. Alf's vote only makes a difference to the outcome if it is the decisive vote. So, if Alf is an American, and it matters tremendously to him that the Democrats win the election—and they do, by a mere 250,000 votes—what did Alf's vote do? Nothing. In terms of the outcome, whether or not Alf voted, the overall result would have been the same. Alf would have received the same payoff (Democrats win) even if he did not vote, so his vote couldn't have made a difference. And if it made no difference, he paid those small costs for nothing at all. No matter how small, it isn't rational to pay something for nothing.

The expected utility from voting $EU(V)$ can be understood as the probability (p) that one's vote will be decisive in electing your favored party or candidate A—call casting the decisive vote for A, D_A—times the utility that Alf will gain from A winning, over what you would have had if the other Party B had won—call this $EU(W_{A-B})$. That is, the *difference* in utility between your favored party winning and the other party winning. It is important that you cannot simply calculate on the basis of how much utility you would receive if your favored party wins, since you would get much of that utility even if the other party was victorious, at stake in the election is *only the difference* in the utility you receive if your favored party wins. So, assuming a purely instrumental account of political rationality, we get the result depicted in figure 9.7.

$$EU(V) = p(D_A)(EU(W_{A-B}))$$

FIGURE 9.7. Expected Utility of Voting

If $EU(V)$ is less than the costs of voting (C), voting is irrational on this account. Voting then is instrumentally irrational if $EU(V) < C$.

The probability that your vote will be decisive depends on two factors. First, the number of other people voting and second, the anticipated closeness of the election. Suppose we say it costs \$1 to vote, which includes all the time you give up, gas, etc. Suppose that Betty is planning on voting for candidate A: how much utility would she have to receive from candidate A winning—rather than B winning—to make the expected utility of voting exceed the cost of \$1? To calculate the probability that you will be decisive, you must know the expected number of voters and the anticipated size of the majority. Lomasky and Brennan's important work show how these two variables—the expected number of voters and size of the anticipated majority—interact to show that the expected payoff "ranges between vanishingly small and infinitesimal."[40] Because expected benefits are so low, it is almost always irrational to vote as a way of securing one's favored outcome.

Once we discount the possibility that you will be the decisive voter, the question of whether to vote is simply a multi-person Prisoner's Dilemma as in table 9.4 (in ordinal utility, I = best, IV = worst).

TABLE 9.4. Voting Dilemma

		All Others	
		A Gets Enough Votes	**A Doesn't Get Enough Votes**
Alf	**Votes**	Alf gains from A winning, but has to pay part of the cost for it II	Alf pays the cost of voting, and doesn't gain from the result IV
	Doesn't Vote	Alf gains from A winning, and pays nothing I	Alf doesn't gain from the electoral result, but at least he doesn't pay anything III

As in all Prisoner's Dilemmas, "defect" is the dominant strategy and no matter what others do, Alf should not vote. Of course, each voter occupies the role of Alf, playing this Prisoner's Dilemma against everyone else. Thus, it seems that if all voters are rational, no one will vote.

40. Lomasky and Brennan, "Is There a Duty to Vote?," 66.

Nevertheless, many people do vote! In the 2020 presidential election in the United States, more than 239 million people (roughly 70% of eligible voters) voluntarily voted for president. Were they making a mistake? If we think that it is categorically irrational to vote, we need to explain why so many people nevertheless decide to vote. Can the rationality of voting be "saved"? Let us briefly consider several suggestions.

Non-Electoral Utility

Downs worried about the apparent irrationality of *Homo economicus* voting—it certainly seems to undermine a theory of democratic politics based on rational *Homo economicus*! Downs proposed adding another value to voting—the advantage that accrues to people living in a democracy: it is a system of government that ensures that the policies of government respond to the utilities of the citizens. In the previous chapter we explored social welfare functions (SWF) and collective choice rules (CCR) that take the set of individual preferences and yield a social decision. We all think that making decisions on the basis of a CCR or SWF that represents the preferences of the citizens is better than having a dictator: one of the reasons that Arrow's theorem is so worrisome is that only a dictator can formulate a SWF that always gives a transitive result, and that always satisfies the Pareto principle and the Independence condition (IIA). For all of that, few readers of Arrow become fans of dictatorship. As Downs recognized, we all get some utility from living in a democracy where the social choice reflects a wide range of individual preferences. So, we don't want a dictatorship—the result of everyone defecting (no one voting). We don't want the democratic CCR to collapse. But if no one votes, it will collapse.

Downs thus argues that there can be some utility gained by the mere act of voting regardless of the outcome: it can help ensure that the democratic CCR carries on, and that is to one's advantage. There is, he would like to say, utility simply from casting a vote—it doesn't matter for whom, namely the utility one gains by supporting democratic institutions.

> One thing that all citizens in our model have in common is the desire to see democracy work. Yet if voting costs exist, pursuit of short-run rationality can conceivably cause democracy to break down. However improbable this outcome may seem, it is so disastrous that every citizen is willing to bear at least some cost in order to insure himself against it. The more probable it appears, the more cost he is willing to bear.[41]

41. Downs, An Economic Theory of Democracy, 257.

Since voting is one form of insurance against this catastrophe, every rational citizen receives some return from voting per se—call this the utility from casting a ballot, $U(B)$. So, Downs proposes what amounts to the outcome depicted in figure 9.8.

$$EU(V) = p(D_A)(EU(W_{A-B})) + U(B)$$

FIGURE 9.8. Expected Utility of Voting
with Decisiveness

Combining this model with what we learned from Brennan and Lomasky, the total utility that a person expects from voting will be a function of four factors:

1. How much she values living in a democracy
2. How much she cares about the outcome
3. How close she thinks the election will be
4. How many other citizens she thinks will vote

The problem with Downs's proposal is his claim that utility attaches to the mere *act* of casting a ballot, rather than the *outcome* that one is seeking to bring about: a functioning democracy. Downs is aware that a person can get the benefit of living in a democracy without voting, noting that "[The voter] will actually get his reward even if he does not vote as long as a sufficient number of other citizens do."[42] Living in a democracy thus is a public good. If the democracy survives the election—that is, if some people vote—then not only the voters, but the nonvoters as well, get the benefits of living in a democracy. Any rational agent would prefer to be a free rider than a contributor.

Two possibilities must be distinguished: (1) saving democracy requires many people to participate in an election; and (2) democracy would be saved even if only one person voted. If (1) is the case, we have the same problem all over again about decisiveness; the odds that your vote will be the one necessary to save democracy are almost zero. What if (2) is the case—democracy will be preserved if even a single person votes? Then we are in a public good game of Chicken: someone should vote, but not everyone. Of course, it is unlikely in the extreme that anyone's vote alone would affect whether democracy is saved or not saved, healthy or not healthy, etc. The most plausible account is that saving democracy is just another multi-person Prisoner's Dilemma, as in table 9.5. The same reasoning that leads people not to vote to

---

42. Downs, An Economic Theory of Democracy, 270.

secure the victory of their party leads them not to vote to secure the continuation of democracy.

TABLE 9.5. Voting to Save Democracy Dilemma

		All Others	
		Enough Others Vote and Democracy Is Saved	**Not Enough Vote and Democracy Isn't Saved**
Alf	**Votes**	Alf gains from living in a democracy, but has to pay part of the cost for it II	Alf pays the cost of voting, and doesn't gain from living in a democracy IV
	Doesn't Vote	Alf gains from living in a democracy, and pays nothing I	Alf doesn't get utility from living in a democracy, but at least he doesn't pay anything III

If our concern really is saving democracy, let $U(M)$ be the utility of living in a democracy, then it seems like Downs should be advocating something like what appears in figure 9.9.

$$EU(V) = [p(D_A)(EUW_{A-B})] + [p(D_M)(EU(M))]$$

FIGURE 9.9. Expected Utility of Voting with Non-Electoral Utility

That is, the total utility of one's vote is the utility one gains by one's preferred party or candidate winning, times the probability that one's vote is decisive in causing its victory, plus the utility one gains by living in a democracy, times the probability that one's vote will be decisive in securing a democracy.

Operating within a pure Downsian theory of political rationality, there is one easy way around these problems, namely, to follow Australia in making voting compulsory by attaching a fine for not voting.[43] The problem that we have been exploring is generated by the small costs of voting being outweighed by the tiny expected benefits. But if there are costs to *not* voting, say a $50 fine, then clearly it will be rational for almost everyone to vote. Note, though, this

---

43. On the many reasons for and against compulsory voting, see Brennan and Hill, Compulsory Voting: For and Against.

would not make it rational for them to become informed voters, who spend time understanding the issues and candidates. Given that their aim is to simply avoid the monetary fine for not voting, the rational thing to do is to show up at the polls and cast a blank ballot, thus saving the time it takes to check the various boxes! Many Australians (as many as 1%–2% of the electorate) cast what is known as a "donkey vote" by just ranking the candidates in the order that they are presented on the ballot in order to fill out the ballot as quickly as possible.

The Act and Expression of Voting

The apparent irrationality of voting depends on a conception of rationality that only considers outcomes, not the value of acts. If the act of voting itself is valued—if it is itself one of the elements in our utility function—then voting may well be rational. So, the equation from figure 9.8 is just about right after all, though not for the reasons that Downs advanced about saving democracy, but because we can put value simply on the act of voting.

Why might one do so? A person might simply value being a good democrat—the sort of person who pulls her weight in cooperative endeavors. Some put this concern in terms of a person's integrity: she lives up to her own view of what she considers the proper thing to do. Any utility that a person attaches to engaging in the cooperative act, doing the right thing, doing her bit, and so on, is apt to be sufficient to make voting rational. Again, remember that the costs are small, so it does not take a great deal of positive utility to outweigh them.

These proposals certainly show that rational utility maximizers can vote—but do they show that *Homo economicus* would vote? Brennan and Lomasky think that voting is *expressive* behavior, like that of a fan at a ball game, "The fan's actions are purely expressive . . . Revealing a preference is a direct *consumption activity*, yielding benefits to the individuals in and of itself."[44] Expressive actions fuse the action and the outcome. One doesn't cheer after a batsman has had a good inning because one hopes to influence the game, but rather to directly express admiration or gratitude.[45]

Given that the probability of decisiveness is so low, Brennan and Lomasky argue that one votes knowing that how one casts one's ballot is almost sure to make no difference—one votes from behind a "veil of insignificance." Thus,

44. Brennan and Lomasky, Democracy and Decision, 44.

45. In football, cheering can actually influence the game on third down if the cheering is loud enough to make it hard for the opposing team to communicate to one another and cause a false start.

Alf may vote to express anger rather than with the aim of selecting the best candidate. Alf can afford to simply let off steam when he votes if he knows that it doesn't really make a difference how he votes. If we all express our anger, everyone might vote in a way that produces a result that no one wants.

We see here that insisting on the distinction between outcome-based and consumption rationality can help us understand that *Homo economicus* has more explanatory power than we might have first thought. If voting is like eating a pizza, *Homo economicus* certainly can do it. Still, it seems a bit of a stretch to see voting as *only* consumption behavior. Over a wide range, *Homo economicus* prefers more rather than less of a consumption good. Although given marginal decreasing utility, voting seems to have a very odd demand curve. In parliamentary systems where governments decide when to call an election, for example, governments are often "punished" for calling an early election, even just a year early.

Now, Brennan and Lomasky's view on this is puzzling. As they see it, those who vote are those who particularly enjoy voting—they are already a self-selecting set of citizens who have a pretty high demand for this sort of thing. It would seem that, if anything, they should reward governments for frequent elections. The costs of elections are spread out over the whole population, and so the voters' consumption is being subsidized. This must be one of the few cases where voters turn on a government for providing a subsidized good. Certainly, pizza eaters would not be so hard on governments subsidizing their favored good!

Conclusion

In this chapter, we moved from the pure logic of collective choice to a more substantial model of politics that models political actors as *Homo economicus*. We can then develop a simple spatial theory of politics. Within this basic model, there are questions about what institutions rational political actors would choose as well as what institutions are best suited for rational political actors. We then raised questions about whether *Homo economicus* really is the best way to think about political actors. Voting poses a bit of a puzzle on this count since, viewed narrowly, the expected returns to voting usually seem to outweigh the benefits. Does this mean that *Homo economicus* shouldn't vote? If so, the *Homo economicus* model of politics would be self-defeating. We saw that the solution to this puzzle is in substance of *Homo economicus*'s utility function. We looked at several explanations that expand the possibilities of what benefit can be gained from voting. Although none of those stories is probably definitive, it gives us a sense of how resilient the *Homo economicus* model is as well as the conditions under which we should reject the symmetry condition.

Discussion Questions

(1) "According to Downs, in a sensible two-party democracy there should be hardly any difference between the parties, so why bother voting?" Explain and evaluate this thought.

(2) Are Downs and Buchanan right that we should assume the same motives in politics as in economic life?

(3) According to Downs, "Hence ignorance of politics is not a result of unpatriotic apathy; rather it is a highly rational response to the facts of political life in a large democracy." Does this mean that you are irrational to be deeply informed about politics? Is it wrong to encourage citizens to know more about politics (are you encouraging them to do what is irrational?).

(4) Is politics a zero-sum game? If it is a cooperative game, what are the best sorts of decision procedures?

(5) Explain Buchanan's ideas of external and internal costs. Do you agree that the best rule is one that minimizes the combined costs?

(6) Who understands simple majority rule better: May or Buchanan?

BIBLIOGRAPHY

Abbink, Klaus, Lata Gangadharan, Toby Handfield, and John Thrasher. "Peer Punishment Promotes Enforcement of Bad Social Norms." Nature Communications 8, no. 1 (September 20, 2017): 609. https://doi.org/10.1038/s41467-017-00731-0.

Akerlof, George A. "The Market for 'Lemons': Quality Uncertainty and the Market Mechanism." *Quarterly Journal of Economics* 84, no. 3 (1970): 488–500. https://doi.org/10.2307/1879431.

Anand, Paul. *Foundations of Rational Choice Under Risk*. Oxford: Oxford University Press, 1995.

Argyle, Michael. *Psychology of Interpersonal Behaviour*. 5th UK edition. London: Penguin UK, 1994.

Arrow, Kenneth J. "Risk Perception in Psychology and Economics." Economic Inquiry 20, no. 1 (1982): 1–9. https://doi.org/10.1111/j.1465-7295.1982.tb01138.x.

———. Social Choice and Individual Values. Revised edition. New Haven, CT: Yale University Press, 1963.

Arrow, Kenneth J., and Gerard Debreu. "Existence of an Equilibrium for a Competitive Economy." Econometrica 22, no. 3 (July 1954): 265. https://doi.org/10.2307/1907353.

Aumann, Robert J. "Correlated Equilibrium as an Expression of Bayesian Rationality." Econometrica 55, no. 1 (1987): 1–18. https://doi.org/10.2307/1911154.

Avery, Christopher, and Peter B. Zemsky. "Money Burning and Multiple Equilibria in Bargaining." Games and Economic Behavior 7, no. 2 (September 1, 1994): 154–68. https://doi.org/10.1006/game.1994.1042.

Axelrod, Robert. "An Evolutionary Approach to Norms." American Political Science Review 80, no. 4 (1986): 1095–1111. https://doi.org/10.2307/1960858.

———. Evolution of Cooperation. 1st edition. New York: Basic Books, 1984.

Barry, Brian. "Is Democracy Special." In Philosophy and Democracy: An Anthology, edited by Thomas Christiano, 321–50. Oxford: Oxford University Press, 2003.

Becker, Gary S. The Economic Approach to Human Behavior. University of Chicago Press, 1976.

Benn, Stanley I. A Theory of Freedom. New York: Cambridge University Press, 1988.

Bentham, Jeremy. Introduction to the Principles of Morals and Legislation in Utilitarianism and Other Essays. Edited by Alan Ryan. Harmondsworth, UK: Penguin, 1987.

Berg, Joyce, John Dickhaut, and Kevin McCabe. "Trust, Reciprocity, and Social History." Games and Economic Behavior 10, no. 1 (July 1, 1995): 122–42. https://doi.org/10.1006/game.1995.1027.

Bernheim, B. Douglas, and Antonio Rangel. "Toward Choice-Theoretic Foundations for Behavioral Welfare Economics." *American Economic Review* 97, no. 2 (2007): 464–70.

Bertrand, Elodie. "The Coasean Analysis of Lighthouse Financing: Myths and Realities." Cambridge Journal of Economics 30, no. 3 (2006): 389–402.

Bicchieri, Cristina. Norms in the Wild. New York: Cambridge University Press, 2016.

———. The Grammar of Society: The Nature and Dynamics of Social Norms. New York: Cambridge University Press, 2006.

Binmore, Ken. Natural Justice. New York: Oxford University Press, 2005.

Binmore, Ken. *Game Theory: A Very Short Introduction.* Oxford: Oxford University Press, 2007.

Boehm, Christopher. Blood Revenge: The Enactment and Management of Conflict in Montenegro and Other Tribal Societies. Philadelphia: University of Pennsylvania Press, 1986.

Boyd, Robert, and Peter Richerson. "Punishment Allows the Evolution of Cooperation (or Anything Else) in Sizable Groups." Ethology and Sociobiology 13, no. 3 (May 1, 1992): 171–95. https://doi.org/10.1016/0162-3095(92)90032-Y.

Bradley, Richard. Decision Theory with a Human Face. New York: Cambridge University Press, 2017.

Brennan, Geoffrey, and James Buchanan. The Reason of Rules. The Collected Works of James M. Buchanan. Indianapolis, IN: Liberty Fund, 1985.

Brennan, Geoffrey, Lina Eriksson, Robert E. Goodin, and Nicholas Southwood. Explaining Norms. New York: Oxford University Press, 2013.

Brennan, Geoffrey, and Loren Lomasky. Democracy and Decision: The Pure Theory of Electoral Preference. New York: Cambridge University Press, 1997.

Brennan, Jason, and Lisa Hill. Compulsory Voting: For and Against. New York: Cambridge University Press, 2014.

Broome, John. "Rationality and the Sure-Thing Principle." In Thoughtful Economic Man: Essays on Rationality, Moral Rules, and Benevolence, edited by Gay Meeks, 74–102. New York: Cambridge University Press, 1991.

Buchak, Lara. Risk and Rationality. Oxford: Oxford University Press, 2013.

Buchanan, James. "Politics without Romance: A Sketch of a Positive Public Choice Theory and Its Normative Implications." In The Theory of Public Choice. Political Applications of Economics, edited by James Buchanan and Roger Tollison. Ann Arbor: University of Michigan Press, 1979.

———. The Limits of Liberty: Between Anarchy and Leviathan. Vol. 7. The Collected Works of James M. Buchanan. Indianapolis, IN: Liberty Fund, 1975.

———. "Social Choice, Democracy, and Free Markets." Journal of Political Economy 62, no. 2 (1954): 114–23.

Buchanan, James, and Gordon Tullock. The Calculus of Consent: Logical Foundations of Constitutional Democracy. The Collected Works of James M. Buchanan. Indianapolis, IN: Liberty Fund, 1962.

Byrne, Richard W., and Andrew Whiten. "Machiavellian Intelligence: Social Expertise and the Evolution of Intellect in Monkeys, Apes, and Humans." Behavior and Philosophy 18, no. 1 (1990): 73–75.

Camerer, Colin F. Behavioral Game Theory: Experiments in Strategic Interaction. Princeton, NJ: Princeton University Press, 2011.

Caplan, Bryan. The Case against Education: Why the Education System Is a Waste of Time and Money. Princeton, NJ: Princeton University Press, 2018.

Charness, Gary, and Matthew Rabin. "Understanding Social Preferences with Simple Tests." Quarterly Journal of Economics 117, no. 3 (August 1, 2002): 817–69. https://doi.org/10.1162/003355302760193904.

Chaudhuri, Ananish. "Sustaining Cooperation in Laboratory Public Goods Experiments: A Selective Survey of the Literature." Experimental Economics 14, no. 1 (March 1, 2011): 47–83. https://doi.org/10.1007/s10683-010-9257-1.

Christiano, Thomas. The Constitution of Equality: Democratic Authority and Its Limits. Oxford; New York: Oxford University Press, 2010.

Coase, R. H. "The Lighthouse in Economics." Journal of Law and Economics 17, no. 2 (October 1, 1974): 357–76. https://doi.org/10.1086/466796.

Coase, Ronald. "The Nature of the Firm." Economica 4, no. 16 (1937): 386–405.

———. "The Problem of Social Cost." Journal of Law and Economics 3 (1960): 1–44.

Cooper, Russell, Douglas V. DeJong, Robert Forsythe, and Thomas W. Ross. "Forward Induction in the Battle-of-the-Sexes Games." American Economic Review 83, no. 5 (1993): 1303–16.

Craven, John. Social Choice: A Framework for Collective Decisions and Individual Judgements. Cambridge: Cambridge University Press, 1992.

D'Agostino, Fred, Gerald Gaus, and John Thrasher. "Contemporary Approaches to the Social Contract." Stanford Encyclopedia of Philosophy, 2019. http://plato.stanford.edu/archives/win2011/entries/contractarianism-contemporary/.

Dietrich, Franz, and Christian List. "What Matters and How It Matters: A Choice-Theoretic Representation of Moral Theories." Philosophical Review 126, no. 4 (October 1, 2017): 421–79. https://doi.org/10.1215/00318108-4173412.

Downs, Anthony. An Economic Theory of Democracy. New York: Harper, 1957.

Doyle, Sir Arthur Conan. "The Final Problem." In Sherlock Holmes: The Complete Novels and Stories, Vol. 1, 642–60. New York: Bantam Classics, 1893.

Dreier, James. "Decision Theory and Morality." In The Oxford Handbook of Rationality, edited by Al Mele and Piers Rawling, 156–81. Oxford: Oxford University Press, 2004. https://doi.org/10.1093/oxfordhb/9780195145397.003.0009.

———. "Structures of Normative Theories." The Monist 76, no. 1 (1993): 22–40.

Duverger, Maurice, and D. W. Brogan. Political Parties: Their Organization and Activity in the Modern State. Translated by Barbara North and Robert North. First American edition. New York: John Wiley & Sons, 1954.

Ellsberg, Daniel. "Risk, Ambiguity, and the Savage Axioms." Quarterly Journal of Economics 75, no. 4 (1961): 643–69. https://doi.org/10.2307/1884324.

Elster, Jon. "The Market and the Forum: Three Varieties of Political Theory." In Foundations of Social Choice Theory, edited by Jon Elster and Aanund Hylland, 104–32. Cambridge: Cambridge University Press, 1986.

Enelow, James M., and Melvin J. Hinich. The Spatial Theory of Voting: An Introduction. Cambridge, Cambridgeshire; New York: Cambridge University Press, 1984.

Epstein, Richard A. Skepticism and Freedom: A Modern Case for Classical Liberalism. 1st edition. Chicago: University of Chicago Press, 2004.

Erev, Ido, and Alvin E. Roth. "Predicting How People Play Games: Reinforcement Learning in Experimental Games with Unique, Mixed Strategy Equilibria." American Economic Review 88, no. 4 (1998): 848–81.

Fehr, Ernst, and Urs Fischbacher. "Why Social Preferences Matter—the Impact of Non-Selfish Motives on Competition, Cooperation and Incentives." Economic Journal 112, no. 478 (March 1, 2002): C1–33. https://doi.org/10.1111/1468-0297.00027.

Felman, Allan, and Roberto Serrano. "Arrow's Impossibility Theorem: Two Simple Single-Profile Versions." Harvard College Mathematics Review 2, no. 2 (2008): 48–57.

Forsythe, Robert, Joel L. Horowitz, N. E. Savin, and Martin Sefton. "Fairness in Simple Bargaining Experiments." Games and Economic Behavior 6, no. 3 (May 1994): 347–69. https://doi.org/10.1006/game.1994.1021.

Freud, Sigmund. "Inhibitions, Symptoms and Anxieties." In On Psychopathology, edited by Angela Richards, 229–315. Harmondsworth: Penguin, 1979.

Gambetta, Diego. Codes of the Underworld: How Criminals Communicate. Princeton, NJ: Princeton University Press, 2009.

Gauriot, Romain, Lionel Page, and John Wooders. "Nash at Wimbledon: Evidence from Half a Million Serves." SSRN Scholarly Paper. Rochester, NY: Social Science Research Network, September 1, 2016. https://doi.org/10.2139/ssrn.2850919.

Gaus, Gerald. The Open Society and Its Complexities. Oxford: Oxford University Press, 2021.

———. The Order of Public Reason: A Theory of Freedom and Morality in a Diverse and Bounded World. New York: Cambridge University Press, 2011.

———. Contemporary Theories of Liberalism. London: Sage Publications, 2003.

Gaus, Gerald, and John Thrasher. "Rational Choice in the Original Position: The (Many) Models of Rawls and Harsanyi." In The Cambridge Companion to the Original Position, edited by Timothy Hinton, 39–58. Cambridge: Cambridge University Press, 2015.

Gauthier, David. "Twenty-Five On." Ethics 123, no. 4 (July 1, 2013): 601–24. https://doi.org/10.1086/670246.

———. "Assure and Threaten." Ethics 104, no. 4 (July 1994): 690–721.

———. "Uniting Separate Persons." In Rationality, Justice and the Social Contract: Themes from Morals by Agreement, edited by David Gauthier and Robert Sugden, 176–92. Ann Arbor: University of Michigan Press, 1993.

———. Morals by Agreement. Oxford: Clarendon Press, 1986.

———. "David Hume, Contractarian." Philosophical Review 88, no. 1 (January 1979): 3–38.

Gibbard, Alan. "Manipulation of Voting Schemes: A General Result." Econometrica: Journal of the Econometric Society 41, no. 4 (1973): 587–601.

Gintis, Herbert. "Social Norms as Choreography." Politics, Philosophy, and Economics 9, no. 3 (2010): 251–64.

———. The Bounds of Reason: Game Theory and the Unification of the Behavioral Sciences. Princeton, NJ: Princeton University Press, 2009.

———. "The Evolution of Private Property." Journal of Economic Behavior and Organization 64, no. 1 (2007): 1–16.

Glymour, Clark. Thinking Things Through: An Introduction to Philosophical Issues and Achievements. Cambridge, MA: A Bradford Book, 2015.

Gneezy, Uri, and Aldo Rustichini. "A Fine Is a Price." Journal of Legal Studies 29, no. 1 (January 1, 2000): 1–17. https://doi.org/10.1086/468061.

Goodin, Robert E., and Christian List. "A Conditional Defense of Plurality Rule: Generalizing May's Theorem in a Restricted Informational Environment." American Journal of Political Science 50, no. 4 (2006): 940–49. https://doi.org/10.1111/j.1540-5907.2006.00225.x.

Grafen, Alan. "Biological Signals as Handicaps." Journal of Theoretical Biology 144, no. 4 (June 21, 1990): 517–46. https://doi.org/10.1016/S0022-5193(05)80088-8.

Guala, Francesco. Understanding Institutions. Princeton, NJ: Princeton University Press, 2016.

Güth, Werner, Rolf Schmittberger, and Bernd Schwarze. "An Experimental Analysis of Ultimatum Bargaining." Journal of Economic Behavior & Organization 3, no. 4 (December 1982): 367–88. https://doi.org/10.1016/0167-2681(82)90011-7.

Hardin, Russell. Indeterminacy and Society. Princeton, NJ: Princeton University Press, 2005. http://press.princeton.edu/titles/7670.html.

Harsanyi, John. "On the Rationality Postulates Underlying the Theory of Cooperative Games." Journal of Conflict Resolution, June 1961, 179–96.

Hausman, Daniel M. The Inexact and Separate Science of Economics. Cambridge; New York: Cambridge University Press, 1992.

Henrich, Joseph, Robert Boyd, Samuel Bowles, Colin Camerer, Ernst Fehr, Herbert Gintis, and Richard McElreath. "In Search of *Homo Economicus*: Behavioral Experiments in 15 Small-Scale Societies." American Economic Review 91, no. 2 (December 2001): 73–78.

Hicks, J. R. "The Foundations of Welfare Economics." Economic Journal 49, no. 196 (1939): 696–712. https://doi.org/10.2307/2225023.

Hindriks, Frank, and Francesco Guala. "Institutions, Rules, and Equilibria: A Unified Theory." Journal of Institutional Economics 11, no. 3 (September 2015): 459–80. https://doi.org/10.1017/S1744137414000496.

Hobbes, Thomas. Leviathan. Edited by Noel Malcolm. Clarendon Edition of the Works of Thomas Hobbes. Oxford: Oxford University Press, 1651.

Hotelling, Harold. "Stability in Competition." Economic Journal 39, no. 153 (1929): 41–57. https://doi.org/10.2307/2224214.

Hume, David. "Of the Independency of Parliament." In Essay: Moral, Political, and Literary, edited by Eugene Miller, 42–46. Indianapolis, IN: Liberty Fund, 1741.

———. A Treatise of Human Nature. Edited by David Fate Norton and Mary J. Norton. Oxford Philosophical Texts. New York: Oxford University Press, 1739.

Hutteffer, Simon, Justin P. Bruner, and Kevin Zollman. "The Handicap Principle Is an Artifact." Philosophy of Science 82, no. 5 (2015): 997–1009.

Jeffrey, Richard. Subjective Probability: The Real Thing. Cambridge: Cambridge University Press, 2004.

Jeffrey, Richard C. The Logic of Decision. 2nd edition. Chicago: University of Chicago Press, 1990.

Joyce, James M. The Foundations of Causal Decision Theory. Cambridge; New York: Cambridge University Press, 1999.

Kahneman, Daniel, and Amos Tversky. "Choices, Values and Frames." In Choices, Values, and Frames, edited by Daniel Kahneman and Amos Tversky, 1–16. New York: Cambridge University Press, 2000.

———. "On the Psychology of Prediction." In Judgments Under Uncertainty: Heuristics and Biases, edited by Daniel Kahneman, Paul Slovic, and Amos Tversky, 48–68. Cambridge: Cambridge University Press, 1982.

———. "Prospect Theory: An Analysis of Decision under Risk." Econometrica 47, no. 2 (1979): 263–92.

Kalai, Ehud. "Proportional Solutions to Bargaining Situations: Interpersonal Utility Comparisons." Econometrica 45, no. 7 (1977): 1623–30. https://doi.org/10.2307/1913954.

Kalai, Ehud, and Meir Smorodinsky. "Other Solutions to Nash's Bargaining Problem." Econometrica 43, no. 3 (1975): 513–18.

Kaldor, Nicholas. "Welfare Propositions of Economics and Interpersonal Comparisons of Utility." Economic Journal 49, no. 195 (1939): 549–52. https://doi.org/10.2307/2224835.

Kaplow, Louis, and Steven Shavell. Fairness versus Welfare. Cambridge, MA; London: Harvard University Press, 2006.

Kerr, Benjamin, Margaret A. Riley, Marcus W. Feldman, and Brendan J. M. Bohannan. "Local Dispersal Promotes Biodiversity in a Real-Life Game of Rock–Paper–Scissors." Nature 418, no. 6894 (July 2002): 171–74. https://doi.org/10.1038/nature00823.

Kimbrough, Erik O., and Alexander Vostroknutov. "Norms Make Preferences Social." Journal of the European Economic Association 14, no. 3 (2016): 608–38. https://doi.org/10.1111/jeea .12152.

Knetsch, Jack. "Endowment Effect and Evidence on Nonreversible Indifference Curves." In Choices, Values, and Frames, edited by Daniel Kahneman and Amos Tversky, 171–79. Cambridge: Cambridge University Press, 2000.

Kovash, Kenneth, and Steven D. Levitt. "Professionals Do Not Play Minimax: Evidence from Major League Baseball and the National Football League." National Bureau of Economic Research, September 10, 2009. https://doi.org/10.3386/w15347.

Ledyard, J. "Public Goods: A Survey of Experimental Research." In The Handbook of Experimental Economics, edited by J. Kagel and Alvin E. Roth, 111–94. Princeton, NJ: Princeton University Press, 1997.

Levine, Michael E., and Charles R. Plott. "Agenda Influence and Its Implications." Virginia Law Review 63, no. 4 (1977): 561–604. https://doi.org/10.2307/1072445.

Lewis, David. Convention: A Philosophical Study. Cambridge, MA: Harvard University Press, 1969.

Lin, Po-Hsuan, Alexander L. Brown, Taisuke Imai, Joseph Tao-yi Wang, Stephanie W. Wang, and Colin F. Camerer. "Evidence of General Economic Principles of Bargaining and Trade from 2,000 Classroom Experiments." Nature Human Behaviour, August 3, 2020, 1–11. https://doi.org/10.1038/s41562-020-0916-8.

List, Christian, and Philip Pettit. "Aggregating Sets of Judgments: An Impossibility Result." Economics and Philosophy 18, no. 1 (2002): 89–110.

Lomasky, L., and G. Brennan. "Is There a Duty to Vote?" Social Philosophy and Policy 17, no. 1 (2000): 62–86. https://doi.org/10.1017/S0265052500002533.

Luce, R. Duncan, and Howard Raiffa. Games and Decisions: Introduction and Critical Survey. New York: John Wiley & Sons, 1957.

Mackie, Gerry. "Social Norms Change: Believing Makes It So." Social Research: An International Quarterly 85, no. 1 (2018): 141–66.

———. "Social Norms of Coordination and Cooperation." Social Philosophy and Policy 35, no. 1 (ed. 2018): 77–100. https://doi.org/10.1017/S0265052518000109.

———. Democracy Defended. New York: Cambridge University Press, 2004.

———. "Ending Footbinding and Infibulation: A Convention Account." American Sociological Review 61, no. 6 (1996): 999–1017.

Madison, James. "Federalist No. 62." In The Federalist, edited by George W. Carey and James McClellan. Indianapolis, IN: Liberty Fund, 1788.

Martin, Christopher Flynn, Rahul Bhui, Peter Bossaerts, Tetsuro Matsuzawa, and Colin Camerer. "Chimpanzee Choice Rates in Competitive Games Match Equilibrium Game Theory Predictions." Scientific Reports 4, no. 1 (June 5, 2014): 5182. https://doi.org/10.1038/srep05182.

May, Kenneth O. "A Set of Independent Necessary and Sufficient Conditions for Simple Majority Decision." Econometrica 20, no. 4 (October 1, 1952): 680–84. https://doi.org/10.2307/1907651.

Maynard Smith, John. Evolution and the Theory of Games. Cambridge: Cambridge University Press, 1982.

McCabe, Kevin A., Stephen J. Rassenti, and Vernon L. Smith. "Reciprocity, Trust, and Payoff Privacy in Extensive Form Bargaining." Games and Economic Behavior 24, no. 1 (July 1, 1998): 10–24. https://doi.org/10.1006/game.1998.0638.

Menger, Carl. Principles of Economics. Translated by James Dingwall and Bert Hoselitz. Grove City, PA: Libertarian Press, 1994.

Mill, John Stuart. Principles of Political Economy. Volumes 2 and 3, Collected Works of John Stuart Mill. Indianapolis, IN: Liberty Fund, 2006.

———. On Liberty. Edited by Elizabeth Rapaport. 8th edition. Indianapolis, IN: Hackett, 1859.

Moehler, Michael. Minimal Morality: A Multilevel Social Contract Theory. Oxford: Oxford University Press, 2018.

———. "Orthodox Rational Choice Contractarianism: Before and after Gauthier." Politics, Philosophy & Economics 15, no. 2 (2015): 113–31. https://doi.org/10.1177/1470594X15599102.

Morgenstern, Oskar. "The Collaboration Between Oskar Morgenstern and John von Neumann on the Theory of Games." Journal of Economic Literature 14, no. 3 (September 1, 1976): 805–16. https://doi.org/10.2307/2722628.

Mueller, Dennis. Public Choice III. Cambridge: Cambridge University Press, 2003.

Munger, Michael. Tomorrow 3.0: Transaction Costs and the Sharing Economy. Cambridge: Cambridge University Press, 2018.

Nash, John. "Two-Person Cooperative Games." Econometrica: Journal of the Econometric Society 21, no. 1 (January 1953): 128–40.

Nash, John F. "The Bargaining Problem." Econometrica 18, no. 2 (1950): 155–62. https://doi.org/10.2307/1907266.

Nisbett, Richard E., and Lee Ross. Human Inference: Strategies and Shortcomings of Social Judgment. First printing edition. Englewood Cliffs, NJ: Prentice-Hall, 1980.

North, Douglass C. Institutions, Institutional Change and Economic Performance. Reprinted. Cambridge: Cambridge University Press, 1990.

Nowak, Martin, and Roger Highfield. Super Cooperators: Altruism, Evolution, and Why We Need Each Other to Succeed. Reprint edition. New York: Free Press, 2012.

Nozick, Robert. The Nature of Rationality. Princeton, NJ: Princeton University Press, 1993.

Okun, Arthur M., and Lawrence H. Summers. Equality and Efficiency: The Big Tradeoff. Revised edition. Washington, DC: Brookings Institution Press, 2015.

Ostrom, Elinor. Governing the Commons: The Evolution of Institutions for Collective Action. Cambridge University Press, 1990.

Padover, Saul K. Thomas Jefferson on Democracy. Eighth printing edition. New York: Mentor Book/New American Library, 1961.

Pearl, Judea, and Dana Mackenzie. The Book of Why: The New Science of Cause and Effect. 1st edition. New York: Basic Books, 2018.

Pinker, Steven. How the Mind Works. New York: Norton, 1997.

Pollock, John L. Thinking about Acting: Logical Foundations for Rational Decision Making. Oxford; New York: Oxford University Press, 2006.

Poundstone, William. Prisoner's Dilemma: John von Neumann, Game Theory, and the Puzzle of the Bomb. 1st edition. New York: Anchor, 1993.

Rawls, John. A Theory of Justice. Revised edition. Cambridge, MA: Belknap Press, 1999.

———. Political Liberalism. Paperback edition. New York: Columbia University Press, 1996.

Ridley, Matt. The Red Queen: Sex and the Evolution of Human Nature. New York: Harper Perennial, 2003.

Rigdon, Mary L., Kevin A. McCabe, and Vernon L. Smith. "Sustaining Cooperation in Trust Games." Economic Journal 117, no. 522 (2007): 991–1007.

Riker, William. The Art of Political Manipulation. New Haven, CT: Yale University Press, 1986.

———. Liberalism Against Populism: A Confrontation Between the Theory of Democracy and the Theory of Social Choice. Reissue. Long Grove, IL: Waveland Press, 1982.

Robbins, Lionel. An Essay on the Nature & Significance of Economic Science. 2nd edition. London: MacMillan, 1945.

Romer, David. "Do Firms Maximize? Evidence from Professional Football." Journal of Political Economy 114, no. 2 (April 1, 2006): 340–65. https://doi.org/10.1086/501171.

Rousseau, Jean-Jacques. "Discourse on the Origin of Inequality." In The Basic Political Writings, edited and translated by Donald A. Cress, 25–110. Indianapolis, IN: Hackett, 1755.

Rubinstein, Ariel. "Perfect Equilibrium in a Bargaining Model." Econometrica 50, no. 1 (1982): 97–109. https://doi.org/10.2307/1912531.

Samuelson, Paul. Economics: An Introductory Analysis. 6th edition. New York: McGraw-Hill, 1964.

Samuelson, Paul A. "Consumption Theory in Terms of Revealed Preference." Economica 15, no. 60 (1948): 243–53. https://doi.org/10.2307/2549561.

Sandler, Todd. Economic Concepts for the Social Sciences. Illustrated edition. Cambridge, UK; New York: Cambridge University Press, 1997.

Satterthwaite, Mark Allen. "Strategy-Proofness and Arrow's Conditions: Existence and Correspondence Theorems for Voting Procedures and Social Welfare Functions." Journal of Economic Theory 10, no. 2 (April 1, 1975): 187–217. https://doi.org/10.1016/0022-0531(75)90050-2.

Savage, Leonard J. The Foundations of Statistics. 2nd revised edition. New York: Courier Dover Publications, 1954.

Schelling, Thomas. The Strategy of Conflict. Cambridge, MA: Harvard University Press, 1960.

———. "For the Abandonment of Symmetry in Game Theory." Review of Economics and Statistics 41, no. 3 (1959): 213–24.

Schmidtz, David. The Limits of Government: An Essay on the Public Goods Argument. Boulder, CO: Westview, 1991.

Schotter, Andrew. The Economic Theory of Social Institutions. New York: Cambridge University Press, 2008.

Schwab, David, and Elinor Ostrom. "The Vital Role of Norms and Rules in Maintaining Open Public and Private Economies." In Moral Markets: The Critical Role of Values in the Economy, edited by Paul J. Zak, 204–27. Princeton, NJ: Princeton University Press, 2008.

Sen, Amartya. Collective Choice and Social Welfare: An Expanded Edition. Cambridge, MA: Harvard University Press, 2018.

———. "Maximization and the Act of Choice." In Rationality and Freedom. Cambridge, MA: Harvard University Press, 2002.

———. "The Impossibility of a Paretian Liberal." Journal of Political Economy 78, no. 1 (1970): 152–57.

Senior, Nassau William. An Outline of the Science of Political Economy. 5th edition. Edinburgh: Charles Black, 1864.

Shepsle, Kennneth. "Rational Choice Institutionalism." In The Oxford Handbook of Political Institutions, edited by R.A.W. Rhodes, Sarah A. Binder, and Bert A. Rockman, 23–38. Oxford: Oxford University Press, 2006.

Sherratt, Thomas N., and Mike Mesterton-Gibbons. "The Evolution of Respect for Property." Journal of Evolutionary Biology 28, no. 6 (2015): 1185–1202. https://doi.org/10.1111/jeb.12648.

Sidgwick, Henry. The Principles of Political Economy. 3rd edition. London: MacMillan, 1901.

Simon, Herbert A. "Theories of Decision-Making in Economics and Behavioral Science." American Economic Review 49, no. 3 (1959): 253–83.

Sinervo, B., and C. M. Lively. "The Rock–Paper–Scissors Game and the Evolution of Alternative Male Strategies." Nature 380, no. 6571 (March 1996): 240–43. https://doi.org/10.1038/380240a0.

Skyrms, Brian. The Stag Hunt and the Evolution of Social Structure. New York: Cambridge University Press, 2004.

———. "The Stag Hunt." Proceedings and Addresses of the American Philosophical Association 75, no. 2 (2001): 31–41. https://doi.org/10.2307/3218711.

———. Evolution of the Social Contract. New York: Cambridge University Press, 1996.

Smith, Adam. An Inquiry into the Nature and Causes of the Wealth of Nations. The Glasgow Edition of the Works & Correspondence of Adam Smith. Indianapolis, IN: Liberty Fund, 1982.

Smith, Vernon L., and Bart J. Wilson. Humanomics: Moral Sentiments and the Wealth of Nations for the Twenty-First Century. New York: Cambridge University Press, 2019.

Smithies, Arthur. "Optimum Location in Spatial Competition," Journal of Political Economy 49, no. 3 (1941): 423–39.

Spence, Michael. "Job Market Signaling." Quarterly Journal of Economics 87, no. 3 (August 1973): 355–74.

Sterelny, Kim. "Cooperation, Culture, and Conflict." British Journal for the Philosophy of Science 67, no. 1 (March 1, 2016): 31–58. https://doi.org/10.1093/bjps/axu024.

Stigler, George Joseph. The Economist as Preacher, and Other Essays. Chicago: University of Chicago Press, 1982.

Sugden, Robert. The Community of Advantage: A Behavioural Economist's Defence of the Market. Oxford: Oxford University Press, 2018.

Sunstein, Cass R. Free Markets and Social Justice. New York; Oxford: Oxford University Press, 1999.

Thrasher, John. "Evaluating Bad Norms." Social Philosophy & Policy 35, no. 1 (2018): 196–216.

———. "The Ethics of Legislative Vote Trading." Political Studies 64, no. 3 (2016): 614–29. https://doi.org/10.1111/1467-9248.12205.

———. "Uniqueness and Symmetry in Bargaining Theories of Justice." Philosophical Studies 167, no. 3 (February 1, 2014): 683–99.

Thrasher, John, and Gerald Gaus. "On the Calculus of Consent." In Oxford Handbook on Classics in Political Theory, edited by Jacob Levy. Oxford: Oxford University Press, 2017.

Thrasher, John, and Toby Handfield. "Honor and Violence: An Account of Feuds, Dueling, and Honor Killing." Human Nature 29, no. 4 (2018): 371–89.

Trivers, Robert L. "The Evolution of Reciprocal Altruism." Quarterly Review of Biology 46, no. 1 (March 1, 1971): 35–57. https://doi.org/10.1086/406755.

Tversky, Amos, and Daniel Kahneman. "Rational Choice and the Framing of Decisions." In Choices, Values, and Frames, edited by Daniel Kahneman and Amos Tversky, 209–23. Cambridge: Cambridge University Press, 2000.

———. "Belief in the Law of Small Numbers." In Judgments Under Uncertainty: Heuristics and Biases, edited by Daniel Kahneman, Paul Slovic, and Amos Tversky, 23–31. Cambridge: Cambridge University Press, 1982.

Vanderschraaf, Peter. "War or Peace?: A Dynamical Analysis of Anarchy." Economics and Philosophy 22, no. 2 (2006): 243–79.

———. Strategic Justice: Convention and Problems of Balancing Divergent Interests. Oxford Moral Theory. Oxford; New York: Oxford University Press, 2018.

Von Neumann, John, and Oskar Morgenstern. Theory of Games and Economic Behavior. Princeton, NJ: Princeton University Press, 1944.

Waldron, Jeremy. Law and Disagreement. Oxford; New York: Oxford University Press, 1999.

Walker, Mark, and John Wooders. "Minimax Play at Wimbledon." American Economic Review 91, no. 5 (December 1, 2001): 1521–38. https://doi.org/10.1257/aer.91.5.1521.

Walzer, Michael. "Political Action: The Problem of Dirty Hands." Philosophy and Public Affairs 2, no. 2 (1973): 160–80.

Wang, Zhijian, Bin Xu, and Hai-Jun Zhou. "Social Cycling and Conditional Responses in the Rock-Paper-Scissors Game." Scientific Reports 4, no. 1 (July 25, 2014): 5830. https://doi.org/10.1038/srep05830.

Weinstein-Gould, Jesse. "Keeping the Hitter Off Balance: Mixed Strategies in Baseball." Journal of Quantitative Analysis in Sports 5, no. 2 (May 1, 2009). https://doi.org/10.2202/1559-0410.1173.

Wicksteed, Philip. The Common Sense of Political Economy. Edited by Lionel Robbins. Vol. 1. 2 vols. London: Routledge & Sons, 1946.

Williamson, Oliver. "The Economics of Organization: The Transaction Cost Approach." American Journal of Sociology 87, no. 3 (1981): 548–77.

Wilson, Bart J. "Social Preferences Aren't Preferences." Journal of Economic Behavior & Organization, On the Methodology of Experimental Economics, 73, no. 1 (January 1, 2010): 77–82. https://doi.org/10.1016/j.jebo.2008.09.013.

Zahavi, Amotz. "Mate Selection—a Selection for a Handicap." Journal of Theoretical Biology 53, no. 1 (1975): 205–14.

Zandt, David E. van. "The Lessons of the Lighthouse: 'Government' or 'Private' Provision of Goods." Journal of Legal Studies 22, no. 1 (January 1, 1993): 47–72. https://doi.org/10.1086/468157.

INDEX

A NOTE ON THE TYPE

This book has been composed in Arno, an Old-style serif typeface in the
classic Venetian tradition, designed by Robert Slimbach at Adobe.

GPSR Authorized Representative: Easy Access System Europe - Mustamäe tee
50, 10621 Tallinn, Estonia, gpsr.requests@easproject.com

www.ingramcontent.com/pod-product-compliance
Ingram Content Group UK Ltd.
Pitfield, Milton Keynes, MK11 3LW, UK
UKHW042250300325
456820UK00002B/16